DIRTY BUSINESS

DIRTY BUSINESS
Exploring Corporate Misconduct

Analysis and Cases

MAURICE PUNCH

SAGE Publications
London • Thousand Oaks • New Delhi

© Maurice Punch 1996

First published 1996. Reprinted 1999

SAGE Publications Ltd
6 Bonhill Street
London EC2A 4PU

SAGE Publications Inc
2455 Teller Road
Thousand Oaks, California 91320

SAGE Publications India Pvt Ltd
32, M-Block Market
Greater Kailash – I
New Delhi 110 048

British Library Cataloguing in Publication data

A catalogue record for this book is
available from the British Library

ISBN 0 8039 7603 8
ISBN 0 8039 7604 6 (pbk)

Library of Congress catalog card number 96-070156

Typeset by M Rules
Printed in Great Britain by
The Cromwell Press, Trowbridge, Wiltshire

For Julio

Contents

Part Three   Conclusion

Foreword

In the late 1970s I carried out research on police corruption in Amsterdam which drew me into a consideration of 'organizational deviance' (Punch, 1985). As I was working in a business school (Nijenrode, The Netherlands School of Business), I was unable to teach in my main areas of interest – police corruption, corporate crime and organizational deviance; but it proved possible to smuggle some topics on business deviance and control into courses on Public Policy and Social Responsibility in Business, Social Issues in Management, Business Ethics and Management of Crisis. From disparate sources I started to collect data on scandals, accidents, mismanagement, business leaders, and cases of serious corporate misconduct. Much of this comprised clippings from newspapers and magazines (often with intriguing titles that caught the eye such as 'Light Sentences for Fraudulent Nuns in Belgian Convent', where the nuns had fraudulently diverted money, roughly $5 million, from a hospital to build an indoor swimming pool and to place TV sets in every cell of a new luxurious convent; *de Volkskrant*, 1 November 1984). As someone wrote in another context, it's almost enough to restore your belief in original sin.

An earlier attempt to write up this material foundered on an institutional upheaval at Nijenrode, where it was made difficult to work on anything for over a year, but this did lead to exit and a new life as an 'independent scholar' that has given me both time and a renewed motivation for writing. I can now look back at sixteen years among business students and managers as a form of covert observation and as a rich source of data and anecdote. There was the Belgian manager horrified at the prospect of having a delegation of prospective clients from the Middle East; it meant nursing them around the fleshpots every evening until deep into the night. There was no hint of moral reserve but simply frustration at the boredom, physical exhaustion and waste of working time that these jaunts would involve. Also most Dutch managers exude an aura of Calvinist respectability and are straight-faced in a formal setting, where they deny everything; there's no meaningful Gallic shrug, no cynical Latin smirk, and no highly symbolic Mediterranean body language to convey ambivalence and duplicity. But after class, and after a few drinks in the bar, they would open up on their predicament. One told me that when he was sent to a Latin American country he had to construct a double book-keeping system in order to create a hidden economy for informal purposes (such as bribes); but the accountants at headquarters 'didn't want to know' and hence the shadow finance had to be cleverly camouflaged. It's the classic managerial dilemma and also the standard justification for rule-bending ('I had no alternative'). In addition, it was considered all right to do it abroad but you would never try it on home ground. Similarly, a leading Dutch captain of industry addressed one of my MBA classes; a student asked him, 'Do you bribe?' (Nijenrode MBA'ers are noted for their subtlety); without a flinch he stated, 'No, of course not, never', and then added, 'but if you want to do business, say in [he mentioned a country in the Far East], and you haven't got a million dollars in your back trouser pocket then you're a very naïve manager.'

When I was teaching MBA students it was often difficult to visualize their becoming bent. Many were sharp, lively and well informed and also pleasant people to be with socially. Indeed, over the years I've seen female students in particular getting really angry about the Dalkon Shield case (this intrauterine device caused its users to suffer a wide range of disorders); heard people state they would never work for the tobacco, weapons, or nuclear industries; had students who became quite genuinely distressed at tackling the Bhopal case (the massive accident at the Union Carbide chemical plant in India); and witnessed disbelief when students were confronted with Stanley Adams in person telling his account of his imprisonment in Switzerland for espionage when he 'blew the whistle' on Hoffmann La Roche. At the same time, if I asked them to draw up a list of crises, ethical dilemmas, or significant problems that they had encountered in their work experience then most groups would come up with a colourful and quite impressive list of cock-ups, mismanagement, near accidents, sexual intimidation, abuse of power by the leadership, deceit, cooking the books, unwarranted risk-taking, back-stabbing, and incompetence. One British engineer told me that he heard on the news of a tunnel collapse near a construction site above the London Underground and in a blind panic drove to his own site because he was petrified that his company might have caused it; in fact, the roof fall was elsewhere. He made it sound just like Goodrich.

In general, my students in class discussions were often more sensitive to ethical issues and sympathetic to 'social responsibility' in business than you might expect from budding executives. Yet if you gave them a simulation which asked them to take a risk in order to achieve an important goal, then almost without exception they would jump right in and take the risk. Clearly, the classroom is not reality but it was noticeable how, in a role-play or simulation, these bright young people would almost instantly revert to the gung-ho, 'go-for-it' management style. If you then explained that they had just replicated decision-making in the 'Challenger' case (by pushing for performance over safety and by filtering out warning signals), then they would say things like 'Yes, I should have seen that coming, that was dumb of me, but I've been there before and you do go into meetings and take decisions where you simply blind yourself to the consequences.' And then they would add, 'But of course our decisions never harmed anyone.'

Another source of insights and indirect data for me was gained by attending the Management of Disasters and Civil Emergencies course at the Police

Staff College, Bramshill, UK. When you have sat through the graphic and grisly presentations on the series of British disasters – the fire at the King's Cross Underground Station, the train crash at Clapham, the terrorist bomb aboard the PanAm Boeing above Lockerbie, the capsizing of the *Herald of Free Enterprise* at Zeebrugge, the plane crash on the M1 motorway at Kegworth, the fire at the Bradford football stadium, the accident on the River Thames when the sand-barge *The Marchioness* ran into a crowded pleasure-boat at night, and the crushing of fans at the Hillsborough football ground – then it sharpens your mind considerably on the issues of safety, risk, recklessness, negligence, and corporate accountability. We heard an extensive account, for instance, of the failure to secure a conviction against P & O (the parent company of Townsend Thorensen) for corporate manslaughter in the courts in relation to the Zeebrugge disaster. The police inquiry had generated sixty volumes of evidence; it contained a 43-page glossary of nautical terms to enable detectives and lawyers to understand the jargon of seamen who were interviewed; the report was virtually an extended exercise in industrial sociology that recreated the discrepancies between the formal world of rules and procedures and the informal social world of the crew on a cross-Channel ferry. Afterwards a policeman turned to me and said, 'I'll never travel on a car-ferry again.' Indeed, it was difficult to know which form of transport to take on leaving Bramshill and there was something of a general reluctance to enter a train, boat, or plane.

Then, just before I left Nijenrode, I was asked if I would like to invite Ernest Saunders, who figured in the Guinness case, to lecture to my students. Saunders had been sentenced to five years for a number of offences related to market manipulation. In prison he developed symptoms that appeared to be a form of Alzheimer's. Given an early release on medical grounds he was doing the rounds of the business schools telling his story (which he had also done prior to his conviction, at the leading European business school, INSEAD in Fontainebleau, for instance). Since then he has appealed successfully to the European Commission on Human Rights that his trial was unfair (*The Economist*, 24 September 1994). The four suspects in the Guinness case have now been given the right to appeal against their convictions, and if the sentences are quashed then multi-million pound compensation claims could follow (*Daily Mail*, 23 December 1994). Saunders illustrates how resilient and combative those involved in white-collar crime cases can be, how determined Saunders was to broadcast his innocence (and to spread the message in the business schools of Europe to aspiring managers), and how he had the power to influence his case in a way that is unthinkable for most people who wish to protest their innocence of 'common' crimes. Indeed, the ambition, resourcefulness, and drive that executives displayed in their business careers can stand them in good stead when faced with trial and/or bankruptcy; some make successful comebacks and are clearly aided by the social and cultural 'capital' that they enjoy; their companies may also lend financial and other support during prosecution as well as later during rehabilitation. I did not invite him.

While I was writing, a lot of interest was aroused in Britain about 'sleaze' (conflicts of interest and back-handers for politicians; the *Guardian*, 21 October 1994), norms of conduct in public life, 'bungs' for soccer managers and goalkeepers taking a tumble in football matches for cash (is nothing sacred?), government deviance in tying construction deals in Malaysia to overseas development funds and dubious arms sales to Iraq prior to the Gulf War (cf. the Scott Inquiry and the so-called 'super-gun' affair; *The Economist*, 18 December 1993). In Italy 'Operation Clean Hands' has revealed a vast network of illegal transactions between business, politicians, and organized crime.

> By the end of 1993 magistrates had traced just over 620 billion lire ($390 m) in bribes to politicians alone. Between February 1992 (when a Milanese police investigation called 'Operation Clean Hands' first brought the corruption to light) and February 1994, 4,800 Italians were arrested on 'Tangentopoli' ['Bribesville', as Italians refer to the scandal – MP] charges. Of these 930 were businessmen in private or state-owned companies. The industries hit hardest include advertising, insurance, mineral water, telecommunications and office equipment – virtually all those, in other words, that depend on public contracts or permits. Two industries that have depended particularly on good will are construction and pharmaceuticals. More than 2,000 arrests have been connected to corrupt building contracts and permits; just under 400 of those arrested were businessmen. (*The Economist*, 2 July 1994)

In Japan there have been a whole series of political and financial scandals during the last twenty years. Some twenty-five people were recently indicted for insider trading in the Nippon Shoji case; a number of people died after taking the drug Sorivundine together with cancer drugs, and members of the drug industry started dumping shares based on unpublished information about the fatal side-effects of Sorivundine (*Japan Times*, 21 December 1994; I would like to thank John Kerr of Tsukuba University for drawing my attention to this and other cases). Also considerable evidence has emerged about the role of organized crime, particularly the drug syndicates, infiltrating the straight financial world in order to launder vast sums of dirty money (Ehrenfeld, 1992). Hopefully, the revelations surrounding these affairs and scandals will further stimulate the study of organizational crime and deviance in business, government, and non-profit organizations.

Completion of this book has, alas, been a more than usually prolonged and painful process. In the last phase of writing both my parents died one shortly after the other, and I would like to record my gratitude to them both for all that they did for me. I have been fortunate, however, in receiving valuable comments on drafts from Nic van Dijk, Bob Hoogenboom, Ralph Crawshaw, Geoffrey Markham, Henk van Luijk, John Kerr, Jeff Gaspersz, Aaldert van der Vlies and Mike Chatterton (also from a number of anonymous reviewers, while Dick Bennett and Roger Price provided some useful materials and references). In particular I was kept going by the valuable comments and strong encouragement of Mike Useem, the judicious criticisms of Michael Clarke, the whip-cracking enthusiasm of John Van Maanen (who wrote presciently, 'it will certainly not make you the featured speaker at the next Academy of Management Meetings'), and the patience and support of Sue Jones at Sage. In the past I enjoyed a number of discussions with Al Reiss, Jr, who has been influential in mapping out the area of 'organizational crime' and whose advice was valuable and stimulating. And I've always gained a lot from discussing ideas, books, and approaches to my work with Derek Phillips after our weekly game of squash. I'm really most grateful to them all. Then, in times of acute culture conflict, I could always seek solace in the curries at Bobby Khawaja's Pakistan Restaurant, and welcomed a string of itinerants from abroad, but particularly Buddy Ungson from Oregon, as an excuse to over-indulge on the lamb chops and butter chicken. I would also like to thank Christa Been and Julie de Jong for typing the manuscript so professionally. And when the going got rough I could always rely on my children, Julio and Maria, to deride my efforts (they were particularly caustic about the unmanageable piles of press-clippings). Fortunately, there was always Corry to fall back on for coffee and moral support; her Dutch common sense, resilience, and affection were essential to keeping me going through the dark and gloom-laden periods. In return I will really have to fulfil the twenty-year-old promise to reserve Sunday mornings exclusively for bike rides and walks on the beach. Together we are involved in a foundation that plans to set up a rehabilitation project for young ex-psychiatric patients suffering from schizophrenia, and the proceeds from this book will go to supporting the 'One in a Hundred Foundation'.

Maurice Punch

Acknowledgements

Doubleday and Co. gave permission to quote generously from K. Vandivier's 'Why Should My Conscience Bother Me?' (originally published in R.L. Heilbroner, *In the Name of Profit*, New York: Doubleday, 1972), as I exceeded the number of words normally allowed for citation in my summary of the article. Case no. 9 on Calvi and the Banco Ambrosiano appeared in a nearly identical form as 'Bandit Banks: Financial Services and Organized Crime' in *Contemporary Criminal Justice*, 9: 3 (August 1993), and I appreciate the permission of editor-in-chief George E. Rush to reproduce it in this volume.

PART ONE
INTRODUCTION

1

Management and Organizational Misbehaviour

Business has a dirty side. On those occasions when the veil of corporate respectability and probity is lifted, we are able to witness a world where managers lie, cheat, manipulate, dissemble, and deceive. In terms of everyday social interaction, in which we *all* engage in a measure of concealment and impression management (Goffman, 1959), this makes managers no different than the rest of us. The difference lies in the control over powerful resources that managers enjoy and the potentially deleterious consequences of their misconduct in the corporations that they run. This must raise our acute concern, because some companies have killed, maimed, gassed, poisoned, and blown up people while others have robbed us. There are, in contrast, 'clean' and reputable firms with exemplary reputations (Punch, 1992). But there is an accumulating body of evidence that some managers, in order to control their markets and environments (and for a broad spectrum of other motives), will consciously and forcefully employ almost any means – devious, foul, or downright illegal – to achieve their ends. The reasons why managers lend themselves to deviant activities, and the seeming inability of business, government, and regulatory agencies to control effectively such misbehaviour, are problematic and worrying. This is largely because the subjects of business crime and corporate deviance have been sadly neglected by criminologists in favour of other areas such as street crime, low-level law enforcement, and the prison system. The predilection for delinquency on the street, as opposed to 'crime in the suites' (Timmer and Eitzen, 1989), has distorted our image of what some see as the 'real' crime problem. As Box (1983: 2) asserts, the most serious offences are committed by persons in positions of power and privilege and it is they who cause the bulk of avoidable deaths, injury, and deprivation.

This means that we must cast our gaze *upwards*. In essence, the central focus of this work lies in interpreting deviance in business organizations by analysing the moral, managerial, and business component in human behaviour within organizations. The aim is to rectify the imbalance in the criminological and socio-legal literature which is overly slanted to external views of corporate deviance, particularly in relation to legal control and penal sanctions. All too often the behavioural and organizational component is missing, and it is this which creates the social and moral dilemmas that managers have to solve. In contrast, I shall locate business deviance in the institutional context in which it occurs. In a nutshell, the western business organization operates within the structure of advanced capitalist society and in a culture of competition that provides opportunities, motivations, and rationalizations for rule-breaking (Coleman, 1989). This context is dynamic, shifting and culturally diverse but a crucial element is the use of organizational power, trust, and impression management in order to employ the organization as a tool in deviant activity and as a shield against discovery, enforcement, and prosecution (Jamieson, 1994). And I would argue that the corporation, and the business environment, are potentially criminogenic.

This book, then, is concerned with exposing upper-world crime and deviance in the upper levels of business organizations. A crucial concern is that the power of business is expanding and that the potential for abuse of that power is increasing. A number of structural changes – globalization of the economy, advanced technologies, economies of scale (leading to industrial concentrations), and the diminishing power of governments – mean that new opportunities for deviance have opened up while the potential for damage has been amplified (Perrow, 1984; Ross, 1992; Allison, 1993). Furthermore, the new-found muscle of big business enables it to manipulate regulation and to impose its interpretation of events on the media. The work presented here is based on the assumption that, in order to explain why executives in organizations bend, break, and exploit the laws (and even their own self-imposed rules of professional and corporate conduct), we have to enter the social world of the manager. That means placing the manager in a moral, social, cultural, and organizational context, because the offences concerned are *organizational* crimes in which the organization provides the location, the means, and the justifications for misconduct (Tonry and Reiss, 1993). I am particularly interested in critically examining the almost taken-for-granted idea that managers break the law for the 'good' of the company and are, therefore, somehow 'honest crooks'. Recent research has cast serious doubt on this assumption in the white-collar crime literature and some cases, such as Maxwell and the Savings and Loan Scandal, reveal a predatory and rapacious 'looting' of the organization. And the response – or lack of it – from regulators and controllers must also be analysed in terms of organizational and inter-organizational relationships (related to capture, co-optation, collusion, power, resources, and mandates; Hawkins, 1984).

The accounts that I will be drawing on, and the cases that I will be presenting, are based largely on secondary sources related to well-known scandals. The cases have been carefully selected to illustrate a wide range of deviant organizational activity in diverse industries. Some of the cases are 'classics' and are reproduced here because they represent standard dilemmas for organizations and executives that recur time and time again in the literature.

Indeed, it can happen that a case is revived many years later and returns to haunt the company. This happened with Guinness who took over Distillers. Twenty years earlier Distillers had been involved in the Thalidomide affair and had contributed to a trust fund for the victims. This fund needed a reinjection of cash to secure its future, and Guinness, faced with the lobbying of the Thalidomide Action Group and with publicity on a highly charged issue, decided to top up the fund with £37.5 million (*Daily Mail*, 4 May 1995). Also they provide particular insight into the social psychology of decision-making processes. And a number of foreign cases have been added to accentuate the cross-cultural component in placing cases in a specific cultural context and to avoid an over-reliance on North American cases. The advantage of such well-publicized affairs is that they break open the façade, or organizational front, presented to the outside world to reveal the 'underside' of business activity. As such they tell us how business really gets done as opposed to the filtered versions released by firms for public consumption. In scrutinizing that reality behind the façade, it is of interest to examine the extent to which business requires a measure of trust, integrity, and confidence in order to function. At times the business world may be highly competitive and aggressive, but there must also be a degree of consensus to avoid a Hobbesian 'war of all against all', to attract investors, and to allay the suspicions of watch-dogs. Scandals tend to reveal that that trust has been abused, and, generally, business hastily endeavours to restore its image in order to persuade us that what we have seen is an aberration and that we can have confidence in our business leaders. What are generally swiftly passed over are precisely the factors in the business environment at the time, together with informal patterns of conduct and norms allowing tolerance of deviance, that caused the law-breaking in the first place.

My perspective is informed by the traditional sociological view that things are never quite what they seem to be, that it is our task to be iconoclastic and sceptical, and that we are involved in unmasking the 'secret worlds of the powerful' (Bouchier, 1986: 1). In brief, this works seeks to combine my criminological interest in a neglected but increasingly important social problem, why managers in business organizations deviate from the law, with my sociological curiosity about the relatively closed world of management. It is this combination of perspectives that is largely absent in the literature and which represents the major contribution of this book to the field. I intend penetrating the everyday world of the business corporation by focusing on the social and moral dilemmas faced by managers at their work within organizations that lead them to tackle their problems with deviant solutions. Why do they turn to crime and other forms of rule-breaking?

The Myth of Management

In order to explore the ideas above I wish to look first at the nature of management and then examine a number of business scandals. This will enable me to see if there is a discrepancy between what we think management is about and what it really is; and also to hold up scandals in order to pick out a number of variables that seem relevant to law-breaking in business organizations and to the difficulty of combating that illegality.

On the surface, corporations are all about formulating strategy, winning market share, gaining competitive edge, introducing innovative products, and establishing coherent planning. They are the essence of dispassionate *rational* calculation, judiciously weighing the most efficient means for achieving explicit goals, and they often exude respectability. Some speak in glossy and expensive brochures of being good corporate citizens, of valuing the environment, of contributing to charities, of investing in communities, and of following ethical codes. Their senior executives are well educated, impeccably turned out, engage in public service activities, and are role-models in terms of the work ethic, healthy ambition, respectability, and the trappings of success. Ostensibly the corporation and its managers are subject to a battery of controls and are besieged by alert interest groups and nosy media. Their documents have to pass the scrutiny of sophisticated professionals and suspicious regulators so that they are stamped with their approval. What could possibly go wrong?

In trying to peer through this smokescreen of probity it is not only clever PR that waylays us but also a traditional view of the manager as a neutral technocrat engaged in a relatively mechanistic coordination of productive activity. This stereotype has persisted partly because of our ignorance of what really happens in the boardroom (Galbraith, 1986a: 6); despite their increasingly strategic position in society we know relatively little about the world of managers. As Reed (1989: 79) notes, 'the inner sanctum of the company boardroom and the senior management enclaves within corporate hierarchies still remain a largely closed and secretive world.'

The relatively few empirical studies of what managers actually do that have been conducted using observational techniques tend to paint a picture of managerial practice quite at variance with the rational planning and control model: Mintzberg's (1973) influential study revealed the manager as a non-reflective, day-to-day doer, constantly negotiating on his feet or on the phone (preferring not to bother with tiresome correspondence). And it was, then, preponderantly a 'he' (Kanter, 1977). The characteristic of managerial work was that it was highly contingent and diffuse. Fluctuating circumstances meant that the manager was constantly, and largely intuitively, reacting to pressures and conflicts that presented him or her with 'competing and even contradictory demands' (Reed, 1989: 75). A number of other studies charted the inherently political nature of the corporate environment and noted that the manager had to engage in power plays to achieve routine ends (for example, Dalton, 1959; Pettigrew, 1973; Kotter, 1982). Faced by conflict and insecurity the manager sought alliances, and this constant negotiation for position required

> high-level skills in constructing and reconstructing organizational networks and agendas through which organizational dependencies can be established and the legitimacy of personal aims secured. Expertise in the use of informational and symbolic resources, as well as in the manipulation of formal organizational designs, becomes the 'sine qua non' of managerial success. (Reed, 1989: 76)

Recently attention has been paid to the symbolic element in management and its contribution to moral and political legitimacy. This alerts us to the nature of 'shared meanings' and 'collective myths' and their relation to domination and control (Reed, 1989: 77):

> The management of meaning refers to a process of symbol construction and value use designed both to create legitimacy for one's actions, ideas and demands, and to delegitimise the demands of one's opponents. (Pettigrew, 1985: 44)

Undoubtedly corporate management remains locked into an ostensible concern with strategy formulation and planning related to survival, long-term continuity, return on investment, a reputable image and the application of the latest and most sophisticated techniques of managerial practice (Johnson and Scholes, 1993). But under that coherent and apparently ratio-nal effort there is a world of power struggles, ideological debate, intense political rivalry, manipulation of information, and short-term problem-solv-ing. Viewed in this light, managers emerge as something of amoral chameleons, buffeted by moral ambiguity and organizational uncertainty, and they survive this 'messy, not to say dirty' environment by engaging in Machiavellian micro-politics (Jackall, 1988; Reed, 1989: 78). Of course we should also continually bear in mind that there is a huge diversity in styles and practices of management *within* corporations, between various areas of business, and particularly cross-culturally.

But I wish to emphasize throughout this book the contingent, ambiguous, contradictory, manipulative, and essentially 'political' nature of management as a social enterprise. Managers are shaped by their complex environment but they are also busily reconstructing it. And the business organization, while presenting a coherent and unified front to outsiders, is in practice a political arena where reality is constantly defined and redefined. For the purposes of my analysis I wish to hold on to the view, summarized by Reed, that

> the picture of the work behaviour and relations of the managerial elite that emerges from this review of empirical studies is one of a highly complex – and often divided – group attempting to secure long-term profitability in the face of environmental uncertainty and organizational conflict. (1989: 84)

I have argued, then, that there is a considerable discrepancy between the surface solidity of the business organization and the fluctuating and even turbulent reality of managerial 'backstage' behaviour (Goffman, 1959). One way of exploring that divergence is to examine a number of scandals where the practices and mechanisms of deviance have been exposed. This also enables me to look at a number of features of organizations that turn to illicit solutions for the dilemmas that they face, and also at the regulatory response.

Three Contemporary Cases: Maxwell, BCCI, and the S & L Débâcle

'Captain Crook': Robert Maxwell

> I always say confidence is like virginity – it can only be lost once.
>
> (Maxwell, quoted in Greenslade, 1992: 217)

Robert Maxwell was born in Czechoslovakia (Haines, 1988; Thompson and Delano, 1989; Bower, 1989). He escaped before the war, joined the British Army in which he earned a commission, and fought courageously (he was awarded the Military Cross for bravery). After the war he began a successful business career centred on academic and scientific publishing and, in particular, he built up the Pergamon Press (which attracted the Queen's Award for Industry in 1966). The breakdown of a business deal with an American partner in 1969, however, led to questions being raised with the City of London Takeover Panel and to an investigation by the Department of Trade and Industry (DTI). The DTI inspectors issued three reports; the first contained the damning sentence, 'We regret having to conclude that notwithstanding Mr Maxwell's acknowledged abilities and energy, he is not in our opinion a person who can be relied on to exercise proper stewardship of a publicly quoted company' (Greenslade, 1992: 42). The reports spoke of his 'lying, exaggerating, distorting, concealing and general company law-breaking' (*Observer*, 8 December 1991). Maxwell managed to evade prosecution for his 'creative accounting' but many believed he was finished.

Yet, he managed against the odds to regain control of Pergamon, and this resurrection earned him the nickname of the 'Bouncing Czech'. He also entered Parliament as a Labour Member but had an undistinguished political career. In the 1970s and 1980s he built up an empire of companies, including the Labour-orientated tabloid newspaper the *Daily Mirror*, became a household name (he was involved in a number of soccer clubs and revelled in publicity), and moved in the highest circles domestically and internationally. By the early 1990s, however, his empire was facing a debt crisis. In 1991 he apparently fell overboard from his luxury yacht and was found dead floating in the sea off Tenerife. Tributes poured in from all over the world and Maxwell was given a 'quasi-state' funeral in Jerusalem (his name had often been linked to espionage and gun-running for Mossad).

Soon after his death speculation mounted that he had committed suicide. Then came the real bombshell. Faced by massive debts Maxwell had literally 'looted' his companies and, in particular, the Mirror Group Pension Fund. The scale of the fraud was colossal and led *Newsweek* to call him the 'Crook of the Century' while the affair was soon dubbed 'Mirrorgate'. Maxwell controlled a large empire of private companies, Maxwell Communications Corporation (MCC), and a public enterprise, Mirror Group Newspapers (MGN). The former comprised a web of trusts of which the ownership was concealed and which exploited the secrecy and company laws of Liechtenstein, Switzerland, Panama, the Virgin Islands, and Gibraltar. Many transactions occurred between the businesses in this opaque network and allowed an element of creative accounting and massaging of profits. The underlying financial fragility was put under substantial pressure in the late 1980s by an accumulation of elements including raising interest rates, recession, falling profits, and mounting debt. Exposure was threatened when Maxwell could not deliver security against a loan which effectively had him cheating on the Swiss Bank Corporation, First Tokyo Bank, Crédit Suisse, and Lehman Bros. Faced by public humiliation and bankruptcy he engaged in an illegal share-support operation, began to plunder his companies, and looted the pension funds (particularly of MGN).

Within a three-month period some £300 million (roughly $500 million) was missing from the pension funds. The family debts were later estimated at £1.4 billion and the banks faced losses of £1.2 billion. In December 1991 accountants reported that £770 million was missing from his companies and that £430 million had disappeared from pension funds. Robert Maxwell had perpetrated one of the greatest individual frauds of the century. A duped pensioner said, 'We feel like digging him up and hanging him' (Greenslade, 1992: 393).

Now let us stand back and itemize a number of factors of significance in the Maxwell affair. First, Maxwell was a man of huge energy, gifted and talented in many ways, and he could have basked in the reputation of the penniless immigrant who became one of Britain's most successful post-war entrepreneurs. Second, he had undoubted charm but he was also, according to inside accounts, a rude, aggressive, and cruel tyrant. He intimidated employees, harried opponents, manipulated the media, bullied his family, and ruthlessly removed threats to his dominance. Maxwell had total control of his private companies; outside directors posed no effective control, board meetings were a sham, and minutes were a fiction. In particular, Maxwell was not loath to use the legal weapon and was a champion at 'writ-slapping' to stall critics. Third, despite the warnings of the DTI he did manage to run some 150 companies and to win cooperation from major banks and brokers. He was not even a particularly good manager – there was no coherent strategy behind his acquisitions, he did not understand the newspaper business, his decisions were capricious and meddlesome, and he mistrusted his personnel (secretly tapping their phone conversations). But, with a mixture of shrewdness and cunning, he just pushed on relentlessly, juggling with his companies and people (usually acquiring the former and discarding the latter).

Referred to as 'Cap'n Bob', the weird world he created around him was dubbed 'Maxwellia' by the people who had to function in it. He ran roughshod over all the rules of modern management as well as the logic of business (often paying far more than was necessary for companies); but he was – at least on the surface – hugely successful. Fourth, he created a near impenetrable web of companies and holdings fully utilizing the opportunities provided by 'off-shore' and other tax havens protected by secrecy. Fifth, and most importantly, almost all that he did was cloaked in *legality* and sealed with the approval of lawyers, accountants, and bankers. He was only exposed as a fraud on a grand scale after his death. The DTI had labelled him in pejorative terms but, in general, the regulators simply failed to nail him down and the financial establishment of the City of London continued to support him right up to the end.

In effect, Maxwell represents one of the most dangerous and elusive types of corporate deviant. He was indistinguishable on the surface from the classic ambitious and aggressive entrepreneur; he had the social power to build influential relationships and create positive images; he had the corporate and legal muscle to cow opponents and bamboozle the regulators; and he shrewdly constructed a façade of *legality and respectability*. At the same time he was typical of corporate leaders for whom the organization is an extension of their ego (treating them as their personal fiefdoms) and the cut and thrust of business dealings is addictive. He was a speculator, gambler, risk-taker, and juggler. People, and companies, are means, not ends. Rules are there to be bent or manipulated. And the game is all about power, domination, and control. This implies that a 'bent' businessman can get away with a great deal as long as no one inside the organization dares to challenge his power and no agency outside the organization can get a grip on this illegality. This multiple failure was expressed in the words of the chairman of the Parliamentary Select Committee on Social Security;

> If the regulators had acted with a proper degree of suspicion, if the directors had carried out their duties fully, if professional advisers' common sense had been commensurate to their fees, if insiders had been brave enough to resign and talk, if newspaper editors had been prepared to stand up to Maxwell's bile and legal attacks, if brokers and merchant bankers had cared about their tasks as much as they did about their fees, if parliament had not been so beguiled by its own rhetoric about the special status of trust law, the Maxwell pension funds would have been secure. (Quoted in Greenslade, 1992: 392)

Maxwell was a confidence trickster but a very good and highly successful one, for he consistently managed to convince the business community that he was something that he was not. Despite the residue of suspicion from the DTI inquiry, and despite the fact that many considered him 'dodgy' (Greenslade, 1992: 12), he consistently generated sufficient trust and confidence to continue his business activities and to keep the watch-dogs at bay.

Finally, it is valuable to raise two aspects of corporate crime in relation to the Maxwell case. One is that the Maxwell affair dispels the widely held notion that corporate criminals do it for 'the good of the company'. Maxwell literally *looted* his own companies and did it solely in his own interests. The other is that much corporate crime is relatively harmless and 'victimless'. The collapse of the Maxwell empire caused harm and created *multiple victims* – among banks, investors, employees, and in a highly vulnerable group, pensioners. Maxwell had often openly pledged his loyalty to those reliant on his pension funds ('Do you honestly believe I would put my hand in the pension fund and steal it?' he had asked a meeting in 1985, and someone had called out 'Yes'), but he ruthlessly ripped them off. The charismatic maverick, the rogue elephant of British business, the great survivor, the philanthropist, the socialist entrepreneur had left them penniless. As one paper put it, the captain had mugged his own crew (*Daily Mail*, 5 December 1991).

Maxwell, the robber-baron, had dominated his organization, had crushed any opposition, had outwitted the regulators, and had taken his friends and associates for a ride. And he succeeded in keeping up the pretence of legality for a hell of a long time. The banks, the merchant banks, the brokers, the auditors, Goldman Sachs, the Stock Exchange, and the DTI had all failed to pick up the signals and the warnings. The self-regulating institutions in the financial world of the City of London not only had egg on their faces but they had also been badly burned. They had been conned on a massive scale; but then '"trust" is just the kind of City concept Maxwell despised' (Greenslade, 1992: 302). The watch-dogs had failed to bark because Maxwell had charmed them to sleep.

BCCI: A 'Full Service' Bank

> This indictment spells out the largest bank fraud in world history. BCCI was operated as a corrupt and criminal organization throughout its entire nineteen year history. It systematically falsified its records. It knowingly allowed itself to be used to launder the illegal income of drug sellers and other criminals. And it paid bribes and kickbacks to public officials.
>
> (Robert Morgenthau, New York District Attorney, 29 July 1991)

If Maxwell was the lone maverick, a one-man band wreaking havoc predominantly in the City of London, then BCCI was a large, intricate financial institution that exposed, and profited from, the weaknesses of global banking supervision. It is a convoluted and breath-taking story of a 'bank' – variously known as the 'Bank of Crooks and Criminals International' or the 'Bank of Cannabis and Cocaine International' – that attracted and was used by terrorists, security services, drug-barons, arms dealers, dictators, bent businessmen, and politicians, as well as thousands of legitimate businessmen and depositors, many of them from Asian countries. The Bank of Credit and Commerce International was set up in Luxembourg in 1972 by the Pakistani financier Agha Hasan Abedi and it was shut down by the Bank of England, in concert with regulators in other countries, in July 1991. In its nineteen years of existence it had indulged in nepotism, money-laundering, mismanagement, bribery, corruption, evasion of foreign exchange regulations, false accounting, misappropriation of depositors' money, blackmail, and massive fraud ('Kerry' Report, 1992). The collapse of BCCI was the largest bank closure in history (Adams and Frantz, 1992; Beaty and Gwynne, 1993). How could it happen and why were the regulators so tardy?

Origins   Agha Hasan Abedi registered BCCI in Luxembourg in 1972. He worked hard, possessed charm (and, for some, charisma), was a devout Muslim, and believed in building up powerful contacts wherever he operated but particularly among the leaders of Arab states. The largely Pakistani managers that he gathered around him were 'driven', worked long hours, and were adept at making their clients feel comfortable and at ease. His right-hand man, Swaleh Naqvi, was a 'brilliant banker' and the brains behind the operation, and it was he who 'devised the banking systems and kept the internal books' (Kochan and Whittington, 1991: 31). BCCI pushed itself as a 'Third World bank, a Third World voice'. There was a 'Third World Foundation' that published a glossy magazine, *South*, and that organized sumptuous conferences with leading keynote speakers; there were educational scholarships to

Cambridge University for children of the Third World; and there was a 'Third World Prize' which was awarded to Willy Brandt, Nelson and Winnie Mandela, Bob Geldof, and Gro Harlem Brundtland (Kochan and Whittington, 1991: 62).

Growth was spectacular, from $2.5 million capital in 1972 to 400 branches in 70 countries with a $23 billion capital base at the end, making it the world's *seventh* largest bank. Its centre of operations was London; there was the 'charity' ICIC, 'a bank within the bank', registered in the Cayman Islands (but ostensibly not linked to BCCI); there were shell companies in the Caymans and the Netherlands Antilles; the major depositors were in Arab countries; and the Luxembourg holding was not supervised by the Luxembourg authorities because it was not technically a 'bank'. BCCI also operated in the USA and secretly acquired the First American Bank in Washington, DC. It was a 'global' bank that cunningly evaded effective international supervision (Potts et al., 1992).

At this stage it is difficult to discern whether or not Abedi and Naqvi set out deliberately from the beginning to construct an illicit empire; some detractors were convinced that this was the case but it may well be that a combination of deviousness and mismanagement led to criminal solutions. What is apparent is that a number of features contributed to the growth of deviancy. First, there was the highly personal, autocratic style of leadership. When Abedi spoke at the annual conference it was a 'one man show', 'mesmeric', 'hypnotic', and there was an air of 'religious fervour' about the event (Kochan and Whittington, 1991: 53). Second, the Islamic bond between many employees induced a strong sense of loyalty and all the three main aspects of eastern culture – loyalty, nepotism, and hospitality – were 'taken to extremes' (Kochan and Whittington, 1991: 49). Third, traditional Asian practices of banking, such as 'Hundi' or 'Hawalla' (based particularly on illegal cash flows between the Indian subcontinent and other countries related to avoidance of exchange controls), were continued under the guise of modern western banking. Fourth, the highly personalized style of operating, allied to precipitous expansion, drew in unscrupulous operators, crooks, and security services who all saw BCCI as a convenient vehicle for their own devious schemes. Fifth, the cavalier attitude to paper and accounts, the opportunities for corruption, the tendency to buy off internal critics, and the wide-scale falsification of documents all made it increasingly difficult to steer the operations while also allowing considerable internal abuse. The accountants Price Waterhouse uncovered a treasury within the treasury which 'traded disastrously'; this evaded normal auditing and its losses were concealed by creative accounting. Furthermore, the treasury, according to the accountants' report to the Bank of England of 1991, 'had misappropriated depositors' money without their knowledge, misappropriated funds deposited by shareholders of BCCI Holdings, and created entirely fictitious loans of "no commercial substance"'. Price Waterhouse estimated that some £1.3 billion had passed through the treasury. In a follow-up letter to the Bank of England dated 4 July 1991, they summed up their report as follows: 'We believe that the report reflects the general scale and complexity of the deception and falsification which have undoubtedly taken place over many years' (Kochan and Whittington, 1991: 139, 182). And, sixth and last, the fragmented, opaque structure was difficult to oversee and granted near total power to the man at the top.

There were, then, a number of forces pushing BCCI towards crime and permitting it to thrive unchecked. At the same time there were hundreds of honest employees unaware of these criminal machinations; to them it was a normal bank. There were thousands of legitimate depositors who thought their money and investments were safe. For BCCI was run by sophisticated and even brilliant bankers, the branches were well situated and opulent, and the staff were polite, fast, and understanding. A representative of the Asian business community of East London lamented, 'For many, it was more than a bank, it was a central part of their business life' (*Daily Mail*: 15 July 1991). Indeed, some depositors and employees retained their faith in the bank; they blamed the regulators and, in particular, the Bank of England. Why had the watch-dogs waited so long before going public on the disturbing evidence that something was seriously amiss at BCCI? Why had the accountants not cried 'wolf' earlier? Many were embittered that the delay had caused them to lose their jobs, their savings, their livelihood.

A Litany of Villains   Rapid expansion, pressure for results, unscrupulous managers, and a non-western cultural base all conspired to draw BCCI into a web of intrigue and deception that included most of the notorious 'folk devils' of the last two decades. In effect, BCCI allowed its branches to be used for the following:

● Manuel Noriega amassed a personal fortune by stashing in western banks some $300 million which he had acquired illegally by fraud in Panama and by involvement in drug-smuggling. According to the indictment against him,

    The operations of the BCCI Group in its dealings with Manuel Noriega constitute a racketeering operation of unparalleled scope, international in its reach and totally ruthless in its evasion of banking, fraud, disclosure and common and code laws of numerous nations, including the United States. (Kochan and Whittington, 1991: 108)

● BCCI operated as a conduit for the funds from the Colombian Medellín and Cali cartels earned from the cocaine trade, largely with North America, and it 'laundered' their money for them.
● BCCI was used by arms dealers, terrorist groups, and secret services for dubious and even bizarre transactions, as strange bedfellows met in the world of intrigue and covert operations. Mossad, Hezbollah, Abu Nidal, and the CIA were all cavorting around in curious deals while there were interconnections to Irangate, Adnan Kashoggi, Oliver North, the Contras, the Mujaheddin of Afghanistan, and the Pakistani nuclear industry.

The bank apparently had its own secret service, known as the 'black network', and this operated as a 'global intelligence operation and enforcement squad' (Kochan and Whittington, 1991, 130). But there was undoubted involvement with the secret services of several countries and their bag of 'dirty tricks', while the bank itself was alleged to have used bribery, secret surveillance, blackmail, and intimidation ('Kerry' Report, 1992).

Ironically, it was ostensibly a 'legitimate' business relation that helped to pull BCCI down. The three Gokal brothers were Pakistanis and Shi'ites, and they expanded their family business until, for a number of years, Gulf Shipping and Trading had the largest merchant fleet in the world. Like BCCI, Gulf was run by 'charismatic, all-powerful individuals and both shared a culture of opulence and optimism' (Kochan and Whittington, 1991: 42). The Gokals ran 750 accounts with BCCI and their turnover was $15 billion within a fifteen-year period; but from early on these major customers of the bank ceased to repay their loans and, when the Gokals' empire showed the strain of rapid expansion and uncoordinated diversification, it threatened to drag BCCI into dangerous waters. The Gokals could get almost unlimited credit from BCCI, and transactions were not recorded; bank employees took a rake-off; and Gokal people lined their own pockets. The cavalier attitude to loans and accounts was sketched by a former Gulf employee:

> We used to go round to BCCI and pick up a bag of money to pay somebody off. I would go to 101 Leadenhall Street (the BCCI headquarters) and see a man called —. He would smile at me, and say, 'Sign this piece of paper.' I would write 'Mickey Mouse' on a piece of tissue paper which was then thrown away. He handed me a bag of money which I would then take back and distribute. (Kochan and Whittington, 1991: 44)

The Gokal 'empire' eventually got out of control, loans escalated, debt mounted, and this all proved highly damaging, if not fatal, to BCCI.

Coming Apart   There has been a fair amount of speculation as to how long BCCI could have continued to operate if it had not indulged in excesses, such as the unbounded largesse accorded to the Gokals. In retrospect there may seem something inevitable about the collapse of this financial house of cards, but the major mistake was to operate in the country with relatively tough and tenacious regulators – the United States. BCCI was pushing its luck in illegally acquiring an American bank. Yet the law enforcers initially stumbled on BCCI almost as a coincidence. For it was a 'sting' operation in Miami that finally brought the launderer's dirty washing into public. BCCI took over the First American Bank by using 'shell' constructions in the Caymans and Netherlands Antilles that concealed their ownership of CCAH and CCAI (a holding company and a 'charity' respectively). It employed prestigious lawyers to plead its cause and used prosperous Saudi and other Arab dignitaries as nominee investors. This enabled it to fend off complaints to the SEC (Securities and Exchange Commission). The bank cultivated powerful allies through donations and charities and was linked in particular to associates of former President Jimmy Carter. Although the Federal Reserve received signals that all was not quite correct with BCCI in 1981, it took some *ten years* for formal charges to be brought against the bank. And it was only in 1988 that the Federal Reserve began a serious investigation into the illegal take-over of First American. BCCI had contrived to stave off the financial regulators for over a decade.

But other regulators were at work in the area of drugs and drugs money (Pearce and Woodiwiss, 1993). The US Customs, for instance, mounted 'Operation C-chase' and used a spectacular 'scam' when a wedding celebration set up by undercover agents was employed as a cover to arrest eighty-five suspects. As a result BCCI and nine of its officers were charged with laundering drug money to the tune of $18.8 million (Kochan and Whittington, 1991: 105). The bank decided to enter a guilty plea and was fined $14.8 million, while several executives were jailed with sentences reaching fourteen years. This was the first investigation in the USA to lead to the successful conviction of an international bank. The evidence indicated that senior officials of the bank had deliberately broken banking regulations, had consciously bought influence, and had colluded in crooked enterprises. From then on the bank was attacked by negative publicity as its connections with Noriega, drug dealers, arms traders, terrorists and secret services began to leak out. It was linked to Duvalier, Somoza, Saddam Hussein, and Marcos and it was connected with the Iraq-gate scandal and the Iran-Contra affair. The regulators began to close in for the kill.

The whole process of control was, however, retarded by interference and by politics. There were inter-organizational rivalries, failures of communication, and complex legal issues that sometimes undermined the swift and coordinated investigation and prosecution of highly complex cases (Passas and Groskin, 1993). Many agencies were involved and there were accusations of lack of resources, poor leadership, and lack of resolve – not to mention interference and even corruption; but a key element seems to have been that the prosecutory focus was fixed on money-laundering and not so much on the breaking of banking laws. BCCI was also known as the 'bank of the CIA', and it is almost certain that security considerations in several countries prolonged its existence. Then in 1990 and 1991, when the pressure for interference was mounting, the conflict in the Gulf War meant that western governments did not want to alienate their Arab allies. Indeed, the Bank of England had its doubts about BCCI earlier, refusing it a full licence way back in 1978, but in April 1990 it was presented with an accountant's report that 'certain accounting transactions were false and deceitful' (Kochan and Whittington 1991: 149). At this stage the Bank of England wanted more evidence before any move that might cause a run on the bank, particularly as BCCI was restructuring and receiving injections of new capital from Abu Dhabi. Later the then Governor of the Bank of England, Robin Leigh-Pemberton, justified his reticence before a parliamentary Select Committee with the words, 'Our view was that even if these transactions added up to individual acts of fraud, it did not add up to systematic fraud. . . . If we closed down a bank every time we had a fraud, we would have rather fewer banks than we have' (Kochan and Whittington, 1991: 151).

What changed the Governor's mind was a secret examination of the books by accountants Price Waterhouse that unearthed vast, almost inconceivable, frauds. The Bank of England had no alternative but to take action and it moved to close down BCCI on 5 July 1991 (following consultation and coordination with the US authorities who might even have embarrassingly pre-empted its action). The liquidators Touche Ross moved in immediately, and later the Serious Fraud Office was involved leading to a series of investigations and prosecutions. It was the largest bank closure in history, the 'largest bank fraud in world financial history' (according to Morgenthau, the New York District Attorney), and Leigh-Pemberton now publicly labelled the culture of the bank as 'criminal' (Kochan and Whittington, 1991: 168). Some critics might have used that label to castigate the Bank of England's tardiness, and an official report documented a series of errors by the Bank of England ('Bingham [Report; MP] Blames the Bank'; *Observer*; 25 October 1992; 'Bingham' Report, 1992).

This was distressing news for the thousands of employees, investors, pensioners and businessmen who had lost their money and who felt that they had been duped by the lack of warnings. There was particular acrimony directed at the Bank of England; but BCCI had successfully thwarted the regulators for years. And it enabled them to perpetuate a fraud of unimaginable proportions – the New York indictment spoke of a $20 billion swindle from depositors around the world (Kochan and Whittington, 1991: 168).

Implications   BCCI represented a profound shock to the financial system. It is of especial interest for three main reasons. First, it was rooted in Third World countries and it imported traditional Asian practices into western banking; for example, Kochan and Whittington (1991: 217) write of 'Hundi' and 'Hawalla' banking that BCCI 'were doing nothing more than institutionalizing what Indians and Pakistanis have been doing for decades, namely, passing money across the world using an underground banking system which worked on trust and close family networks'. Second, it became essentially a *criminal* organization posited on massive manipulation of accounts. The bank was controlled by a number of devious and fraudulent men; they were aided by influential customers who acted in collusion with them; and cooking the books had become 'a way of life' (Kochan and Whittington, 1991: 212). Price Waterhouse, for instance, reported that, 'It appears that account manipulation began at this stage, and to this end a "special duties" department was set up to oversee these accounts. This was a full-time occupation which involved the manufacture of documentation, inflation of account takeover, concealment of fund flows, etc.' (Kochan and Whittington, 1991: 47).

To date, a number of BCCI bankers have been prosecuted and sentenced to terms in prison, but Abedi has evaded arrest by living abroad in Pakistan (*de Volkskrant*, 29 September 1993); Naqvi pleaded guilty to a number of charges having been extradited to the United States and was sentenced to eleven years' imprisonment (*de Volkskrant*, 20 October 1994). The former head of BCCI's treasury division was jailed for six years at the Old Bailey in London in 1993 following his admittance to sixteen charges of false accounting (the prison term was relatively light as he cooperated fully with the authorities, and he was released within two years; *Daily Mail*, 1 September 1995).

Third, BCCI used secrecy, deception, off-shore constructions, and influential friends to circumvent regulation. With pretensions to being a global bank, BCCI thrived largely because there is no effective global regulation of financial services (*Business Week*, 22 July 1991). And also because an incredible cast of characters – dictators, drug dealers, arms traders, terrorists, and spies – *needed a bank*; it was their subterranean interests that kept the bank in existence longer than necessary. And also helped in duping thousands of people involved in this 'full-service' bank.

Bilkers in the Night: the Savings and Loan Débâcle

> We built thick vaults; we have cameras; we have time clocks on the vaults; we have dual controls – all these controls were to protect against somebody stealing the cash. Well, you can steal far more money, and take it out the back door. *The best way to rob a bank is to own one.*

> (Commissioner of California Department Savings and Loan, quoted in Calavita and Pontell, 1990: 321; emphasis in original)

Background   The Savings and Loan (S & L) scandal represents almost certainly one of the greatest cases of mismanagement and fraud in this century (Pizzo et al., 1989; Mayer, 1990). The sheer magnitude of the affair, with an impact on every American inhabitant to the tune of $6,000, is almost beyond belief (and 'represents a monetary loss greater than the direct cost of crime over a lifetime for all but a very small fraction of American individuals or families', Zimring and Hawkins, 1993: 256). Indeed, reflection on it has helped to alter our thinking on corporate deviance. If previous work tended to focus on corporate deviance as being born from a wish to enhance a company's interests, then this has to be revised in the light of the S & L cases where often the conscious aim was precisely to 'loot' the firm. In blunt terms, some owners ripped off their own institutions on a grand scale.

The Savings and Loan (or 'thrifts') financial network was designed to take deposits and to offer mortgages (White, 1991). Substantial regulation of the industry was created in the wake of the Depression as part of the New Deal arrangements in order to guarantee low-interest mortgages. Restricted in terms of loans and interest rates, these thrifts expanded and prospered in the post-war boom, survived the increase in interest rates of the 1960s, but were severely hit by the double-digit inflation of the 1970s and by the higher interest rates offered by the commercial banking sector. By the end of the decade most were losing money and collectively they were burdened by a negative net worth of $17.5 billion (Pizzo et al., 1989: 11). The election of Ronald Reagan to the presidency accelerated an ideology and rhetoric of deregulation which held that business should be freed from undue rules and restrictions and that market forces should be given a freer rein to enhance competition. Deregulation was seen, for instance, as a cure for the ailing thrift industry and much of the mechanism of control was dismantled. Over a decade later a significant minority of thrifts have failed, the cumulative losses are astronomical, and this national scandal has fostered accusations of mismanagement, undue risk-taking, 'looting', and widespread criminal activity (Day, 1993). How could this happen and what went wrong?

The Débâcle   The move to deregulate the thrift industry meant that interest rates were no longer tied to a low ceiling, that investments and loans could be given for consumer and commercial purposes, that 100 per-cent financing could be offered with no down payment, and that a single entrepreneur could own and operate a S & L (White, 1991; Adams, 1990). In effect, these developments opened up a rich vein of opportunity for unscrupulous and crooked businessmen who moved in and exploited the thrifts for their own devious purposes. They discovered not only a virtual licence to print money but also they could rely on government backing to do so! For there was a fatal flaw in the deregulation move in that it was founded on a central contradiction: legislation both loosened controls on thrifts but at the same time it raised the limit of federal protection on deposits to $100,000. These 'brokered deposits' meant that brokers could make commissions on them, investors received higher interest rates, and the S & L attracted new funds while enjoying a federal safety net; according to Calavita and Pontell (1990: 313) they were 'the critical factor in creating pressure to engage in misconduct and in providing unprecedented opportunities for fraud'.

The deviance inspired by this new opportunity structure was rich and creative. It inspired a new cynical vocabulary of terms such as 'land flips', 'dead cows, dead horses', 'daisy chains', and 'cash-for-trash' (Hagan and Benekos, 1990). Some quipped that S & L stood for 'Squander and Liquidate'. The regulatory agency for thrifts (the Federal Home Loan Bank Board or FHLBB) reported to Congress in 1988:

> Individuals in a position of trust in the institution or closely affiliated with it have, in general terms, breached their fiduciary duties; traded on inside information; usurped opportunities for profits; engaged in self-dealing; or otherwise used the institution for personal advantage. Specific examples of insider abuse include loans to insiders in excess of that allowed by regulation; high-risk speculative ventures; payment of exorbitant dividends at times when the institution is at or near insolvency; payment from institutions' funds for personal vacations, automobiles, clothing, and art; payment of unwarranted commissions and fees to companies owned by a shareholder; payment of 'consulting fees' to insiders or their companies; use of insiders' companies for association business; and putting friends and relatives on the payroll of the institutions. (US General Accounting Office, 1989: 22)

In terms of these fraudulent practices Calavita and Pontell (1990: 316f.) categorize them under three main concepts: 'unlawful risk-taking', 'looting', and 'covering-up'.

The thrifts were suddenly thrust into a highly competitive environment, endorsed risky speculative ventures and also 'long-shot investments with the potential for high pay-off' (Calavita and Pontell, 1990: 317). There was a circular, addictive element to this response to market change. Thrifts could attract large sums of money by offering high interest rates but the inflow of funds was often used to postpone problems; and the deeper the trouble, the higher the interest rates, 'And, like a drug the most desperate institutions needed the most and paid the highest interest rates. In a perverse contortion of the theory of the survival of the fittest to which the free market deregulators subscribed – in this environment it was the weakest thrifts that grew the fastest (1990: loc. cit.).

One area where this behaviour was evident was speculative real estate development, particularly in those states (such as Texas) where no ceiling was set for 'ADC' loans (Acquisition, Development, and Construction). The scramble to enter real estate, and to advance loans, fostered the colloquial expression 'cash-for-dirt loans'. But, in essence, the lifting of restraint led to rampant competition and rabid rule-bending. 'The "cure" turned out to be worse than the disease; deregulation had triggered an ever-escalating competition for deposits, and pressed some thrift operators into high-risk, often unlawful, loan arrangements' (Calavita and Pontell, 1990: 319).

Then there was 'looting'. Calavita and Pontell dub this 'collective embezzlement', which refers to 'the siphoning off of funds from a savings and loans institution for personal gain, at the expense of the institution itself and with implicit or explicit sanction of its management. This "robbing of one's own bank" is estimated to be the single most costly category of crime in the thrift industry, having precipitated a significant number of the thrift insolvencies to date' (1990: 321).

Forms that this looting took were buying luxury goods, lavish entertainment, private jets and extravagant yachts, exorbitant salaries and excessive bonuses, but particularly 'special deals'. Often by using a 'straw borrower' outside of the thrift, a loan could be obtained for someone usually involved in the thrift – the owner of one S & L in Texas set up an 'intricate network of at least 30 subsidiary companies for the express purpose of making illegal loans to himself' (Calavita and Pontell, 1990: 323). In 'land flips', property was juggled back and forth to increase its value artificially and to secure loans on the basis of inflated real estate worth. One parcel of real estate at Lake Tahoe went from $4 million to $40 million, while another in California was assessed at under $1 million but had risen to over $80 million two years later after a series of 'flips' (Calavita and Pontell, 1991: 99). 'Daisy chains' or 'linked financing' involved making a deposit, borrowing on the strength of that deposit, and then defaulting on the loans. And everyone profited (except the taxpayer); the brokers were granted virtually free cash, 'middlemen obtain a generous "finder's fee"; and thrift operators record hefty deposits and inflated assets, which spell extra bonuses and dividends for thrift executives' (Calavita and Pontell, 1990: 325).

There was something of a looting epidemic and the S & L's vulnerability represented a field day for con-men and crooks who sensed easy money;

> The Commissioner of the California Department of Savings and Loan described the pressure to engage in fraud in the competitive environment dominated by brokered deposits: 'f you have got a lot of money, high-cost money pushing you, and

you have to make profits, you have to put it out awful fast'. But the words of an unidentified witness best sum up the formula that produced an epidemic of unlawful risk-taking in the thrift-industry: 'If you put temptation and the opportunity, and the need in the same place, you are asking for trouble'. (Calavita and Pontell, 1990: 319).

With mismanagement, negligence, risk-taking, fraud, and insolvency widespread in the industry, it was inevitable that a great deal of energy had to be expended on concealing the real situation by 'cooking the books' (Hagan and Benekos, 1990: 13). Calavita and Pontell maintain that this 'covering up' was 'perhaps the most widespread criminal activity of thrift operators . . . . At one savings and loan studied by the GAO [General Accounting Office, MP], three irreconcilable sets of records were kept – two on two different computer systems and one manually' (1990: 26). The intricate rule-bending and extensive rule-breaking spawned a massive manipulation of accounts, books, and records that covered the deviants' tracks and that aimed to bamboozle the regulators.

What also emerges with considerable clarity from the evidence is that some thrifts did *not* turn to deviance, that some sought the deviant solution only as a desperate attempt to ensure survival, but that some attracted unscrupulous characters whose *sole aim* was to milk the thrifts for all they were worth.

In the anger and vengeful frustration that accompanied debate on the débâcle it was probably inevitable that the fraudulent and criminal element would dominate perceptions. White (1991: 4) argues that this is misleading. It was the rapid expansion of a minority of thrifts – whose 'executives were overly aggressive, excessively optimistic, careless, ignorant, and/or fraudulent and criminal' – that underlay the crisis;

> There is no question that rule violation did occur in many thrifts. . . . The bulk of the insolvent thrifts' problems, however, did not stem from such fraudulent or criminal activities. These thrifts largely failed because of an amalgam of deliberately high-risk strategies, poor business judgements, foolish strategies, excessive optimism, and sloppy and careless underwriting, compounded by deteriorating real estate markets. These thrifts had little incentive to behave otherwise, and the excessively lenient and ill-equipped regulatory environment tolerated these business practices for far too long. (White, 1991: 117)

In the public eye, however, it was often the rapacious 'looters' who attracted attention. An owner of one particular Savings and Loan institution 'earned' over $34 million for himself and family members in five years. The closing of this thrift, delayed because of the successful lobbying of five Congressmen, cost the taxpayer around $2.5 billion (Hagan and Benekos, 1990: 10). Another owner made his jets and yacht available to members of Congress, ran up exorbitant expenses, and extracted with his associates some $40 million while 'squandering' $350 million of Vernon's assets (1990: 21). Unlike the old-style corporate criminal of the standard literature, who was ostensibly something of a straight character pushed into deviance to aid the company and to ensure its continuity, these new-style 'casino capitalists' had, like professional gamblers, one main aim – namely, 'get in and out of the "house" with as much of the "pot" as possible' (Calavita and Pontell, 1990: 336).

In addition there can be no doubt that fraud and crime played a significant role in the demise of a significant minority of thrifts. While the thrift industry had largely recovered by the end of the 1980s, it was the rapid expanders or 'flameouts' – who entered new lines of business, who attracted new entrepreneurs, and who speculated on the commercial real estate boom of the early 1980s (particularly in Texas and some south-west states) – who were 'disproportionately responsible for the wave of insolvencies and their huge costs to the FSLIC (the federal provider of insurance to depositors)' (White, 1991: 101f.). For example, in 1987 more than 6,000 cases were referred to the Justice Department in relation to S & Ls, and in 1988 the number was in excess of 5,000. When the GAO (Government Accounting Office) scrutinized twenty-six thrifts that had failed, the conclusion was that criminal activity was central in the demise of *all twenty-six* (Calavita and Pontell, 1991: 98).

The House Committee on Government Operations reported in 1988 that crime had been a major factor in 80 per cent of the insolvencies then up for support; and the Resolution Trust Corporation (the FSLIC's successor as federal insurer of deposits) maintained that fraud was the cause of failure in 450 thrifts for which the agency had become responsible. Pizzo et al. concluded their analysis of the débâcle by asserting that

> a financial mafia of swindlers, molesters, greedy S & L executives, and con men capitalized on regulatory weaknesses created by deregulation and thoroughly fleeced the thrift industry. While it was certainly true that economic factors (like plummeting oil prices in Texas and surrounding states) contributed to the crises, S & Ls would not be in the mess they are today, but for rampant fraud. (1989: 289)

This judgement is shared by Calavita and Pontell (1991: 98): 'regardless of the actual percentage of the final bill that can be traced directly to crime, there is no doubt that substantial crime and fraud have permeated the industry in the last decade and have contributed to its collapse'. The thrifts had been looted and, in some cases, even been 'killed' by their marauding owners.

The Conspiracy of Factors   This national scandal arose from a complexity of factors. First, market changes in the 1970s pushed the S & L sector into a disadvantaged position in relation to the commercial institutions. Second, the government's response to this was deregulation, but the 'fatal formula' combined measures of deregulation with *increased insurance protection* of deposits (White, 1991). This conspired to create rich opportunities for widespread deviance. Third, the effect of the remaining regulation and enforcement was weakened by inadequate resources, overlapping responsibilities, the magnitude of the task (which often meant a reluctance to intervene), ambivalence in terms of both controlling and promoting the industry, the poaching of regulators by the thrifts, and political interference. There was an element of 'capture' in the relationship but also a built-in fear of tough action in case rumours led to a run on thrifts that would expose their weakness and possibly reverberate into the commercial branch. The financial sector is vulnerable to rumour and nervously apprehensive of a 'domino' effect. Regulators were reluctant to deflate the 'soap bubble' in case the whole shaky house of cards came crashing down around them. Some 489 thrifts went on to record losses of $42 billion while continuing to operate *after* insolvency (Calavita and Pontell, 1991: 98). The FSLIC (which itself became insolvent as its funds proved inadequate to the task) became a holding-tank for 'zombie' thrifts which were warehoused until they could be dealt with (White, 1991: 133). Criminal prosecutions were lengthy and uncertain, while civil actions often foundered on insolvency and an inability to recover any assets. And fourth, the thrifts lobbied energetically, enjoyed some strong links with politicians, and could rely on political support to deflect enforcement. Congressmen were entertained royally by the thrifts and could rely on them for campaign contributions. All of these factors combined to ensure that the S & Ls were not deregulated but 'unregulated'; they were 'victimized by congressional incompetence and regulatory ineptitude' (Pilzer and Deitz, 1989: 126).

There emerged a web of vested interest that profited from prolonging the agony. And that raised dramatically the cost of the rescue and extent of the final bill (affecting some 1,600 thrifts – *Business Week*, 2 August 1993). In effect, the unintended consequence of government policy had been the creation of a criminogenic market which had proved too tempting for a minority of thrifts. The 'iron triangle' of Congress members, career bureaucrats, and special interest lobbies was finally broken by 'whistle blowers, journalists, and an insider (Chairman Gray of the FHLBB)' (Benekos and Hagan, 1990: 28). The complacency, indecision, and paralysis that accompanied political and regulatory response to this financial and institutional débâcle meant that many people were unaware of the extent of the crisis until it was too late; as Benekos and Hagan (1990: 28) caustically observe, 'We were told that the S & Ls had venereal disease when in fact they had AIDS.'

The Significance of the S & Ls Scandal

> If you didn't do it, you weren't just stupid – you weren't behaving as a prudent businessman, which is the ground rule. You owed it to your partners, to your stockholders, to maximize profits. Everybody else was doing it.

> (Texan S & L consultant quoted by Calavita and Pontell, 1990: 320)

In this brief overview of one of the white-collar crimes of the century I wish to focus on three main points. First, the financial capitalism of the 1980s (the 'casino economy', as Maurice Allais, the Nobel Prize-winning economist, called it) created new opportunity structures for deviance. Financial institutional fraud – centred on violation of trust, self-dealing, insider trading, and so on – took trust, plus the stewardship of other people's money for 'some ephemeral service in the future', and exploited the near limitless opportunities virtually to mint money (Calavita and Pontell, 1993: 540). Second, these opportunities magnified rapidly with the withdrawal of much regulatory restraint, and this spawned an incredible array of cases of mismanagement, undue risk-taking, speculative investment, looting, fraud, and creative accounting. Weaknesses in enforcement, and self-serving political reluctance to intervene, stymied those who did wish to tackle a situation which deteriorated to disastrous proportions (with estimates of the final bill reaching $1.4 trillion).

Third, and most crucially, the S & L affair helped to reshape our perception of corporate crime, particularly through the work of Calavita and Pontell (1990, 1991, 1993; Pontell and Calavita, 1993). This was not deviance designed to enhance corporate interest, conducted on behalf of the company, and with the manager situationally resorting to law-breaking as a means to increase profits or to ensure continuity and not directly profiting financially from it. Rather, the misconduct was premeditated, highly organized, and continuous. The criminal and fraudulent element in the S & L affair revealed a strong element of *premeditated looting* for personal gain. Unscrupulous people flocked to the industry in order to fleece it. Only the absence of violence and intimidation separated this behaviour from that of organized crime (if by that we refer to illegal, syndicated enterprises based on criminal intent and control of illicit markets, but almost inevitably 'mob money' did enter the thrift circuit: Pizzo et al., 1989: 230). But in a sense this *was* a form of 'organized crime'; except in order to plunder the bank you bought it first. In the S & L case the organization was the weapon and, at the same time, the victim. The thrifts were 'ideal vehicles for their own victimization' (Calavita and Pontell, 1993: 542).

The thrifts affair forces us to revise our notion of corporate crime. In the new opportunities of the 1980s, 'cowboy capitalists' plundered their own businesses in their own interest; they not only stripped them ruthlessly but they even threatened to undermine the health of an entire financial sector with possible serious repercussions for banking as a whole. Yet in a strange way it was also an 'almost painless public catastrophe', because the comprehensive insurance scheme meant that this was the 'first major institutional failure in American history subject to 100 per cent government reimbursement' (Zimring and Hawkins, 1993: 256). This may have reduced the demand for tough criminal prosecution, particularly as the government had deliberately doubled the bill by not choosing a politically unpalatable short-term solution. Indeed, the government emerges almost as an accomplice to crime; it created such seductive opportunities for deviance that these virtually amounted to entrapment, while 'the discussion of the causes of the S & L failures is the first time we can recall when the failure of the regulatory system has been widely seen as a principal cause of large-scale criminal conduct' (Zimring and Hawkins, 1993: 281). This, then, was crime *by* the corporation *against* the corporation, encouraged by the state; and with the taxpayer as the ultimate victim (Calavita and Pontell, 1991: 100).

2

Business, Society, and
Corporate Deviance

The three highly dramatic cases of Maxwell, BCCI, and the S & Ls are doubtless far removed from the world of much small-scale business deviance
(Barlow, 1993). But because of the detailed attention they have aroused, they
do help to blow apart the rational and respectable myth of management to
reveal parts of business as having a pervasive underside where top managers
manipulate their companies, the regulators, and their environments for devious ends. More generally, accidents, scandals, public inquiries, and
'whistle-blowers' have helped expose misconduct in a broad spectrum of business organizations. For example, a number of well-known cases in recent
decades have alerted us to deviance in certain industries and in relation to
specific deviant practices: it is important to perceive the wide range of companies involved, and the considerable impact on public perceptions of
corporate misconduct, that the following cases represent.

Mini-cases: from Bhopal to Barings

Industrial Accident at Bhopal

On 3 December 1984, the world's worst industrial accident happened at the
Union Carbide chemical plant at Bhopal in India (Shrivastava, 1987; Weir,
1987; Jones, 1988). An explosion at the factory released poisonous gas (methyl
isocyanate) into the atmosphere and this killed between 3,000 and 5,000
people and injured more than 200,000. In recent commemorations of the disaster it has emerged that many survivors are still suffering considerably as a
result of the accident; thousands have incurred permanent damage and their
illnesses have been related to 'damaged eyes, chronic lung disease, brain damage, cancer and birth defects' (*Japan Times*, 4 December 1994; *de Volkskrant*,
3 December 1994). Union Carbide had wanted to sell the plant and it was
being run down; there were reports of poor maintenance, turnover of personnel, and a number of minor accidents, but these signals met with a lack of
interest from corporate headquarters in the USA. Faced by a massive accident
on another continent, Carbide went into a defensive posture and ran through
a repertoire of explanations and excuses – Union Carbide India was completely independent of the American corporation (which was not the case), a
disgruntled employer had committed sabotage, Sikh extremists had carried out
a terrorist attack, and safety at the plant was at the same level as the 'identical'

plant in the USA (which was later changed to the Bhopal unit being 'identical but different'). Union Carbide defended its safety record and that of the chemical industry; won a crucial legal victory when the court case was transferred to India (if the case had gone against Carbide in the American courts then UC could have been bankrupted); and came to a final settlement with the Indian government of $470 million. As the settlement is still being contested in the Indian courts the victims have not received a cent of UC's money. Ironically, UC escaped the takeover rage of the 1980s, and the tentacles of an ambitious competitor, because Bhopal operated as a 'poison-pill' (no one was interested in taking on UC's potential liabilities). UC actually emerged 'leaner and meaner' and, when the settlement with the Indian government was announced, its stocks soared; the rise of UC's shares on Wall Street plus insurance cover meant that the Bhopal tragedy had cost Carbide 'nothing' (BBC Television documentary, 'The B-Word', 1991). The Bhopal tragedy raised issues related to industrial safety (UC had produced the deadly m.i.c. in Virginia and safety in North American plants was a major media focus), the transfer of technology by multinationals, the level and reliability of regulation in less developed societies, the legal muscle of western corporations and their influence via the media, and the ethical responsibility of management for a disaster in one of their plants abroad. The level of human suffering at Bhopal was immense; in contrast, the value placed on an Indian's life was revealed to be pitifully low compared to that calculated by insurers and lawyers for a western life.

Product Liability and the Ford Pinto

This is probably one of the most widely debated cases in business ethics (and cf. Cullen et al., 1984). The American car industry faced foreign competition from small cars in the late 1960s and Lee Iacocca, president of the Ford Motor Corporation, decided to launch a sub-compact built to tough specifications on size and cost (Iacocca, 1986). The petrol tank was placed behind the rear axle and, in tests, it proved vulnerable to rupturing and igniting following a rear-end collision (Buchholz, 1989: 167). The controversy centred on documents which could be interpreted as contributing to decision-making based on a cost-benefit analysis of the costs of a design change balanced against anticipated insurance claims for deaths and injuries. Iacocca dismissed the suggestion that senior management callously pushed ahead with production in order to keep the price competitive while fully aware of the hazards: 'The guys who built the Pinto had kids in college who were driving that car. Believe me, nobody sits down and thinks: "I'm deliberately going to make this car unsafe". In the end, we voluntarily recalled almost a million and a half Pintos' (1986: 172).

The difficulty in interpreting many business decisions that have led to intense public debate and even court cases is that you cannot fully reconstruct the motives and interaction of executives in a board-room meeting. Motives may be mixed, documents which appear in the public arena and are held to have been influential may not have played a highly significant role, and the 'collective conscience' of the board – prompted by legal counsel and media advisers – may rally around *post hoc* defensive rationales for decisions. Then the consequences of decisions are related to thousands of documents of technical data that require expert analysis. Ford was attacked on the safety record of the Pinto but argued that it was no worse than other models produced by other companies. At the time there was often an adversarial relationship between large companies and the media as well as the regulators, and Ford was doubtless determined to defend its product and reputation against what it saw as bias and the selective quoting of documents. The controversy on car safety had been launched by Ralph Nader's *Unsafe at Any Speed* which critically examined the record of General Motors' Convair model.

The Pinto went into production in 1970 as a 'carefree little American car'. There were later a number of accidents causing horrendous injuries and deaths by burning, following rear-end crashes with Pintos. In Indiana in 1978 three young women died in a flaming Pinto and Ford was taken to court for 'reckless homicide'; 'it was the first time a major American corporation would go to trial for murder' (Mokhiber, 1988: 381). The prosecution proved unsuccessful. Subsequent civil court cases led to far higher damages than Ford had calculated, while there was also a wave of negative publicity; a 'Mother Jones' article entitled 'Pinto Madness' spoke of a 'fire-trap' and of '500 burn deaths' (Dowie, 1977; 'but nothing in Ford records supported the contentions in the article', according to *Harvard Business School*, Case 383-129, 1983:1). Ford had vigorously opposed some of the NHTSA's (National Highway Traffic Safety Administration) standards on safety and had adopted an adversarial relationship with it; now Ford also strongly defended its product: 'there is no serious fire hazard in the fuel system of the Ford Pinto' (Ford news release, September 1977). But criticism mounted and was accentuated by a $125 million punitive damages case involving a teenage passenger in a Pinto who had been severely burned and who had required sixty different operations after the accident (*Harvard Business School*, Case 383-129, 1983 – the judge reduced this sum, following a Ford motion to set aside the award, to $3.5 million; Mokhiber, 1988: 379). Class action suits demanding the recall of the early Pintos and the modification of their tanks together with further criticism from the NHTSA forced Ford, after years of strenuously defending the safety of the Pinto's fuel system, to recall more than 1.5 million cars.

The government wished to avoid a prolonged legal battle in the courts and shelved its investigation without a final determination in the face of Ford's willingness to announce a recall; Ford continued to defend its product in relation to comparable cars, but Henry Ford II did state, 'the lawyers will shoot me for saying this, but I think there's some cause for concern about the Pinto' (*Fortune*, 11 September 1978).

Environmental Pollution and the Exxon Valdez

There have been a number of major ecological calamities caused by the spilling of massive quantities of oil following accidents at sea. And when oil-tankers run aground it is almost as if they seek out areas of outstanding natural beauty do so: the *Amoco Cadiz* off Brittany (1978), the *Torrey Canyon* in the English Channel (1967), the *Aegean Sea* off La Coruña in Spain, and the *Braer* (1993) in the Scottish Shetlands, all contaminated attractive coast-lines (Keeble, 1991). When the *Exxon Valdez* hit the rocks in Prince William Sound it released 40 million litres of oil that spread along 1,200 kilometres of the Alaskan coast-line (Keeble, 1991). This was a region of almost unblemished beauty, of rich flora and fauna, of abundant wild-life and a prolific salmon industry, and with communities of fishermen and native Americans dependent on the sea.

The *Valdez* had departed in perfect conditions. The captain, Hazelwood, went below to rest and handed over to the unlicensed third mate before the *Valdez* had cleared the Sound's channel; the Lieutenant Governor of Alaska later remarked,

> It took an almost impossible situation to have that tanker hit what is probably the most obvious piece of real estate in all of Prince William Sound. Any boy plying his daddy's motorboat in Prince William Sound knows the ultimate consequences of striking that reef. (*Management Review*, April 1990: 15)

A navigational error, compounded by a failure to pick up this danger on the Coast Guard radar, led to the accident. Exxon reacted slowly as did Alyaska, the pipe-line consortium responsible for clean-up operations. Confusion about responsibility for the clean-up, and lack of preparation for such a large spill, exacerbated the extent of the disaster. Exxon was pilloried for minimizing the calamity, for its seeming indifference to the environment, for its initial miserliness in offering funds for the clean-up, and for its lack of openness with the media. The negative publicity darkening Exxon's reputation was amplified when it emerged that Hazelwood had a history of alcohol problems (but he was acquitted on a recklessness charge by an Alaskan jury).

> After the accident, Exxon fired Hazelwood. Contrary to general belief, he was not fired for drunkenness on duty – a charge difficult to prove – but for not being on the bridge of the ship as company regulations require. Having been convicted of a negligent discharge of oil, Hazelwood was sentenced, a year after the accident, to 1,000 hours of community service helping clean up the oil spill. A jury had acquitted him of three more serious charges: criminal mischief, reckless endangerment, and operating a vessel while intoxicated. (Hartley, 1993: 221)

Exxon was hounded by civil claims in the courts that may reach $16 billion but it is estimated that the disaster has already cost Exxon some $3 billion ($1.1 billion in fines and $2 billion for the clean-up: *The Economist*, 18 June 1994).

This was by far the worst oil-tanker disaster in the history of the United States. It ranked as the thirtieth largest spill in the world – the *Amoco Cadiz* had lost 70 million gallons – but it was four times larger than any other spill in the USA and it happened to a hugely successful American corporation, with a state-of-the-art tanker, with an American crew, under American supervision, in American waters, and under ideal conditions (*Management Review*, April 1990). Questions were raised about personnel policy and selection of captains (also about compulsory alcohol and drugs tests for crews); about the industry's state of preparedness for a major spill; about the oil companies' apparent lack of concern for the environment; about bureaucratic infighting and passing the buck on responsibility which weakened the emergency response; and about the industry's reluctance to replace its fleet with double-hull tankers that would be better able to withstand a grounding. Although no humans died, Exxon was savaged by environmentalists and by ordinary citizens, who returned their Exxon credit cards in large numbers, because it was held morally responsible for the moving images of wild-life expiring under an enveloping layer of crude oil.

The Dalkon Shield

The Dalkon Shield intrauterine device (iud) was brought on to the market by the A.H. Robins Corporation in 1971. This was despite the fact that a number of officials in the company 'expressed concern about the lack of thorough testing to support the effectiveness of the model that was about to be sold in the marketplace' (Buchholz, 1989: 194). Despite this, the national advertising campaign which launched the iud spoke of a 1.1 per-cent pregnancy rate. The brochure stated, 'you can relax and enjoy the luxury of a truly superior birth-control method' (1989: 195). Within a year the Dalkon Shield had taken 60 per cent of market share in the USA. Some evidence emerged that the pregnancy rate might be higher; furthermore, there was an accumulating wave of medical complaints. Despite some very strong signals on infections and on the pregnancy rate, Robins merely amended its advertising and labelling. By 1973 the deaths of six women were attributed to septic or infected abortions in relation to the iud. Disorders included punctured and destroyed uteri, unwanted pregnancies, and pelvic infections (sometimes related to 'wicking problems' – the wick on the device attracted infections: Mintz, 1985).

With pressure mounting for recall Robins first hesitated on legal advice, in case the move would be interpreted as a 'confession of liability' (Buchholz, 1989: 198), but then voluntarily withdrew from the market on 28 June 1974. But Robins did not make a formal recall. Law-suits began to mount against the company and many women had complaints related to the period *after* recall. Robins took a tough, adversarial, and strictly legal stance to answering its opponents; women plaintiffs, for instance, were aggressively questioned in court about their sexual activities. Robins was found guilty of perjury when an expert witness for the company admitted lying to the court on the firm's behalf; and compensation cases were dragged out interminably by hard-nosed corporate lawyers. By 1985 Robins had paid out $378.3 million in relation to more than 9,000 cases, and with thousands more cases in the offing the company went into bankruptcy under Chapter 11 which effectively halted most claims. The Dalkon Shield had been extremely profitable and had also been the largest selling iud world-wide. It was claimed to be still in use in Latin American countries a decade after its withdrawal by Robins.

Defence Procurement Fraud

The General Dynamics Corporation is a major defence contractor for the US government. Following a number of investigations by the Defense Department, the Internal Revenue Service, the Senate, and the Securities and Exchange Commission, it emerged that the company had not always been straight in its dealings with officialdom. General Dynamics attracted a good deal of public criticism but the practices were held to be symptomatic of the defence industry in general in America. Evidence has emerged from a number of official inquiries that some companies have indulged in 'cost overruns, fraud, faulty workmanship, questionable dealings with Washington officials, bill padding, mismanagement, overseas bribery, and tax evasion (Hartley 1993: 96; DOD Report to Congress, 1990; Packard Commission, 1986; and 'whistle-blowers' account of malpractice between Pentagon and defence contractors: Burton, 1993). For example, General Dynamics was to build the nuclear-powered SSN-688 submarine with Trident missiles for the Navy; but the Navy pushed for a fixed-price contract which was risky for General Dynamics. Indeed, the corporation filed in 1976 for $843 million in cost overruns and blamed the Navy for mismanagement of contracts. Although the Navy coughed up most of the money it did dispute some of the claims, and in the aftermath of increased attention and scrutiny there emerged the revelations of fraud and mismanagement. There were accusations of 'sweeteners', bill-padding (claiming 90 per cent of the $22 million for air travel to the company chairman's weekend retreat in Georgia), and gross mismanagement,

> Numerous internal documents compiled by congressional investigators revealed the complaints managers at all levels had about the company: poor supervision, low morale, materials not ordered on time, proper records not kept. The documents also suggested that the company had long had a strategy of recouping its losses through false expense claims. Other allegations concerned attempts to manipulate the value of General Dynamics' stock, illegal wiretapping, and improper reporting of income taxes. (Hartley, 1993: 99)

As a result, some contracts were cancelled, the company was fined, and a number of officials resigned, including the chairman. But essentially little had changed.

The defence industry and the Pentagon are inextricably locked together and this interdependence easily leads to abuse. That General Dynamics was not on its own can be illustrated by the forty-five defence contractors under investigation for criminal charges in 1985; *Newsweek* (11 February 1985) spoke of flaws 'deeply embedded in defense procurement'; 'Some problems ranging from faulty products to overcharges, seem endemic to defense contractors – especially the giant aero-space, electronics and high-tech companies that make up the bulk of what has long been known as the military-industrial complex.'

The scandal of defence procurement can be related to a highly competitive industry, to the enormous costs of developing modern weapon systems, to the complexity of the contracting process, to the risky nature of long-term technological projects, and to the strong reliance of the Pentagon on a number of major contractors. Some of the over-billing, fraud, and mismanagement seems to be related to the nature of the industry, to the two-sided malpractices of contractors and the military within their incestuous relationship, but also to the feeling that it is legitimate to rip off the government and to spread the burden over millions of taxpayers. In effect, Hartley (1993: 106) notes, 'the defense procurement process lends itself to abuses and taxpayer fleecing.'

Challenger and NASA

The disaster on 28 January 1986, when the Challenger space-shuttle exploded shortly after launching, causing the death of all seven crew members, is indelibly etched in the minds of millions as it was transmitted live on television, and the pictures have been repeated many times since. It also led to a number of exhaustive inquiries. (There is also a pedagogical package with documents, videotapes, and a replica of the O-ring, produced by J.M. Maier, SUNY, Binghamton, 1992.) The President's Commission (1986) referred to an 'accident rooted in history' and retraced the decision-making background (Charles, 1989). NASA (the National Aeronautics and Space Administration) had an impressive record in space exploration and rocket technology; it had achieved world-wide kudos for putting the first person on the moon. In the mid-1980s, however, it was having to push hard for continued government support and was in need of some well-publicized success. The launch of the STS 51-L, Challenger, had been postponed several times. Some O-ring corrosion in the rocket booster motors had been uncovered on previous launches in cold weather. The weather on 28 January was to be the coldest for a launch yet encountered. Several engineers of the Morton Thiokol Corporation, the subcontractors for the solid rocket-boosters, expressed their concern. When conveyed to NASA, these objections, supported by detailed data on O-ring failure at low temperatures, were not always circulated effectively internally. And Thiokol's no-launch advice on the day prior to launching elicited the response from one official, 'My God, Thiokol, when do you want me to launch, next April?' (President's Commission, vol. 1, 1986: 96).

There was a lot of conferencing, much detailed and technical discussion, and some confusion; but 'at Thiokol not one engineer in a non-management position made any positive statement supporting a launch' (Charles, 1989: 153). Then a senior manager at the Thiokol meeting said, 'we have to make a management decision', and he asked a colleague 'to take off his engineering hat and put on his management hat' (1989: 154). Thiokol agreed to recommend the launch. Even then the Thiokol representative at the Kennedy Space Center voiced his concerns about the flight and refused to sign the authorization on Thiokol's behalf. During the night another contractor, Rockwell, became anxious about the temperature and ice formation at the launching site; Rockwell sent messages that they opposed the flight. Failures of internal communication again meant that vital information did not get to top NASA officials. The Space Shuttle Challenger was launched at 11.38 a.m., and after seventy seconds it exploded; 'obviously a major malfunction' according to the understated response at the control centre (1989: 141).

Analysis of the tragedy focuses on the commercial pressures on Thiokol to translate an engineering decision into a 'managerial' one; on the political vulnerability of NASA to budget cuts and its need for visible success; on a self-confident management style that served to undermine professional accountability and to enforce an autocratic, top-down style; and to failures in internal and external communication that filtered out negative signals. For instance, there was the letter signed 'Apocalypse' that was written two months after the disaster, which stated:

> it has been apparent for some time that the Flight Readiness Review process developed by ———— [senior NASA managers] simply was not doing the job. It was not determining flight readiness. Rather, it established a political situation within NASA in which no center could come to a review and say that it was 'not ready'. To do so would invite the question 'if you are not ready, then why are you not doing your job? It is your job to be ready'. (Charles, 1989: 159)

NASA did its job; but six astronauts and a civilian woman teacher died in front of an audience of millions. One of the most sophisticated operations in the world had failed in terms of communication, responsibility, and decision-making.

Industrial Espionage

In some cases the victims and targets of corporate malfeasance are external to the business community – consumers, the government, the environment, the general public, Third World countries, or the unborn child. In other cases companies *victimize one another*. An excellent example of inter-company skulduggery is 'industrial espionage.' There were the embarrassing photos of Japanese executives being led away in handcuffs because they had bought IBM computer secrets from an American consultancy firm on behalf of, amongst others, Hitachi (*de Volkskrant*, 25 June 1982 and 27 July 1982). This was said to be part of a concerted effort by Japanese companies to acquire confidential data on the American computer industry in order to apply it in the production of clones to challenge the Americans who at that time were well in advance of the Japanese. In Britain, two men 'handed out millions of pounds in bribes to persuade senior executives "at the heart" of oil giant BP to "sell their company down the river"':

> During their two-months trial, the court heard how they took part in large-scale industrial espionage by bribing top managers at BP to reveal confidential plans about projects the company was planning in North Sea oil-fields. Then the men approached huge engineering companies in Europe and Japan and offered to sell them the information to ensure that their bid for a particular project was accepted.

The judge, in sentencing them to three years in prison, said, 'what you did struck at the very root of business probity and has to be treated very seriously indeed' (*Daily Mail*, 27 April 1993).

In the Netherlands many victims of espionage do not report this to the police; there is increasing concern about the damage done to companies and about the role of 'malafide information brokers' (Schaap, 1995). Two private detective agencies in the Netherlands reported handling between 80 and 100 investigations of espionage a year on behalf of companies (Broer and Gielen, 1993). Probably the most publicized case of the last few years has been that of José Ignacio López, 'the strangler of Rudelsheim' (Rudelsheim is the head-quarters of Opel, General Motors' subsidiary in Germany).

López built up a reputation as a tough cost-cutter in Germany and was brought to General Motors in Detroit as head of purchasing. Then in March 1993 he was poached by European rival Volkswagen. There were soon claims that confidential material had been taken to Volkswagen despite a written guarantee by López to GM. López had just attended top-level strategy meet-ings at Opel at which future models were discussed; he took a posse of colleagues with him to Germany; and it was rumoured that Volkswagen employees took days to enter into their computer system 'boxes' of docu-ments brought over from GM (*de Volkskrant*, 16 August 1994). The commotion between GM and Volkswagen led the Volkswagen chairman Piëch to speak of a 'dirty war' in which anything was permitted, as if Rudelsheim was deliberately spreading malicious insinuations. The German Minister of Economic Affairs even intervened, and urged both companies to exercise restraint and to refrain from phrases such as 'war, battle, and slaugh-ter'. But Opel top-executive Graeb insisted that documents had been 'systematically and consciously' removed, and they included, 'a secret Opel-project for a small car, 70 to 90,000 computer print-out pages of detailed information on all European suppliers with part-numbers and purchase prices and a photo of the new Vectra which will only be on the market in four years' time' (*de Volkskrant*, 30 July 1993).

The case was being investigated by the Justice Department in Darmstadt and by the FBI. López has denied the allegations, his company has sup-ported him, and the investigations have not led to a prosecution at this point. The defection of López from GM to Volkswagen saw car-makers at each other's throats. The loss of trade secrets to a competitor could be extremely damaging to a company. This case brought questions of industrial espionage into the full light of day. How do you keep secrets 'secret'? How far do you go in poaching top talent from a competitor? How do you guarantee that depart-ing executives will not take confidential data with them (*Business Week*, 23 August 1993)? And if they do it to you, do you do it to them?

Market and Price Manipulation

Some companies and industries have a history of price-fixing. Pharmaceuticals is one of them (Braithwaite, 1984). Stanley Adams was a British citizen who had made a career with the Swiss pharmaceutical company, Hoffmann La Roche. It was almost unknown for a foreigner to reach high rank in the com-pany, but Adams had made it as seemingly the stereotypical corporate executive. Then his conscience began to give him trouble. He noticed illegal clauses in contracts fixing prices and promising kickbacks. If an influenza epidemic was predicted in Asia, then he was ordered to reduce production of medicine. When the demand subsequently rose, prices were raised and the company benefited doubly; from increased sales and from increased profits based on an artificially created shortage. Adams decided to blow the whistle. He took his complaints under a guarantee of anonymity to the European Commission in Brussels. Although Switzerland is not a member of the European Union the company had been trading with firms in EU countries and this made it liable to EU law. Hoffmann La Roche was prosecuted and fined.

Somehow Adams' name was leaked to Hoffmann La Roche. By this time Adams had left the firm and was setting up a farming business in Italy. On crossing the Swiss border for a Christmas vacation with his Swiss wife's family, he was arrested and charged with espionage (Swiss companies' confidential material is strongly supported by the Swiss criminal law). While he was in prison his wife was put under pressure to confess as his accomplice; she committed suicide. Adams was not allowed to attend her funeral. On release from prison he was declared a bankrupt in Italy, his farming enterprise collapsed, and his passport was impounded. He managed to get out of Italy, risking imprisonment, and went to Britain with his daughters, where he began a long campaign for compensation from the European Commission. Eventually he was awarded £500,000, of which some £300,000 went on legal fees. In a presentation to MBA students at Nijenrode in 1990 he emphasized the rapaciousness of the large drug companies, their *total lack of ethics* (he was particularly insistent on this point), and their ruthlessness towards whistle-blowers (cf. Adams, 1984). Adams was a whistle-blower who clearly still carried the scars of trying to expose illegality in a large Swiss drug company.

Singapore Crash: the Bank that Lost its Bearings

> We all thought he was unbeatable.
>
> (Japanese broker on Leeson, *Daily Mail*, 28 February 1995)

The financial services industry had taken a drubbing from the Wall Street and other scandals as well as the BCCI affair. One response was to increase internal control and also to improve the technology of regulation through computerized systems that could more easily trace suspect share dealings on the markets. There was a feeling that the excesses of the past had been countered by sophisticated checks and balances. Another response, which was related to the volatility of the financial markets in the 1980s, was to shift to 'derivatives' that promised a higher measure of predictability. (Derivatives are financial market instruments whose value is *derived* from an underlying asset such as a product or shares that have a value and a fluctuating price.) They were initially designed to *reduce* risk and became attractive because traders can take large positions at a fraction of the cost of buying on the cash market. Futures and options are relatively simple instruments, but some others require complex mathematical formulae, leading some US companies to recruit analysts from NASA, the space agency. Professional dealers speculate on the movement of markets and prices in relation to these instruments (*Sunday Times*, 5 March 1995; *Independent*, 28 February 1995). The deregulation of financial services in the 1980s and the increasing globalization of the economy altered the nature of the industry. Financial institutions became more complex and offered varied services, there were mergers and acquisitions creating new players, competition became fiercer, the speed of transactions increased, and the image of the industry changed (Zey, 1993). The City of London, for instance, had always been considered a preserve of the well-bred and the privately educated, but increasingly people were recruited from widely diverse backgrounds providing they could learn the skills of the trade quickly and could take the pace and the pressure of dealing on the exchanges. The attraction was fast promotion and high rewards. You could make a mint and retire early.

A reputable and seemingly rock-solid player in the London financial world was the merchant bank, Barings. This was an aristocratic, respected, professionally led institution with a lineage of over 200 years. The family influence was still present, the chairman was Peter Baring, and the bank attracted the accounts of the blue-blooded and of the royal family. To the outside world it was a stable, successful, discreet, reserved, and somewhat stuffy bank (it was referred to in the City as 'OverBarings'). Barings had also moved into derivatives, had long held a strong interest in Asian markets, and had taken on a number of people who had not travelled the orthodox upper-class path of boarding school, Oxbridge, and the Guards.

One of these new boys was Nick Leeson. After a fairly undistinguished career he joined Barings and worked in the 'back office' (where deals are cleared administratively but which is also the first line of defence against fraud and fiddling). Because he failed to disclose a couple of county court debt injunctions on his application to join the London stock market he was banned from working on that exchange; Barings sent him instead to the burgeoning market of Singapore. He was 25 years old. His rise was meteoric and he became a major operator on the Singapore International Money Exchange (SIMEX) and on the Japanese exchange of Osaka. He was ostensibly responsible for handsome profits in 1993 and the prospects for 1994 looked excellent. Leeson was enjoying the privileges of expatriate life and was notching up substantial bonuses. A great emphasis was later made in the British press of his humble background. There was also an effort to portray him as bumptious, boozy, and sexist (*Sunday Times*, 5 March 1995). Not surprisingly, his friends and family preferred to see him as restrained, considerate, pleasant, and honest. In fact, that was precisely how he came across in an interview with David Frost on BBC Television in September 1995. He was being held on remand in a German prison awaiting the result of extradition procedures. Leeson calmly stated that he was prepared to go to prison (preferably in the UK), was ready to cooperate with the authorities, and was proposing to admit to a number of offences (which he understandably could not specify in advance on legal advice). He claimed that he had opened the now infamous 88888 account to help out a young female colleague who had got herself into difficulties on an account; he made it sound like a casual, off-hand, coincidental move just to help out a friend in distress.

But what is clear is that he soon built up an impressive volume of work in Singapore. In essence, his job was to lay bets on the movement of the Nikkei Index (which monitors the movement of major Japanese companies on the stock exchange). He decided that the Nikkei was likely to rise and in anticipation of this he was committed to roughly £18 billion ($27 billion) in Singapore and Osaka; with over 40,000 contracts between the two exchanges he was indisputably the major player. In one year he was said to have brought in £36 million for Barings, and was telling his colleagues that he expected a bonus of one million pounds. This 'play-boy of the eastern world', turbo-arbitrageur and 'almost miracle worker' claimed he was in 'heaven' (*Independent*, 28 February 1995; *Financial Times*, 19 July 1995).

But what was he actually doing? In effect, his job was to play the markets. Ironically, companies had turned to derivatives on a large scale over the last decade in order to build in more predictability for investments and products (since the abandonment of fixed exchange rates in the early 1970s the financial markets had become increasingly volatile). However, a number of firms had been badly burned on futures and options so that the warning of danger was there (companies that had been hit hard included Metallgesellschaft in Germany, Bankers Trust, Kidder Peabody, Procter and Gamble, Chemical Bank, Orange County in the USA; and Shava Shell and Allied Domecq in Britain: *de Volkskrant*, 27 February 1995). This reveals that the work of a dealer is still essentially a form of legitimized gambling and that he or she can make horrendous mistakes. The logic of the game is to hedge your bets so that you come out ahead most of the time, that you do not overcommit yourself, and that you realize you cannot beat the market. Some dealers lead long and successful lives, but there is an element of pressure meaning that some get out early; there is a stereotype of young, brash, ambitious, and ruthless people who can get rich very fast on bonuses or else they can fail dramatically and drop out of the game. The successful ones end up handling vast sums of money and a few key people can be responsible for most of a bank's profit; 'it is an adrenalin-charged life gripped by twin demands: greed and fear of imminent disaster' (*Sunday Times*, 5 March 1995). In the trading room, it is said, you need the 'killer instinct' plus 'a strong sense of personal and corporate greed. Ruthlessness. Single-mindedness. Intolerance' (*Daily Mail*, 28 February 1995). Dealers are supposed to be 'loud, brash and flash' but there is doubtless an element of journalistic hype in the rhetoric surrounding financial dealing; it is the case, however, that Leeson was seen as a 'ruthlessly aggressive trader' (*Daily Mail*, 28 February 1995). Normally the substantial risks taken are monitored by internal supervision and external regulation. Yet these back-up brakes on excess and over-commitment dramatically failed to function in Singapore.

Leeson's world began to unravel on 17 January 1995 when Kobe in Japan was hit by a substantial earthquake, causing the Nikkei to dip. He made the assumption that the market would pick up as funds were pumped into the reconstruction of Kobe and consequently he committed Barings up to the hilt. For quite other reasons the Nikkei did not recover but slumped even further. Leeson had been burned yet he could have pulled out then with his damages severe but limited. Instead, he made the fatal decision of trying to fight the market as if he on his own could force it back up. This desperate, almost irrational, risk has been seen as typically the 'action of a gambler, one last chance to recoup his losses' (*Sunday Times*, 5 March 1995: 12). It was at the time rumoured that to support him Barings transferred some £400 million to Singapore within six weeks (the Bank of England report states that this happened 'without any real murmur' but that London was not fully aware of the destination and use that Leeson had for these payments, *Guardian*, 19 July 1995; 'Barings' Report, 1995). This was to no avail and Leeson was facing a gaping hole of more than £400 million or $600 million. This was far in excess of the bank's reserves. After 233 years of exuding reliability and integrity, Barings was facing financial melt-down. Leeson left a note on his desk saying 'sorry', and walked out of the office a few days before his 28th birthday. He was later arrested in Frankfurt on his way to England and was held in Germany until he was extradited to Singapore in November 1995.

How could one man escape the controls and cause the sixth largest merchant bank in Britain to simply crash out of the blue? As with many cases of corporate deviance and company crisis there were warnings and signals.

- Leeson's apparent success was bringing in a lot of apparent profit for the bank. He was granted a great deal of autonomy and operated not only in the dealing room but also in the back office, whereas these two functions should be effectively separated in order to enhance control. Barings seemed blinded by Leeson's good fortune and he enjoyed private channels to London over the heads of his local supervisors in Singapore. His boss there complained to London, 'My concern is that once again we are in danger of setting up a structure which will subsequently prove disastrous and with which we will succeed in losing a lot of money or client goodwill or probably both' (*Sunday Times*, 5 March 1995). This was in August 1994.
- In the later phases his excessive commitment ought to have been plain to SIMEX, Osaka, and London, and some dealers started to ask, 'What's going on?' (*Sunday Times*, 5 March 1995). The Osaka Exchange regularly publishes figures of transactions, and Leeson could have been seen to be considerably more exposed than any other player. But again this was not picked up.
- When warning lights began to flash in London an audit of Leeson's activities was undertaken (because his eye-catching results seemed to be just too good); this was discussed in September 1994. The board was faced with a report which stated that the controls over Leeson were minimal, that there

was a fudging of responsibility between the trading side and the 'back office' (meaning that Leeson was 'watchdog of his own deals'), and that there was an 'excessive concentration of powers' and a 'danger of overriding the controls' (*Sunday Times*, 5 March 1995). Barings permitted Leeson to continue trading.

The news of Leeson's disastrous dealings and of his disappearance were transmitted to London on Thursday, 23 February. During the weekend, crisis meetings were held at the Bank of England to see if a consortium of banks could mount a rescue operation, but this was apparently not helped by the insistence of Barings that they could not guarantee the size of the hole (then around £650 million). On Sunday the news broke in the papers.

The rescue failed and the Bank of England decided not to intervene to prop up Barings, and on Monday, 27 February, the receivers were called in to oversee the bankruptcy of this proud bank. Its chairman claimed to the press that Barings had been the victim of a criminal conspiracy, and that there may have been a deliberate effort to wreck the bank so that others could profit from its demise (although he produced no evidence for this allegation; *Sunday Times*, 5 March 1995). The Chancellor of the Exchequer, making an announcement in Parliament, spoke of 'a specific incident unique to Barings centred on one rogue dealer in Singapore' (*Daily Mail*, 28 February 1995). Had one man, acting alone, put 4,000 jobs at jeopardy, risked the investments of thousands (including the Queen of England), and brought down a famous bank?

The Bank of England ordered an investigation into the collapse, and the inquiry was conducted by the Board of Banking Supervision which issued the 'Barings Report' in mid-1995. The report maintained that, on arrival in Singapore, Leeson began almost immediately to act beyond his authority and to conceal the extent of his activities using concealed computer account 88888 to hide the extent of his dealings (*Financial Times*, 19 July 1995; 'Barings' Report, 1995: 53–77). The Singapore authorities argued for extradition on the grounds of fraud and forgery; the Serious Fraud Office in London proved lukewarm about pursuing the matter although Leeson publicly offered to talk to officials from the SFO in an attempt to avoid trial and imprisonment in Singapore; in the end Leeson faced the music on his own and was sentenced to six-and-a-half years in a Singapore jail (*Financial Times*, 4 December 1995). But what is of essential concern in the interaction between the plasterer's son from unfashionable Watford (outside of London), the Asian exchanges, and blue-blooded Barings is what this tells us of the world of business and management.

For this 'one-man demolition job' revealed 'arrogance, corporate greed, management failure and supervisory incompetence on a grand scale' (*Independent*, 4 March 1995). Financial dealing is known to be inherently risky, and there had been a number of warnings on Asian markets (as in the collapse of the Malaysian Bank Negara). Yet Leeson was given wide autonomy and was encouraged with substantial rewards; he could evade control and go over the heads of his local supervisors; London was blinded by his success, and powerful allies there supported him and deflected criticism; the several warning signals from various sources were not heeded and the board continued to support Leeson up to the end; and the board's interest in the takeover of the prestigious brokers Cazenove, for which it needed to build a substantial 'war-chest', may have distracted its attention from Leeson's activities. In short, a reputable bank with a penchant for caution and with limited reserves allowed a 28-year-old to dictate its strategy and to commit it to 60,000 contracts representing £4.4 billion on the Asian markets. This was seen as 'incompetence on a cosmic scale' and, '"Some of the Barings' management will find it very difficult to prove that they were not utterly incompetent", predicted a senior director of a high street bank' (*Sunday Times*, 5 March 1995: 11).

Light was shed on many of the open questions in the official report of over 300 pages on the Barings collapse which placed the blame firmly on Leeson's shoulders but sketched the 'managerial confusion' and 'serious problems of control' at Barings (*Independent*; *Guardian*, 19 July 1995; 'Barings' Report, 1995). This was echoed by the Chancellor of the Exchequer's speech in Parliament where he mentioned that Leeson had engaged in systematic concealment but that there had been no effective management control of his activities and a considerable element of chaos and confusion at Barings. The Bank of England's report asserted that there had been an 'absolute' failure of controls at Barings, that managers did not do their jobs properly, and that some did not understand their own business (*Financial Times*, 19 July 1995).

> Barings' collapse was due to the unauthorised and ultimately catastrophic activities of, it appears, one individual (Leeson) that went undetected as a consequence of a failure of management and other internal controls of the most basic kind. Management failed at various levels and in a variety of ways, described in the earlier sections of this report, to institute a proper system of internal controls, to enforce accountability for all profits, risks and operations, and adequately to follow up on a number of warning signals over a prolonged period. Neither the external auditors nor the regulators discovered Leeson's unauthorised activities. ('Barings' Report, 1995: 250)

Newspaper comment on the collective failure, of a major bank – and the regulators – was savage: 'The scale and breadth of incompetence – at Barings, in the Bank of England, and at the auditors – almost defies imagination. . . . .The scandal derives from the ease with which Mr Leeson was able to deceive his masters and the lack of care that they and their regulators exercised' (*The Times*, 19 July 1995).

There was, then, a personal failure that was compounded by a managerial one but also a regulatory one; one senior figure in the banking world told *The Times* (19 July 1995) that 'most bank supervisors were "the old regime." He claimed they lacked a deep understanding of the business, the products, the nature of the risk, the geographic diversity and the fast-moving nature of the industry.'

The Bank of England, having been heavily criticized in the BCCI and Johnson Mathey affairs, was again under fire:

> Reading between the lines, the Board of Banking Supervision has concluded that the Bank of England was simply not up to supervising these strange animals because it did not understand them. . . . But, of course, the real villains of this report, apart from Nick Leeson himself, are the Barings managers who let it happen under their noses. It was a free-wheeling, adventurous and risk taking organisation where incompetence defies belief. (*Independent*, 19 July 1995)

More broadly the Barings crash can also be perceived as a lesson in terms of the following:

- *Individuals* – in high-risk occupations there are psychological mechanisms at play that should be taken into account. Leeson was young and apparently successful. He went against the advice of other analysts and perhaps believed in his own omnipotence. He may even have convinced himself that he had backing for his efforts and had been encouraged by the substantial rewards. He was considered to be a 'star performer' ('Barings' Report, 1995: 121). But what Leeson did manage to do was to beat the system of controls, as is clear from the Bank of England report on the collapse.
- *International financial markets* – although major investors seek solid returns for their investments there is still an element of fragility in financial dealings because risk and judgement are not always well matched and the opportunities for major errors and/or deviance have been enhanced by structural changes such as competition, speed of transactions, and the reward structure (Zey, 1993; Hutton, 1995). Or, as the *Guardian* (19 July 1995) put it, 'The real issue of the Barings' collapse is not, however, incompetence at the Bank of England or the failure of audit and internal controls, although that is bad enough. It is that our financial leaders have allowed the world, in the name of free capital movements, to drift into the equivalent of a global crap-shoot, in which there are no final arbiters and in which all our savings can be put so easily at risk.'
- *Regulation and control* – the dangers inherent in playing with large sums of money have fostered a battery of internal and external controls. After each scandal these mechanisms are improved and there are assertions that 'this sort of thing could not happen again'. But it did happen; the control system in this case did not work to prevent these massive losses. The industry had 'failed to control its own gamble' (*Independent*, 28 February 1995). The 'Barings' Report spelt out implications for management and regulators (1995: 250–64).
- *The culture of British banking* – in a sense this was a revelation that Barings, a bank of reputation and integrity, had taken on new-style whizz-kids for the dealer room but had expected them to behave under the tight, informal control of a clubby world that had largely disappeared. The combination of a an old-style management with young, thrusting new blood on the rapidly expanding Asian markets, and with a reward structure of juicy bonuses for large deals, proved disastrous.

In the immediate aftermath Barings was bought by the Dutch financial conglomerate ING for £1 (and the losses taken over probably cost them £860 million), Peter Baring and several other senior managers resigned (including one official at the Bank of England), and leaked reports of the receivers' investigation spoke of incompetence and negligence at the top (*de Volkskrant*, 5 April 1995). There were strange holes in the bookkeeping and a profound failure of internal control which enabled Leeson to act in the way he did.

The important lessons are related to banking, business, and management. Financial services remain risky areas, and the institutionalized gambling that this implies is enhanced by an excessive reward structure; business seeks predictability and solid rewards but structural change and a fierce culture of competition produces volatility and risk-taking; and reputation, integrity, and controls can all be undermined by a management that refuses to change, refuses to face up to reality, becomes blinded by success, becomes seduced into short-term decision-making, ignores warning signals, and that indulges in scapegoating and conspiracy theories when confronted with the consequences of its own incompetence. It is difficult to legislate for greed and stupidity.

But greed and stupidity are social and cultural constructs that are enhanced by specific times and particular settings. The Governor of the Bank of England said, 'it could have happened to anyone'; but it would almost certainly not occur in a Dutch bank, for instance, because they operate with a quite different structure, culture, and reward system (personal communication: Dr N. van Dijk, a consultant with experience of the Dutch banking environment). It just happened to be an aristocratic British merchant bank, in an Asian market, with a young man from a working-class background. That combination, which brought about the humiliating collapse of a seemingly solid institution, is of value in informing us about the fragility of financial markets, about the vulnerability of control systems, and about the weaknesses that can afflict management. Of course, if Leeson had been right in his judgement, he would now be a rich hero. And he would not be sitting out a prison sentence in a spartan Singapore cell.

Systemic Deviance in Business?

In commenting in general on the above cases, and many other cases, it could be argued that they provide considerable evidence of sustained and often deliberate corporate deviance in various ways related to products, consumers, employees, markets, competitors, regulators, politicians, the media, the environment, foreign officials, government subsidies, and particularly with regard to tax, company, regulatory, and criminal law. The mass of evidence from these cases indicates that certain deviant practices were not individual or incidental but were pervasive, sophisticated, even *systemic*; and often highly damaging (in terms of victims, the environment, politics, and the economy). All of this raises serious questions about the internal and external control of business organizations.

Increasing Recognition of Corporate Deviance

There exists a complex and shifting relationship between government, business, and society that leads to an intricate, triangular negotiation in response to societal change, economic power, institutional control, and vested interests (Fisse and Braithwaite, 1993; Tonry and Reiss, 1993; Wells, 1994; Jamieson, 1994). Here I would like to touch on one or two central themes that have contributed to altering the attention paid to corporate deviance.

Generally, western economies experienced growth and expansion in the relatively stable post-war period but ran into considerable turbulence in the 1970s and 1980s (related to the oil crises, the Japanese challenge, government regulation, consumer and ecological movements, technological change, inflation, and labour problems). The 1980s have witnessed a fundamental shake-out in the business world and have been characterized by deregulation, mergers and takeovers, globalization, the displacement of industrial activity to less developed societies, de-unionization, the rapid expansion of financial markets (aided by the swift electronic exchange of information), and new organizational forms. In a nutshell, these momentous changes created new opportunities for business deviance – to a certain extent enhanced by specific aspects of deregulation – which sponsored abuses and, in turn, public debate on controlling the new business world. That debate, moreover, has brought business deviance to the forefront of the socio-political stage as a considerable social and ethical problem.

This contrasts strongly with earlier protestations that business violations were not taken seriously. Sutherland's writing had an undertone of moral outrage, undoubtedly related to his Baptist background (cf. Geis and Goff, 1983), and this was fuelled by his anger at the unwillingness of society to tackle white-collar crime with any vigour. Thirty years later Box was equally if not more caustic in his comments on the 'huge cynical black-comedy' of society's failing to put brakes on corporate crime; it was not only enmeshed in 'ignorance, mystification and misinformation' but also was 'not viewed as a pressing, serious social problem' (Box, 1983: 65, 17). What can be said to have changed the situation in the last decade? Among the many, complex factors that have played a role, three in particular were of vital importance.

First, the merging of illegal and legitimate business interests began to bring discredit on business. And this was especially related to the loopholes and opportunities provided by international arrangements (in offshore banks in the Caribbean, in countries like Panama, in the secretive vaults of Switzerland, but also in the major financial institutions of several western countries). This was no more evident than in the banks' laundering of money for drugs cartels, while Levi also relates it to other areas of illegality:

> The organization of fraud and laundering of the proceeds of commercial fraud, tax evasion, political corruption, terrorism, and narcotics are intimately linked via the need for secrecy and immunity from law enforcement that they require. Increasingly, this has been achieved by the use of international tax havens as

conduits for money and as legally registered bases for operations. It has also been achieved through using professionals – lawyers and accountants – as intermediaries in the perpetration of crime. (1987: 277)

The American public's attitude to economic violations also stiffened noticeably; their views were influenced by the impact of the crime on others and by physical damage caused, while in some cases types of fraud and corruption were considered worse than burglary (and people declared themselves in favour of tougher treatment of white-collar criminals than the courts: Wolfgang et al., 1985).

Second, business crime became a political issue and governments which had peddled deregulation, and which could be seen as 'soft' on business, became potentially vulnerable. This was notably the case in the UK, where the Conservative government was closely identified with the financial centre of the City of London and where scandals could easily become politically damaging. Clarke (1990) surmises that if it did not legislate for the City 'then the right was perhaps handing a major political gift to the left on a plate'; hence we have a Conservative minister making the following strong statement aimed to reassure public opinion: 'We want the public to realise we are in deadly earnest about stamping out City fraud. The City fraudster is just as much a professional criminal as is the large-scale bank robber, and motivated just as much by greed' (Clarke, 1990: 15).

But in the USA too there was the President's Commission on Organized Crime (1986), and a 'war on drugs' by the newly elected President Bush, and in most western countries there was an 'anti white-collar bug' (Levi, 1987: 115).

And third, business deviance began to undermine the basis of *trust and legitimacy* which is essential to a healthy transaction of economic conduct. As economies moved from an old industrial base to a new financial one, as more and more people were encouraged to purchase shares, and as the new 'enterprise culture' became imbued with almost moral values, then it became less and less tolerable to accept fraud, manipulation, greed, recklessness, incompetence, and professional misconduct. Scandals could mean that stockholders felt they had been ripped off, that the media could have a field day exposing sexy 'upper-world' intrigue, and the credibility of venerable institutions could be severely dented. The City of London, for instance, has become absolutely crucial to the future of the British economy, and in the intense global competition in financial markets it is of essential concern that its position is maintained in relation to New York and Tokyo. (In 1985 half the new jobs in the British economy were related to the financial services sector, especially in the City of London, and roughly two million people work in the financial services sector in the UK: Clarke, 1990.) It could be said that when business deviance begins to hurt badly business's own long-term interests for relatively healthy, predictable, and trustworthy economic relations, then that is the time when control of business deviance is really taken seriously.

My case, then, has been that the 1980s witnessed a growing consciousness of the infiltration of legitimate business institutions by organized crime, an emerging awareness of the political dimension of corporate deviance, and, especially, a self-protecting response that business itself was suffering considerable damage (Sterling, 1994). In a sense, the costs to business and government of accepting a certain level of economic deviance had simply become too high; the astronomical sums involved were damaging to national economies and the undermining of trust was too corrosive of the basic level of predictability, calculability, and trustworthiness that is considered essential to healthy economic life. It is debatable whether or not the victims of economic deviance had much influence in pushing for reforms compared to the macro interests of corporations and governments; but Levi is convinced that we are not just seeing a cynical political exercise in rattling sabres on controlling corporate crime but that the 1980s ushered in a genuine shift in societal opinion on the issue (1987: 285).

Management Studies and Researching Business Deviance

Just about everyone working in the area of corporate deviance bemoans the fact that very little research is conducted on this subject. That work which is done tends to be carried out by sociologists, legal scholars, and criminologists (and especially by some tenacious and well-informed journalists). And, not surprisingly, business schools and management studies often avoid the nasty and naughty aspects of business life. But earlier it had been the McCarthy era, functionalism, and the predilection for quantitative research that all conspired to dampen down enthusiasm for research on corporate deviance from within sociology departments in the USA (Geis and Goff, 1983). In North America, moreover, it is most unusual to find sociologists in business schools; the schools may recruit faculty directly from the corporations (in the 1980s a number of schools favoured appointing deans who had held high managerial positions in business and industry); and business donates substantial sums of money to universities in general and to the business schools in particular. In many ways the ethos of the business school – the formal attire of the faculty and their mercenary preoccupation with consulting, the open competitiveness and ambition of the students and their unquestioning industry, the punitive work-loads that reflect an uncritical and unreflective 'boot-camp' approach to graduate studies, the emphasis on impression management in the classroom, the intimidatory style of teaching, and so on – can all be seen as exuding anticipatory socialization for the tough demands of corporate life. Perhaps this 'gung-ho' model is only true of a small number of top graduate schools, with the Harvard Business School as the paradigm (Van Maanen, 1983). There has been some debate recently, for instance, on the 1980s' generation of business school graduates brought up to believe in the wholesomeness of greed and ambition, who had gone avariciously into the financial world with its escalating rewards, and who had come unstuck on account of their total lack of moral restraint.

But in general it is possible to say that in university business schools there are often strong links with business that may readily inhibit research, for practical and 'ideological' reasons, on the less savoury side of corporate practice. The sociological tradition of dispelling mystification and debunking institutions is plainly not likely to be tolerated willingly in a vocational education that strongly reflects the values of the occupation and institution for which it is moulding students (cf. Cohen, 1974). In the curriculum there may well be courses in Ethics, Social Responsibility, Legal Environment, and Public Policy, but these may be seen as 'soft', marginal areas that are interesting to reflect on in classroom discussions but which are overwhelmed by the importance attached to the core courses perceived as essential to the 'real' conduct of business, such as marketing, finance, production, and strategy. Indeed, management studies as a disciplinary area is characterized by fragmentation (it is considered a theoretical 'jungle'), a subservience to practitioners, an openness to fads and fashions, and a measure of naïve and unreflective empiricism (Whitley, 1984; van Dijk and Punch, 1985).

Apparently, in some business schools epithets such as 'theoretical', 'academic', and even 'articulate' are virtually terms of abuse – and the negative stereotyping is reflected in the UK where management studies may still be considered rather disreputable (Thomas, 1989: 8). A healthy pragmatism, suitable for money-making executive programmes for practitioners sceptical of theoretical knowledge but overawed by academic status, reflects the strong ambivalence between academically produced knowledge and the burgeoning industry of popular management texts:

> Non-academic business-book publishing remained a backwater until the early 1980s. By now the 'once staid world (of business-book publishing) has been transformed into one where sales run into hundreds of thousands, sometimes millions, royalties are in six figures, business-titles are best-sellers, and authors command huge sums as guest-speakers at conferences'. (Menkes, 1987: 163)

> Business is booming in business publishing and especially in popular business publishing, something which seems to have been sparked off by the appearance of *In Search of Excellence*. (Peters and Waterman, 1982)

> With world-wide sales of over 10 million copies, this could well be the most influential management text ever, but the 'One Minute Management' series, with UK sales of 500,000, is also high on the list of best-sellers. (Thomas, 1989: 27)

In contrast to academic knowledge – often perceived as 'useless' by practitioners (cf. van Dijk and Punch, 1985) – there is, then, a vast amount of practical knowledge posited on simplicity, common sense, experiential validity, and a sprinkling of wisdom from the ancients – often Machiavelli but preferably Lao-tzu (the alleged founder of Taoism). The case method itself, widely used in business studies, purveys an ahistorical, atheoretical style of treating business practice as encrusted in limited descriptions of corporate dilemmas that are seen largely as didactic tools depended on for rounding out in classroom discussion. But they are presented almost as universally applicable nuggets of data, implicitly containing some lightly concealed message of business wisdom, that do not need placing in a specific societal, historical, or time framework. Generally, we do not learn much about the company, the industry, or about the wider implications of the case for management, work, organization, and control. Even in more extensive organizational analyses it is often the case that the functionalist paradigm predominates and there is a neglect of disharmony and conflict (Burrell and Morgan, 1979). In brief, the social organization of management studies does not usually lend itself to critical, penetrating, cross-disciplinary studies of business practice that might also illuminate the darker side of that practice. The dirty side is largely ignored.

These deficiencies are magnified if we consider the problems of access to corporations and the methodological difficulties of studying senior managers. Many businesses are secretive – particularly about strategy and data that ostensibly might be valuable to competitors – and zealously guard access to sensitive regions. Argyris was turned down by umpteen banks before he found one willing to grant him an opening for research (Van Maanen, 1978: 63); and Jackall (1988: 13) was refused permission for his study by *thirty-six* corporations before informal channels, chance meetings, and doctoring of his research proposal (to make it anodyne enough to be non-threatening), helped him gain access.

Consider how even more difficult it is, then, to make a direct approach about researching corporate deviance. Do you approach senior executives of major corporations and say you are interested in bribery, corruption, industrial espionage, fraud, and manipulation of accounts to hoodwink external auditors, and would be quite willing to undertake research for them within their companies? And that you would fully acknowledge their cooperation in subsequent publications? That is to ask for trouble (it's a bit like approaching the Medellín drug cartels in Colombia for access to study their investment portfolios). Most business organizations do not want to recognize openly the existence of such problematic areas. And even if one could get inside, then the practical dilemmas of researching these issues may be almost intractable because managerial 'deviants' are likely to be clever, conspiratorial, and secretive, their activities will be 'concealed behind walls or locked doors', and they will not only be unwilling to cooperate – having been forewarned about 'snoopers' – but will simply deny that any nefarious practices take place at all (Downes and Rock, 1982: 27).

This might lead to the conclusion that only covert observation, such as Dalton (1964) carried out, can hope to penetrate the deviant labyrinths of the corporation. But nowadays that clashes with codes of ethics that enshrine 'informed consent' for participants in research and that restrict academics in the interests of their own profession's respectability and its continued access to other areas for research (Punch, 1994a). Even if one could overcome the handicaps of access and informed consent, there are the intrinsic methodological difficulties of studying senior managers. Although they may engage in a lot of informal interaction in the office, their actual work may be carried out individually behind a desk and be largely composed of phone-calls, reading memos, and correspondence. It may simply not be possible to share easily in these activities. Even if one was granted access to meetings, documents, and phone calls, then there is the problem of out-of-work socializing that may be essential to clique cohesion and to visible participation in the networking associated with office politics (cf. Jackall, 1988; Dalton, 1959).

In effect, we may have to acknowledge that we are perhaps dealing with institutional regions that are unresearchable by conventional, and ethical, means (Punch, 1994b). It implies that we are highly reliant on scandals, the media, public inquiries, police investigations, and 'whistle-blowers' for glimpses of the concealed world of top management and particularly its involvement in 'dirty tricks'. Occasionally a renegade may lift the veil on the company he has just left (for example, De Lorean's unflattering portrait of General Motors: Wright, 1979); an investigative journalist may penetrate in disguise the hidden practices of business (the speciality of Gunther Wallraff in West Germany: cf. Wallraff, 1979); or a high-status journalist may have the legitimacy and clout to raise the most sensitive of issues with highly placed persons (as Anthony Sampson has consistently done in his popular books on various segments of the modern corporate world, such as *The Money Lenders: Bankers in a Dangerous World*, 1982). It is also possible to conduct research via surveys, as Levi has done, and to interview businessmen anonymously (which is the predominant technique in the work of Kanter and Jackall, and was used to spice the surveys of Levi and of Clinard and Yeager).

In brief, anyone wishing to tackle directly the area of business deviance encounters considerable methodological and ethical difficulties related to access, ethical codes, studying desk-bound senior personnel, getting at the data of informal networks and hidden practices, and almost certainly with reaching publication. Braithwaite's (1984) study of corporate crime in the pharmaceutical industry was delayed for two years by lawyers representing the managers he had interviewed; he was forced to answer 300 empirical claims that might be raised in court; and he argues for always interviewing with two questioners and/or a tape-recorder as some managers – who claimed to be identifiable – also denied that they had ever said what he had printed (1985b). Much research relies, then, on published secondary sources. This book is no exception, and restraints of time precluded surveys and interviews; but rather it seeks to place the cases, which form the bulk of the book, in a specifically sociological, criminological, organizational, and managerial framework that locates the managers in a context constrained by work, culture, situational norms and values, moral dilemmas, occupational identity, organization, and the nature of business.

Research Perspectives

This final section is designed to bring the broad focus on corporate deviance and control down to a few essential strands that will inform the rest of this book. In essence, the research spotlight is aimed at a central question: why do managers break the law and their own rules of professional and corporate conduct? And, indeed, what can we do about it? This overly simple question is, in fact, capable of opening up extremely complex, wide-ranging arguments that do not lend themselves to plain answers and simple solutions ('the complexity behind the decisions of corporate executives to engage in illegal behaviours cannot be underestimated', Jamieson, 1994: 98). To examine deviance and control, for example, takes us into the analysis of rules, conformity, sanctions, rewards, rule-makers, rule-breakers, rule-enforcers, labelling, and so on. To place that deviance in a societal context requires looking at social change and how that affects business, government, and attempts at regulation. A certain amount of selection and reduction is unavoidable to keep this work within acceptable bounds and, as such, the following assumptions will be implicit throughout the rest of this work.

The first assumption is that types of, and opportunities for, business deviance will alter with social, economic, and technological change. For instance, Levi (1987) accentuates the interlinked innovations occurring in the swiftly fluctuating world of financial and business transactions (in terms of economic, financial, technological, and organizational change) and their relationship to fraud. The second is that societal attitudes to business deviance will be dependent on complex negotiations of rules between business, government, and other vested interests, making that process essentially 'political.' In a classic book on the corporation, Drucker hammers home the fact that the large corporation has become 'our representative social institution' (with an insistence that echoes Orwell's 'Big Brother');

> In other words, Big Business is the general condition of modern industrial society irrespective of the forms of social organization or the political beliefs adopted in particular countries. Even to raise the question whether Big Business is desirable or not is therefore nothing but sentimental nostalgia. The central problem of all modern society is not whether we want Big Business but what we want of it, and what organization of Big Business and of the society it serves is best equipped to realize our wishes and demands. (1972: 18)

Given the immense and growing power of business, who can control it particularly if governments release their grip via deregulation and especially if multinationals evade effective national control?

The third assumption is that the phenomenon of business deviance, and business crime, is *inseparable from the legitimate conduct of business.* The essence of business is pursuit of legitimate self-interest in transactions circumscribed by rules that protect the parties involved and the relationship of those private parties to the interests of the public, society, the state, and regulatory agencies (Clarke, 1990: 8). Another way of putting this is to say it is about the exercise, and abuse, of power. And the fourth is that to understand business deviance requires an examination of the business world – and on developing insights into the corporate world and the milieu of managers. In addition, I wish to emphasize strongly four further aspects that flow from these suppositions.

Corporate and Common Crime

In much of the literature there is a strong contrast drawn between two almost distinct systems of detection, prosecution, and sanctioning; namely, that there exist considerable discrepancies – leading to accusations of bias, discrimination, injustice, and classbound justice – between mechanisms for coping with common crime compared to white-collar crime. This raises issues such as reporting crime, policing, prosecution, trial, sanctions, stigma, sentencing, deterrence, rehabilitation, incapacitation, and control and enforcement strategies (Reiss, 1983). That contrast and those discrepancies will also inform this work. Although it has been established that a great deal of corporate deviance is never classified as 'crime', and the law plays a minor role in its regulation, it is vital to appreciate that perhaps the greatest discrepancy between common and white-collar violations is that corporations have the power to mobilize in order to influence the rules which cover their own conduct. (The Insolvency Act of 1985, for instance, which arose from a concern about the abuse of the corporate form to escape personal liability in Britain, encountered 'enormous resistance in the House of Lords and an impressive lobby organized by the Institute of Directors and representatives of the merchant banks': Levi, 1987: 85). This can be done by lobbying power when the rules are being established initially or by utilizing clout to influence and contest directly or indirectly the whole enforcement process. In many of the cases, then, we can observe the corporation actively defending its interests in ways that would normally be unthinkable for a 'common criminal'. Much of that defence is aimed specifically at getting offences out of the criminal system and into informal, private, and civil dispute settlement.

Everyday Deviance and the World of Work

It is doubtless unavoidable that a loaded term like 'business crime' will excite titillating images of exotic, conspiratorial intrigues, of Swiss bank accounts, laundered money, lavish entertainment, dramatic suicides, and nearly unfathomable double-dealings in sophisticated financial circles. But to explain the origins of those practices requires getting down to the daily reality of managers and the dilemmas they face in the modern corporation. Work, culture, and organization shape the experience of the manager, and I would concur with Kanter's (1977: 10) remark that 'behaviour in organizations can only be fully understood when there is adequate appreciation of the self-perpetuating cycles and inescapable dilemmas posed by the contingencies of social life'.

Building on the work of Kanter, Dalton, and Jackall, among others, I wish to place the manager centrally in a social and moral context where deviance may be embedded in the daily practices and understood meanings of routine organizational reality. Only when this level of analysis is appreciated is it possible to perceive the almost intractable dilemmas of enforcing effective control at the micro level. This is because people are ingenious at avoiding control mechanisms and, indeed, their response is in a sort of symbiotic reaction to the form of control. As a consequence analysis should focus on dilemmas generated by work and the extent to which corporate culture condones and legitimates deviance, and should note that the organizational structure may permit deviance and inhibit control.

Complexity and Levels of Analysis

It is difficult to avoid stating *ad nauseam* that this is a wide-ranging and diffuse area, but it is essential to emphasize again that corporate deviance does not fit neatly into a disciplinary compartment, that it does not readily lend itself to quantification, and that necessarily research on corporate deviance involves touching on society, inter-organizational relations, legal systems, ethics, politics, the media, culture, work, identity, and change over time. In effect, the material to be presented later in this book will be analysed at several levels and will concern multiple variables. Just to take the Thalidomide tragedy (related to a drug that caused deformities in babies, cf. Case no. 7), for example, it would be necessary for an analysis to take into account social, legal, and ethical aspects related to monitoring of drugs, legal battles for compensation, freedom of the press, standards of pharmaceutical research, the relationship between commercial marketing of drugs and the medical profession, the manipulation of academic publications, the intimidation of critical spokespersons, the responsibility of government in relation to the drug industry, the relationship between drug companies and regulatory agencies, the nature of medical innovation, and the human ethical responsibility of management towards the unborn child who is exposed to potential handicap through the serious side-effects of certain drugs (Knightley et al., 1980; Braithwaite, 1984). When the interests of powerful corporate institutions, government, regulatory agencies, and concerned groups in the wider society (such as consumers and the media) clash, then the ensuing struggles may be bitter, prolonged, and difficult to unravel (Reiss, 1983). Analysis is necessarily wide-ranging, multilayered, and, of course, open to multiple interpretation.

Avoidance of Naïvety

The researcher in this area should avoid naïvety (in a sense this is related to the previous point about complexity). On the one hand, revelations of deviancy in corporations should alert us to the fact that we are concerned with a wide spectrum of activities; some will be genuine accidents, unavoidable incidents, and 'human errors' (that elastic term often used to rationalize away complex causation in accidents: Wagenaar, 1992). But when it comes to deliberate, persistent deviance – particularly that which causes damage and creates victims – then we should not be incredulous about the cunning, ruthlessness, and deviousness of managers. And it must be obvious that these are senior, competent, respectable, and established executives; they are not usually dangerous, 'criminally'-orientated mavericks but eminent members of the business community who break rules ostensibly in the interests of the company (Levi, 1987: 341) – but also in their own interests, as we have seen above in the cases of Maxwell, BCCI, and the S & Ls.

Yet on the other hand, we should also not fall into simplistic 'conspiracy' explanations. It is possible to see a strong relationship between segments of the 'power elite' (Mills, 1956) whereby business influences government to legislate and to enforce laws that minimally hinder the conduct of trade and the long-term interests of industry. You do not have to be a Marxist to understand that the social construction of laws reflects the interests of powerful groups and that governments are ambivalent about controlling business in advanced capitalist society (Wells, 1994). Reisman (1979: 43) speaks of 'lex imperfecta', of laws not really meant to be enforced fully or effectively, and it is possible to be highly critical of the powers and functioning of regulatory agencies (their selective enforcement, reluctance to prosecute, and feeble sanctions). Yet it is also possible to see legislation as a result of a genuine debate on how to control business without damaging economic interests from which many benefit (often a considerable dilemma for ostensibly 'anti-business', left-wing governments when they are elected to power). Furthermore, one can view enforcement as resulting not from pusillanimity and servile sloth but from choices based on realistic appraisals of the effectiveness of certain strategies. (When Schrag, an aggressive leader of the consumer movement, was given a post in a New York regulatory agency he found that an adversarial approach was simply time-consuming, expensive, and counter-productive and he could achieve far more through a conciliatory, persuasive approach: Braithwaite, 1985a: 10.)

I am conscious that this sort of discussion leads to a quicksand of semantics and circular arguments – of course mild enforcement is 'realistic' when your regulatory budget is low, your personnel has just been reduced, your sanctions are pathetic, the courts will not convict, and you are dependent on the industry anyway to get your information. But perhaps I can short-cut the morass and state baldly that the two essential points are that, while exposure of business deviance often does reveals conspiracy, this is not sufficient to employ conspiracy as a blanket explanation for corporate misbehaviour and its 'lenient' treatment. (For example, how does one explain periodically 'tough' approaches as in the Wall Street cases; is it all a massive charade and, if so, why bother?)

Second and finally, the material presented in the rest of this book will be informed by a sociological and organizational perspective. By that I mean the following. First, I consider that the analysis of organizational deviance should consider the *spectrum* of occupational and organizational practices embedded in a concrete situation in order to determine the complex web of formal and informal rules, boundaries of tolerance and legitimacy, rights and privileges, rewards and sanctions, and so on, which comprise people's working world. Second, we should concern ourselves with how people *experience* organizational reality (Kanter and Stein, 1979). My emphasis, then, is on the complexity and fluidity of situations and how these need to be understood in terms of the *meanings* people attach to them. Third, I wish to avoid simplistic notions of unambiguous legality, and somehow mechanically imposing social control, and of swiftly labelling organizations deviant, which leads to crude assumptions that all businessmen are criminals and that all organizational members share in deviant practices or a deviant identity. In practice, deviance, control, and labelling are related to norms and practices that are differentially dispersed within the organization, and control can spark off intense, prolonged, and varied debate and 'political' machinations that are intricate and complex and which are not readily visible. But, in essence, we are concerned with deviancy related to, and facilitated by, people's work and by their organizational setting.

It is to be hoped that this work will lead to a better understanding of business deviance and of how to control it. At one level it poses the issue: how serious is society about dealing with corporate crime and deviance? For instance, there is an increasing sophistication in corporate deviance and a measure of powerlessness in control agencies (particularly in the international arena); does this then encourage deviance – on the grounds that the 'deviant' is the one who *conforms* to the law and suffers economic losses as a result – and lead to further impotence in control? At another level it raises the question which is the elemental issue of how can we explain 'ordinary' people's involvement in foul or devious deeds (Hughes, 1963). Why *do* 'good' managers engage in 'dirty' business; and does their conscience really never bother them?

3

White-Collar Crime and Organizational Deviance: Consequences and Control

Literature and Concepts

Virtually everyone writing on the subject of white-collar and corporate crime commences with the obligatory and repetitive observation that there is a lamentable paucity of substantial work in this area. By this people mean not so much that little has been written (cf. Coleman, 1989: Croall, 1992), but rather that there has not been a great deal of conceptual and theoretical work, while the concept of 'white-collar crime' defies delimitation in a way that might create a coherent sub-field within Sociology or Criminology. Margolis (1979: 403) wrote of the 'immaturity' of theory in the field which had 'not developed much since Sutherland'; and a decade later Clarke (1990: 7) states that the area is 'very weakly organized intellectually'.

Equally inevitable is the due reverence for Sutherland's genuinely innovative work, which popularized the concept of 'white-collar' crime. His speech to the American Sociological Association in 1939 gave immediate currency to the concept, and he established himself as the pioneer of the field with his corner-stone book *White-Collar Crime* (Sutherland, 1949). He stated unambiguously,

> Corporations have committed crimes. . . . These crimes are not discreet and inadvertent violations of technical regulations. They are deliberate and have a relatively consistent unity. . . . Even when they violate the law, they [businessmen] do not conceive of themselves as criminals. Their consciences do not ordinarily bother them. (Sutherland, 1983: 217)

This makes it clear that Sutherland was not just talking about individual 'white-collar' crime but also about 'corporate' crime. Sutherland established that in corporations illegal practices were persistent and extensive, that proof of violations was difficult to obtain, that cases against corporations were often 'fixed', that managers expressed contempt for the law, government, and regulatory personnel, and that businessmen who were caught did not necessarily lose status (unlike the stigma attached to 'common' criminals). Sutherland had not only launched a new term into the academic and lay vocabulary (one that has been picked up in many languages) but he had also expressed a devastating critique of American business. His study examined the records pertaining to seventy of the largest private corporations and fifteen public utilities, and he named names; fear of libel, however, meant that the uncut version, with the names of the companies included, had to wait thirty-four years before it could be published (Sutherland, 1983). Without a doubt Sutherland had opened up an entirely new research area for the social sciences.

But Sutherland did not establish a 'school' or a research tradition. For almost twenty years there was low output and weak interest in following up his initiative (apart from work by Hartung, 1950; Clinard, 1952; Cressey, 1953; Geis, 1967). This was reflected in the lack of attention paid to white-collar crime in textbooks (cf. Clinard and Yeager, 1980: 13, who detail this neglect, which echoes a 1975 survey of 4,000 post-war criminological publications of which only 2.5 per cent dealt with white-collar or corporate criminality: Wolfgang et al., 1975). Undoubtedly, the drama of Watergate, with its highly publicized trials and series of exposures (fuelled by President Nixon's resignation and autobiographies penned by the leading participants), stimulated considerable interest in governmental deviance. A spin-off was the insight into illegal corporate contributions to Nixon's re-election campaign, and then later there was Senator Church's Senate Sub-Committee on the Multinationals (Sampson, 1976).

In American society this generated deep scepticism and wide mistrust of large organizations and it also coincided with Nader's sustained and telling attacks on corporate misconduct, with the rise of militant action groups and more critical media, and with a number of official investigations which exposed deviancy in the intelligence services, widespread domestic and foreign bribery in business, and illegal contributions of business to political parties (Ermann and Lundman, 1978). Clinard and Yeager (1980: 171) observe that 'The investigation of foreign payments or bribes, perhaps more than anything else, reveals the ingenuity and the deviousness of large corporations in violating business ethics and often laws.' This led to a rapid increase in the academic interest in the structured faults of major institutions, and this interest was reinforced by the emergence of radical theories that scrutinized the 'crimes of the powerful' (Quinney, 1977; Pearce, 1976; Krisberg, 1975; and Taylor et al., 1973).

A string of publications emerged from sociologists, criminologists, legal scholars, and political scientists that was wide-ranging, diffuse, and divided in its attention between political and business deviance (Reiss and Biderman, 1980; Sherman, 1979; Ermann and Lundman, 1978, 1982a, b; Geis and Meier, 1977; Geis and Stotland, 1980; Johnson and Douglas, 1978; Stone, 1975; Douglas and Johnson, 1977). Braithwaite (1985a) provides a concise and insightful review of the literature.

Probably the best-known piece of research in this stream, and the closest to Sutherland's legacy, was the substantial survey undertaken by Clinard and Yeager (1980). They focused on 582 of the largest publicly owned corporations in the USA and, covering a period of two years, examined legal violations brought by twenty-four federal agencies. Their definition of 'corporate crime' was restricted to those *successful* actions brought by the state under administrative, civil, or criminal law. The 582 corporations were responsible for a total of 1,554 'crimes', with at least one sanction imposed on 371 firms. Clinard and Yeager also observed that some businesses are more likely to violate than others (while some 40 per cent have 'clean' records); that this can be related to structural and market considerations and to corporate culture (the oil, automobile, and building industries were confirmed 'recidi- vists'); and that 'corporate violations are exceedingly difficult to discover, to investigate, or to develop successfully as legal cases because of their extreme complexity and intricacy' (1980: 6).

Their evidence unambiguously displays that often decisions on malpractice were taken at the highest corporate levels, that records were destroyed or ingenuously doctored by executives and their accountants, and that the out- comes of these decisions can have serious economic, financial, political, personal, and even physical consequences. Clinard and Yeager's research establishes, then, that the majority of America's largest companies had been successfully prosecuted at least once in a period of two years. This is clearly a substantial underestimate as they are reliant on offences that were detected, reported, and brought to court with success on behalf of a limited number of agencies. This leaves a virtually undiscoverable 'dark number' of unreported and unprosecuted offences. There have been other attempts to assess the extent of corporate deviance (Ross, 1980), but these are beset with method- ological and conceptual difficulties (the most encyclopaedic effort being by Reiss and Biderman (1980).

The field is clearly dominated by the sheer volume of North American studies and publications, which do, however, tend to be rather insular if not parochial. With some exceptions, only lip-service is paid to comparative research, because the focus is almost exclusively on one society, the USA (and because many American academics have poor foreign-language skills compared, for instance, to most continental European academics). Some studies are overly broad (encompassing a messy spectrum of organizations), some are related to specific industries or specific laws, and others are limited to legal violations. Three alternative sources have enriched the area recently. First, some excellent work has been conducted by British and Australian academics which helps to bring a fresh, comparative element to the debate. Levi's research on fraud (1987), Clarke's material on regulating the City of London (1986), and Braithwaite's (1984) study of the pharmaceutical indus- try are welcome additions to the field. Braithwaite (1989), in particular, has gone on to produce important and valuable work (cf. Fisse and Braithwaite: 1993). Also a large number of wide-ranging cases are reported in the business ethics literature (Buchholz, 1989; Hartley, 1993; Donaldson and Werhane, 1979; Ferrell and Fraedrich, 1991; Matthews et al., 1985). Second, the area of disasters and corporate culpability and response has begun to attract increas- ing attention (Perrow, 1984; Regester, 1987; ten Berge, 1990; Meyers, 1988; Shrivastava, 1987; Comfort, 1988).

Third, there is a growing volume of empirical studies of regulation, com- pliance, inspection, and institutional control of business and industry (Carson, 1982; Hawkins, 1984; Richardson et al., 1983). This material generally scrutinizes specific control agencies in relation to particular industries in a national, regional, or local context. They help shift the focus away from crime and on to 'compliance' and self-regulation. There are, however, very few cross-national studies, which is not surprising given the difficulty of comparing legal and control systems in different societies; but this gives rise to acute definitional problems. In short, we are ignorant on the nature and extent of business deviance in many countries outside of a few English-speaking countries.

There may well be a substantial number of studies in foreign countries which never emerge into the English-language literature in this area. The Netherlands, for instance, has had its share of scandals, but most of these are not reported outside of the country – unless, of course, the case has international dimensions, as with the example of Prince Bernhard and Lockheed ('Donner' Report, 1976; Sampson, 1978), largely because very few non-Dutch journalists and academics read Dutch. This is likely to be true too of 'minority' language countries in Europe which often have relatively deferential media, no tradition of academic research in this area, and a language that acts as a barrier to communication with outsiders – for example, the Scandinavian countries, Finland, Portugal, and Greece. Even then a number of scandals, renowned in a specific 'major' European society, may not be well known outside of those countries (the journal *Corruption and Reform* is a good source for many European and other cases). For instance, the Flick affair in Germany sparked off a long-running scandal related to dubious payments by businessmen to politicians (eventually two leading politicians and a businessman were sanctioned for tax-evasion charges). Although the corruption charges were dropped for lack of evidence, the scandal caused considerable political and social shock-waves, and was seen by one commentator as 'one of the most serious challenges to the authority of the Bonn Republic since the creation of the West German state in 1949' (Glees, 1987). Yet who has ever heard of Flick outside of Germany?

One reason is related to what is considered worth reporting internationally; another is that social scientists tend to write about their own society and in their own language. But what these comparative studies reveal is that there are wide national and cultural variations in business–government relations, in regulatory regimes, in implementing legislation, and in notions of risk, blame, culpability, responsibility, and morality. Japanese executives often resign in response to mistakes made by their companies and may still even commit suicide. In the legally orientated climate of the USA it is unusual for managers involved in accusations of deviance to express regret, contrition, atonement, or shame unless to impress the judge or jury before sentencing. In Europe in some countries there is a high tolerance of business deviance and little serious attempt to control it.

Nevertheless, it should be accentuated that even in Great Britain the number of people working in this area can be counted on one hand and until quite recently, only a single textbook – Box's (1983) feisty, critical but oversimplified treatment that has as its major focus the systematic neglect of elite crime and the 'system's' overemphasis on 'common' crime – dealt with the issue of corporate crime. Most British criminological and deviancy research still predominantly highlights street crime, fear of crime, victimization, prisons, and policing and rarely attends to the crimes of the powerful. Ironically, the more pronounced radical criminological tradition in Britain (certainly in comparison with that in the USA) led to a focus on repressive measures, particularly by the police, the judiciary, and the prison system, against the working class rather than looking *upwards* at elite deviance which could be seen as helping to exploit the working class. As such, the development of the discipline led academics away from upper-world crime, and this imbalance has only recently begun to be rectified by a few lone rangers – notably Levi (1987) and Clarke (1990).

And yet there still exists a great deal of conceptual confusion surrounding the concept of white-collar crime and organizational deviance. Geis and Stotland (1980: 11) are not atypical in neatly side-stepping the quicksand when they frankly admit, in introducing their selection of articles, 'we deliberately have avoided the conceptual and terminological issues involved in white-collar crime definitions'. Sutherland, for instance, attributed white collar crime to a 'person of respectability and high social status in the course of his occupation' (1983: 7). His aim was to refute the prevalent views of criminals as being predominantly poor, working class, and mentally unstable when businessmen who were well-off, well-educated, middle- or upper-class, and ostensibly mentally healthy, were also responsible for crime. This raises immediately the query as to the definition of 'respectability'; someone of high status can be guilty of common crime (theft, rape, robbery and so on), while some white-collar crimes (such as fraud and embezzlement) can also be committed by people of low status.

To what extent, then, can we speak of 'crimes'? Some academics have argued that we can only refer to crime when criminal sanctions have been applied (Tappan, 1947). For instance, Clinard's and Yeager's (1980) work refers to cases that were perhaps for only *1 per cent* criminal (Levi, 1987: xxiv). But Sutherland argued that 'an unlawful act is not defined as criminal because it is punished but by the fact that it is *punishable*' (1983: 49, my emphasis); and this would also include actions brought against a corporation by private litigants. Clinard and Yeager, however, define corporate crime as 'any act committed by corporations that is punished by the state, regardless of whether it is punished under administrative, civil, or criminal law' (1980: 16). This narrows prosecutions to those brought by the *state* alone, but widens their survey to include actions brought not only under criminal law but also civil or administrative law, which are far and away the majority of cases.

The rationale for continuing to use the highly emotive word 'crime' for cases that do not reach criminal proceedings is that much behaviour which could be defined, and processed, as criminal is, for a multiplicity of reasons, shunted into the non-criminal legal system. And, it is argued, a murder is a murder whether or not it has been solved and a murderer is a murderer even if he or she has not been caught. Reiss and Biderman argue for the retention of the white-collar concept (as does Braithwaite, 1985a) but avoid the use of the term 'crime':

> White-collar law violations are those violations of law to which penalties are attached and that involve the use of a violator's position of significant power, influence, or trust in the legitimate economic or political institutional order for the purpose of illegal gain, or to commit an illegal act for personal or organizational gain. (1980: 4)

This definition has a number of advantages over previous ones. First, it avoids the use of the loaded word 'crime' in favour of 'violations'. Second, by not defining the area of law it opens up the area of *private* law (namely, how organizations and institutions impose private systems of justice on their members; for example, via professional codes or through rules of membership of, say, the stock exchange). At the same time the use of the terms 'law' and 'illegal' assume formal codes with sanctions, and this precludes areas of deviance and unethical conduct that remain uncodified. Third, it refers to legitimate enterprises and therefore excludes business set up with the sole purpose to defraud (cf. Levi, 1981, on 'long-firm' fraud where fake companies are set up as fronts to entice large quantities of goods on credit from manufacturers). And, fourth, it includes acts committed *on behalf of* the organization and not simply for personal gain.

The latter helps to place white-collar crime and deviance firmly in the context of not only the individual offender, such as the embezzler, but also of 'organizational' crime and deviance of which business crime and deviance is a sub-set (in the sense that governmental deviance can also be seen as a sub-set of organizational deviance). This concept should not be confused with 'organized crime'; even relatively primitive forms of common crime may have a measure of organization while some, such as project-crime, requiring team-work, planning, and technical know-how as in safe-breaking (Punch, 1989a), plainly demand a high level of organization and even sophistication (McIntosh, 1975). But 'organized crime' is normally used of criminal syndicates such as the Mafia, which endeavours to monopolize areas of 'inelastic demand' (vice, gambling, drugs) through force, intimidation, illegal organizational forms, and illicit manipulation of legitimate organizations.

But can an organization commit a crime? And what do we mean by 'organizational' deviance? No behaviour is intrinsically deviant, but where you have rules you have deviance. Cohen (1966) maintains that deviant behaviour is behaviour which violates institutionalized expectations, by which he means expectations shared and recognized as legitimate within a social system. The social audience is crucial in defining deviance – meaning that child pornography or defiling synagogues may be accepted behaviour in certain groups (even though this is quite repugnant to the vast majority of people) – while definitions may also change over time and may be dependent on the power of the accusers to apply successfully the deviant label. In this work I would like to utilize the concept of *organizational* deviance, while cautiously guarding against the trap of reification. Gross (1980: 59) argues, for instance, 'But what must be understood is that organizations, though inventions of biological persons and *thus totally dependent upon the continuous activity of such actors*, nevertheless may take on lives of their own' (my emphasis).

In other words, an organization cannot take a decision; people take decisions. At the same time organizations are legal entities that can be prosecuted and punished; they survive the biological persons that control them; they can successfully process people with relative ease to meet predetermined standards and traditions (as in the military, which massively and routinely turns civilians into soldiers, ready to kill, and to die, within a matter of months); and even the most phenomenological of sociologists continually slips into the vernacular and attributes reality to the gas board, the university, and General Motors (Cohen, 1966: 21).

In turn, however, the concept of deviance opens up a limitless plethora of possibilities, for most organizations are extremely complex social entities containing a bewildering range of formal and informal activities. It is hoped, nevertheless, that some order can be brought to the debate by the following classification of types of deviance commonly found in organizations.

1 *Informal rewards* Perks, fiddles, tipping, discounts, presents, use of company phone/post, etc. These practices may be widespread, can even expand considerably as one moves up the organization, and may almost be considered as a way of life (as in some service industries). Although they are technically against company rules, management sometimes tolerantly views them as acceptable and even legitimate providing they remain within implicitly agreed boundaries.

2 *Work avoidance/manipulation of work situation* Activities designed to make work conditions more comfortable and acceptable (arriving late, sciving, seeking cushy numbers, leisure activities in company time, and so on). This type of behaviour is encountered at all levels, although when it reaches excess proportions, and a crackdown is enforced, it tends to be defined as a 'blue-collar' or a 'lower orders' problem.

3 *Employee deviance: against the organization* Practices such as stealing, absenteeism, neglect, and sabotage are generally perceived as being confined to the lower levels of the organization and are normally seen by management as being highly negative and damaging. Embezzlement and fraud may also hurt the company; and may be conducted by middle- and even higher-level management, but in the interests of the corporation forms of 'private justice' are frequently applied informally and prosecution is avoided.

4 *Employee deviance: for the organization* Workers often bend rules, cut corners, fail to observe safety regulations, etc., in the interest of satisfactory performance (such as enhanced production). These activities can be seen as minor, virtually unavoidable, near universal, but essentially positive. Rules are perceived differentially and some may be respected on ritual occasions, such as inspections, but routinely they are bent, broken, or ignored in an institutionalized 'indulgence pattern' (Gouldner, 1954).

5 *Organizational deviance: for the organization* It is clear that many of the activities dealt with in the literature of business deviance are relatively serious and deliberate practices conducted with a measure of deception, stealth, and cunning (in relation to internal and external formal control agencies) in order to achieve formal or informal organizational goals. These can be acts of commission or omission and they are frequently supported, overtly or covertly, by senior management.

6 *Managerial deviance: against the organization* In a number of cases senior management has victimized its own company and 'looted' it in their own interests. Serious predatory deviance at the top which is not in the long-term interests of the company is probably the most potentially damaging behaviour for a corporation because of its vulnerability to insider deviance by powerful people.

There is a considerable literature on categories 1–4, which can be included in the concept 'occupational deviance' (Ditton, 1977; Henry, 1978). But my concern will be *predominantly with 5 and 6*. Essentially we are concerned with influential people who utilize their power or resources for ends which some other people define as illicit, and then, not infrequently, employ that power or those resources to protect themselves from the consequences of social control.

This relates not to trivial matters such as executives fiddling expenses, but to serious issues such as bribery, secrecy, deception, falsification, industrial espionage, black markets, abuse of power, negligence, intimidation, conspiracy, price-fixing, and so on. This leads me to concur to a large extent with Ermann and Lundman, when they state that

> organizational deviance is consistent with normal organizational routines. The deviant behaviours are not produced by dramatic or aberrant actions of a few isolated individuals, but instead are an integral part of the organization. Deviance thus exists alongside legitimate organizational activities and frequently serves to advance important organizational goals. (1982a: 91)

But in a number of cases, as we have seen, the deviance may be directed at the corporation itself and may effectively *undermine* formal organizational goals.

The essence of my use of the term '*organizational* deviance' is not meant to convey any form of reification or determinism, that somehow impersonal forces irresistibly dictate behaviour to pliant puppets; but, rather, that organizations may create climates where collective deviance is an acceptable answer to perceived institutional dilemmas, and where the organizational culture, resources, and facilities are intrinsic to the development of the deviance (Tomy and Reiss, 1993).

In short, we are concerned with a complex, diffuse, wide-ranging area where we are basically interested in corporate deviance, that is, with significant deviance that takes place in the legitimate business world. This refers not solely to technically defined 'criminal' behaviour but also deals with a wide range of significant violations against external and internal rules and regulations. But that does not mean that we should avoid ever using the term 'crime' because some corporate behaviour is criminal in intent, in its consequences, and in its prosecution. Clarke (1990) provides a comprehensive and useful analysis of the characteristics of business crime which also helps to explain why much potentially criminal behaviour is dealt with *privately and informally*, because enforcement is intimately related to the nature of the offences concerned. These features can be compared with street crimes which generally are physically threatening, take place in public places, lead to complainants who inform the police, and are near universally condemned as indisputably criminal offences, while the perpetrator is unambivalently seen as a 'criminal'. Successful prosecution will mean a criminal trial and penal sanctions.

This can be contrasted with the characteristics of business crime (Clarke, 1990: 20–31).

- It takes place within the business environment and hence in a *private* context.
- Business offenders are *legitimately present* at the scene.
- There is *not necessarily an immediate complainant*. 'Insider-dealing' may pass unnoticed while the offenders can even 'manipulate the victims' perception of what happened so that it may not occur to them that they have been victimized improperly or criminally' (Levi, 1987: 24).
- Because there is no public order violation it is *less threatening* than 'common' crime.
- Detection and control are initially *internal* to the organization and hence private.
- The *law plays a limited role* and private, informal solutions may prevail over public/formal ones.
- There is a *fundamental ambiguity* about business crime which is 'profound and pervasive'.
- *Business offences are 'political'* because of their 'essentially contested character' and this can lead to protracted struggles in the public realm involving the mobilization of considerable and powerful resources by the contending parties.
- There is a *great diversity of sanctions*.
- The power of consumerism, and the need to ensure business accountability, has led many *states to intervene* considerably in the regulation of business conduct.
- And it raises in acute form debate about the balance between the *'private interest'* and the *'public good'*; 'the danger of unfettered private enterprise is that it degenerates into greed, ruthlessness, and deceit to the oppression of those insufficiently cunning, skilled, wealthy or powerful to protect themselves, and so polarises the haves from the have-nots' (Clarke, 1990: 31).

One might also add a number of additional factors such as the fact that the consequences of business crime can be considerable; that the evidence is complex and open to manipulation; that offences can be *longitudinal* and spread over several locations; that juries are often reluctant to convict businessmen accused of crimes; and that the victims of business crime are, among others, often *other businesses*.

The Deleterious Consequences of Corporate Behaviour

That business kills, maims, pollutes, and corrupts is a powerful theme in a critical stream of condemnatory literature (for instance, Mokhiber's engaged and hard-hitting *Corporate Crime and Violence*, 1988). Activists, journalists, and academics have been deeply concerned that business's search for economic results is bought at the price of physical, economic, political, social, and human suffering and damage. To specify the precise extent of that damage is, however, extremely difficult. There may simply be no reliable statistics available (for example, on infant mortality in Third World countries); impressive-looking data on industrial injuries are flawed because an unknown number of accidents are not reported or not recorded; some anti-business groups may have political and ideological reasons for inflating figures, which then become rhetorical devices; and business may simply continue to dispute the validity of any evidence which damages its reputation or threatens its continuance – for instance, the tobacco industry has persistently challenged the medical evidence on the causal relationship between smoking and cancer (Buchholz, 1989: 174–90; Miles, 1986).

The point of this section is threefold. First, to document the damage and suffering caused by economic activity, some of which is avoidable; second, to suggest that this is related to the management of business; and, third, to note that there is continual negotiation between business on the one hand, and government together with societal groups on the other hand, as to the benefits and negative side-effects of economic progress and their collective ability to control those side-effects.

But no lack of valid statistics can conceal the magnitude of the deleterious effects of economic activity in advanced industrial society and, increasingly, in Third World countries. Indeed, this is especially pertinent because economic and industrial progress has reached a crucial stage where it has begun to threaten the very balance of nature, with potentially severe and debilitating consequences for human and animal existence on our planet. Acute, then, is the complex sociopolitical issue of steering the further expansion of legitimate economic activity; this is even more the case with illegal economic behaviour that is damaging people and the environment (such as the adulteration of consumer goods and the illicit dumping of poisonous waste) and that successfully evades control. Of course, in all economic activity – and this has been evident since the commencement of the industrial revolution – there is an equation of advantages and disadvantages to be drawn up for society which means that businessmen, and political and societal watch-dogs, always engage in a debate which involves compiling a balance sheet in the form of *risk assessment* (for instance, modern society permits the extensive production of automobiles, tobacco, and alcohol although all three are highly injurious to health).

While business, unavoidably but also avoidably, harms consumers and workers, it is also evident that some illicit economic activity is highly damaging to business itself, as with fraud, counterfeiting, and stock manipulation. This is related to the threshold of trust and confidence which people need to have for healthy economic activity to persist and which may be undermined by manipulation of the market, by the infiltration of financial institutions by organized crime (for example, by those institutions performing willingly economic functions for international drugs cartels), and by banks which take undue and irresponsible risks – such as Continental Illinois which had to be rescued to the tune of $4.5 billion contributed from other banks and $4.4 billion from the Federal Deposit Insurance Corporation (Meyers, 1988: 22–6). Trust may be further undermined if it is discovered that business is corruptly buying into markets or protecting its interests by manipulating the political process.

But there can be no doubt that business activity, legitimate and illegitimate, can have serious and negative effects on the environment, the public, consumers, workers, communities, politics, and the financial-economic order itself. Here an attempt will be made to specify some of the consequences of business behaviour while recognizing that many of the data in this area are unreliable and contentious and need to be treated with reserve.

Human Suffering and Environmental Damage

As early as 1973, Bell, in his *The Coming of Post-Industrial Society*, lamented that corporate performance had made society 'uglier, dirtier, trashier, more polluted, and noxious' (p. 272). Since then matters have grown worse almost exponentially although there is a growing acceptance of the urgent need for drastic measures to prevent further ecological deterioration. This raises a fundamental and almost intractable issue related to the continual struggle between the profit-seeking goals of business and the protection of the interests of employees, consumers, communities, the general public, and the environment. Safety, negligence, and accidents are matters directly related to managerial policies, investments, infrastructure, internal and external control, and industry's compliance with regulation. And the differential implementation and enforcement of rules and regulations can clearly create victims and cause immense physical and psychic damage.

Most people nowadays, even including ostensibly deregulatory politicians of the right, are acutely aware that air and water pollution threaten our rivers, seas, lakes, and forests; that the consumption of finite hydrocarbon energy sources not only depletes energy reserves for future generations but also releases carbon dioxide which alters climatic conditions with far-reaching consequences for sea-levels and for agricultural production; and that toxic waste, pesticides, fertilizers, and hazardous chemicals are potential time-bombs which pose severe dangers for the physical and social environment. This makes industrial accidents especially contentious when the damage is considerable and when controversy arises over neglect (on occasion related to cover-up and misinforming the public and the authorities). Chernobyl had global consequences for the environment, while the accident in the nuclear power plant at Three Mile Island (Harrisburg, Pennsylvania) could have been equally disastrous (cf. Case no. 5). The explosions at the chemical plants in Seveso (Italy) and Bhopal (India), as well as the fire at the Sandoz plant in Basle (Switzerland) which led to considerable pollution of the Rhine, raised critical questions on safety, maintenance, contingency plans, cooperation with the emergency services, compensation for the victims, and misinformation of the public (Regester, 1987; ten Berge, 1990).

Business, in short, creates victims and damages the environment. The automobile industry has produced cars with debatable safety records while the pharmaceutical industry has marketed drugs with dangerous side-effects; and the 'dumping' of chemicals and other waste products has caused an ecological calamity in a number of communities (Levine, 1982). Allied Chemicals was fined $13.24 million on criminal charges for depositing Kepone, a toxic pesticide, into the James River in Virginia for several years, with subsequent detrimental effects on the fish population and also on the health of those who consumed the fish (Mokhiber, 1988: 248, 57; Yeager, 1993: 97).

If we take the 19,000 deaths related to street crimes recorded by the FBI in 1985, then we can compare that to the yearly total of victims of 'corporate crime and violence' in the USA (Mokhiber, 1988: 3):

- One hundred and thirty Americans die every day in automobile crashes. Many of those deaths are either caused by vehicle defects or are preventable by available crashworthiness designs.
- Almost 800 Americans die every day from cigarette-induced disease.
- Over the next 30 years, 240,000 people – 8,000 per year, one every hour – will die from asbestos cancer.
- An estimated 85,000 American cotton textile workers suffer breathing impairments due to cotton dust (brown lung) disease.
- 100,000 miners have been killed and 265,000 disabled due to coal-dust (black lung) disease.

Product-related accidents are said to cause 28,000 deaths and 130,000 serious injuries; there are annually 5.5 million injuries in the work place (of which 3.5 million require hospital treatment); and some 100,000 deaths have been related to exposure to dangerous chemicals and 390,000 deaths to occupational diseases (Mokhiber, 1988: 16). The figures are staggering, and shocking, and these are only for *one* country. On a world-wide scale, the amount of suffering and damage, partly unavoidable but also partly avoidable, is immense, virtually beyond measurement, and almost beyond comprehension.

Herald of Free Enterprise The issues related to 'harm' and corporate accountability revolve around the key question as to the relationship between the pursuit of profit and managerial concern with, and responsibility for, safety, workers, consumers, and the environment. For instance, the ferry-boat *Herald of Free Enterprise* capsized outside Zeebrugge in 1987 because the front loading-doors on this 'roll on/roll off' ship were left open upon sailing; water rushed in, destabilized the ship, and in the ensuing calamity 197 passengers and crew were killed. It was claimed that speed of turn-around was emphasized in this highly competitive industry and that this led to the rapid departure of boats; also to the design of such ships, which makes them highly unstable because comfort and convenience take precedence over safety.

The last desperate movements of the ship took it out of the harbour's channel and into shallow waters so that it capsized half-submerged on to a sand-bank, enabling people to escape and the rescuers to work from the exposed hull; a few minutes later the *Herald* would have been in open water and the loss of life would doubtless have been far greater. This was tragically illustrated by the sinking of the *Estonia* in September 1994, which lost its bow doors when crossing the Baltic Sea from Estonia in heavy weather and which sank rapidly to the sea-bed with a toll of some 900 lives (*Daily Mail*, 5 October 1994; *Financial Times*, 30 September 1994). The ship foundered so quickly that the SOS message was cut off in transmission, the life-boats could not be launched, and the few survivors had to abandon ship quickly into the cold waters as the *Estonia* disappeared within minutes (*Daily Mail*, 29 September 1994).

Following the Zeebrugge accident, there had been recommendations for improved safety aboard 'ro-ro' ferries, but many companies still had to implement the alterations; indeed, safety checks on the ferry fleet to and from Britain made after the *Estonia* calamity revealed that '21 of the 58 British-registered ships and 14 of the 49 sailing under foreign flags needed repairs' and that a third of ro-ro ferries leaving British ports had faults on doors (*Daily Mail*, 8 November 1994). In a feature article entitled 'Why These Ferries Are Still Not Safe', one newspaper stated, 'Experts say that a roll-on/roll-off ferry will capsize in European waters once every five years. The cause is simple, the effect – as witnessed on the *Estonia* – catastrophic' (*Sunday Telegraph*, 2 October 1994). The loss of life on the *Herald* was the highest for a British vessel in peacetime since the sinking of the *Titanic* in 1912. (This account is based on the 'wreck commissioner's' court of investigations proceedings – 'MV *Herald of Free Enterprise*', 1987; and on presentations at the Police Staff College, Bramshill, by the Kent County Coroner who presided over the inquest into the cause of death of the victims at Zeebrugge, and by the senior investigating officer of the Kent County Police who conducted the inquiry into the liability of Townsend (Car Ferries Ltd) for the accident and who presented the case in court.)

The report of the Court of Investigation detailed a whole series of contributing factors related to management, personnel and procedures ('MV *Herald of Free Enterprise*', 1987). Mr Justice Sheen, the 'wreck commissioner', assisted by two legal advisers and two damage experts, held the investigation in London under the Merchant Shipping Act of 1894. There were frequent crew and officer rotations; there had been previous instances of ships sailing with bow doors opened but no management directives on this practice had followed; meetings between managers and masters were infrequent; and there were a whole series of technical matters related to passenger overloading, underestimation of vehicle weights, inability to read draughts, water ballast and instability ('MV *Herald of Free Enterprise*', 1987: 17–29); Boyd, 1990: 141–4). In fact, the ship was not designed for the Zeebrugge route but had been diverted there by management,

> Another aspect of the accident had to do with the question of why the water entered through the open doors, which were several meters above sea level. Here it appeared that the 'Herald' was originally designed for the Dover-Calais connection. The ramp in Zeebrugge differed from the ramp in Calais; at high tide it was not possible for the cars to reach the upper deck. Therefore, the nose of the ship had been lowered a few meters through the filling of the ballast tanks. The ballast pumps did not have a sufficient capacity for emptying the tanks in a short time. The 'Herald' had docked in Zeebrugge five minutes late, but was requested to arrive in Dover 15 minutes early. Therefore, there was no time for waiting till the ballast tanks were empty. Instead, the 'Herald' left the harbour with the nose 3 meters down, and at full speed, which created a high bow wave. And so the 'Herald' capsized, in perfect weather, and on a practically waveless sea. (Wagenaar, 1992: 272)

The report stated that the Board of Directors must accept a 'heavy responsibility for their lamentable lack of directions. Individually and collectively they lacked a sense of responsibility. This left a vacuum at the centre' ('MV *Herald of Free Enterprise*', 1987: 15, 74).

In essence, the official inquiry of 1987 laid the blame firmly on 'serious negligence' within the company, as well as specific members of the crew, and Mr Justice Sheen came to the conclusion that the management of Townsend was complacent, neglectful of its responsibilities, and 'that all concerned in management, from the members of the Board of Directors down to the junior superintendents, were guilty of fault in that all must be regarded as sharing responsibility for the failure of management. From top to bottom the body corporate was infected with the disease of sloppiness' ('MV *Herald of Free Enterprise*', 1987: 14). But the Department of Transport did not recommend a criminal prosecution.

It was only after a verdict of 'unlawful killing', brought in by an inquest jury against the coroner's instructions, that the Kent County Police mounted a criminal inquiry. This led to the attempt to take Townsend (via its parent company P & O) to court on a charge of 'corporate manslaughter' for causing the deaths of 197 people at Zeebrugge. The prosecution failed in court. At the time of departure the assistant boatswain responsible for closing the doors was asleep in his bunk; the officer who was supposed to oversee the assistant boatswain was not at his post because operating instructions required him to be in two places at one time and he was on the bridge; and the captain had no mechanical means of knowing that the bow doors were shut despite several requests from masters for a warning device to be fitted on the bridge ('MV *Herald of Free Enterprise*', 1987: 8–10, 17–24; presentation by Kent County Police officers on criminal investigation into the accident).

The reason that the judge dismissed the case early on in the proceedings was because of the difficulty of tracing culpability from the failure to close the bow doors of the ferry to managerial decision-making on safety (cf. Swigert and Farrell, 1980/81: on the difficulties of defining 'corporate homicide'). The judge expressed his difficulty in defining 'the mind and will' of the corporation from the evidence (*de Volkskrant*, 20 October 1990); this is related to the chain of command and who can be held to be the 'embodiment' of the company;

> As Lord Justice Bingham said in R v. H.M. Coroner for East Kent; ex parte Spooner (1989) 88 Cr. App. Rep. 10, DC:

> It is important to bear in mind an important distinction. A company may be vicariously liable for the negligent acts and omissions of its servants and agents [i.e. for civil negligence], but for a company to be criminally liable for manslaughter it is required that the mens rea and the actus reus of manslaughter be established not against those who acted for or in the name of the company, but against those who were to be identified as the embodiment of the company itself. (Sturt, 1993)

It should also be said that there is a long nautical tradition of treating captains as primarily responsible for accidents to their vessels; Fisse and Braithwaite (1993: 39) point out that such traditions can lead to the avoidance of responsibility at the right, managerial level. And when the prosecution failed against the company (P & O), then the charges were also dropped against the individuals who had been implicated in the accident.

In short, the criminal law tends to experience difficulty in attributing blame to *organizations* even when they may be held to have committed violent acts leading to suffering and death (Tonry and Reiss, 1993). One explanation is that the criminal law tends to reflect reliance on an 'individual model of responsibility', while 'there is still a structural and ideological resistance within the legal system to the notion of criminal liability for that type of offence [corporate violence – MP]' (Wells, 1994: vii). No company has ever been convicted of the crime of manslaughter in Britain (*Guardian*, 1 February 1994).

The extensive research conducted by Carson (1982) on the North Sea oil industry is posited on the argument that economic interests, supported by British governments of both political persuasions, demanded rapid exploitation of the wells and this was bought at the cost of safety. That offshore drilling is extremely hazardous was indelibly illustrated by the explosion on the Piper Alpha rig off the coast of Scotland (in which 168 workers died); yet, while it is plain that it is not in the industry's interest to be faced with an accident (and major accidents are rare), Carson persuasively maintains that the hazards for workers reside not so much in the exceptional conditions (frequent storms in the North Sea and depths of up to 600 feet) as in the weak regulation and enforcement of safety and the *constant pressure* on workers to get on with the job (Carson, 1982; Clarke, 1990).

Thus, it is precisely pressure to get on with the job that can lead to injuries and death. In response, business would doubtless point to the general benefits of economic progress and to their constant, genuine concern for consumers, workers, and the environment. My intention here is not to explore the credibility of those claims but merely to indicate a form of social and eco-logical 'fall-out' that causes suffering and damage. That damage can be to consumers, workers, the environment, the general public, and to specific communities.

Of course there are costs too for the companies concerned (loss of facilities and production, legal and court costs, and hidden costs in terms of manage-ment time and energy diverted to coping with the crises). As noted above, Exxon faced clear-up costs in Alaska of $2 billion; and the A.H. Robins Company, maker of the Dalkon Shield, was forced to pay out millions of dol-lars in damages and chose the Chapter 11 bankruptcy procedure in the face of millions of pending lawsuits. A similar resort to Chapter 11 was taken by the Manville Corporation, which was faced by actions brought by workers who had suffered from asbestos-related diseases (in some cases related to exposure up to forty years previously), and which made a 'high projection' of 120,000 suits at a liability of more than $5 billion (nearly five times the com-pany's net worth: Buchholz et al., 1985: 333). Chapter 11 defers and virtually protects companies from civil liability and its use by certain companies has raised important ethical questions (Buchholz, 1989: 152–66).

Corporations, governments (as revenue collectors), and shareholders (tech-nically the owners of corporations), are also themselves hurt by business deviance. Companies that bribe officials may reduce competitors' profit mar-gins and even drive them into bankruptcy; and illegal mergers and takeovers and other 'shady financial manoeuvres may result in many shareholders being defrauded' (Box, 1983: 30). The 'grey market' is said to be worth $7 billion in North America; it involves the diversion of goods bought cheaply from wholesalers abroad to the American market in order to undercut domestic distributors; this trade is partly conducted with the connivance of some firms, but others, however, are the victims of 'sophisticated scams': 'And with the grey market a low priority for law enforcement agencies, these companies must find their own ways of penetrating a murky world of dummy companies, fake invoices, off-shore accounts, and sometimes outright bribery' (*Business Week*, 7 November 1988).

For instance, diversion's 'dirty side' was revealed by an FBI and congres-sional investigation into the appearance of counterfeit birth-control pills in drug-stores in 1985:

> they found a vast underground economy in prescription drugs. Hospitals were over-ordering to take advantage of volume discounts, then selling the surplus to brokers who peddled the drugs to discounters. Doctors were selling free samples to repackagers, who put them in authentic-looking bottles, sometimes changing the expiry dates. (*Business Week*, 7 November 1988)

Two executives of Bindley Western Industries Inc. pleaded guilty to fraud charges, and admitted they had bought from diverters whom they were aware had bribed government officials in Haiti and Bulgaria to place large orders with pharmaceutical companies: 'The FBI probe also led to more than 100 fraud convictions of pharmacists, doctors, and brokers across the country' (*Business Week*, 7 November 1988).

The airline industry's association, IATA, has claimed that half the profits made by the industry world-wide in 1985, some £500 million, were lost through fraud. Counterfeiting of products (watches, clothes, videotapes and compact discs, perfume, and so on, costing $60 billion globally: *Newsweek*, 21 April 1986) causes considerable damage to reputable companies and leads not only to loss of money but also to loss of jobs. Adulteration of foodstuffs can cause much suffering and even deaths among its victims (and there have been cases of tampering with Italian wine, of Russian caviar and tinned Indian curry; while the olive-oil scandal in Spain allegedly caused more than 400 deaths and affected some 20,000 people, of whom more than 700 are permanently handicapped: *de Volkskrant*, 19 May 1989). Such practices can sponsor market collapse for a product, as in the case of Austrian wine, which was virtually unsaleable when it emerged that wine had been adulterated with antifreeze.

In Britain, the black economy is estimated conservatively at £500 million (with other sources mentioning £28,000 million: cf. Levi, 1987: 24) and it means deleterious consequences for government revenue and legitimate business's share of economic activity. Banking frauds reported in 1985 to the two London Police Fraud Squads (of the Metropolitan and City forces) amounted to £1,349 million. And, in the 1980s, the failures of the Carrian and Pan-Electric corporate groups in Hong Kong, Malaysia, and Singapore were 'accompanied by proven allegations of widespread fraud' with arguably 'disastrous short-term effects upon their national economies' (cf. Levi, 1987: 25–46).

Clearly, business deviance can hurt business badly, and also society, and the sums involved are astronomical; 'flight capital' in Swiss banks in 1984 was said to amount to 100 billion Swiss francs, but by definition adequate data on 'secret money' is hard to come by: 'In general no-one has even a remote idea of the size or direction of global secret money flows or of the identity of those involved' (Walter, 1986).

Political Consequences

Corporate tax evasion and avoidance depletes the government's coffers and effectively means that ordinary people are forced to pay more taxes. In Great Britain, evasion of Value Added Tax (VAT) by companies was said to have cost the exchequer £300–500 million in 1986 (Levi, 1987: 24). In the USA, a Department of Justice estimate put the loss to the taxpayers 'from reported and unreported violations of federal regulations of corporations at $10 billion to $20 billion each year' (Mokhiber, 1988: 15). In 1983 America's Internal Revenue Service calculated that anything between $20 and $135 billion was illegally leaving the country for secret destinations abroad. In West Germany some DM 1,500 million escape from the exchequer in dividend payments annually. In France it is asserted that tax evasion is put at 7.85 billion francs. The underground economy of Italy is *officially* recorded in the statistics as 15 per cent of GNP; but this is dwarfed by the proportion in Third World countries (in Peru, where the underground economy is reputed to be the largest in the world, it is said to amount to 60 per cent of GNP: Walter, 1986).

These losses are considerable financially and economically, but a different sort of damage can arise when interconnections between government and business, based on bribery, corruption, favouritism, and conflicts of interest, are exposed, thus setting off political repercussions. In Mexico and Italy controversy surrounded the consequences of corruption in politics and the building industry which was said to have brought about sub-standard housing, not built to adequate safety standards, and which therefore collapsed, causing unnecessary death and injury in earthquake zones (Levi, 1987: 24). The Lockheed scandal had far-reaching political consequences in several countries, including the Netherlands (where the Queen's threat of abdication caused a constitutional crisis and where Prince Bernhard was publicly, albeit mildly, disgraced but not prosecuted); in Italy (where two defence ministers were implicated); and in Japan (where the prime minister was arrested, tried, and sentenced to prison); while in West Germany a previous defence minister, Franz-Josef Strauss, evaded scrutiny when documents 'disappeared' from the defence ministry (Boulton, 1978; Sampson, 1978). In Japan there have been a series of political scandals related to payments and connections with business and these have led to a number of resignations, prosecutions and criminal sanctions (cf. 'Recruitgate': Saito, 1990; *The Japan Times*, 23 February 1995).

In conclusion, this brief and inevitably selective overview indicates that illicit economic activity can deplete national income and financial resources and can also undermine political legitimacy.

Finally, I would like to add two comments to this section. First, business can create fortunes but it can also destroy them, and a number of senior businessmen have either lost fortunes, or their reputation, or their personal freedom because of their involvement in shady practices. One thinks of Michael Milken, Robert Maxwell, Roberto Calvi, Michele Sindona, Ivan Boesky, and David Levine. Entanglement in business deviance can, then, have severe personal consequences for some of the actors concerned. Second, perhaps the most damaging impact of business deviance is *the lack of trust and confidence* that it may foster. Scandals in Wall Street, in the City of London, and in the Hong Kong Stock Exchange (where an ex-chairman and two of his associates were arrested on suspicion of corruption), undermine the trust which is fundamental to financial institutions and the conduct of business. A member of the Wall Street financial community spoke of a cancer that threatened the integrity of financial markets, and that cancer was greed; indeed, the conduct of affairs in Wall Street was a financial 'time-bomb' because no less was at stake than a climate for healthy investment, the reinvigoration of industry and the maintenance of jobs, and the ability of America to compete with Japan (Rohatyn, 1987: 213).

Business has the capacity to damage people, the environment, reputations, even societies, but also itself. Here it has only been possible to skate swiftly over a vast subject to give an impressionistic account of an intricate area; but an underlying assumption is that *pressure* – to get work done, to deliver the goods, to bring in a contract, to raise economic performance, to achieve financial goals, and to amass personal fortunes – in some way generates motivation and willingness to break or bend rules and the law.

Control, Compliance, and the Corporation: National Styles and International Dimensions

Control

Let me recapitulate briefly; the characteristics of business crime and other types of violation of the law are that they take place *within* the business environment, during the course of *legitimate* business, and they have an ineluctably ambiguous nature that leads to a high measure of *contestability* (Clarke, 1990). Almost invariably executives accused of illegality deny it; they not only argue their innocence but also forcefully contest the illegality of their behaviour, as did Saunders in the Guinness case. From the first two features we can conclude that in many cases the deviant behaviour will in the first instance inevitably be detected and dealt with inside business organizations and by internal control mechanisms. To the extent that violations are brought outside of the corporation – by competitors, by audits, by inspections, by tracing pollution to its source, by the media, by partners in crime falling out (and by jilted partners seeking revenge for broken promises – 'disgruntled wives or lovers are the downfall of many a tax fraudster': Levi, 1987: 165) – then we can expect, when the matter is contested, a battle of wits between the corporation and external control agencies.

With regard to internal control it is possible to be sceptical about its ability to detect effectively sophisticated deviance, which is cleverly designed to evade that control and which may be perpetrated by senior managers who are difficult to tackle (precisely because of their social power and internal political influence over control mechanisms). Furthermore, corporations may have powerful interests in keeping violations within company walls (to avoid negative publicity the management allows miscreants to depart quietly and, apart from being squeezed out, without further sanctioning them; in some cases, even *rewarding* them to keep them quiet).

But then with regard to external control it is also possible to paint a highly depressing picture of the unequal battle between powerful corporations and minuscule, impotent, and demoralized control agencies. Major corporations frequently possess immense social, economic, political, and legal clout. A control agency may be tiny and weak in comparison; it may have limited personnel (civil servants with low remuneration, low occupational mobility, and poor training), a tight budget, curtailed legal powers, feeble sanctions, and an understandable tendency to avoid confrontation and prosecutions. Its critics may complain that it has been 'captured' by the industry it is meant to control and the relationship is one of deference and even servile accommodation to the corporations. The agency's response might be to say that confrontation would involve asking emaciated midgets having to grapple with sumo wrestlers (Ralph Nader asserted that some cases were almost 'untryable'; for instance, the anti-trust suit involving IBM which lasted eighteen years and in which the 50 million pages of documents brought forward by IBM to defend its case could potentially have swamped the court: Braithwaite, 1985b: 304). This is effectively an uneven competition with a depressingly predictable outcome.

A critical spectator of this one-sided struggle might legitimately protest that this allows companies to get away with murder (sometimes literally), and that it is rank injustice to see corporations go unpunished, or to witness managers being lightly treated by the courts, and to observe that businessmen can break the law and yet avoid social stigma. Corporate lawyers can utilize every legal trick in the book to delay legal proceedings so that court cases can drag on for years. This is all in shrill contrast to the perpetrator of a common crime who is dependent on forms of legal aid and relatively inexperienced legal representation, who is immediately incarcerated on arrest to await trial, who is refused bail, who is relatively severely punished, and whose reputation is blighted for life (once, that is, he is released from a lengthy period in a highly custodial prison).

Perhaps the answer is to be much tougher on business? For instance, Clarke (1990: 224f.) argues that if we look at substantial frauds then they are usually carefully planned conspiracies and often involve 'serious losses to customers, creditors, employees and the state, and involving sometimes great suffering for the victims, such as those who entrust their savings to crooked investment or franchise operators'. Surely, he continues, 'the only appropriate recourse for such obvious villains is criminal prosecution, expropriation of assets, and imprisonment'? His own reply is that this response is *irrelevant and impossible* for the majority of cases, that a vigorous prosecution policy often makes little or no contribution to *prevention*, and that a lot of prevention already takes place *within* business.

Building on this viewpoint, and combining it with the work of others in this field, I wish to make three points here which are relevant both to this section and, indeed, to the cases which illustrate these themes in the rest of the book. First, that we are greatly and unavoidably reliant on internal control mechanisms to detect initially deviance within business, between business, and against business. Second, that external control agencies do, within certain limits, have a favourable impact on corporations. This is often achieved precisely by non-confrontational tactics; and, furthermore, that to expect an adversarial and prosecutorial policy from many agencies is to misunderstand radically their mission, culture, and operating style. And, third, that some people argue that the emphasis should come to lie on 'compliance' – on the complicated and seemingly almost intractable question of how we can persuade corporations to *comply* with the law – rather than on imposing external control on business organizations in an effort to enforce the law (with a philosophy of 'deterrence': Tonry and Reiss, 1993).

In the rest of this section I intend to look more closely at the dilemmas of external control agencies and at the issue of compliance and control; I shall do this by briefly touching on material from the USA and the UK, and also by looking at some inter-business control mechanisms and at new forms of international business deviance that appear almost to defy current regulation. But first let me clarify what is meant when talking of business violations of the law. In the previous section it was seen that offences by business concern competitors, governments, consumers, employees, the general public, and the physical environment. Clinard and Yeager (1980: 113f.) maintain that six main types of corporate illegal behaviour were found in their research – administrative, environmental, financial, labour, manufacturing, and unfair trading. And their research examined violations of administrative, civil, and criminal law. As such we are dealing with an immense body of law, with a myriad of control agencies, and with three levels of formal, codified judicial action.

Criminal law is concerned with public wrongs, with culpability ('beyond a reasonable doubt'), and courts can impose penal sanctions (leading to a criminal 'record') that include fines, incarceration, restriction of freedom, probation (and/or forms of community service), and ultimately the death penalty. Civil law relates to civil or private wrongs (such as the recovery of assets/money or settlement of damages); cases are decided on a balance of probabilities and can be ended before completion if the contending parties agree to a settlement (and can be conducted in secret through 'consent decrees'); 'losers' do not carry the stigma of a criminal conviction and cannot be imprisoned; and penalties are in the form of fines, injunctions to refrain from action or to return money or property, and revocations of a licence to conduct business. In that last sense civil courts can put organizations to 'death'; indeed, Reiss (1983) asserts that 'more organizations are put to death by civil and administrative actions than are individuals for capital crimes'; in the UK in 1985, for instance, there were 5,761 enforced liquidations of companies (Levi, 1987: 163). Administrative law concerns violations of administrative orders, and courts can issue warning letters, decrees not to repeat the offence, orders to compel compliance, can order the seizure of goods or the recall of products, and can impose fines.

Three points are of importance here. First, the sanctions overlap to a large degree. Second, there are certain difficulties under criminal law in dealing with corporations as legal entities responsible for a crime (Wells, 1994). And third, and most crucially, whether or not an offence is dealt with criminally or civilly is not dependent purely on the nature of the offence but rather on an intricate set of filters that canalize the case through different segments of the judicial system: 'Yet it has been shown repeatedly that much behaviour which is formally similar in its occurrence is treated as legally different solely because legal processing systems differ in their flexibility, efficiency, or other evaluative criteria' (Reiss, 1983: 79).

But something essential is missing here. That is that a great deal of detection, enforcement, prosecution, sanctioning, prevention, and so on, goes on *outside* of these systems. As Reiss (1983: 90) puts it, 'our inattention to private policing has ignored the role of private employers in law enforcement and of the policing of illegal behaviour in private places by a private police'. In other words, institutions like the stock exchange, industry organizations (such as the British Travel Agents Association), and professions (as in medicine, the law, and accountancy), all have contractually binding codes of conduct which can lead to investigations and sanctioning of deviants without recourse to public systems of law. A great deal of *private policing* takes place in business which may be in some respects just as effective, if not more effective, than public mechanisms of control.

In practice, then, the control of business deviance takes place in criminal, civil, and administrative judicial systems but there exist also private systems of control (and, of course, *informal* and hence usually hidden forms of dispute resolution). Often the emphasis in research has been on the legal aspects of regulations, or on the outcomes and consequences of the interaction between agency and industry (leading to disparaging conclusions about the dithering and toothless records of regulatory agencies: cf. Box, 1983), whereas here the focus is on examining that interaction sociologically in terms of the work, culture, and organization of agencies and corporations and the societal response to issues of deviancy and control. One element of that interaction will be the national culture in which deviance and control takes place, and consequently I wish to touch briefly on control in two societies, the USA and the UK.

Tough or Tame? the USA and the UK

The United States   A broad, and doubtless wild, generalization would be to assert that regulatory agencies in the United States are tougher, more aggressive and combative, and certainly more litigious than their counterparts in most European countries. But that is not the whole picture and has certainly not always been true (cf. Yeager (1993) on water pollution, where there is a high dependence on the industry leading to collusion, particularly as the government itself is a major polluter). First, enforcement policies are subject to change over time (depending on the political party in power, on the swell of public opinion, and on the exigencies of election for prosecutorial and other officials), and between states. Reisman (1979: 106), for instance, discerns a pattern of 'crusades' in relation to commercial bribery in which periodic displays of 'sound and fury' are succeeded by 'business as usual'. Second, the sometimes adversarial stance of some agencies in the 1960s and 1970s has become somewhat muted in the 1980s. But it was the case that corporations saw particularly some of those new regulatory organs as anti-business, felt that media coverage had become increasingly hostile to them, and winced under the lashes of Ralph Nader and his 'Nader's Raiders' (often aggressive young lawyers who were perfectly willing and capable of taking companies to court, including the criminal courts, on behalf of their network of watch-dog and consumer agencies). Industry mounted a powerful and sustained lobby that argued that the combative approach to regulation was not only inappropriate but also damaging to American economic interests, and Reagan's presidency ushered in a period of deregulation – or, more accurately, 'regulatory flux'; budgets and personnel were often cut, as happened with the EPA (Environmental Protection Agency) – but the rhetoric of deregulation did not always mean practical deregulation, as Braithwaite (1993: 27) makes clear in relation to nursing homes where there was 'unparalleled regulatory growth'. And, third, the 'sound and fury' of public clashes between corporations and regulators covers up the reality that much regulatory activity is highly selective and is based on negotiation, persuasion, advice, education, feeble sanctions, a reluctance to prosecute, and even on cordial and cooperative relations.

However, there is a tendency to argue that there are globally two visibly different styles of enforcement between regulatory agencies in the USA and the UK (Clarke, 1990). The FDA (Food and Drug Administration) and the SEC (Securities and Exchange Commission) are generally acknowledged to be paradigmatic for control agencies in comparable branches elsewhere. The FDA has the advantage, compared to some other agencies – such as OSHA (Occupational Safety and Health Administration), which has to control five million companies covered by job safety laws (Buchholz, 1982: 309) – that it is concerned with a limited number of companies with which it is in regular contact, that it regulates an industry that has a very high public profile (and is also highly profitable), and that it enjoys substantial administrative powers for licensing drugs and other medical products. Braithwaite's (1984) research on the pharmaceutical industry makes it clear that the FDA displayed weaknesses in the past, leading to disasters and near disasters (MER/29 and Thalidomide – see Case no. 7), because it was largely dependent on the research of the drug companies. It could not afford the high cost of its own evaluations but was, in fact, helped by negative publicity surrounding the excesses and malpractices of the companies (some of which indulged in the falsification of test results) which provided a political mandate for the agency.

The reinvigoration of the FDA emerges in three ways. First, the FDA obtained improvements by 'exercising the enormous leverage it has over the licensing of new products and by being able to recall batches of products if manufacturing defects are detected' (Clarke, 1990: 215). Second, the key to exerting control was to insist on the quality of research. This was done, for example, by negotiating improved internal control structures, such as quality assurance units within the research laboratories. Third, a company that drags its heels or behaves dubiously is pressured to comply via 'a blitz of inspections, complaints, citations and requirements to improve, which can cost the company dearly in executive time, in production lines at a standstill, and in additional expenses to implement remedies' (Clarke, 1990: 216). However, and this is important, the FDA very rarely has recourse to *criminal* prosecution.

The effectiveness of the FDA has rebounded on it to a certain extent as it has come under considerable criticism recently for being too slow and cautious:

Is the FDA Too Slow and Too Rigid?
Although the FDA has good reason to be concerned about the safety and effectiveness of drugs, the approval process winds up being very lengthy, as much as 15

years from Stage I to approval for human use. In certain cases the FDA bans drugs that are in use in other parts of the world or takes 7 to 10 years longer to approve drugs than other countries do. Clozapine, for example, was continuously available in the rest of the world while people with chronic schizophrenia could not receive it here [in the USA – MP] because of FDA safety concerns. In addition, drugs that are marginally effective against schizophrenia in general but that might have the potential to be very useful for a subgroup of people with the disorder often have a hard time receiving approval. The recent uproar involving the Alzheimer's disease drug Tacrine (also known as THA and marketed as Cognex) is an example of a potentially effective although imperfect drug having a hard time reaching the public.

While the FDA has had a crucial role in protecting the public from danger and useless drugs, critics have suggested that it is more concerned with paperwork and adherence to protocol and routine than with people's lives. Over the past few years, however, the FDA has shown itself to be more responsive to concerns about its excruciatingly slow approval process, with the AIDS crisis leading to a substantial increase in its flexibility. (Keefe and Harvey, 1994: 157)

But its strength depends on adequate staffing, strong licensing powers, and the compliance of the majority of the companies (Braithwaite, 1984). Indeed, compliance is seen as actually enhancing a company's reputation and nowadays FDA approval may even be bandied around as a seal of quality.

The SEC is also seen as a relatively sophisticated, tough, and effective agency. But then it does have the considerable advantage that to a large extent financial services and securities require public and investor confidence and are thus hurt by scandals and exposures.

To a certain extent, then, the highly visible regulators of the FDA and SEC tend to be seen by foreigners as tougher and more sophisticated than many of their counterparts elsewhere. For instance, the FBI has mounted 'sting' operations against banks and used 'scam' methods against businessmen (most notably in the case of John De Lorean who was acquitted after two court hearings on charges related to involvement in drug transactions set up by the police and recorded on video; the jury clearly had difficulty accepting the Justice Department's use of 'entrapment'-style methods: *Newsweek*, 27 August 1984). Yet, despite their relative strength, the agencies are still minuscule compared to the industries they regulate; and an agency such as the Office of Surface Mining, which is far less well-known than the SEC, and enjoys far less lobbying 'clout', can easily fall victim to deregulation with staff and budgetary cuts, limitation of powers, and political appointees parachuted into top positions (Shover, 1980; Clarke, 1990: 207; Curran, 1994). In practice, moreover, enforcement tends to be based on persuasion, compromise and settlement, highly selective and infrequent prosecution, but with the occasional dramatic campaign to expose excesses and aimed at encouraging others to comply.

For most agencies – given their history, mandate, cultures, resources, powers, and relation to the industry – that is probably the maximum that can be expected. Whether or not it is 'effective' – in truly exerting control on embedded abuses and on the daily conduct of business – is, of course, a moot point and I shall return to this in Part Three.

The United Kingdom   Although the picture is complex and varied, then, it does appear that some major American regulatory and judicial agencies are more proactive, more adversarial, and tougher in sanctioning than agencies in many other countries; and this is certainly true if a comparison is made with the UK. This can be illustrated by the financial institutions of the City of London (Lloyd's, the stock and other exchanges, the merchant banks, and the 'jobbers' and 'brokers' of the investment houses) which were highly self-regulating, which experienced several scandals and considerable criticism in the 1980s, and which were exposed to far-reaching proposals for reform. Clarke (1990: 162) makes clear that the new regulatory system, with the Financial Services Bill of 1985 demanding an equivalent of the SEC, met with 'vehement opposition':

> The British securities industry had always done without a state regulatory agency, and the SEC was always looked upon with fear and loathing by the British practitioners as representing formalism, legality, bureaucracy and heavy-handedness that was the antithesis of the successful British regime.

Clarke's research also illuminates three features of regulation in the City. First, it was traditionally geared to discipline exercised *by members over members*, and cohesion and control were reinforced by the small, exclusive, upper-class, club-like nature of the financial world. Second, dramatic changes in the late 1970s and early 1980s in financial markets, spiced by a number of scandals and some conspicuous failures of control, made reform almost inevitable. And, third, the cosy, gentlemanly amateurism of the past was clearly going to have to make way for tougher, less 'British' styles of control.

These developments have been followed closely by two academics in particular, Clarke (1981, 1986, 1990) and Levi (1981, 1987). Let me turn first to Levi (1987) who, in his research on fraud, has argued cogently that we have neglected to pay attention to *non-police* regulatory agencies in the control of business crime. In practice, the police have no monopoly of control on fraud cases. The Inland Revenue, Customs and Excise, the Office of Fair Trading, and the Department of Trade and Industry (DTI), for example, can all be concerned with fraud. This multi-agency involvement can sponsor demarcation disputes; rivalry and confusion can result, where 'inter-agency competition and divergence of approach may be fuelled by conflicts of personality or by bureaucratic empire-building' (Levi, 1987: 117).

Although it is difficult to summarize Levi's wide-ranging work succinctly and to do justice to his detailed analysis, I shall attempt to condense his findings into four general points. First he maintains that British enforcement styles tend to be more reactive, cautious and accommodative than American ones. Units may be ill-equipped and under-staffed (and even be subject to shrinkage due to economies in public spending); for instance, there was low confidence among businessmen for the DTI, and one interviewer asserted that the DTI's resources and attitude on fraud were 'pitiful and disgraceful' (Levi, 1987: 179). In contrast, the SEC, with a staff of 2,000 and an annual budget of $100 million, is seen as forceful and proactive. An attempt to sharpen the teeth of public enforcement arose with the creation of a new agency, the Serious Frauds Office, which was set up in 1987 and which is a statutory body responsible directly to the Attorney-General (making it independent of the Director of Public Prosecutions). It has an annual budget of about £4 million, employs eighty people (accountants, lawyers, investigators, and clerical staff), and is geared to unravelling serious fraud cases (Levi, 1987: 284; hereafter page numbers refer to Levi, 1987).

Second, he astutely analyses the limitations of public policing in this area in relation to the joint Metropolitan and City Police Company Fraud Department in London where manpower shortages, turnover of personnel, the prevalent reward system, and weaknesses in training, motivation, skills, knowledge, and so on, all militate against a really effective organizational response to corporate crime. In general, the police do not give a high priority to fraud compared to common and especially violent crime; fraud is scantily dealt with in training (whereas one quarter of FBI recruits are public accountants); attachment to a fraud squad is not a popular assignment (cases are long, complex, involve a laborious 'paper trail', and may lead nowhere); and most officers serve for only two to five years before being transferred – while it probably takes eighteen months just to get accustomed to the intricacies of the work (p. 150). Manpower allocated to fraud squads in 1985 in the whole of the UK was 588 while numbers actually *declined* in London – in 1985 the combined London squads numbered 190 compared to 211 in 1982 (p. 138). Given the low effectiveness of police enforcement up to the mid-1980s Levi maintains that it is nearly 'miraculous' that anyone was prosecuted at all. As a result of all this Levi argues that,

> Given limited resources the police do not normally adopt a proactive intelligence gathering strategy and they ration their priorities in relation to judgements about what enquiries are likely to lead to successful prosecution and the sorts of pressures they experience from senior officers, the public, and the media. The general consensus is that frauds upon the 'the public' are the most serious types of fraud, but these may be the object of less high-profile 'public pressure' for clear up than sensational and 'complex' City frauds'. (p. 182)

Third, fraud trials tend to be expensive, may collapse suddenly after lengthy proceedings – the acquittal rate in 1984 was 30 per cent (p. 204); juries find them difficult to understand, while there is also a pattern of delays, of bail leading to the defendant absconding abroad, and of defendants not turning up for trial. Imprisonment is exceptional and fines rarely exceed £1,000. Sentencing then, tends to be lenient, and courts take into account the social stigma of public disgrace and the loss of employment if a company should fold due to the imprisonment of its boss; if prison should ensue, then it will almost certainly be an open prison and application for parole will usually be honoured because of the 'good conduct' of the prisoner; Levi concludes, 'thus we see British fraudsters generally benefiting from what one might term their low "evilness rating" – a construct combined from moderate offence seriousness and comparatively light criminal records – and good behaviour inside prison' (p. 261).

Fourth, and of considerable interest, is the light Levi sheds on self-regulating organizations (sro's). These are quasi-judicial agencies that enforce rules for members of a particular professional institution. For instance, the Stock Exchange Disciplinary Committee can impose suspensions and expulsions, as can Lloyd's (but enforcement applies only to members, and sanctions cannot include imprisonment, although sro's can act as a filter for prosecutions later via the criminal justice system). Suspension from trading and expulsion as a member can mean stiff economic consequences – in the case of one person, involved in the dubious purchase of a Swiss bank 'obtained through re-insurance premiums paid to Panamanian companies controlled by Liechtenstein trusts' (p. 244), his six months' suspension from Lloyd's might have cost him £350,000 (given his annual salary of £700,000, while his defence is said to have cost at least £130,000). In another case a broker was expelled from Lloyd's, given a £1 million fine, and ordered to pay £125,000 costs; certainly in comparison with penalties in the common courts those are pretty stiff financial sanctions (while Lloyd's investigations are conducted at criminal standards of certainty). Sentences may also be imposed for breaches of rules unrelated to fraud.

But where the offence is not seen as blatantly negligent or conspiratorial, and where the offence is followed by cooperation and immediate recantation, then the only sanction may be a reprimand with no other public record of the incident. Although these forms of *private* policing could be objected to on the grounds that professionals prosecuting professionals, particularly in the clubby, elite world of London's City institutions, are unlikely to be severe on one another, there is also a case to be made that sro's, under certain conditions, can be more effective than public policing. For instance, Levi's businessmen maintained that they would only call in the police when the case was relatively uncomplicated and the company had conducted a thorough internal investigation first, because otherwise the police would probably not understand it and would mess up the case (and, they added, who knows what else they might inadvertently turn up if they crashed around inside a company!). Opinions were that the police are 'not very good at keeping things quiet', that they 'would not have a clue in looking at fraud in the Stock Exchange or in a stockbroker's office', and that because the police did not fully understand the complexity of the system they were unlikely to get convictions. This meant that they would probably not be called in to deal with stock-market fraud, and, in addition, 'the disastrous effects that calling in the police would be likely to have upon the firm's trading position would increase his [the interviewer's] inhibitions against reporting' (p. 132). There are plainly mechanisms at work that keep certain business offences away from formal policing.

A fundamental issue arises, then, of the credibility and effectiveness of sro's in controlling, deterring, and prosecuting violations of business codes of conduct and legally binding rules for carrying out business. Whether or not an sro is more capable and swift in its enforcement than a public agency, it could be argued that, given the nature of business offences, they are a major, if not essential, component for controlling business. In the 'clean-up' of the City it was important to provide legitimacy for the sro's, and this was sought by the establishment of the Securities and Investments Board following the Financial Services Act 1986. The SIB, with its members appointed by the Secretary of State for Trade and the Governor of the Bank of England, has become the 'licensing and accreditation authority for a series of sro's covering various sectors of the City'; eventually there were five sectors as well as the professional bodies and investment exchanges – Lloyd's had been exempted by the Lloyd's Act of 1982 (Clarke, 1990: 159). The SIB employs some 200 people and has an annual budget of around £15 million (personal communication: M. Clarke).

And yet, as Clarke has made clear in his research, even statutory, public enforcement agencies are apt to be restrained and sparing in the use of their powers. (Levi uses the word 'dainty' in comparing UK with US regulatory styles). For instance, although tax evasion and avoidance by individuals and companies occurs on a massive scale and is highly damaging to the state's finances, revenue services generally present examples of regulatory agencies with quite extensive powers that are nevertheless used most selectively and quite cautiously. In Britain, the Inland Revenue rarely undertakes prosecutions unless the case is 'serious' (usually defined as financially substantial and also probably involving conspiracy, forgery, accountants, tax advisers, and so on) and where preliminary investigations have led only to persistent, uncooperative denials. When the Service does prosecute, then conviction rates are high and can lead to fines and/or imprisonment. There is also a prevalent view that if a company is exposed to a detailed investigation, then that works preventively and the operating style is to convince people 'that honesty and cooperation are the easiest way out of trouble' (Clarke, 1990: 120). This apparently lenient approach emerges from the inherent difficulties of discovery and enforcement: 'unless given draconian powers of investigation, as well as vastly increased personnel, it [Internal Revenue] will remain simply unable to extract the whole truth from all tax payers' (Clarke, 1990: 112; hereafter page numbers refer to Clarke, 1990).

Customs and Excise is another agency with extensive powers (particularly of entry and arrest) that are normally used highly cautiously. The agency's focus is divided between specialized units for serious crime (such as drug and bullion smuggling) and a more general emphasis on negotiation and on settling cases without prosecution. In the latter case the prime target is *revenue collection* and criminal prosecution is secondary (p. 119). It could be argued from this analysis that the tax authorities in Britain are exercising their powers with a 'caution that borders on trepidation' (p. 120); and this view tends to be reinforced by the knowledge that large companies employ considerable personnel and sustained ingenuity in exploiting the complexity of the rules and the loopholes provided by exemption clauses and by offshore tax havens. Customs probably does not begin to tackle a VAT (Value Added Tax) evasion case below £30,000, which effectively permits a fair amount of substantial fiddling (Levi, 1987: 166).

But Clarke argues that tax authorities are dependent on a substantial degree of willing compliance 'from the taxpayer in order for the system to function effectively', and, furthermore, that those authorities 'would be grotesquely expensive if they were to have resources for comprehensive rather than selective enforcement' (p. 120). In effect, even control agencies with substantial powers may use them cautiously because they see their role as revenue *collectors*, because they do not believe that severe sanctions are a deterrent, because they feel that negotiation and settlement rather than prosecution is more effective in eliciting compliance, and also because full enforcement could only be attempted with the massive and expensive apparatus of a police state, which is unacceptable in democratic societies.

This picture is reinforced with considerable clarity if we look at enforcement in less publicized and less well-known areas such as health and safety. Some of these established, long-standing regulatory agencies, concerned largely with standards and conditions in industry and with damage to the environment, indicate that generally their inspectorates adopt a policy and working style based on persuasion. Given limited manpower and resources, inspectors and regulators have developed a practical, pragmatic approach based on 'law in action', as opposed to 'law in the books', and the working philosophy and style is that persuasion, backed by threats, is more realistic and effective than choosing the path of coercion and prosecution. Indeed, prosecution may be taken by control officials themselves as evidence that the *agency* has failed. The essential aim is to achieve *long-term compliance* (Clarke, 1990: 186; Hawkins, 1984).

It should also be recognized that regulatory agencies may often have a dual function; not only to 'control' an industry but also to protect its interests (for example, in the balance between safety and continued production, aviation authorities may be reluctant to ground a whole class of aeroplanes following a serious accident because of the damaging economic effect on the commercial carriers). In general – for the area of regulatory control is vast and multifaceted and changes constantly over time – control agents see themselves as *advisers* rather than 'policemen':

> inspectorates are reluctant to use their legal powers to impose sanctions, especially sanctions involving legal proceedings, and above all criminal proceedings, upon manufacturers and businessmen. Rather they seek to gain the confidence and cooperation of industry to manage an agreed regime. (Clarke, 1990: 200)

The daily work of the inspector is largely to persuade, to advise, and to negotiate; while prosecution may be used in cases of excessive and/or persistent rule-breaking, it may be more often true that turning to legal sanctioning is perceived as a form of defeat; an adversarial and combative relationship with business and industry is seen not only as time-consuming but as largely counter-productive. In Great Britain in 1982, for example, there were 1.6 million conventional criminal cases dealt with by the courts as opposed to only 17,602 regulatory offences; this reveals a reluctance to prosecute, while offences were generally heard in the magistrates' courts and led to low fines (cf. Braithwaite (1993: 27), where he records that 'a three year study of 96 Australian regulatory agencies found that a third had not launched a single prosecution during that time'. Wells (1994: 1994: 41–2) notes that a death at work in the UK led to an average fine of £1,940 where a violation had occurred under Health and Safety legislation, and goes on to state that 'not only are the maximum penalties low, and the actual fines lower still, the offences themselves as we have seen do not reflect the gravity of the harm caused'. In practice, then, the courts are also demonstrably reluctant to impose stiff penalties. While there are often differences in style between different agencies – related to historical background, relationship to the industry, recruitment and training of personnel, and so on – and even wide variations in policy *within* agencies (based on regional differences, local council interference, and a strong urban–rural divide), the major impression is one of officials using predominantly persuasion and only very occasionally threats; or, as Hawkins (1984) puts it in his research on water pollution control, 'bargain and bluff'.

In brief, then, the dominant regulatory style in Britain – to paraphrase Theodore Roosevelt – is to talk softly and to carry a big stick, which is carefully concealed and only most reluctantly wielded.

Inter-business Control and Internationalization of Deviance

Given that the victims of violations of law and rules related to business are often other businesses, it is plain that corporations themselves will have recourse to the law in order to protect their interests. For instance, Texaco agreed in 1987 to pay Pennzoil $3 billion following a takeover dispute (*Business Week*, 11 August 1987); this enabled Texaco to avoid paying $10.3 billion damages awarded by a court and also to avoid bankruptcy. In 1988 the Hunt Brothers were found guilty in a federal court of manipulating the price of silver and were ordered to pay Mipeco (the Peruvian state mine) $134 million (*de Volkskrant*, 23 August 1988). These dramatic, well-publicized cases, involving large sums of money, are extreme examples of many inter-business disputes fought out in the courts. Through 'consent decrees' they may be heard in closed court; agreement to settle out of court can end proceedings before they come to a conclusion; and restitution in some form can be used to avoid having severe damages imposed. As such, it may appear as if the court system is conducive to corporate dispute resolution and to evading final judgement on blame.

But the courts are the preserve of corporate lawyers who, in the interests of their clients, will exploit every loophole, and employ every delay, that they can find. Often, then, proceedings in court are cumbersome, costly, and slow. This is even more the case if a company turns to a control agency and asks for cooperation in prosecuting someone who has victimized it. Then all the deficiencies of control agencies – which can be seen to work in favour of the corporation when individuals, groups, and other agencies grapple with business deviance – now work against the interests of the corporation. If a bank, for instance, turns to the police and asks them to investigate a fraud, then the bankers may end up complaining bitterly about their slowness, lack of resources, low commitment, poor skills, inadequate manpower, and a failure to reach a successful prosecution. In Britain, for example, policing in the provinces is far less sophisticated in fraud detection than is the work of the two experienced London fraud squads, and Levi points out that those who assert that the criminal justice system is the 'handmaiden' of capitalist institutions will have to explain the irony that often 'the most powerful victims receive the most dilatory service' (1987, 139).

As such it may well be the case that business takes the 'law' into its own hands and mobilizes itself in order to combat more effectively deviance against it. Clarke (1990) provides an illuminating example in terms of the insurance industry in three countries. Changes in the insurance market have led to more claims and more losses through false claims. In the USA fraud is exercised by well-organized and skilled groups who move from state to state; fraud was estimated to cost the industry $5 billion in 1987. Initially the industry's response was cautious and confined to individual companies (the working style was basically to trust claimants, to fear obtaining a negative reputation as a suspicious company, and to be secretive about company losses and release of confidential information). Persistent, flagrant, and widespread fraud elicited a change in response. For instance, in 1971 the Insurance Crime Prevention Unit was established with lawyers, doctors, and ex-policemen on its staff. By 1984 its investigations had enabled 11,000 people to be arrested on fraud charges and with an 80 per-cent conviction rate. The Association of American Insurers runs advertisements on fraud to make claimants aware of its efforts against false claims. Data banks have been established across company boundaries allowing liaison with federal and other agencies. The Arson Information and Management Systems Program established in 1984 helps to coordinate efforts with industry, government, and communities to identify arson-prone communities, to enhance technical detection and control methods, and to increase public, corporate, and political awareness of the problems surrounding arson by means of publicity, training, lectures, and lobbying. Through an index system, carrying 30 million entries, the companies can trace bad risks.

Companies have also installed Special Investigation Units (SIUs) which have successfully emphasized internal measures for fraud control and which exhibit a primary orientation to settlement and a basic avoidance of prosecution. Clarke concludes:

> Overall, the striking features of the American response to insurance fraud are its comprehensiveness, its recognition that political and publicity aspects are an important complement to the technical detection and control side, its national scope even though many schemes and institutions started locally, and the willingness of industry and companies in it to build fraud awareness and control into their everyday routines. (1990: 77)

Two additional points are of importance; first, that the industry has created separate institutions which do have a law-enforcement investigatory style but whose very existence works preventively; and, second, that, while there is increasing cooperation with the police and government, this provides an excellent example of an industry 'that clearly wishes to retain control of the problem in its private interests' (Clarke, 1990: 78).

In turning to the experiences of insurers in two other countries, France and Britain, it becomes clear not only that there exist wide divergences in approach across national cultures but also that most control measures are not geared to tackling the increasing internalization of business crime. In France, for example, there existed a somewhat fragmented structure of many, small insurance companies which did not cooperate greatly and which ran duplicated control measures (with three separate registers for automobiles). Increasing recognition of losses (running at 9 billion francs per annum) showed the need for a nationally coordinated system of control. A national investigatory agency, APSAIRD, employing ex-policemen, has been set up to deal with fraudulent claims related to vehicles and there is liaison with the police and with the Ministry of the Interior. In brief, then, Clarke claims that the French have built a 'national and quite sophisticated fraud control system' (1990: 82) but that the system remains in the control of the industry.

In contrast, Britain is taken to illustrate a situation where there exists 'a reluctance of insurers to recognize and respond to fraud in a coordinated and effective fashion without overwhelming and compelling evidence' (Clarke, 1990: 83). The reactions of industry to fraud tend to be slow, hesitant, and cautious. The point is that there are differences in approach across cultures that are related to the nature of the problem, its perception by the industry, and the willingness to adopt national efforts at investigation, data collection, and prevention (legislation on privacy can also play an important role).

In looking at business deviance, then, it is possible to see differences in approach between industries, between control agencies on an urban–rural dimension (Miles, 1986), and also in variations across national borders. These begin to give a highly varied picture of deviance and control – and of success under certain circumstances in one particular society – but that picture changes dramatically if one examines the *international* dimension of business crime where offences are often difficult to detect and even more difficult to prosecute. A good example is that of maritime fraud, the investigation of which is characterized by

> confusing cross-border traffic, incomplete or incorrectly completed papers, scarce controls, mysterious accidents at sea, conflicting statements of witnesses, political aspects, interference in the judicial process, years of preparation, networks of companies that stretch from Europe to the Far East, willing bankers. (Bakker, 1985: 48)

By the late 1970s growing concern with the rising cost of such fraud brought the International Chamber of Commerce to set up the International Maritime Bureau in 1980. The task of the IMB is coordination with other agencies, prevention, data collection, preparation of cases for prosecution, and publicity and information campaigns for the industry. The almost intractable nature of the issue facing the IMB and industry emerge in Conway's (1981) book *The Piracy Business*, in which she states:

> There may never be a perfect crime, but there is an ideal one. It is a minimum risk, maximum profit affair, easily adaptable to prevailing conditions, relatively simple to operate, difficult to detect, and, even if detected, still more difficult to prosecute successfully in court. The ideal crime in short, is maritime fraud. And never has it been a more profitable and secure proposition than during the past five years when it has taken to the sea in a big way.

Eric Ellen, head of the IMB, has asserted baldly that he is involved in an unequal battle with the fraudeurs; the criminal is always 'two, three or even four steps ahead . . . he uses organisation advisers, accountants, lawyers, and computer experts. He continually changes his scene of operations. It's proving increasingly difficult for us to keep tracks of the key actors' (Bakker, 1985: 51).

The complexity of the maze created by such cases emerged in the affair of the *Salem*:

> It concerned a Liberian registered ship with Greek officers and a Turkish crew. The oil, loaded in Kuweit through an Italian company, was sold in turn to a British-Dutch concern (Royal Shell) and was supposed to be delivered in France. It was in fact unloaded in South Africa, the ship was deliberately scuttled in international waters off the Senegal coast, and involved were, among others, an American, a German, and a Dutchman. It's a miracle that people could find a judge qualified to sit on the case. (Bakker, 1985: 53)

In 1979 some 193,000 tons of oil were illegally delivered to South Africa, after which the tanker *Salem* disappeared, leading to a fraudulent insurance claim. Two of the main participants were successfully prosecuted and jailed in America and Greece respectively but another suspect was set free by a court in Rotterdam in 1987 almost eight years after the incident. Part of the delay was due to the fact that the South African authorities were uncooperative and crucial witnesses could not be spoken to, or communicated with, in South Africa. In the last resort the Dutch judicial authorities were unable to construct a convincing ease against the suspect and, six years after his initial arrest in 1981, he was set free from prosecution. The case reveals the complexity of such maritime frauds and the difficulty of mounting a successful prosecution (although two other suspects had been sentenced elsewhere, while South Africa had also agreed to pay Shell $30 million as part compensation for its $52 million loss in what Scotland Yard described as the 'oil fraud of the century'; *de Volkskrant*, 29 October 1987; 12 November 1987).

There are two main aspects to this international facet of business crime. One is that companies can employ every legal, and illegal, device to evade control by fully exploiting the loopholes in the international net of judicial and other supervision (for example, international law evasion, Swiss banks, tax havens, pollution havens, and international dumping: cf. Braithwaite, 1985a). And the second is that regulatory agencies experience considerable difficulty in international cases in terms of detection, evidence, prosecution, jurisdictions, sanctions, and cooperation between authorities and governments. Indeed, in economic crimes restitution may be as important as, if not more important than, prosecution (which is a long, intricate, and insecure path that often strands on non-cooperation of banks); thus Eric Ellen of the IMB often negotiates settlements with suspects, which means that his client at least sees some return on a lost investment. Prosecution may seem a poor option in comparison.

Finally, this section has examined some aspects and dilemmas of deviance and control in business. It has raised a number of complex and broad issues. Let me endeavour to summarize this section briefly with three points. First, it is possible to see societal attempts to control and to regulate business as feeble and ineffective. From a purely control point of view this can be supported by a great deal of evidence, but, if we shift the emphasis to compliance, the agencies may be able to exert a corrective influence on corporations to conform to the law. Although there are wide differences in styles of enforcement between agencies, many opt for persuasion and negotiation rather than prosecution (Reiss, 1983). Second, business itself can considerably enhance prevention, detection, and prosecution by reforming internal procedures and by setting up industry-wide agencies to collate and coordinate inter-company efforts to combat damaging economic crime (such as fraud). But, third, there is less optimism about the dilemmas of controlling companies that seek to evade regulation by operating internationally and about successfully detecting and prosecuting intricate and sophisticated international crimes that almost defy effective investigation under current laws and conditions. In a sense, then, this section has raised the question as to what is really an effective control system in the business world.

Two themes have emerged that will be explored further in this book. One is that we are perhaps mesmerized by *law* when we think of deviance and control, whereas the law may not play such an important role in internal and external control and in dispute resolution. The other is that 'compliance' – encouraging and stimulating corporations to conform to the rules, and investing in self-regulation as a matter of self-interest, rather than having control imposed from outside – may be more effective than expensive, cumbersome, and inherently weak regulatory agencies. The strongest motivation for business to pursue the latter is that self-control in an industry is beneficial in reducing damage done by business deviance to that industry. For, as Ellen of the IMB caustically remarked about maritime fraud, 'crime sometimes pays very well indeed'.

The Central Issues – and Using the Cases

Summary

Before moving to Part Two, and the ten cases of corporate misconduct, I wish to summarize the major issues explored in this book. First, I concur with Tonry and Reiss (1993: 1–5) when they write that organizations 'are central offenders in many violations of law', and form a 'major class of victims'; further, organizational deviance 'involves the use of an organization's position of significant power, influence or trust' while it may also be pursued through the 'organizational power created by a network of organizations' (as in price fixing, insider trading networks, public construction contracts, and so on). Second, we have seen that the orthodox view of business crime as being 'for the organization' has to be altered in the light of cases where the managerial deviance was directed *against* the organization and was highly damaging to it. Third, the nature of harm caused by corporate misconduct has highlighted the fact that it can create multiple victims and bring about significant suffering; in no sense are we talking of 'victimless crimes'. Fourth, I have emphasized that we should not become mesmerized by the criminal law and formal policing of organizations because a great deal of control, regulation and sanctioning takes place informally and through private systems of 'justice' and control. Throughout, then, I wish to accentuate the *organizational* dimension in corporate misconduct because the organization is the offender, the means, the setting, the rationale, the opportunity, and also the victim of corporate deviance. And, as Tonry and Reiss (1993: 8) express it, 'a central problem of modern societies is to control the behaviour of organizations in the public interest'. That brings me to my fifth and final point; namely, that business deviance has to be socially constructed in terms of opportunities, options, selection, motives, implementation, and rationalization. A number of managers have to be persuaded that the dilemma they are facing warrants a 'deviant' solution, in terms of violating a law, rule, or code, and they have to adapt to that stance organizationally, socially, and morally.

The Cases

It is on the basis of the features above that the cases have been chosen, and that is why the underlying theme of the commentaries is the social psychology of managerial decision-making in constructing deviance. The cases presented here have a twofold function. They have been designed and presented as pedagogical devices for classroom teaching. They contain a wide range of issues that the teacher can tailor to the nature of the audience, be it one composed of sociologists, criminologists, business students, or executives. But second, and in a way more importantly, the ten cases in Part Two, and the 'mini-cases' elsewhere in the book, are subject to a reinterpretation in the light of the themes raised in Part One and considered further in Part Three. As such, the cases serve also as illustrations of the analysis, and they are each placed in a context that raises the industrial and social setting, the opportunities presented, the mechanics of implementation of the deviant solution, the personalities involved, the dynamic moving them towards violations or malfunction, and also the consequences of managerial behaviour and corporate decisions. Like all cases, they are not cast in stone; rather they are meant to provoke discussion and stimulate thought. This means that the reader is invited to grapple with the intricate issues that run through these cases in order to come up with his or her own answers and solutions. Why do *you* think that 'organizations' violate laws and rules, and managers engage in dirty business?

PART TWO
CASES

4

Ten Cases of Corporate Deviance

Case No. 1: the Goodrich Brake Scandal

> But bills aren't paid with personal satisfaction, nor house payments with
> ethical principles.
>
> (Vandivier, 1982: 114; page numbers refer to Vandivier, 1982)

This, next to that of the Ford Pinto, is probably one of the most widely used
cases in business schools because of its value in highlighting group dynamics,
responsibility, ethics, and the contrasting frameworks in which managers and
professionals operate in an organization. And this was a decision that potentially endangered human lives. As such it presents us with the quintessential
double-bind predicament; you are damned if you do and you are damned if
you do not. It is a predicament that recurs in many cases and that effectively
poses the issue 'What would *you* do?' The central dilemma in the case makes
it a highly relevant and useful example of distorted decision-making and this
generally induces considerable and widely divergent discussion in the classroom. This makes it suitable for adaptation as a role-play based on the
characters – their personalities, organizational positions, motives, and behaviour under pressure. The cast:

John Warren	engineer	assigned to brake project
Searle Lawson	engineer	responsible for production design
Robert Sink	manager	project manager
Kermit Vandivier	lab data analyst and technical writer	
Ralph Gretzinger	engineer	test lab supervisor
Van Horn	manager	design engineering section
Russell Line	manager	test lab fell under his responsibility
Bud Sunderman	manager	senior engineer
Jeter	lawyer	counsel for Goodrich

The Brake

The Goodrich brake case is interesting for two main reasons. First, it concerns an industry that has to work to hair-fine specifications, that employs

high-quality and well-qualified engineers, and that delivers a product upon which human lives depend. Professional norms and professional pride, coupled with the client's demand for safety and reliability, must surely minimize deviation in the quality of goods delivered. And, second, it provides an *inside* account of the dynamics, and the personalities, involved in a situation that led to the manipulation of test data. That account focuses strongly on the pressure exerted on individuals to bend the rules in the ostensible interests of the company.

At the time of the case the B.F. Goodrich Company was a leading manufacturer of aircraft wheels and brakes. In June 1967, LTV Aerospace Corporation ordered a brake for a new Air Force aeroplane. Goodrich was very keen to make a success of this order because some years before they had lost LTV as a customer and wanted it back. Although the initial order was minuscule it could represent a major contract as, once a manufacturer has opted for a particular brake for a specific plane, it is also·committed to buying all replacements from the supplier and, particularly with a defence contract, that could mean substantial, long-term profits. The message went out at the Troy plant in Ohio: 'we can't bungle it this time, we've got to give them a good brake, regardless of the cost' (p. 103).

Goodrich had promised LTV a light brake comprising four discs. John Warren, a highly capable engineer, was assigned the project. He was known to resent criticism and people tended to be wary of his short fuse; no one queried his design for the A7D brake. A young newcomer aged 26, Searle Lawson, was responsible for final production design and he approached his first real project with gusto. Before production the brake would have to be subject to extensive tests in the plant's lab, and the military contractors lay down minute specifications on how these trials are to be conducted. The simulated breaking stops and other tests are written up finally in a qualification report. The brake can go into production after successful completion of these hurdles, but it will also be subject to extensive test flights before approval is granted for routine use in military aircraft.

Lawson began testing immediately using a prototype and with special attention paid to linings and to temperatures generated (temperatures can reach 1000 degrees or more on landing). When Lawson began his first simulated landing 'the temperature of his prototype brake reached 1500 degrees. The brake glowed a bright cherry-red and threw off incandescent particles of metal and lining material as the temperature reached its peak' (p. 105). After a few such stops the linings were found to have disintegrated almost totally. Lawson tried new linings but, once more, high temperatures were recorded and the linings crumbled. He soon came to the conclusion that the fault lay with the design itself; the brake was simply too small.

The dilemma facing Goodrich was clear. They could dump the brake and begin again with design and testing but using a five-disc brake. But that spelled out delay, and deadlines for delivery of parts and for test flying were approaching rapidly. Goodrich had assured LTV of swift delivery and had even intimated that the tests were successful. Warren did not want to admit to any error and to his exposure by a youngster fresh out of college and insisted that the problem must be with the linings. The four-disc brake *was* viable, and that was that.

The Problem Moves up the Hierarchy

Lawson now decided to take his story one more rung up the corporate hierarchy and approached the project manager, Robert Sink. Although he only had a high-school background, Sink had worked his way up from draughtsman to supervisory position, which was resented by some of the well-qualified engineers; 'but though Sink had no college training, he had something even more useful: a fine working knowledge of company politics' (p. 107). On examining the calculations it must have been clear to Sink that Lawson was correct and that the abortive results indicated the failure of the four-disc brake. Sink had to face up to the possibility of conceding that Warren had been wrong, to explaining the difficulties to superiors not only at Troy but also at headquarters in Akron, and taking back his repeated assurances to LTV (issued on the strength of Warren's judgement) that the brake was virtually ready for shipment.

Sink's answer to the dilemma was to express confidence in Warren, to minimize the problem, and to advise Lawson to keep on testing. But, once more, tests saw linings crumble as great heat was generated – new linings proved no better – and despite expert advice from lining manufacturers, Lawson always faced the same result: failure. By now it was March 1968 and test flights were programmed in seventy days' time. Twelve attempts to qualify the brake had failed and no one could realistically avoid the sombre conclusion that the brake was a complete failure. Only a major redesign could retrieve it. Panic set in.

Facing Defeat

Lawson was downcast. Warren was reticent. Sink was unusually interested in the tests and conferred in undertones with Warren. A team from LTV arrived but, fortunately, the real situation was concealed from them. In April, the thirteenth attempt at qualification commenced but by this stage there was no real attempt made to follow the methods demanded by military specifications, and, regardless of how it was to be done, the brake was going to be 'nursed' through the required fifty stops. In addition, fans were constructed to aid cooling, pressure was reduced to allow the wheel to 'coast', and, after the stops, parts were examined and any disfigured parts were machined to remove signs of overheating. The methods were seriously at odds with military specifications but even then the brake could not meet all the requirements, and, on one occasion, the wheel rolled for 16,000 feet, nearly 3 miles, before the brake could halt it (although the normal distance was around 3,500 feet).

On the day of the thirteenth test Kermit Vandivier was called in. He worked in the test lab as a data analyst and technical writer; he transcribed data for the engineering department and put together the qualification report following successful tests (which were then issued to customers and defence officials). At once he spotted irregularities in the data, including the miscalibration of the instrument for recording brake pressure, done in order to downplay the actual pressure.

Gretzinger Takes a Stand

The test logs were taken by Vandivier to Ralph Gretzinger, the test lab supervisor, who said that Lawson had ordered the miscalibration on Sink's instigation. The reasons for this, according to Gretzinger, was that they knew the brake was too small and was not going to work but 'they're getting desperate, and instead of scrapping the damned thing and starting over, they figure they can horse around down here in the lab and qualify it that way' (p. 110). Gretzinger was a top-flight, innovative engineer who was also renowned as a 'stickler for details and he had some very firm ideas about honesty and ethics' (p. 110). Vandivier returned to Lawson, who unburdened himself;

> 'I just can't believe this is really happening,' said Lawson, shaking his head slowly. 'This isn't engineering, at least not what I thought it to be. Back in school, I thought that when you were an engineer, you tried to do your best, no matter what it cost. But this is something else.' (p. 110)

Lawson went on to warn Vandivier that he too would become involved because 'win or lose, we're going to issue a qualification report'. Despite the stringent requirement of the military, the brake was going to be qualified, regardless of its test performance, and these were exactly the words used by Sink at a meeting with Van Horn (manager of the design engineering section). Sink had sought an ally and the result was, apparently, a determination to issue a falsified qualification report. On hearing this Gretzinger vehemently assured Vandivier that 'under no circumstances' would he accede to such a report being issued; the report would be accurate and 'no false data or false reports are going to come out of this lab' (p. 111).

In May, the fourteenth attempt to qualify the brake was undertaken, and despite the illicit methods aimed at nursing it through, the brake was again a failure. Lawson asked Vandivier to start writing the report but he refused and took the matter to Gretzinger. Gretzinger was furious and stormed out of the room to confront a senior manager, Russell Line, part of whose responsibility was the test lab.

> In about an hour, he returned and called me to his desk. He sat silently for a few moments, then muttered, half to himself, 'I wonder what the hell they'd do if I just quit?' I didn't answer and I didn't ask him what he meant. I knew. He had been beaten down. He had reached the point when the decision had to be made. Defy them now while there was still time or knuckle under, sell out. 'You know', he went on uncertainly, looking down at his desk, 'I've been an engineer for a long time, and I've always believed that ethics and integrity were every bit as important as theorems and formulas, and never once has anything happened to change my beliefs. Now this . . . Hell, I've got two sons I've got to put through school and I just . . .' His voice trailed off.
> He sat for a few more minutes, then, looking over the top of his glasses, said

hoarsely, 'Well, it looks like we're licked. The way it stands now, we're to go ahead and prepare the data and other things for the graphic presentation in the report, and when we're finished, someone upstairs will actually write the report.'

'After all', he continued, 'we're just drawing some curves, and what happens to them after they leave here, well, we're not responsible for that.' He was trying to persuade himself that as long as we were concerned with only one part of the puzzle and didn't see the completed picture, we really weren't doing anything wrong. He didn't believe what he was saying, and he knew I didn't believe it either. It was an embarrassing and shameful moment for both of us. (pp. 111–12)

Kermit's Troublesome Conscience

Vandivier felt uneasy and took his case to Russell Line, the senior executive in the section, who was a sociable, well-respected import from headquarters who was probably being groomed to take over the top position. Vandivier argued that to protect the reputation of the company they should take the issue further up the hierarchy, to 'Bud' Sunderman the chief engineer, where people would surely veto matters when they realized what was going on. Line laughed and felt there was no sense in disturbing Sunderman, 'because it's none of my business and none of yours. I learned a long time ago not to worry about things over which I had no control. I have no control over this.' Vandivier enquired about his conscience if a test pilot should be injured or killed during tests.

'Look', he said, becoming somewhat exasperated, "I have just told you I have no control over this thing. Why should my conscience bother me?' His voice took on a quiet, soothing tone as he continued. 'You're just getting all upset over this thing for nothing. I just do as I'm told, and I'd advise you to do the same.' He had made his decision and now I had to make mine. (p. 113)

At 42, with several jobs behind him and with a comfortable home for his wife and seven children, Vandivier had settled in to Goodrich and to Troy. Now he saw that he was being asked to engage in a fraud but refusal could only mean resignation or being fired. Perhaps he should let someone else write the report because at least then he would have the satisfaction of not being implicated: 'But bills aren't paid with personal satisfaction, nor house payments with ethical principles' (p. 114). He informed Lawson that he was prepared to go ahead and asked him if he was fully aware of what they were doing:

'Yeay', he replied bitterly, 'we're going to screw LTV. And speaking of screwing', he continued, 'I know now how a whore feels, because that's exactly what I've become, an engineering whore. I've sold myself. It's all I can do to look at myself in the mirror when I shave. I make me sick.' (p. 114)

The Conspiracy Develops

Uneasily they both set about constructing the report. Elaborate charts and graphs purported to show the results of tests, temperatures were dropped a few hundred degrees (or raised to fit military specifications), brake pressures and distances were tailored to needs, and some tests were simply 'carried out' on paper. As they worked on the report they discussed culpability and even referred to the Nuremberg war crimes trials after the Second World War (when the standard German response to accusations was to deny guilt because 'I was following orders'). Lawson felt that what they were doing was 'downright dangerous', and, on occasion, Vandivier would needle Warren with barbed remarks including one on fraud. Warren then consulted the law section of a handbook for the engineering profession and looked up the definition of fraud:

> 'Well technically I don't think what we're doing can be called fraud. I'll admit it's not right, but it's just one of those things. We're just kinda caught in the middle. About all I can tell you is, do like I'm doing. Make copies of everything and put them in your SYA file.'
>   'What's an "SYA" file?' I asked.
>   'That's a "save your ass" file.' He laughed. (p. 115)

In fact both Vandivier and Lawson had been keeping SYA files since the beginning as they were concerned that the data might be otherwise 'lost'. In June the report went to Gretzinger, who delivered it to Sunderman for final editing in the engineering department. But Sink had got to Sunderman fist. The report was bounced to Gretzinger for completion. He refused. Soon afterwards Line rushed in:

> 'What the hell's all the fuss about this damned report?' he demanded loudly. Gretzinger explained the situation and also his resolution not to work on the report. Line shut him up with a wave of his hand and, turning to me, bellowed, 'I'm getting sick and tired of hearing about this damned report. Now, write the goddam thing and shut up about it!' He slammed out of the office.
>   Gretzinger and I just sat for a few seconds looking at each other. Then he spoke.
>   'Well, I guess he's made it pretty clear, hasn't he? We can either write the thing or quit. You know, what we should have done was quit a long time ago. Now, it's too late.' (p. 116)

Vandivier felt they were now all deeply implicated and actually writing the report would not increase his guilt.

> Still, Line's order came as something of a shock. All the time Lawson and I were working on the report, I felt, deep down, that somewhere, somehow, something would come along and the whole thing would blow over. But Russell Line had crushed that hope. The report was actually going to be issued. Intelligent, law-abiding officials of B.F. Goodrich, one of the oldest and most respected of American corporations, were actually going to deliver to a customer a product that was known to be defective and dangerous and which could very possibly cause death or serious injury. (p. 117)

He completed the report and ritualistically added a negative conclusion, knowing that this would be altered to a positive one before publication. Vandivier, Lawson, and Warren refused to sign the report, while Sink also managed not to sign.

Real Trouble Intrudes

In June 1968, the report was officially distributed to all concerned and test flights commenced. Lawson represented Goodrich, but he was back at the plant within a fortnight because the flights had been cancelled after a number of unusual incidents. Brake trouble had caused several near crashes on landing and once the brake was welded together by the intense heat and the plane skidded for 1,500 feet. Hearing this, Vandivier decided to go to an attorney and subsequently to the FBI, as did Lawson later. They were told to say nothing to anyone and to go on reporting developments. The FBI probably tipped off the Air Force because the Air Force demanded the test data from the trials.

Now panic really broke out at Goodrich. Vandivier, Lawson, Warren, and Sink met to confer on a Saturday morning. Sink stated they were going to 'level' with LTV and tell the 'whole truth'. Vandivier asked if it would not be difficult to admit that they lied.

> 'Now, wait a minute,' he said angrily. 'Let's don't go off half-cocked on this thing. It's not a matter of lying. We've just interpreted the information the way we felt it should be.'
> 'I don't know what you call it,' I replied, 'but to me it's lying, and it's going to be damned hard to confess to them that we've been lying all along.'
> He became very agitated at this and repeated his 'We're not lying,' adding, 'I don't like this sort of talk.' (p. 119)

When the meeting reconvened, some forty-three discrepancies were located in the report – most of which Sink dismissed as minor (or by saying it would not be wise to open that 'can of worms') – but these were reduced to three. Conferences continued throughout the summer in a deteriorating atmosphere of frayed tempers. Then Lawson submitted his resignation and Vandivier followed him. In his letter of resignation addressed to Line, Vandivier wrote of the qualification report:

> As you are aware, this report contained numerous deliberate and willful misrepresentations which, according to legal counsel, constitute fraud and expose both myself and others to criminal charges of conspiracy to defraud. . . . The events of the past seven months have created an atmosphere of deceit and distrust in which it is impossible to work. (p. 120)

This led to his being summoned to Sunderman's office, and Sunderman accused him of making 'shocking' and 'even irresponsible charges' and demanded an explanation. What was the fraud and how could he possibly accuse the company of such a practice?

> 'There's nothing wrong with anything we've done here. You aren't aware of all the things that have been going on behind the scenes. If you had known the true situation, you would never have made these charges.' He said that in view of my apparent 'disloyalty' he had decided to accept my resignation 'right now', and said it would be better for all concerned if I left the plant immediately. As I got up to leave he asked me if I intended to 'carry this thing further'.
> I answered simply, 'Yes', to which he replied, 'Suit yourself.' Within twenty minutes, I had cleaned out my desk and left. Forty-eight hours later, the B.F. Goodrich Company recalled the qualification report and the four-disc brake, announcing that it would replace the brake with a new, improved, five-disc brake at no cost to LTV. (p. 121)

Kermit Blows the Whistle

Several months later, on 13 August 1969, Vandivier testified before Senator Proxmire's Economy in Government Subcommittee of the Congress' Joint Economic Committee. Lawson's testimony supported Vandivier, and both the Air Force and GAO (General Accounting Office) investigators considered that the brake had not been tested properly and was dangerous. This expert testimony was not accepted by Goodrich, who were represented by the firm's counsel and by Sink, both of whom denied any wrongdoing on the part of Goodrich. Sink claimed not to have been involved in writing the report or of directing any falsification, that he was away at the time it happened, and that Warren had supervised the writing. Vandivier was denigrated for his lack of technical training and Lawson was portrayed as young and inexperienced – 'we tried to give him guidance,' Sink testified, 'but he preferred to have his own convictions.'

> About changing the data and figures in the report, Sink said: 'When you take data from several different sources, you have to rationalize among those data what is the true story. This is part of your engineering know-how.' He admitted that changes had been made in the data, 'but only to make them more consistent with the over-all picture of the data that is available.' (p. 122)

Jeter (counsel for Goodrich) pooh-poohed the suggestion that anything improper had occurred, saying: 'We have thirty-odd engineers at this plant . . . and I say to you that it is incredible that these men would stand idly by and see reports changed or falsified. . . . I mean you just do not have to do that working for anybody. . . . Just nobody does that' (p. 122). The four-hour hearing adjourned with no real conclusion reached by the committee. But, the following day the Department of Defense made sweeping changes in its inspection, testing, and reporting procedures. A spokesman for the DOD said the changes were a result of the Goodrich episode.

Kermit concluded:

> The A7D is now in service, sporting a Goodrich-made five-disk brake, a brake that works very well, I'm told. Business at the Goodrich plant is good. Lawson is now an engineer for LTV and has been assigned to the A7D project. And I am now a newspaper reporter. At this writing (1972), those remaining at Goodrich are still secure in the same positions, all except Russell Line and Robert Sink. Line has been rewarded with a promotion to production superintendent, a large step upward on the corporate ladder. As for Sink, he moved up into Line's old job. (p. 122)

Comment

Inter-personal Dynamics The Goodrich brake scandal is a particularly valuable case because it provides a rare inside account, written by a 'whistle-blower' (Vandivier), of the mechanisms leading to corporate deviance. It also tells us something of the actual people involved so that they do not remain shadowy figures, as in so many cases, while Goodrich is not an abstraction but a concrete world of conflicting personalities and subjectively experienced pressures.

Goodrich is a reputable company, employing well-qualified engineers who are used to working to exacting standards and to strict procedures for testing. This is not a second-rate firm, producing shoddy goods and living with the hazard of rejections of low-quality products, but a market leader employing top-class professionals. The pressure involved, then, is *self-imposed* – to get the contract 'at any cost' – and this goal is elevated almost to that of a mission.

The individual personalities involved are visible actors whose age, training, status, role, and qualifications all play a part in determining the course of events. There is an element of 'passing the buck' up, and around, the corporate hierarchy and manoeuvring to avoid blame. Although we are told that the Troy plant is small, a one-storey building employing 600 people, it is highly segmented with an advanced division of labour and poor communication between units. People shield superiors from knowledge, manoeuvre to deflect blame, and prepare for the day when the 'shit hits the fan'. There is too a notable division between the engineers and the managers, between the professionals and the 'politicians': the former endeavour to work to externally imposed norms and regulations whereas the latter are conscious of making the firm look good, of keeping up appearances, of compromise, and of personal survival. And individual error (Warren's) leads to institutional involvement and the necessity to cover up so that the top imposes conformity on subordinates, forcing them to shelve professional norms – and their consciences.

When the initial panic about delay breaks out the actors take steps which move them beyond the 'point of no return' in which their involvement enables them to falsify data, to deflect the inevitable reality of eventual exposure, and to accept Van Horn's order that regardless of the test the brake would be qualified. There is a form of 'group think' at work in which the participants refuse to face up to the patent defects and, instead, espouse an almost irrational commitment to pursuing the project in the conviction that it will come out well in the end. Warren's irrationality, in refusing to admit a mistake, escalates to become institutionalized irrationality, when Van Horn orders people to continue by ignoring the facts.

Inter-personal dynamics are crucial, and a pivotal moment is when Gretzinger first gets beaten down by Line. The man of personal conscience and professional integrity folds before a tougher personality, and before the bread-and-butter consequences of taking a firm stance. People begin to think of families and mortgages and wonder if they would get another job (presumably they are well qualified enough to find positions elsewhere but are concerned about a stigma preceding them or of Goodrich people, on whom they perhaps rely for a reference, putting the word around that they are not 'reliable'). Indeed, Vandivier's personal predicament in having seven children to care for may be the fundamentally mundane key to this case! But, then, there is also Warren's temper, Lawson's inexperience, Sink's instinct for the realities of institutional 'politics', Gretzinger's lack of backbone, and Line's adeptness at social climbing and survival.

Rationalizations and Justifications   As the actors become more deeply implicated they seek rationalizations (inaccuracies become 'interpretation' and
cooking the books is 'engineering licence'), employ vocabularies of motive, and
evade responsibility with the 'I do as I am told' argument. The recalcitrants are
virtually coached in the appropriate vocabulary to be used in assuaging their
consciences. Yet the deviance engaged in is bound to be discovered at a later
stage, while 'traces' of the cover-up are present in documents (this is a high-vis-
ibility, easily detectable, offence, making it almost all the more staggering that
these engineers could succumb to it). They know it is dangerous, become
aware that it is probably criminal, and yet let themselves be shouted down for
a second time by Line ('write the goddam thing and shut up about it') when
they start to get cold feet. For several days, moreover, they are able to put on
a charade to hoodwink colleagues from LTV.

When the inevitable external reality does intrude in the form of near
crashes during test flights, the response is to rally around and to think in
terms of loyalty and disloyalty. External control agencies become involved
and are met with denials, distortions, scapegoating (Vandivier and Lawson),
and the 'I wasn't there when it happened' routine. The inquiry seems to be
inconclusive, and it may well be that the parties involved are playing a public
ritual of symbolic penitence. Perhaps Goodrich is seen as a 'good' company
that just slipped up and, as it will undoubtedly continue to play an important
role in defence contracts, it is salutary enough to administer a symbolic slap
on the wrist. But apparently administrative procedures of external control
were tightened up as a result. No real sanctions are imposed, no criminal
prosecutions evolve, and it soon becomes 'business as usual'.

Indeed, it is, ironically, precisely the 'loyalists' who are rewarded for their
devotion to the company, and the 'deviants' are the trouble-makers who are
filtered out of the system. At Goodrich you were apparently rewarded for
your mistakes. And the sanctions were reserved for those who 'made waves'
that 'rocked the boat'.

Conscience versus Individual Self-interest   In essence, then, I perceive this as
a case revolving around 'inter-personal dynamics'; if one or two of the main
participants had shown more backbone or 'bottle', and less fear of losing
face, then they might easily have prevented an incident escalating into a
scandal. It also illustrates potently that professional integrity and individual
conscience can give way under company pressure and personal interests.
The actors were asked *to put the company first and their consciences second.*
The origin of the deviance is the pressure imposed on people to produce a
difficult product under a tight time schedule which scarcely allows for delays
(meaning that the moral must be not to promise what you cannot deliver).
Given that top-class engineers were prepared to falsify data, it is difficult to
conceive of watertight testing procedures which are not amenable to manipulation if people are really intent on changing records. The promised DOD
changes in inspection, testing, and reporting were, then, likely to be cosmetic
changes rather than foolproof devices. It is also doubtful whether tougher

external sanctions would have inhibited the participants. Prevention probably needs to be seen in internal terms of ethical codes, programmes on social responsibility, and grievance procedures. Vandivier was forced to go outside with his dilemma, whereas an ethical committee might have been able to handle the problem internally and to protect him from any reprisals from superiors.

One's final thought is that tightening procedures is unlikely to be effective against intelligent and determined men, bent on conspiring to falsify data. For these were honourable men; yet between them they lied, covered up, falsified data, and endangered the lives of test pilots. The frightening prospect is, then, what forms (and in what magnitude) does 'engineering licence' take in less reputable firms than Goodrich?

Case No. 2: the Heavy Electrical Equipment Anti-trust Cases

These historical court cases are interesting for two main reasons. First, the offences were *long-term conspiracies* designed to help regulate markets in a specific industry. And second, the 'perpetrators' were model citizens for whom the criminal stigma was clearly painful to accept. Although price-fixing is a crime, the practice had become so routine that the managers had great difficulty perceiving their activities as criminal, while their public exposure forced them to articulate a number of vocabularies of motive. This was 'pure' business deviance in the sense that its aim was to regulate competition between companies and, as such, it was conducted for 'the good of the company'. Ostensibly, the defendants did not gain by it and no one was 'hurt'.

At least that seemed to be the message conveyed by the original case (cf. Senator Kefauver's Subcommittee on Antitrust and Monopoly, 1961). When Geis initially reported on the heavy electrical equipment cases in 1967 he helped to shape the definition of white-collar crime as being largely in the interests of the company; for since then Geis has become a prominent and productive scholar who has strongly set forth the tradition of Sutherland. Only recently, as we have seen above, has this widely held view been challenged. Anti-trust cases – related to cartel-forming, monopolies, price-fixing, bid-rigging, and other anti-competitive practices – have a measure of irony in that business normally espouses free and open competition yet can be seen to manipulate markets under certain conditions. The evidence in this area is complex and not always clear in relating market conditions to corporate behaviour, but in general there is an assumption that corporations tend to enhance predictability in a turbulent or insecure environment by engaging in networks to interfere with the workings of a freely competitive environment. For instance, Jamieson scrutinizes a wide range of evidence and argues that,

In situations where the declining health of a specific line of business threatens overall corporate profit goals, a pursuit of an improved market position by illegally manipulating the environment may be the most rational and cost-effective strategy for securing elusive resources. (1994: 61)

Anti-trust cases have often revealed the difficulty of pursuing corporate giants, as in the ATT and IBM cases (which took years to complete, with the IBM case being dropped after eighteen years), while anti-trust violations have been exposed in dairy firms rigging milk prices, in the shoe industry, the folding carton industry, among uranium suppliers, and recently in Europe in the cement industry. In Europe a number of cement companies tend to dominate the domestic markets and these markets were protected by price agreements among more than forty companies and agencies; a company that insisted on selling in another country had to adjust its prices to those of the local 'price leader' (the violations attracted a record fine of 535 million guilders or some $340 million: *de Volkskrant*, 1 December 1994). In general, the larger the organizational network of conspirators the more difficult it is likely to be to maintain the conspiracy without detection (Jamieson, 1994).

This case focuses our attention, then, on why business organizations misuse their position to interfere with the workings of a competitive market, and on the rationalizations of executives accused of criminal activity. Is it really the case that they seek no reward for breaking the law?

Conspiracy of Gentlemen

> No one attending the gathering [of the conspirators] was so stupid he did not know the meetings were in violation of the law. But it is the only way a business can be run. It is free enterprise.

> (Manager: in Clinard and Yeager, 1980: 298)

The heavy electrical equipment anti-trust cases of 1961 were considered at the time to be the most serious offences prosecuted under the anti-trust laws (which had originally been enacted in the 1890s). The defendants appeared in a federal courtroom in early 1962 and they included a number of vice-presidents of General Electric Corporation and Westinghouse Electric Corporation, then the two largest firms in the industry. A journalist covering the trial saw them as 'middle-class men in Ivy League suits, typical businessmen in appearance, men who would never be taken for law breakers' (p. 59; page numbers refer to Geis, 1978). Furthermore, a number of them were 'deacons or vestrymen of their churches'.

> One was president of his local chamber of commerce, another a hospital board member, another chief fund raiser for the community chest, another a bank director, another a director of the taxpayers' association, another an organizer of the local little league.
> The attorney for a General Electric executive attacked the government's demand for a jail sentence for his client, calling it 'cold-blooded'. The lawyer insisted that government prosecutors did not understand what it would do to his client, 'this fine man', to be put 'behind bars' with 'common criminals who have been convicted of embezzlement and other serious crimes.' (p. 59)

In other words, these were apparently upstanding members of the business and local community; and, it seemed, their defence counsel could not perceive their offences as 'serious'.

Yet the most glaring aspect of the anti-trust conspiracy was precisely its seriousness because it was clearly 'wilful and blatant'; the offences were not marginal and inadvertent but were 'flagrantly criminal' and broke quite deliberately the articles of the Sherman Antitrust Act of 1890 which prohibited price-fixing as a restraint on trade (p. 61). In making his analysis Geis was reliant on secondary sources because the records of the grand jury hearing were not open to the public. But apparently the federal government's attention had been brought to the fact that certain manufacturers were entering identical bids for electrical equipment. Eventually some 196 people were subpoenaed and twenty indictments were issued, concerning forty-five defendants and twenty-nine corporations. Most defendants pleaded guilty, while companies entered pleas of *nolo contendere* ('no contest', which does not involve an admission of guilt). Fines of nearly $2 million were doled out – $1,787,000 for the companies and $137,000 for managers. But seven defendants were sentenced to thirty days in jail – 'four were vice presidents, two were division managers, and one was a sales manager' (p. 62).

Like other defendants sent to jail they were handcuffed, fingerprinted, and issued with prison garb. At the county jail they were described as 'model prisoners'; several were allowed to work on the prison farm, and a warden described them as 'the most intelligent prisoners' he had encountered (p. 62). They wished to receive no visitors, and earned a five-day remittance for good conduct. The other defendants, who had been put on probation, were prematurely released from probation by the judge who had earlier imposed the sentences, on the grounds that it was scarcely appropriate in these cases.

Although the fines were pinpricks to huge companies like General Electric, there were also civil suits for treble damages as allowed by the anti-trust legislation. Initially, General Electric was determined to oppose these suits, and argued in justification:

> We believe that the purchasers of electrical apparatus have received fair value by any reasonable standard. The prices which they have paid during the past years were appropriate to value received and reasonable as compared with the general trends of prices in the economy, the price trends for similar equipment and the price trends for materials, salaries, and wages. The foresight of the electrical utilities and the design and manufacturing skills of companies such as General Electric have kept electricity one of today's greatest bargains. (p. 63)

But by 1964 it was estimated that the vast majority of the 1,800 claims had been settled for around $160 million, which makes the fines appear tiny. Much of the sum paid in claims was, however, tax-deductible.

The Mechanics of Market Manipulation

In piecing together *how* the managers went about constructing their network of alliances and illicit agreements, it emerges that they were fully aware of the need for secrecy: 'Like most reasonably adept and optimistic criminals, the antitrust violators had hoped to escape apprehension. "I did not expect to get caught and I went to great lengths to conceal my activities so that I would not get caught", one of them said' (p. 65). Another manager went on to reveal some of the methods employed to conceal their activities: 'It was considered discreet to not be too obvious and to minimize telephone calls, to use plain envelopes if mailing material to each other, not to be seen together when travelling, and so forth . . . not to leave wastepaper of which there was a lot strewn around a room when leaving' (p. 65). The participants were cloaked by false names and innocuous-looking codes (the 'attendance roster for the meetings was known as the "Christmas" card list and the gatherings, interestingly enough, as "choir practice"' (p. 65)). They used public rather than office phones, met at trade conferences, or at inconspicuous sites. To cover up their real purpose they falsified their expense accounts to camouflage the cities they had visited. But no one took the opportunity to claim a cent more than was due to him. It may be legitimate to cheat the customer, but you do not rip off your own company. That, presumably, is a matter of conscience.

During the concealed negotiations the market was parcelled out to the companies, so that everyone could expect a proportion of the trade available, and this calculation usually reflected the already existing division of the pie among the leading companies. A company would then be allowed to submit the lowest bid for tenders proportionate to its share of the market and the remainder would bid at slightly higher levels. (Tenders for contracts are meant to be confidential and the system is designed to avoid price inflation and to ensure low costs for contracts by choosing the lowest bidder.) For a number of reasons,

> debate among the conspirators was often acrimonious about the proper division of spoils, about alleged failures to observe previous agreements, and about other intramural matters. Sometimes, depending upon the contract, the conspirators would draw lots to determine who would submit the lowest bid; at other times the appropriate arrangement would be determined under a rotating system conspiratorially referred to as the 'phase of the moon'. (p. 66)

Justifications

Of particular interest in this case is the attempt by the participants to justify their behaviour. Most agreed that their conduct might have been 'technically criminal', but they endeavoured to evade the full impact of the criminal label by maintaining that their offences were not criminal in intent or in their consequences. Indeed, their actions were even claimed to have had a 'worthwhile purpose by "stabilizing prices" (a much-favoured phrase of the conspirators)' (p. 67). As well as putting an altruistic gloss on their motives, the managers also argued that they were unaware that certain acts were criminal; or they maintained that acts with positive consequences should not be defined as criminal. This viewpoint was explicated by a Westinghouse executive before a Senate Subcommittee:

> *Committee Attorney:* Did you know that these meetings with competitors were illegal?
> *Witness:* Illegal? Yes, but not criminal. I did not find that out until I read the indictment. . . . I assumed that criminal action meant damaging someone, and we did

not do that. . . . I thought that we were more or less working on a survival basis in order to try to make enough to keep our plant and our employees. (p. 67)

Essentially, the managers argued that no one was harmed by the offences, that they were not fully convinced that anti-trust law had actually been broken (they had been operating in a 'grey area'), and there was nothing extortionate in a device that aimed to get just value for their products. One manager articulated several of these points:

One faces a decision, I guess, at such times, about how far to go with company instructions, and since the spirit of such meetings only appeared to be correcting a horrible price level situation, that there was not an attempt to actually damage customers, charge excessive prices, there was no personal gain in it for me, the company did not seem actually to be defrauding. Corporate statements can evidence the fact that there have been poor profits during all these years. . . . So I guess morally it did not seem quite so bad as might be inferred by the definition of the activity itself. (p. 68)

The characters of the men involved were not at dispute; rather, they had succumbed to corporate pressure.

A Way of Life

Almost all the men were at pains to point out that, when they started their jobs, they simply inherited price-fixing virtually as a way of life in their branch. They were introduced to it by their superiors and 'drifted' into it almost unquestioningly, accepting it as the firm's s.o.p. (standard operating procedure); 'every direct supervisor that I had directed me to meet with competition. . . . It had become so common and gone on for so many years that I think we lost sight of the fact that it was illegal' (p. 68). Price-fixing obviously had become an integral, and routine, part of their jobs.

But what if they refused? General Electric, for instance, had issued a directive in 1946 which was even tougher than the wording of the anti-trust laws, but executives seemed to feel that this was really only for 'public consumption'. One of its signatories followed his conscience and refused to engage in the forbidden practices; he was shunted aside and his successor was told that the man had obviously not been 'broad enough' for his job. In short, the successor had spelt out to him that he was gaining promotion to do precisely what his predecessor had refused to do and, in addition, that if he was not 'broad enough' then another would take his place: '"If I did not do it, I felt that somebody else would", said one [General Electric witness], with an obvious note of self-justification. "I would be removed and somebody else would do it"' (p. 69).

Westinghouse kept on its managers but General Electric decided to dismiss those involved in court proceedings. Westinghouse justified its decision on the grounds that the managers did not seek personal gain but operated in the 'misguided belief' that they were promoting their company's interests; that they had already been harshly punished and an additional sanction was pointless; each one of the convicted managers was 'in every sense a reputable citizen, a respected and valuable member of the community and of high moral character' (p. 70); and it was most unlikely that they would repeat the offence. In contrast, General Electric maintained that its managers deserved dismissal because they had broken both the law and company policy. Some felt that this was scapegoating to protect top management and that the men had been 'thrown to the wolves' (p. 70).

Not surprisingly, the witnesses had spoken of the negative consequences of non-compliance with the directives from above; but none mentioned the *rewards* for taking part. The judge, however, was unequivocal. He graphically portrayed the companies as undoubtedly the leading miscreants but went on to shed a far less favourable light on the participants than they themselves had done:

> They were torn between conscience and an approved corporate policy, with the rewarding objective of promotion, comfortable security, and large salaries. They were the organization or company man, the conformist who goes along with his superiors and finds balm for his conscience in additional comforts and security of his place in the corporate set-up. (p. 71)

Their principal motivation, then, was comfort and security, according to the judge. The retired company president spoke with hostility of the 'monkey business' he encountered early in his career when he was asked to bid for a contract that had already been fixed. And the then president, Ralph Cordiner, thought that the practices were fuelled by 'drives for easily acquired power':

> Cordiner's statement is noteworthy for its dismissal of the explanations of the offenders as 'rationalizations': 'One reason for the offences was a desire to be "Mr Transformer" or "Mr Switchgear" . . . and to have influence over a larger segment of the industry. . . . The second was that it was an indolent, lazy way to do business. When you get all through with the rationalizations, you have to come back to one or other of these conclusions.' (p. 71)

One of the Perpetrators

One offender denied that it was price-fixing at all and claimed they were just 'recovering costs': others blamed decentralization, which pressured the divisions to achieve profit (which was then linked via 'incentive compensation' to bonuses); yet others believed that the 'dog-eat-dog' mentality that permeated their branch was also partly responsible. But one executive cut through the verbiage and stated baldly, 'I think the boys could resist everything but temptation' (p. 72).

One of the offenders who had been jailed had previously been tipped as a prospective president of GE. He was a graduate, a naval veteran, an active member of the community, and was married with three children. In short, he exuded the stereotype of the active and law-abiding citizen, the family man, and the industrious executive. Following sentence he issued a statement that his conduct had been interpreted as infringing some technicalities of the complex anti-trust laws, that the company and the community would survive this ordeal, and that he had received a great deal of support from all over the country. Later he regretted the fact, in rather bitter terms, that the support of his own company had not extended to paying him while he was a 'guest of the Government'. He had joined GE after graduation, and had risen rapidly to the point where he was singled out for promotion to general management. In 1946 he had first been initiated into price-fixing practices by his superior.

The meetings he attended were often punctuated by disputes. It was vital to disguise continually the nature of the discussions from the 'manufacturing people, the engineers, and especially the lawyers', but, apparently, 'commercial transactions remained unquestioned by managerial personnel so long as they showed a reasonable profit' (p. 73). These meetings took place between 1946 and 1949, at which point a federal investigation forced a clamp-down on the illicit gatherings. The meetings were reconvened at the instigation of this manager's superior, who was described as

'a great communicator, a great philosopher, and, frankly, a great believer in stabilities of prices', [and who] decided that 'the market was getting in a chaotic condition' and that they had better go out and see what could be done about it.' He was told to keep knowledge of the meetings from Robert Paxton, 'an Adam Smith advocate', then the plant works manager, because Paxton 'don't understand these things'. (p. 74)

On promotion in 1954 he had been invited to meet the GE president, who told him to comply with company policy and the law on anti-trust, and to ensure that his subordinates followed suit (the message was felt necessary because he was known as a 'bad boy'). On return to his office, however, his own boss instructed him, 'now, keep on doing the way that you have been doing but just . . . be sensible about it and use your head on the subject' (p. 74). Over-production following the end of the Korean War spelt out the need for continued price-fixing but this practice became more difficult as foreign companies began to enter the market with low bids.

In 1957 the witness gained promotion to vice-president. Once again he received a sermon from the president on price-fixing but this time, his 'air cover gone', he avoided further involvement in such practices. On going back to his plant he 'issued stringent instructions to his subordinates that they were no longer to attend meetings with competitors. Not surprisingly, since he himself had rarely obeyed such injunctions, neither did the sales persons in his division' (p. 74). Under interrogation about his moral feelings he stated that he had been forced to re-examine his conduct because of the effect on his family, the sensationalising of the case by the media, and the stigma of a prison sentence. But, implicitly, he admitted that he had not seen the practices in moral terms until *after* exposure to sanctions.

With regard to his resignation he was fairly philosophical; that was 'the way the ball had bounced' and he felt no bitterness (p. 75). He wished the others good luck and merely hoped he could get a job somewhere in American industry. Just over a month later he was president of a large corporation.

Comment

Conspiracy   The heavy electrical equipment anti-trust cases of 1961 illuminate several important features of certain corporate deviance. They revealed
that businessmen engaged in a *long-term, deliberate, sophisticated conspiracy*
which endeavoured to regulate strategically the market in an entire industry.
Those involved were senior executives who were model corporate, and community, citizens. They resisted, and resented, the label 'criminal'. Their
conduct and motives could not be deduced from the transcript of the court
proceedings, which was secret, but Geis was able to base his oft-quoted analysis on several books about the cases, academic articles, newspaper reports
(particularly in the *New York Times*, the *Wall Street Journal*, *Fortune*, and
local papers), and, most vitally, on Senator Kefauver's Subcommittee on
Antitrust and Monopoly (the hearings of which were published and before
which many witnesses involved in the conspiracy appeared). These sources
provide a good insight into how the conspiracy was conducted and also as to
the motives of the participants.

Criminality   The reaction to the cases at the time seems to have revolved
around the implication of the label 'criminal' applied to reputable businessmen whose offences did not appear to be 'serious'. But as several
commentators, including Senator Kefauver, pointed out, these were very serious offences indeed, and *indisputably criminal*. Kefauver said they made a
mockery of the law, and spoke of sealed secret bids to ensure competition,
while a representative of the American Bar Association stated:

> it should now be clear that a deliberate or conscious violation of the antitrust
> laws . . . is a serious offence against society which is as criminal as any other act
> that injures many in order to profit a few. Conspiracy to violate the antitrust laws
> is economic racketeering. Those who are apprehended in such acts are, and will be
> treated as criminals. (p. 76)

The evidence of the witnesses made abundantly clear that the conspiracy
was highly formulated and coordinated, was conducted over a long period of
time, was concealed by subterfuges to camouflage what was going on from
federal investigators, from managers, from other departments within the companies, and from top management (who probably knew of the activity but
who were to be spared any incriminating details). The illicit practices were
protected by secrecy involving the use of telephone, mail, codes, and falsified
expense accounts. The executives' activities were tailored to conditions in the
market which offers an explanation for their conduct:

> The ebb and flow of the price-fixing conspiracy also clearly indicates the relation-
> ship, often overlooked in explanations of criminal behaviour, between extrinsic
> conditions and illegal acts. When the market behaved in a manner the executives
> thought satisfactory, or when enforcement agencies seemed particularly threaten-
> ing, the conspiracy desisted. When market conditions deteriorated, while corporate
> pressure for achieving attractive profit-and-loss statements remained constant,
> and enforcement activity abated, the price-fixing agreements flourished. (pp. 78–9)

Yet despite the publicity, the fines, and the prison sentences, the defendants were treated fairly lightly; the jail sentence was short, was spent on the prison farm (for some), and was reduced for good behaviour (while others had their probation prematurely lifted). The offences might have been serious, but in the eyes of the court these were 'good' defendants who were unlikely to become recidivists and for whom long, custodial sentences were inappropriate.

General Electric's argument in opposing the civil suits for damages placed a rather precious gloss of positive intent and favourable consequences on the price-fixing, which was echoed by the defendants. But there *were* losers, the customers denied honest competition by fraudulent means, and they sought solace through the civil courts to the sizeable tune of $160 million. The managers endeavoured to maintain that it was illegal 'but not criminal' because no harm had been done, because the practices had positive effects, because they had not gained anything personally, or because they were unaware they were breaking the law. These 'vocabularies of motive' were put down by the judge, who emphasized the security, comfort, and rewards that the executives could expect from bonuses and promotion related to their successful illicit behaviour; and, surprisingly, they were also criticized by two senior figures of General Electric, one of whom spoke of men seeking power over the market, which also provided them with an easy, predictable way of doing business.

Embeddedness in a 'Way of Life'   What does emerge with considerable clarity, moreover, is that deviance had become a *way of life*, a part of the corporate (and industry) culture, and was routinely accepted as 'part of the job'. Executives were brought into it and coached by their superiors. General Electric's internal directive against price-fixing was perceived as window-dressing; a warning from the president was taken as a ritual sermon that did not interfere with practice out in the field away from corporate headquarters; and statements from a senior manager were reinterpreted by his subordinates as not to be taken seriously because he had never stuck to the rules himself when he had been in their position. People with a conscience were moved to less sensitive areas, and promotion, it was made clear, implied compliance with the conspiracy or someone else would be found to do it. You were tested and either found wanting (and were shunted aside) or else you joined the fold.

The 'career' of the defendants in these case emerged in evidence which demonstrated they had gone through a learning process in deviant activities. This inheritance of a deviant situation led one senator at the hearings to speak of 'imbued fraud'. When exposed, they found it painful to be labelled publicly as criminals. But Westinghouse imposed no further sanctions on its errant managers and welcomed them back; and, when General Electric dismissed its miscreants, some saw it as merely hypocritical house-cleaning. However, a criminal record did not prevent one manager landing the top position in another company. Business looks after its own.

And, finally, the one thing the managers seemed to have the greatest difficulty coping with was to see their behaviour in moral terms. They expressed shame rather than guilt. After all, they were just doing their job, and one executive, when asked why he attended the meetings, replied, 'I thought it was part of my duty to do so' (p. 68). At the managerial level this raises issues of loyalty and 'duty' and of how far an executive will go in breaking the rules and the law. This case is also important in terms of 'organizational' crime because networks of organizations colluded to manipulate the market. These sorts of violations tend to occur when a company in a near monopoly position feels that its powerful position is threatened or when adverse conditions motivate competitors to coalesce in an illicit alliance to fix prices, rig bids, or exercise control over the industry (Jamieson, 1994). Perhaps 'economic' violations are not seen as especially reprehensible, and this can be reinforced by the fact that much anti-trust legislation is disputed and prosecutions may be resisted forcibly (while the company may pose as the 'victim' as ATT or 'Ma Bell' did in its battle with the Justice Department: *The Economist*, 17 January 1981). Indeed some economists, politicians, and executives argue for the abolition of anti-trust legislation as unjust interference in the workings of what should be a free market. Are, then, these offences 'criminal'? Are managers who violate these laws 'criminals'? And what are appropriate sanctions in this area for organizations and for executives?

Case No. 3: the DC-10 Crash at Paris and McDonnell Douglas

The Pressures

Engineers maintain that they can readily produce a perfectly safe aeroplane; but it would be too heavy to fly. This implies an unavoidable element of *risk* in aviation – risk for the manufacturer, the carrier, the insurers, the area or community in which a plane operates, and, of course, for the passengers and crew. Currently there is considerable debate and concern about safety in the air related to ageing fleets of planes, congestion at airports, and overcrowded skies. And, in the past, there have been aeroplanes dogged with initial problems – the Comet, the Electra, the Boeing 707, the Caravelle, the DC-6 and DC-8 (of which some have gone on to be highly successful). But, surely, no manufacturer would market an aeroplane with safety defects. There is no more visible a sign of failure than a downed airliner with its macabre litter of mechanical and human debris. Even hardened emergency workers can be appalled, and moved to tears, by the carnage caused by a plane that has hurled its passengers to horrifying destruction.

Yet that is precisely what happened to McDonnell Douglas. According to the elite investigatory journalists of the *Sunday Times*, the Insight Team, a defect in the initial model of the DC-10 led to an accident that was predictable (this case draws heavily on their account and reconstruction of events: Eddy et al., 1976). McDonnell Douglas did not cooperate with the reporters and always strongly defended its product:

> We know that we have great responsibilities, and we take those responsibilities very seriously – a Douglas aircraft is always a Douglas aircraft no matter who owns it, how long it remains in service, or what's done with it after it's beyond our control. Our planes are part of our lives and part of our identity; that's one reason why we build them with such care. (McDonnell Douglas Press Release, 1974)

Aeroplane accidents are often highly complex events with a long chain of contributory causes (Weick, 1990). They can happen to well-run and safety-conscious companies flying widely used and highly tested models. Causes may be related to 'pilot error', flying conditions, relations between crew members, sabotage, terrorism, and so on (Perrow, 1984), but one key element in all technical investigations, and much journalistic interest, will always be product failure and possible liability of the manufacturer and carrier.

As with other product liability cases, it is necessary to place this accident in an industry context. Generally civil aviation is characterized by high development costs, a long wait for return on investment, intense competition, and an elongated product life-cycle (there are still DC-3 Dakotas in operation and this plane was designed over fifty years ago, before the Second World War). The pressure to get a contract with a carrier can be intense and the failure to do so devastating. It is a tough business to be in and the stakes are incredibly high. There is an element of pressure, as in other cases of product liability, to push on with production even in the face of misgivings about the quality or safety of the product. Although aeroplanes have tended to become safer, it can be the case that a model contains a structural weakness that is only revealed well into production; thus Boeing has decided to strengthen and replace the pins securing the engines to the wings of a series of 747 'jumbos' after an El Al cargo version of the 747 lost two motors and crashed in Amsterdam in 1992 (Dekker, 1994). The worst commercial aviation accident to date was the collision of two 747 jumbos on the runway of Tenerife in 1977 with the loss of 583 lives; but with industry plans for planes carrying up to 1,000 passengers we have to face the possibility of much higher casualties in the event of an accident.

This case, then, poses the central issue: how do industry conditions place managers under pressure to the extent that their actions lead to bringing a product with a defect on to the market?

Paris, 1974: the Crash

On 3 March 1974, a DC-10 of Turkish Airlines took off from Orly Airport, Paris, with 346 people on board *en route* to London. During its climb over a Paris suburb the plane suffered decompression, leading to the collapse of the floor under which the controls were mounted; the rear cargo door blew open and six passengers were sucked out still strapped to their seats; the pilot lost control of the 300-ton plane which crashed at nearly 500 mph into a wood. The fuselage ruptured and people were hurled out, to be virtually shredded by the trees. Captain Lannier of the local unit of the Gendarmerie was called to the scene from a pleasant family lunch and, expecting that a light aeroplane had come down (possibly belonging to a nearby aeroclub), he was horrified to see the extent and nature of the damage caused by a wide-bodied plane that had disintegrated on impact:

> On my left, over a distance of four hundred or five hundred meters, trees were hacked and mangled, most of them charred but not burnt. Pieces of metal,

brightly coloured electric wires, and clothes were littered all over the ground. In front of me, in the valley, the trees were even more severely hacked and the wreckage even greater. There were fragments of bodies and pieces of flesh that were hardly recognizable. In front of me, not far from where I stood, there were two hands clasping each other, a man's hand tightly holding a woman's hand, two hands which withstood disintegration. (Eddy et al., 1976: 104)

The then worst accident in aviation history had cost 346 lives of people from more than twenty nationalities, it had involved a Turkish carrier and an American manufacturer, and it had occurred in French airspace. As the American Federal Aviation Authority (FAA) began to investigate a history of problems with the cargo door, the company expressed its determination to support the plane by referring precisely to the FAA certification of airworthiness: 'The DC-10 meets all FAA regulations and we have complete confidence in its safety and airworthiness' (McDonnell Douglas press release, 1974). The cargo door, which was found 6 miles from the scene of the main crash, was pointed out as the sole cause of the accident by French authorities within a matter of weeks. Who was to blame? How is blame apportioned following such accidents? What is the predicament of the victims' relatives? And how can we explain the company's behaviour?

To explore these questions requires a look at the aircraft industry, its regulation, at courts and compensation, and at the reactions of management to nursing a plane through design and into operation.

This 'avoidable accident' has to be centred in the intense commercial pressure surrounding aeroplane manufacture in general, and in America in the 1970s in particular, as a new generation of jumbo planes were projected. In the late 1960s Boeing had the 747 nearing service; Lockheed was busily engaged on the 1011 Tristar; and McDonnell Douglas decided to enter the race for the wide-bodied jets which would compete in the ferocious climate for securing orders which characterized selling to the commercial carriers in North America. All three companies were taking huge financial risks, but McDonnell Douglas' real battle was with Lockheed for the medium-sized, all-purpose 'airbus' market (planes for about 250 passengers). But McDonnell Douglas had already lost lead time and it was in a desperate hurry to get the plane into the air before Lockheed. Speed put the development schedule under pressure while, at the same time, a momentous effort was made on the sales side. For, unlike military orders where development costs are covered by defence contracts, the costs of developing a new commercial airliner are astronomical, and represent a considerable gamble because a high level of success is required in order to reap any rewards. McDonnell Douglas was playing a game with extremely high stakes where losing was barely worth considering; 'Its DC-10 was a billion-dollar gamble that the company could not avoid, and could not afford to lose' (*Forbes*, 1 August 1969). Virtually with a sense of mission the engineers got down to work.

The design of the cargo door was sub-contracted to Convair, a subsidiary of General Dynamics. Doors are clearly of considerable importance in aeroplane design because planes fly at high speed and with the cabin under considerable pressure, so that doors represent a potential weak spot; equally floors are crucial because collapse can damage controls. In the DC-10 the controls ran under the floor, and designers opted for three hydraulic systems instead of four, presumably to speed up production (while in the 747 the controls are mounted above the floor of the plane). The designers at Convair argued for a cargo door using hydraulic cylinders to drive the cargo-door latches but McDonnell Douglas insisted on electric actuators. Some, including Dan Applegate at Convair, felt that the latter were intrinsically less safe (but a major consideration was weight and cost for McDonnell Douglas, while the lead carrier, American Airlines, also held that a hydraulically operated door would be too complex in its working parts; and in a buyer's market the first purchaser, or lead carrier, has a powerful position to enforce modifications: *Harvard Business School*, Case 9-383-128, 1984: 4).

Teething Problems

When the first prototype, Ship 1, was rolled out of the hangar in 1970 at Long Beach, California, for a ground test of the pressurized cabin, a section of the floor collapsed. This inauspicious baptism was blamed on the mistake of a mechanic. As the Dutch national carrier, KLM, was considering ordering the DC-10, the Dutch Civil Aviation Authority (RLD) examined the design in 1971 and voiced quite strong reservations about the possibility of a floor collapse leading to a loss of control by the pilot. This was before the plane had been certificated and represented an opportunity to take some sort of remedial action, such as strengthening the floor or moving the controls. McDonnell Douglas countered by maintaining that they had met all regulatory requirements but carried out a number of modifications to prevent depressurization if a door was not properly locked, and the hand-driven door linkages were improved.

On entering service, however, the rear cargo door continued to give problems, and within ten months of service there were over 100 reports of the door refusing to close properly. The most dramatic incident, and almost a forerunner of the Paris accident, occurred with an American Airlines DC-10 over Windsor, Ontario, when the rear cargo door blew off, leading to decompression and floor collapse. Aided by a light load the pilot showed high skill and quick wits in landing safely by using the power of the motors to control the plane. No one was seriously injured but the warning was crystal clear. The plane was vulnerable.

The Company's Response and the Regulators

McDonnell Douglas' reaction was to blame the baggage handler at the airport for forcing the door shut in a way that led to the pins of the locking device not closing properly while no warning light came on in the cockpit indicating partial closure. The cargo door was hinged at the top and closed downwards with bent hooks catching on a bar and being secured with pins; the system was driven by an electrical circuit; but it was possible to get the pins in place by using force even though the hooks were not fully engaged (while this also meant that the door was registered as 'secure' on the cockpit controls). FAA certifying agents did not believe it was possible to force the 'vent door' – a back-up safety system to the cargo door – shut when the door latch safety pins were not properly secured. The 'Windsor Incident' occurred because an American Airlines baggage handler at Detroit had been able to force the vent door shut with his knee (*Harvard Business School*, Case 9-383-128, 1984: 6). The Windsor incident was dismissed as a freak event.

No plane goes into service without certification and this requires looking at the role and functions of the regulators of the industry. There are, in the USA, two agencies which are concerned with regulatory control of airline manufacture and safety, and both could have played a more decisive role in inducing McDonnell Douglas to make modifications. The FAA has potentially considerable power and its main weapon is the Airworthiness Directive (AD) which allows a plane to fly and the suspension of which can ground a plane. In addition, the National Transportation Safety Board (NTSB) can investigate accidents and can make recommendations to the FAA. In the early 1970s, however, both agencies had been weakened by political interference. Both were housed in the US Department of Transportation, but relations had deteriorated between them, as the FAA had paid less and less attention to NTSB recommendations, and they were actually feuding in public on these issues (leading to a loss of personnel at the NTSB and a measure of demoralization). The FAA, moreover, had the dual – and potentially contradictory mandate – of both *promoting* and *policing* the industry. The head of the FAA was a White House appointee who came from the industry and who strongly identified with it. Under those circumstances the revocation of a certificate in the middle of the summer season, with the airlines performing at peak capacity, probably seemed a drastic and unduly hasty step. For it would have grounded every DC-10 in service for some time (which happened after the crash of a DC-10 at Chicago in 1979 when *all* DC-10s of the same type flying within American airspace were grounded for thirty-eight days).

The FAA settled for a compromise. A 'gentlemen's agreement' was reached between the company and the head of the FAA which avoided grounding the plane and which passed the responsibility of modification to McDonnell Douglas. The regional official responsible for the AD was overruled by his top boss in Washington, DC, following the direct intervention of Douglas' president, Jackson McGowen. The weakened position of the NTSB meant that its recommendations had been watered down to a service directive issued by McDonnell Douglas itself which did not appear to carry any sense of urgency. The modification involved putting in a peep-hole, a warning placard on not forcing the door shut, and an adjustment to the vent door.

The Applegate Memorandum

McDonnell Douglas had countered NTSB demands by claiming that they had already met full FAA requirements. As such, the FAA must shoulder some of the blame. But the story might have been altered if the FAA had received some vital information earlier. For in 1972 there emerged grave doubts at the Convair Division of General Dynamics about the safety of the DC-10. These fears were worded in the 'Applegate Memorandum' which predicted the loss of planes because of the cargo door opening.

Dan Applegate, the Convair engineer who questioned Douglas' original cargo door design, was not at all pleased with the FAA–McDonnell Douglas agreement. On June 27 1972, 15 days after that understanding was reached, Applegate wrote a long memorandum to his superiors that began, 'The potential for long-term Convair liability on the DC-10 has caused me increasing concern for several reasons.' The memo outlined in detail Applegate's objections to the way McDonnell Douglas was handling the cargo door safety problem. Applegate was worried that the 'progressive degradation of the fundamental safety of the cargo door latch system since 1968 has exposed us to increasing liability claims'. On the American Airlines mishap over Windsor, he noted that it was 'only chance that the airplane was not lost'. As for Douglas's proposed remedy, Applegate was not convinced that even if implemented it would ensure the safety of the airplane. 'Douglas has again studied alternative corrective action', he wrote, 'and appears to be applying more "band-aids".' Applegate also criticized Douglas for the design of its cabin floor, which he described as a 'fundamental deficiency'. In commenting on the Long Beach test incident, Applegate observed that the DC-10 'demonstrated an inherent susceptibility to catastrophic failure when exposed to explosive decompression of the cargo compartment'. He concluded his memo with a prophetic warning and a recommendation: 'It seems to me inevitable', he wrote, 'that in the twenty years ahead of us, DC-10 cargo doors will come open and I would expect this to usually result in the loss of an airplane. It is recommended that overtures be made at the highest management level to persuade Douglas to immediately make a decision to incorporate changes in the DC-10 which will correct the fundamental cabin floor catastrophic failure mode.' (Mokhiber, 1988: 168),

F.D. 'Dan' Applegate passed on his memorandum to his boss, J.B. Hurt, who appended to the note the comment, 'we have an interesting moral and legal problem here' (and concluded that Convair 'should not risk an approach to Douglas': *Harvard Business School*, Case 9-383-128, 1984: 7; this case draws on evidence given by Hurt of Convair in *Hope* v. *McDonnell Douglas et al.*; Civ. No. 17631, Federal District Court, Los Angeles, California).

Thus the memorandum never reached McDonnell Douglas or the FAA. Convair/General Dynamics, as a sub-contractor, was forbidden to deal directly with the FAA. A signal had been made to McDonnell Douglas by a draft FMEA ('Failure Mode and Effects Analysis') from General Dynamics which included nine hazards that might involve danger to life. One of the nine was door failure and floor collapse in flight.

Turkish Airlines Enter the Market

The modification which McDonnell Douglas made might have been sufficient except for two aspects. One was the nature of the carrier, Turkish Airlines; and the other was the modification itself. McDonnell Douglas was engaged in a desperate battle to sell aeroplanes and had begun to look beyond its traditional purchasers to new markets. In fact the company had several planes

suddenly awaiting purchasers due to a rejection of a provisional order by All
Nippon Airlines. During the aggressive sales campaign across the globe,
known as 'Friendship '72', Turkish Airlines emerged as a likely candidate. It
would be the first carrier outside of North America using the DC-10 on
intercontinental services, and it was almost a matter of national pride that
Turkey would have its national airline flying wide-bodied planes.

But Turkish Airlines was also in a hurry. It wanted the two planes in service rapidly for the stream of pilgrims wishing to be transported to Mecca. In
fact, the McDonnell Douglas instructors were themselves rather concerned
about the short training period and level of technical sophistication of the
Turkish personnel. Flying crews were recruited from ex-pilots of the Turkish
Air Force whose experience was mainly on single-motor, one-pilot, jet fighter
planes. It took some adjustment for them to fit into the civilian team-work of
a commercial multi-jet airliner, where they were no longer captain of their
own plane and where they were expected to conduct (for them) somewhat
menial duties. In particular, there was a shortage of adequately trained flight
engineers. Some extreme errors were observed during the flying instruction. It
was with this background, then, that Turkish Airlines took to the air with its
new DC-10s.

On Sunday, 3 March 1974, flight THY 981 took off from Orly Airport.
There had been a Rugby international in Paris that weekend and many British
supporters were anxious to get home as industrial action had grounded most
planes to London. The Turkish Airlines DC-10 was fully loaded. On its climb
the rear cargo door broke free of the plane and the craft went into a dive. It
crashed into woods in Ermenonville just outside Paris and all on board were
killed instantly. The 'black-box' flight-recorder reproduced the last words of
the crew as they struggled to control the plane as it hurtled towards the
ground. Captain Lannier of the Gendarme reported that not one body was
left intact:

> Although a few heads were still attached to chests, a great many bodies were limb-
> less, bellies were ripped open, and their contents emptied. Everywhere, the scene
> was nightmarish; the Forest of Ermenonville had been turned into a battlefield, it
> was Verdun after the bloodiest battle. (Eddy et al., 1976: 104)

All fatal accidents are gruesome, and here a chain of circumstances had led
to a major catastrophe (this was at the time the worst commercial aircraft disaster in history). Unfortunately, one link in that chain was the fact that the
modification to the Turkish Airlines plane had not been carried out, although
records indicated that it had been made to this particular plane. McDonnell
Douglas issued a news release which stated that 'preliminary evidence indicates the plane's rear cargo door did not incorporate all the approved
changes' (McDonnell Douglas Press Release, 1974). The discrepancy between
the records and the failure to modify the door was never properly clarified
although it was probably related to the complexity of inspections procedures.
But in congressional hearings the company was criticized for its slow response
in implementing the modifications, while the FAA also came under fire for its

easing of certification requirements which may have communicated a lack of urgency to the industry (Oversight Hearings on the DC-10 Aircraft, 1974).

Liability

In the aftermath of the accident, McDonnell Douglas maintained that the DC-10 was as 'safe as any plane flying' and countered press statements by dubbing them 'irresponsible and malicious' (McDonnell Douglas Press Release, 1974). Liability would be a crucial issue for the courts as the relatives of the victims would seek compensation through legal proceedings. As no criminal proceedings arose from the crash the action would take place in the civil courts.

However, civil cases do not continue until the 'truth' has emerged but seek to define liability in a case between parties who can settle before a definitive cause is arrived at. In such cases the insurers, often led by Lloyd's of London, direct the lawsuit on behalf of the company. A contest ensues between the insurance lawyers, whose aim is to agree to the best moment for the company to pay out compensation, and the plaintiff lawyers for the victims' relatives, whose goal is to hang on as long as possible for the highest settlement. Both sides are usually prepared to make a deal at the appropriate moment; the company may wish to rid itself of negative publicity and the relatives may desire financial support (and an end to the emotional strain of continued proceedings related to the deaths of their dear ones). This means that cases can be terminated before a conclusion has been reached and before the matter is fully researched. Even so cases can drag on for years.

In product liability cases involving an American company in a foreign country the first move of relatives is to get the case heard in the USA, where lawyers will represent you for contingency fees (on a 'no cure, no pay' basis), where the media are generally open and critical, and where juries and courts award the highest damages in the world. The company's first move, in contrast, will be to try and avoid litigation in the USA; if that fails, then the lawyers for the insurers will make a swift opening offer in the hope that people will want to settle quickly, and with the added implication that not to do so will initiate a protracted hassle about the amount of the award. The children of an English couple killed in the accident were eventually awarded $1.5 million, which was over five times the initial offer (and which led Lloyd's to complain about 'money-grubbing'!).

The proceedings were complex and involved three companies – General Dynamics, Turkish Airlines, and McDonnell Douglas, as well as the FAA – who were subject to a detailed pre-trial investigation (Brizendine, the CEO of McDonnell Douglas, gave evidence for eleven days and submitted over 1,500 pages of information). The defendants decided not to contest liability (which is not the same as *admitting* liability). One of the lawyers for the relatives was able to quote documents that had not been made public and this forced the defendants to implicate one another in response and to issue mutual denials. The three companies began to sue one another on various grounds.

Eventually, McDonnell Douglas and Convair settled over 300 lawsuits out of court and paid damages estimated to be in the region of $80 million (*Wall Street Journal*, 30 November 1977). Modifications cost McDonnell Douglas another $40 million (*Harvard Business School*, Case 9-383-128, 1984: 10).

But the real answers to the deeper underlying issues were covered over when the cases were settled out of court; they might only have emerged with a public inquiry. Despite the highly professional delving of the *Sunday Times* journalists, the full story will never be wholly revealed; and this is true of many civil cases that end prematurely in a settlement and that do not have to be resolved by pursuing the issue of guilt as in a criminal court.

Comment

The Industry   Although some aeroplanes have better or poorer safety records than others, no manufacturer in his or her right mind would willingly and knowingly produce an unsafe plane. Accidents lead to intense negative publicity, recriminations between the parties involved (including business partners), financially damaging lawsuits, and the possibility of expensive modifications. And yet the DC-10 – a 'great' aeroplane (according to many pilots), made by experienced and expert engineers from a top company – was brought on the market with a design fault. Now it may well be that it is in the nature of the industry that many new planes exhibit teething problems during early service and that this typically involves the 'ironing out of a few bugs'. But in this case there were advance indications of a flaw which was not adequately remedied. How can this be explained?

The DC-10 case has to be centrally located in the high-risk, intense pressure of commercial airliner manufacturing. Three companies were competing in a *race* where they had to commit themselves up to, and almost beyond their necks, in an effort where failure would be devastating. Development costs were enormous, the market for wide-bodied planes was uncertain, and break-even points were hard to predict. McDonnell Douglas, once committed to the challenge, was forced to make an almost superhuman effort if it was to overtake Lockheed with its Tristar. *Pressure and speed* led to questionable decisions on quality and safety.

The ferocious competition between the manufacturers made it a buyer's market, and carriers could not only bargain on price but also on modifications tailored to their needs. American Airlines placed an order for twenty-five DC-10s, which gave McDonnell Douglas an initial boost in the contest, as there had been little to choose between the DC-10 and L-1011, but also made the company amenable to American's preference for an electrically controlled closing mechanism for the cargo door. Convair engineers balked at this but were overruled by the lead manufacturer. Some engineers at Convair were plainly unhappy at this choice and also had misgivings about fundamental issues of safety related to the doors and floor. These concerns were explicitly expressed in the 'Applegate Memorandum' which predicted crashes. But the memorandum itself did not reach McDonnell

Douglas. The company was also legally bound not to communicate directly with the FAA.

Regulation and Control   This legal stumbling-block seems to have been reinforced by political interference and internal dissension. Later, the FAA was severely criticized at congressional hearings, and it had patently become much too deferential to the interests of the industry it was meant to regulate. The NTSB was weakened so that its recommendations had little impact; the industry had clout with the head of the FAA and could lobby successfully for an AD (with the force of federal law) to be shelved in favour of a 'gentlemen's agreement' which reduced the urgency for the modification required (it took eleven months before certain planes were modified: 'Oversight Hearings on the DC-10 Aircraft', 1974). The lack of independence of the FAA, and its bowing to industry pressure on certification, was, then, undoubtedly a further contributory link in the chain of circumstances. Internal supervision of control was also lax at the production level. The FAA delegated its responsibility for inspection to a large extent to the company itself. Whatever the reason, control and supervision failed in this instance and the modification was not made to Ship 29 that was sold to Turkish Airlines (as McDonnell Douglas explained in its Press Release of March 1974).

The Carrier and the Courts   Although wide-bodied jets are now successfully in service throughout the world, at the time there was debate on the ethical question as to whether, in its world-wide sales push, McDonnell Douglas should have sold a sophisticated jet to a carrier like Turkish Airlines, which was then perhaps held to be less technically proficient than many major carriers. Misgivings on this score are certainly strengthened by the shortness of the training programme and the observed weaknesses in the competency of aircrew. Coming from Air Force backgrounds, they were used to flying as pilots in their own plane and had difficulty in fitting in to subordinate roles such as flight engineer. This may have led to a certain disdain for making routine checks. Quality of personnel and training may, then, have played a further contributing role. But Turkish Airlines was also in a hurry. Their haste added to the pressure to get Ship 29 into service as soon as possible, partly for the expected high season of pilgrims and partly as a matter of national prestige.

Plane crashes represent a gruesome human tragedy of torn bodies and lost lives. There follows the painful task of identifying the remains, of claiming insurance, and of relatives considering compensation for those lost in the accident. To a large extent they have to rely on lawyers who are playing a tough game of extracting the maximum concession from equally determined lawyers acting on behalf of the insurers (and the former may hold out for larger claims to increase their own return on a considerable investment in protracted proceedings), and on the courts. But cases can drag on for many years. And they may end when settlement is reached rather than when a full disclosure of cause and liability has been made.

For those concerned with learning the whole truth of the affair, the civil courts were not the place to look. The legal system – in the eyes of a pained relative deeply wounded at the loss of a loved one – is also not an arena brimming with humanity as the worth of a life is calculated, is disputed, and is fought over in an almost unethically cold climate of calculated move and counter-move. There were questions in Congress and the House of Representatives, but probably a full Congressional Inquiry was needed to unearth the entire story. But perhaps the failure of the FAA, and the interference of the White House, were small fry in the light of Watergate, which soon came to overshadow Washington, DC.

The Company and the Failure of Communication   McDonnell Douglas was a company under intense pressure – the commercial rivalry to sell more planes than its competitor in order to reach break-even in a tough market, the haste to get in the air before Lockheed, and the make-or-break gamble of huge investment costs – and people were absorbed with achieving the goal. Indeed, the excellent and painstaking chroniclers of the DC-10 affair, the *Sunday Times* Insight Team, conclude that the root cause was a 'failure of communication'. In this high-pressure context the parties involved seemed to assume that someone else knew the whole story and was doing something about it (this was certainly the position at Convair where Applegate's boss, Hurt, stated in court that 'most of the statements made by Applegate were considered to be well known to Douglas': Eddy et al., 1976: 187; *Hope* v. *McDonnell Douglas*). But the fragmented nature of the communication network seemed to absolve anyone from putting the entire picture together and from bearing ultimate responsibility.

The structure, the culture, and the nature of the work in the competitive and sub-divided plane manufacturing industry meant that there were multiple agencies communicating piecemeal and ineffectively. And this 'conspiracy' of non-communication is perhaps more to blame than a highly conscious and articulated conspiracy of any one party in the affair. And the company went on to modify the plane and to turn it into a successful and widely used airliner. Unfortunately, good engineers produced a 'great' plane, but one marred by a design fault; and a 'failure of communication' cost 346 lives. This case, then, raises complex issues related to product development and product liability, to safety and risk, to regulation and control, to compensation and the courts, and to industry culture.

Case No. 4: Revco, Medicaid, and the State of Ohio

Fraud and abuse of government benefit programmes are widespread in the United States and raise the issue of *organizations 'victimizing' other organizations*. With regard to welfare fraud, for instance, the major emphasis in a number of countries lies with investigating individual recipients who aim to defraud the authorities: but when another *organization* sets out to do so, then this often raises not only complex legal issues but particularly the question of resources within the control agencies adequate to the task of investigation, detection, and prosecution of a large company. Revco, which defrauded the State of Ohio, was a Fortune 500 corporation with 825 stores in twenty-one states and 159 pharmacies in Ohio alone; pitted against it was the state welfare department – hardly, one would think, a repository of investigatory zeal and legal acumen. Central to this case is the manner in which a number of state institutions responded collectively to combating unlawful behaviour in a major business organization.

Also of relevance is the extent to which companies perceive the state (central and/or local) to be a justifiable target for abuse; this rationale is strongly present in Defence Procurement fraud, in overbilling in nursing homes, and in billing fraud by physicians in Medicaid and Medicare fraud (Braithwaite, 1993; Geis et al., 1988). Gradually, as well, we can begin to unravel through the cases the underlying logic of the business and managerial mentality. We have seen the pressure to falsify results in a lab, the attempt to steer the market illegally, and the apparent 'irrationality' of bringing a dangerous product on to the market. This helps to build up a picture of the social, structural, and psychological mechanisms that underlie the managerial choice to select a deviant alternative. For instance, an anonymous reviewer of this book, who clearly has had business experience, wrote: 'Ironically, I felt (having dealt with bureaucratic purchasers) considerable sympathy with the deviants at Revco who were seeking to get what was owed to them (by inappropriate means).' In going through the cases, then, it is important to build a cumulative view of why organizations and managers violate the law and why regulation is often restricted in its response.

Revco retrieves lost revenue

In 1977 Revco was found guilty of defrauding the State of Ohio of over half a million dollars. The fraud was uncovered by chance when a claims analyst in the state welfare department was checking computer print-outs of Medicaid prescriptions for a Revco store. (Medicaid is a scheme for providing medical benefits for people with low incomes and it is administered by the state.) The analyst spotted an irregularity in the sequence of numbers used for prescriptions, and, on further scrutiny, came to the conclusion that the last three numbers of certain prescriptions were being transposed. This occurred in a particular fashion. A prescription was recorded as a claim, and within a couple of days the same prescription turned up again but this time with the last three numbers altered. Revco Drug Stores, Inc., one of America's largest discount drug chains, had been systematically using a computerised double-billing scheme to defraud the Ohio Department of Public Welfare.

The sequence of events leading to this situation began in 1975 when Revco moved corporate headquarters to Cleveland, Ohio. During the reorganization that followed, a number of boxes of Medicaid claims came to light. These were old claims that had been submitted to the Ohio Department of Public Welfare for processing and reimbursing but which had been rejected by the department's computer on grounds of error. Normally these claims would have been resubmitted, and payment was routinely delayed until the corrected claim had been accepted, but these rejected claims had not been examined and reworked. They had simply accumulated in boxes. Revco pharmacists had handed out prescriptions to Medicaid recipients and, of the resulting claims, some 50,000 had failed the screening by computer. The sum involved in outstanding accounts was more than half a million dollars.

Two managers of the company became aware of these arrears and set about rectifying the situation. Rather than establishing a time-consuming and costly procedure to correct the errors for legitimate resubmission, which was feasible but expensive, they decided to hire six clerical people whose task was to rework the rejected claims so that they would pass screening by the computer at the welfare department. Both executives (one a vice-president) had experience, one in computers and the other in pharmacy, which led them to believe that the project could be completed with a low risk of detection. The clerical workers simply rewrote the claims instead of correcting them but with dates and the last three numbers changed (and using successful claims as their models). The plan was devised to accumulate for the company roughly the amount of money owing to it and, when after some twenty months, this had been accomplished, the temporary unit was disbanded. There was no attempt to garner more money than was outstanding to Revco and the managers did not endeavour to enrich themselves in any way from the fraud.

The Agencies and the Investigation

In the investigation that emerged from the analyst's accidentally stumbling on irregularities, there were four agencies involved: the Department of Public Welfare, the State Pharmacy Board, the State Highway Patrol, and the Economic Crime Unit of the Franklin County Prosecutor's Office. Their inquiries demanded considerable secrecy, and over a period of a year they uncovered evidence that, indeed, false prescriptions were emanating from Revco's corporate headquarters, that these were forwarded as Medicaid claims, and that the state had paid Revco for them: 'the evidence was confirmed by the seizure of original prescriptions in a simultaneous execution of search warrants in five Revco pharmacies around the state' (p. 77; page numbers refer to Vaughan, 1980). When the case came to court, both the company and the executives pleaded 'no contest'. Revco was fined the maximum $5,000 for falsification on ten counts and the two executives $1,000 on each of two counts. The company made full restitution to the welfare department, while the two managers 'accepted total responsibility for the falsified claims, stating that their actions had been without the knowledge of any other persons employed by Revco' (p. 79).

Revco as 'Victim'

In effect, two executives of a company had deliberately and systematically set out to falsify documents. But the corporation refused to admit to *criminal* behaviour; moreover, it publicly and forcefully took up the role of *victim*. Revco was able to compile a frustrating history of relations with the state's Medicaid programme. From 1971 onwards there had been difficulties in terms of back-logs of claims, poor communication, and state budgetary problems ('mailings were not made because the state lacked the necessary funds for postage', p. 80); a new computer billing system only exasperated problems and there were further back-logs and delayed payments due to occasional system failure. The welfare department acknowledged these persistent difficulties with computer screening leading to rejections, and 'required major providers to install a presubmission edit system of their own to screen claims before sending them on for reimbursement' (p. 80). Revco did install such a system but it turned out to be much poorer at detecting errors than systems at other providers (on average around a quarter of Revco's claims were rejected and the range ran from 5 to 50 per cent). The department blamed Revco, as their recommendations were not implemented by the company. Vaughan speculates that 'cost and complexity' may have hindered Revco from carrying out improvements (p. 81).

For there is no doubt that the maintenance of a trustworthy presubmission screening programme is quite costly, largely because the information required by the welfare department is highly complex and constantly changing. Given this background, Revco officials engaged in a reasoning that placed the blame squarely with the welfare department. The executives involved in the case saw the pile-up of rejected claims as evidence of one more bungle landed on them by the welfare department, leading to non-payment of claims; it was virtually impossible to correct the claims without incurring undue costs; so to tidy up a 'business problem' the rejected claims were reworked 'to expedite the money the state owed us' (p. 81). In fact, during the subsequent investigation it emerged that claims rejected by Revco's own computer screening system were routinely 'doctored' to make them acceptable.

But what no one seemed to think of was that the falsification was a crime. However, there can be no doubt that the corporation broke the law. In this case two *organizations* are involved and *both* define themselves as victims. But Revco did not cooperate with the research, and Vaughan adds, 'Admittedly, how much of Revco's insistence on their own victimization is rationalization, how much is "real", and how much legal defence is open to speculation' (p. 82). Of course there are significant differences between victim–offender interaction at the micro level, as in street crime, and at the macro level, as in the case of organizations. Here the offences were *longitudinal* and spread over *multiple locations*: they had low visibility, being buried in a mass of data compiled largely by the two organizations' computer systems; and they were conducted within one temporary unit of the parent organization, and ostensibly without the knowledge of most people in the company. It may seem inconceivable that half a million dollars in arrears could go unnoticed, or that temporary personnel employed for fifteen months could continue work and then suddenly disappear without conveying any signal about their task to others, but Revco officials persistently denied any knowledge of the falsification 'factory'. As Vaughan comments, 'delegation of responsibility for decision-making within the organizational structure makes responsibility for decision making difficult to determine and this handicaps interpretation of victim–offender interaction' (p. 84).

Crime between Organizations

Are there, in fact, structural features which lead to crime between organizations? Vaughan identifies three – organizational characteristics, environmental conditions, and supporting ideology – and interaction among these features can foster a situation 'in which organizations can be understood as victimogenic: susceptible to being victimized by crime' (p. 85). First, the large size, considerable wealth, and impersonality of big organizations may encourage deviance against them. Internal structures sponsoring a high hierarchical division of labour can easily create sub-units with considerable autonomy that pose problems of control (perhaps amplified by geographic dispersion). Technology created opportunities for crime in this case and control procedures proved ineffective: 'though the welfare department had a highly sophisticated system, the fraud (over a period of 21 months) went undetected by the computer. Only when the data were painstakingly analyzed by human eyes was the fraud discovered' (p. 87). Diffusion of responsibility throughout the organization can also obscure where decisions are actually taken. In brief, then, Vaughan concludes:

> Generally, it would seem that as organizations have increased in complexity, more opportunities for crime have been generated. Increased size, impersonality, wealth, geographic dispersion, product diversification, division of labour, hierarchical authority systems, specialization, and complex technologies are all organizational attributes that facilitate crime between organizations. (p. 87)

Second, the economic environment in which business operates emphasizes free competition and profit maximization. In practice, however, the latter tends to dominate, as organizational prestige, clout, and ranking are highly dependent on increased profit. Company norms may come to emphasize results over honesty; or, as Shover puts it, 'many times organizations become so preoccupied with the achievement of goals that they virtually give their employees – or demand – carte blanche power to use "innovative" procedures to assure those goals are attained' (1976: 15).

Revco is a Fortune 500 company and, furthermore, Conklin (1977: 45) has remarked on the particularly strong profit emphasis in the pharmaceutical industry. In this case it was matched against a government agency; such agencies tend to be held in low esteem and often carry a negative stereotype of inefficiency and incompetence. Not only were they unequal adversaries but, furthermore, Vaughan maintains that

> the interaction between profit and the drive for public reputation was clear in the Revco case. The 50,000 rejected claims represented outstanding accounts receivable, which cut corporate profits. The false billings were an attempt to bring accounts receivable back in to balance, thus presenting an improved image of the

corporation on paper. The act itself was supported by internal norms that rewarded profitability. The concern with profits and social standing was displayed throughout the case in corporate requests for minimal publicity and speedy settlement. (p. 91)

In brief, Vaughan argues that certain environmental factors foster crime between organizations, such as a discrepancy between free competition and profit maximization, a reputational ranking system based on wealth, and a value system that stimulates and rewards profit maximization, and, often, a perception of a low risk of detection and sanctioning.

Third, collective definitions may exist in societies which focus on specific organizations as 'legitimate targets'. The media exposure of a series of business scandals 'may be generating a collective definition of large organizations as exploitative' (p. 92), particularly where severe economic or physical repercussions are a result of their deviance. The argument is that large organizations have often been seen as inefficient and/or unresponding and, if they are then further labelled as 'criminal', that may lead to a '"rip-off mentality" among certain members of the American public' (Conklin, 1977; p. 92). In addition, it is not only individuals but perhaps also organizations that begin to use – and *feel justified* in using – illegitimate means to achieve ends that elude them by legitimate means. Revco clearly felt that the welfare department was withholding payment due to the company; legitimate means were dismissed in favour of illegitimate ones (the former would have cancelled out the pharmacy's profit-making concern), and there was a firm conviction that the company was justified in utilizing the organization's resources to redress a balance caused by the department's sloth and inefficiency. The Revco managers could adopt their 'innovative' solution not only because they perceived the welfare department as exhibiting weaknesses that made it exploitable but also because they had constructed for themselves a legitimating ideology. That made their fraudulent falsification both an instrumental and justifiable response to rectifying a 'business problem'.

Inter-agency Cooperation

Finally, the Revco case is particularly interesting because of the light it sheds on the establishment and functioning of a 'social control network'. There were not only multiple victims but also multiple control agencies and this had consequences for the conduct of the investigation and sanctioning. There were five agencies involved in what Vaughan calls the 'primary' network. They were:

- Ohio Department of Public Welfare: Bureau of Surveillance and Utilization Review (SUR);
- Division of Data Services (part of the welfare department but treated by Vaughan as separate);
- Ohio State Board of Pharmacy;
- Ohio State Highway Patrol;
- Economic Crime Unit (ECU) of Franklin County Prosecution Office.

Local police were minimally concerned, but 'peripheral' were two powerful and potentially competing agencies, the Office of the State Auditor and the Office of the State Attorney General.

In response to the discovery of falsification and possible fraud, a spontaneous and *ad hoc* control network developed in order to pool resources and expertise in the interests of tackling a complex investigative case. This required planning and coordination – for example, the issuing of search warrants for five locations in four counties was not only unprecedented in the state but also demanded expert execution – while secrecy was imperative; a leak during the more than a year-long investigation would have tipped off Revco and doubtless brought about the destruction of evidence. An over-inquisitive journalist was effectively muzzled by promising him an exclusive on the forthcoming raids of the pharmacies. The four main agencies involved all had possibilities of sanctioning Revco. For example, the welfare department had the authority to disenfranchise Revco as a Medicaid provider, but this was rejected on the grounds that it would also spell hardship and inconvenience for some Medicaid recipients (who would then be further victimized). The Economic Crime Unit, which was the prosecuting authority in the case, had in mind the wider public interests and was careful to minimize the economic impact on the stock market and also for Revco stockholders. Press releases were tightly controlled, the case was conducted with dispatch, and a negotiated plea was accepted to avoid a trial. Although other agencies were involved – such as the State Highway Patrol and the State Pharmacy Board, which might have taken a tougher line – the compromises made by the prosecuting authority were a result of taking the divergent interests of various segments of the public into account. As a result, the sanctions were mild and, one could argue, the potential deterrent impact was diminished.

In effect, Vaughan's work also represents five separate cases of control agencies, rather than simply a case of Revco's deviance, and it sheds light on the compromises that emerge from inter-agency cooperation and crucially, from *inter-agency competition*. In retrospect, there were critical voices raised about the anaemic sanctioning and also about some of the parties getting insufficient public acclaim for their efforts. Why, then, was the prosecution handled so swiftly and so softly?

First, Revco had strong economic and legal reasons for a speedy solution (the value of its shares had suffered on the stock market and it was concerned about a civil suit from the Attorney General's Office) and instantly cooperated in full with the judicial investigation. Second, the Economic Crime Unit faced a complex legal case, a long and costly trial, a formidable opponent, and – in an election year where a public success would be extremely valuable – the fear that the State Attorney General's Office might move in and 'poach' their case. In negotiations between Revco's legal counsel and the county prosecutors, a mutually beneficial deal was hammered out. There would be no trial; the procedure would function via a 'bill of information' that avoided indictment, and a negotiated plea before the county court; Revco and the managers would plead 'no contest' to the misdemeanour of falsification (rather than to the felony of deception); and prison sentences would not be considered for the two managers. This lighter offence actually brought in higher fines for the county than by a felony, but a vital element in the negotiations was *restitution* (which the court could only order under a felony). But by pressurizing Revco with the veiled threat of recourse to a felony charge, the ECU was able to extract full restitution to the welfare department. Although the fines and restitution were the largest in the state's history, they formed a pittance for the company (the fines were less than .001 per cent of gross profits).

Some other control agents believed that the ECU had given the case away; the Pharmacy Board could have revoked Revco's licence for Ohio, the welfare department could have terminated Revco as a provider, and the State Highway Patrol (a more traditional policing agency) could have taken a tougher stance on prosecution. Yet complex social, political, and economic considerations fostered a rapid settlement and a compromise on sanctions. Revco's economic position recovered quickly, and the company fully cooperated with the welfare department in implementing the new screening procedures forced upon the company. Vaughan concludes:

> Thus, although official sanctions appeared to have no long-term effect on the corporation, the origin of the problem was corrected, and monitoring equipment was in place to guard against a reoccurrence. The investigation led to a remedy for the specific problem that generated the unlawful behaviour and close surveillance was initiated as a preventive mechanism. (1983: 53)

Comment

The Suspect – and Who is the Victim?   On a spectrum of 'clean–dirty', the Revco case can be placed at the clean end. No one physically suffered, no blows were exchanged, and the offence was neatly contained within the data of the computer exchanges between two organizations; full restitution was accomplished; and justice was seen to be done (albeit considerably 'underdone' according to some control agents concerned). The case is interesting at several levels. For instance, it involved an offence between two organizations which raised not only intricate legal issues but also the prospect of *both* parties choosing the role of victim. Computer technology, furthermore, was essential to the crime committed. But, above all, the Revco case highlights the dilemmas for control agencies in taking on a corporation and how that interaction sponsors, via intricate negotiations, a settlement that some see as a feeble compromise.

Revco was an ideal 'suspect' offering full cooperation in the judicial investigation and in the post-investigation structural adjustments. Although the raids, the questioning, and the publicity appear to have shocked Revco, the 'paper trail' led to an autonomous and temporary unit, to two highly respected and competent managers working in the 'interests' of the company, and to an offence in which no one tried to line their own pockets and in which the company merely set out to retrieve what was due to it. In short, the offence could be readily located and easily 'exorcised' without contaminating the moral reputation of the company. That the two managers steadfastly asserted that no one else was involved, or had knowledge of their activities, is crucial here, and it may be that they were resolutely protecting colleagues and/or the company. One of them was given a lateral transfer within the company and the other, the vice-president, left Revco to become the vice-president of a company in the same field.

The Social Control Network Of considerable importance is the analysis that Vaughan makes of the complexities of setting up a social control network involving multiple agencies with separate jurisdictions and powers, different cultures and working styles, and each with their own social and political domains. She argues that 'organizational misconduct appears to be a natural accompaniment to the complexity of business organizations and their interactions with other organizations' (1983: 107); that the transaction systems of organizations, which rely increasingly on the electronic transfer of data, create surveillance problems for both companies and control agents (both are potential victims of computer fraud); and that the law may frequently form 'a clumsy tool for penetrating organizational boundaries' (1983: 94).

In this case several agencies, with a couple more competing agencies breathing down their necks, exhibited a commendable degree of cooperation and coordination. The settlement may appear lenient to outsiders, and almost suspiciously favourable to the corporation, but it was considered a highly commendable result by many of those directly involved. However, the outcome was not satisfactory to all concerned, but rather it illustrates the bargaining which leads to a mutually acceptable deal. As lack of communication, and even conflict, can typify the relations between control agencies (with exaggerated claims designed to protect their own 'turf' and reputation), it may be that this temporary liaison was unusual and atypical. But it does indicate what is needed to investigate and prosecute successfully a complex fraud committed by a corporation. And the case did lead to the setting up of a new, federally funded, state Medicaid Fraud Control Unit which helped to put surveillance in this area on a more permanent basis.

The Blurring of Moral and Legal Boundaries One of the many unanswered questions, given Revco's refusal to cooperate with Vaughan's research, is why the two experienced managers employed such an unsophisticated and traceable device for doctoring the rejected claims. Perhaps they simply held the welfare department in such low esteem that they did not believe a more sophisticated scheme, greatly reducing the already low risk of detection, was necessary. And why did they not put the temporary unit to work in a legitimate fashion to recover the money? It can only be speculation, but maybe they chose a deviant solution because that half-million dollars disturbed their managerial sensitivities; it just was not right, and this made it justifiable to con the welfare department. They were killing two birds with one stone. And as Vaughan puts it, 'in the business world the lines between a good business deal and illegality often do become blurred' (1983: 61).

Vaughan's analysis is, then, important and valuable at a number of levels. She alerts us to the structural changes in modern organizations; draws attention to the role of technology as a means of committing organizational crime; and reveals how complicated it is to mount a successful social control network to prosecute a major corporation. Perhaps three more elements can be teased from her case. First, the company's response is clearly one of 'damage limitation'. Revco cooperated with the authorities, plea-bargained a 'no contest' in court which does not involve an admission of guilt, and offered full restitution. Perhaps Revco did not want to lose the contract with the state; but probably more importantly it was the loss of reputation which a pharmaceutical company would suffer if it was seen to be fiddling in the sensitive area of Medicaid where health and the needy are combined. Second, the regulators had a problem in sanctioning Revco. To come down heavily on a provider of health care would also effectively sanction the recipients of that case. What would be a sanction that would hurt the company and not rebound on others (Wells, 1994: Fisse and Braithwaite, 1993)? This is clearly an important matter because it is not easy to find effective sanctions for an organization. Third, and lastly, the Revco case sheds interesting light on the mentality and morality of managers. The two managers faced a 'technical' problem and tackled it in an instrumental way. They doubtless congratulated themselves on doing a good job. It is precisely the underlying logic of business, of the executive mind, that seems to lead to blurred vision on violating the law. The law is a hurdle. Like other business problems it is approached as a challenge to be surmounted. The fact that this is illegal gets shunted aside as an inconvenience in getting the job done.

Case No. 5: Nuclear Accident at Three Mile Island

> You can't think of everything, Carl. You've got to have a little faith in the machine.
>
> (Supervisor in nuclear industry to critical systems analyst:
> Gray and Rosen, 1982)

The Organization as Unintended Offender

We create organizations, and develop advanced technology, and pretend that we can control both. In the 'abstract society' (Zijderveld, 1970), the rationality of large-scale developments becomes taken for granted. But are the constructions we erect fully controllable and steerable? In some cases of industrial accidents there may be no criminal intent but, rather, a process of unconscious rule evasion sets in. The intricacy and complexity of the organization may make it difficult to control effectively and, on occasion, people can lose their grip on the organization. The out-of-control organization may then become an unintended offender in rule violation and causing harm.

For instance, there is no industry that has aroused such bitter and unbridgeable controversy as that of nuclear power. Two central issues dominate the sometimes vitriolic debate; the first concerns safety and the second relates to the disposal of radioactive waste. Although the latter is probably the more intractable problem of the two, it is safety that tends to arouse the most attention. Indeed, the accident at Chernobyl in April 1986 altered the consciousness of the world to the highly deleterious consequences of a nuclear disaster. The credibility of the industry, which in the west continually claimed it was safe, was undermined by the graphic pictures from the east of a severely damaged nuclear plant and the dramatic and dangerous emergency efforts designed to contain the danger. Ironically, the accident at Chernobyl marked the thirtieth anniversary of commercial production of nuclear energy (the earliest plant being Calder Hall in the UK, opened in 1956); an enterprise that had commenced so promisingly as safe and clean has run into operational problems (and into intense political and public opposition), and is floundering badly. In the USA, with 100 plants the world's leading nuclear nation, every proposed plant since 1973 has been cancelled or deferred, and not a single unit has been sold since 1978. The industry encountered a particularly debilitating setback as a result of the accident at Three Mile Island (Harrisburg, Pennsylvania) in 1979. How could an industry posited on the very highest norms of safety, and on seemingly irreproachable standards of performance, explain how things went wrong? What did go wrong, how can we explain it, and what were the consequences?

The Accident

'The most severe accident in US commercial nuclear power plant history' (Mokhiber, 1988: 419) occurred at the Three Mile Island Unit 2 plant at Harrisburg on 28 March 1979. It began in the cooling system. A primary cooling system circulates water through the core where the nuclear reaction is taking place. The water from this system is, in turn, cooled by the secondary system, and it was here that the incident commenced (the interaction of the two systems ensures that the core does not overheat and also produces steam for the turbines which generate electricity). Early in the morning of Wednesday, 28 March, the turbine stopped. A leaky seal had probably allowed moisture to enter the instrument air system of the plant and two valves on feedwater pumps were automatically stopped although, in fact, nothing was wrong. When the flow of water is interrupted the turbine automatically 'trips' (stops). Now, however, emergency feedwater pumps have to come into operation in order to remove the heat from the core. Unfortunately, two pipes involved were blocked, because valves had been accidentally left in a closed position following maintenance some days earlier, and the emergency water was being pumped into closed pipes. But the operators were unaware that the valves were closed and not open. The control switch indicating this was obscured.

Without water in the secondary system, the steam generator boiled dry. As no heat was being removed from the core, the reactor 'scrammed', which means that rods dropped into the core to stop the chain reaction. But the system still produces some heat, which normally would be gradually cooled by the two cooling systems. These, however, were not functioning.

There is an additional safety device to deal with this difficulty called the 'pilot operated relief valve' (PORV), which is intended 'to relieve the pressure in the core by channelling the water from the core through a big vessel called a pressurizer, and out of the top of it into a drain pipe, and down into a sump' (Perrow, 1984: 20). This relief valve failed to reseat after releasing the initial pressure and 32,000 gallons of the radioactive primary coolant poured out. The operators assumed that the controls indicated correctly that the valve had shut down whereas this was not the case; within a few seconds they had encountered

> a false signal causing the condensate pumps to fail, two valves for emergency cooling out of position and the indicator obscured, a PORV that failed to reseat, and a failed indicator of this position. *The operators could have been aware of none of these.* (Perrow, 1984: 22; emphasis in original)

The PORV was open for two hours and twenty minutes, and the subsequent release of coolant caused the pressure in the reactor to drop. This is hazardous unless the temperature decreases rapidly. Yet another emergency system came in to operation, two reactor coolant pumps, but probably the water formed into steam bubbles. The temperature began to rise but, since the core was losing water, pressure in the coolant system declined precipitously. At this stage yet another emergency device was triggered; namely, 'HPI', or high-pressure injection which forces water into the core at a high rate.

> Now came the high drama, the action that has been called the major source of the accident and the key operator error. After letting HPI run for full tilt for about two minutes, they reduced it drastically, thus not replacing the water that was boiling out through the PORV. This meant that the core was steadily being uncovered – the most fearful danger in a nuclear plant, for it will then melt the vessel and perhaps loose radiation on the world. (Perrow, 1984: 23)

Crisis and Confusion

At this point two crucial dials began to display strange discrepancies. Under normal circumstances they should move together, but one showed that pressure in the reactor was falling while the other indicated that pressure in the 'pressurizer' was rising. Gradually, the operators were beginning to distrust their instruments – and as ex-navy men their training was always geared to believing firmly in the instruments – and were becoming increasingly aware of anomalies between their actions and the readings on the dials. But they were following procedures aimed both to protect the core and to avoid a 'LOCA' (loss of coolant accident, usually via a pipe break). What they could not know was that they were already encountering a LOCA and that their actions were making it *worse*.

Under these circumstances, a number of possible indicators of LOCA were ignored (one indicator was situated at the rear of a 7-foot-high control panel which no one thought of checking). The reaction to the impending crisis was to assume that the core was not being uncovered because this had never occurred before; other anomalies were swiftly explained away (for instance, on the grounds of faulty instruments). But with escalating urgency fresh problems arose; the reactor coolant pumps began to vibrate violently and were turned off (this was also a warning message that they were not receiving enough emergency coolant).

Tension began to mount:

> In the control room there were three audible alarms sounding, and many of the 1,600 annunciator lights (little rectangles of plastic with some code numbers and letters on them) were on or blinking. The operators did not turn off the main audible alarm because it would cancel some of the annunciator lights. The computer was beginning to run far behind schedule; in fact it took some hours before its message that something might be wrong with the PORV finally got its chance to be printed. Radiation alarms were coming on. The control room was filling with experts; later in the day there were about forty people there. The phones were ringing constantly, demanding information the operators did not have. (Perrow, 1984: 28)

Almost by coincidence, and perhaps because of a new shift supervisor checking the PORV, the stuck valve was discovered. More as an act of desperation than understanding (according to testimony to the Kemeny Commission) the valve was shut:

> It was fortunate that it occurred when it did; incredible damage had been done, with substantial parts of the core melting, but had it remained open for another thirty minutes or so, and HPI remained throttled back, there would probably have been a complete meltdown, with the fissioning material threatening to breach containment. (Perrow, 1984: 29)

As one threat subsided, an additional danger emerged. An enormous potential hazard was the development of a 'hydrogen bubble' (following a chemical reaction when the 'liner' around the fuel rods overheats and reacts with water) which could lead to an explosion. Indeed, at 1 p.m. on that Wednesday afternoon, a 'soft but distinct bang' was audible to those in the control room and pressure in the containment building jumped rapidly. An operator claimed that they wrote it off as an instrument malfunctioning. Crucially, the containment building had held – at Chernobyl there was no containment building – and by 1 April the bubble began to be bled away. With a cold shut-down the crisis was over. But it had been a damned close-run thing.

The pertinent questions which arise in relation to Three Mile Island are as follows:

- What is the nature of the industry?
- Who regulates the nuclear power industry?
- How did people react in the face of this 'accident'?
- How did management respond to the crisis?
- And what have been the consequences of the drama?

The Industry

The nuclear power industry is concerned with massive initial investments – plants are multimillion dollar investments (Three Mile Island cost $700 million to build) – and with highly advanced technology. The plants are vast; the scale of everything is gargantuan (labyrinths of pipes, 400-ton boilers, 700-ton pressure vessels, enormous volumes of water, and the giant sculpture of massive buildings towering above the skyline). In a sense, the only way to test much of the technology is to try it in practice, so that there is a duality between the multiple layers of safety devices and an inability to predict precisely how plants will function in actuality. The industry is also perpetually immersed in political controversy, and siting, safety, and disposal are matters of prolonged and often bitter public debate. Furthermore, an industry which began so optimistically (its propaganda conveyed the image of a 'brilliant elite leading the world to a bountiful future': Patterson, 1987: 8) has been dogged by policy confusion, by negative publicity on leaks and on costs, and by multiple disappointments:

> The delays, cost-overruns and disappointing performance which beset the industry in the UK and the US, for instance, were in large measure a result of over-optimistic cost estimates, inadequate design work, late delivery of essential components, low productivity, labour disputes on site, and other failures of project management. (Patterson, 1987: 8)

To a large extent, then, we can perceive an industry that involves huge initial costs, that is vulnerable to political and public pressure, and that relies on an image of safety while its practice is littered with incidents that arouse concern about health and the environment. Doubtless this makes it something of a *defensive* enterprise – apt to believe its own propaganda and to denigrate its opponents. For management in individual plants this could readily mean that the pressures are to 'keep the show on the road' – with those huge costs in the back of one's mind (for construction, for operation, and, above all, for non-delivery of energy) – and to rationalize away the arguments of the opposition. It must be difficult to go to work every day if you believe that the plant is endangering your life, that of your children, of your community, and potentially of the global environment.

That pressure – to *keep things running* while ironing out the snags – may be part of the inherent dynamic and logic of industrial enterprises; but that dynamic can perhaps be enhanced in a profit-seeking venture. For, in the USA, nuclear energy is a *private* initiative. Babcock and Wilcox built the reactor, General Public Utilities ran Three Mile Island, and Metropolitan Edison owned it. In fact, the plant had been designed for a site in New Jersey, but, following an attempt at criminal extortion by gangsters operating under the mantle of a trade union, the site had been changed and ownership had been transferred to Metropolitan Edison (the entire design was rewritten in three months with the engineering people working at a 'killing pace' in order to obtain a new site approval from the NRC: Gray and Rosen, 1982: 21). The basic aim was to make a profit from the enterprise by selling energy. Non-availability of a reactor meant a bill for providing alternative energy of some $20,000 per hour. This must have played a role in the minds of the parties concerned, that delay also meant delay in the return on investment. It is possible – but difficult to verify – that a highly subsidized national industry, as in France, experiences the pressure to produce in a less intensive way. Indeed, the Soviets maintained that a socialist state was more likely to enforce stricter safety procedures than a capitalist one where reactors are run on a profit basis. The speciousness of this argument (a combination of ideology and rationalization for cost-cutting with cheaper, less safe plants) was rudely exposed at Chernobyl.

But the suggestion is that the private companies involved in nuclear energy in America have a strong vested interest in promoting their branch and in keeping plants 'on line' because of the underlying dynamic of the profit motive. Of course, safety is a pivotal issue and you would have to be crazy not to take it most seriously; and yet there comes a stage where the only way to test the system is to run it and to iron out the flaws as you go along: 'The system is thus quite new and has not been given a chance to reveal its full potential for danger. Unknown potential cannot be corrected, except by running the plant and taking the risks; without experience, we cannot be sure of the potential for damage inherent in the system's characteristics' (Perrow, 1984: 36).

The Regulators

To guarantee the public interest in relation to nuclear energy, Congress launched the Nuclear Regulatory Commission in 1975. The post-war agency responsible for this initially secretive and sinister area, which grew out of the war-time military involvement in the atomic bomb project, was the Atomic Energy Commission, which had the dual mission of both promoting *and* regulating the fledgling industry. The regulatory, supervisory side of the agency was later hived off to form the NRC. The NRC had the tough task of inspecting and licensing a complex, new technology (that promised cheap and safe energy – an appealing prospect in the aftermath of the 1973 oil crisis). On the one hand, the regulatory bureaucracy built up a vast array of regulations; yet, on the other hand, it did not want to stifle the brave new venture. At times, compromise was considered the most expedient policy.

One particularly critical inspector, Jim Creswell, went so far as to issue a citation for violation of the Nuclear Regulatory Code to the operators of a reactor in Minnesota. His superiors carpeted him.

> Cresswell was called in and reeducated by the senior inspectors. 'A citation is a big deal,' he was told. 'Some of them carry criminal penalties. You don't get cooperation by pounding on people with a baseball bat. This is not a war. We all want safety. And the way to get safety is cooperation, not confrontation. You tell them what you want, and if they don't change, then do something about it. But you've got to give them a chance to clean up their act before you start swinging a club.' Also these citations are a matter of public record. The press tend to exaggerate anything you don't understand. So the citation was quietly withdrawn. (Gray and Rosen, 1982: 49)

This incident reveals the dilemma of many regulatory agencies: that *compromise wins out over enforcement*. Yet, by licensing the reactors, the agency had become a partner in their functioning. Defects in a plant's design, construction, and operation could readily rebound on the competence and skills of the NRC itself. This 'softly, softly' approach emerged at the time of a series of mishaps at the Toledo-Edison Davis-Besse plant at Toledo, Ohio. The most serious was a near rehearsal of the Three Mile Island scenario. The operators of a Babcock and Wilcox reactor were faced with a drop in pressure, a rise in temperature, and the automatic injection of water (HPI). But they were tricked into thinking the system was filling with water, when it was actually emptying, and switched off HPI and cut off half of the emergency cooling pumps (although, in fact, the core was in danger of overheating, causing serious fuel damage). The NRC inspector sent to Toledo after the third incident was Jim Creswell.

The Warning

Creswell's investigations led to a serious concern about operators switching off emergency cooling before they were fully aware of what was going on. Faced with lack of cooperation from Babcock and Wilcox, and hostility from colleagues and superiors, he nevertheless managed to get out a directive to the control operators at Davis-Besse: 'Prior to securing HPI, insure that a leak does not exist in the pressurizer such as a safety valve or an electromagnetic relief valve (the trade-name for the PORV) stuck open' (Gray and Rosen, 1982: 54). This information was *never passed on* to the other seven Babcock and Wilcox units; partly because it was not considered important enough among the unceasing flow of paper surrounding regulation, and partly because it was considered a problem that was probably unique to Toledo.

But it was soon perceived within the NRC that Creswell's 'by-the-book' style represented 'a communication problem' with the industry because he continued to go on and on about the possibility of a reactor meltdown. This irritated both his superiors and representatives of the industry who were insisting on the safety factor and on the minutely low risk of an accident. Faced by this lack of understanding he decided, on the grounds that 'you can always find another job but you can't always find another conscience' (Gray and Rosen, 1982: 66), to take his warnings to the NRC headquarters in Washington. He did so on his day off, paid for his own ticket, and yet felt it worthwhile that he had got his message across to top officials of the NRC. This was 22 March 1979. (By coincidence, the film *The China Syndrome*, which depicted a near meltdown in a reactor plant, had been released on 16 March and had been universally decried by the industry – Dresser Industries had produced the PORV and it sponsored advertisements stating that Jane Fonda, who starred in the movie, was far more dangerous than nuclear plants! (Perrow, 1984: 20).)

Later, during the crisis at Three Mile Island, the NRC became exposed in a decidedly poor light. It proved to be slow, unresponsive, and indecisive. There were failures of communication (internally, but also with the plant, the corporation, and the media), of expertise (not all of its personnel were well equipped to deal with the issues of nuclear power), and, above all, of nerve. For the key to the NRC's reaction was fear of liability; it had licensed the plant to operate.

Creswell's warning to the NRC came too late. His signal to Babcock and Wilcox never got further than the Toledo plant. But there were also warnings within Babcock and Wilcox itself. Some people engaged on the post-mortem into the Toledo accidents became particularly concerned that the control personnel had switched off the HPI before they knew what was going on. Crucial to their reaction was the fact that they had been tricked into believing that the system was filling up when it was actually emptying (because of a design weakness centred on a U-shaped pipe that can create a vapour lock and that can begin to send off false signals into the system). This led a senior engineer to decide to send out a clear directive to operators about the dangers of premature closing of the emergency cooling systems. However, this brought him into conflict with his colleagues in customer service, who blocked his message. Two sets of warnings from engineers were blocked internally and bounced back by the customer service department. Producers and operators were clogged up by the sheer volume of paper-work and the warning was left lying around for thirteen months unattended although the senior engineers involved assumed it had been circulated to the plants. In brief, all sorts of defensive and bureaucratic mechanisms kept the warnings from reaching the reactor operators.

Reacting to Unprecedented Pressure

When the wheel did come off at Three Mile Island, the people concerned were swept along by a chain of events as the crisis unfolded. Their reactions have to be interpreted in the light of dire emergency that puts people under the most intense pressure, in a situation of escalating incomprehensibility, and where the stakes are incredibly high. This was almost a combat situation, with lives, deaths, and personal survival at issue, except here the enemy was the unknown in the heart of the machine. Initial coolness dissolved into near panic. Many of the control personnel were ex-navy men who had been drilled always to stick to their tasks in an emergency. At first, they exuded an air of 'cool professionalism'; then, as events began to slip out of their control, there were the first signs of panic; and eventually the control room was transformed into a 'wall-to-wall Madhouse' (Gray and Rosen, 1982: 123). As one witness graphically recalled, 'bells were ringing, lights were flashing, and everyone was grabbing and scratching' (*Observer*, 9 April 1989).

One important factor in their reaction was that they were encountering a situation for which they had not been prepared – according to Perrow (1984: 27), 'their training never imagined a multiple accident with a stuck PORV, and blocked valves'. Perhaps there was an instinctive reaction – when temperatures soared off the dials, and situations arose that simply were never encountered during the months of preparation on simulators – to minimize the dimensions of what was occurring because these highly programmed operators were led to misread temperature dials, began to disbelieve their instruments, and missed completely the fundamental issue that there might be a connection between the drop in pressure and the boiling of the coolant water. When temperatures at the core reached 3,700 degrees (the computer was only programmed to 700 degrees) and someone suggested that the core might be uncovered, then the answer was 'bullshit!' (Gray and Rosen, 1982: 124). Radiation in the containment building soared to 30,000 R p.m. (roentgen per minute, enough to kill someone within seconds) and then began to be recorded in the control room itself, meaning that the operators had to don protective clothing and breathing apparatus. Under these pressing circumstances, with operators desperately struggling to get a grip on a baffling situation, it is perhaps understandable that they tried to ignore the signals that a hydrogen explosion had occurred inside the containment building. Fortunately for all concerned, the containment building held.

Managerial Response

Within the control room we can explain some of the reactions in terms of panic and pressure in an emergency situation. But, if anything, the company concerned, Metropolitan Edison, simply refused to face up to the seriousness of the situation. At the plant, for instance, procedure dictated that first a Site Emergency be called and, then, as the situation deteriorated, a General Emergency. Messages went out to the state, to the NRC, to emergency services, and, inevitably, the media soon heard of this extra activity.

Yet the corporation was continually issuing denials and endeavouring to minimize the accident; in effect, there was no problem, no danger, and all was following routine. Yet Met. Ed. squads in yellow protective clothing were to be seen in the area employing highly visible geiger counters! Company PR representatives tried to play down the problem; and management insisted on putting a stop to the release of steam because this was visible outside. Yet as news of the probable size of the accident rapidly circulated, the plant and the company were besieged by TV crews, photographers, and 300 reporters (with sixty people turning up from the *Philadelphia Enquirer* alone). An early spokesperson, an engineer, used highly technical language which only confused the journalists; the media became more and more aggressive as they sensed a cover-up, and company officials sometimes became nervous and irritable when they had to run the gauntlet of press conferences that were like entering a snake-pit. The White House and politicians were alerted; people were told to stay indoors and pregnant mothers and small children were advised to leave the area; and there were widespread rumours of a general evacuation (some 100,000 people simply voted with their feet and got up and left the area). It took a long time for Met. Ed. to appreciate the urgency of their predicament.

Both Met. Ed. and the NRC emerged from the crisis with their reputations tarnished. Their responses had been timid, weak, and defensive. Creitz, the CEO of Met. Ed., was shoved aside, Met. Ed. ran into considerable financial problems, but Cresswell did ironically receive an NRC award. General Public Utilities, which ran Three Mile Island, then turned on the NRC and sued it for $4.3 billion.

The Dangers

The extent of the fire at Windscale (now Sellafield) in 1957 was kept secret for thirty years, but it was seven times worse than Three Mile Island; that in turn was dwarfed by Chernobyl, which resulted in over thirty deaths (and 200 seriously injured radiation victims with predictions of eventually 5,000 cancer deaths in relation to radiation). But, although there were no direct deaths or injuries at Three Mile Island, there was talk of a possible explosion equivalent to a 1-megaton bomb and of an evacuation of people within a 20-mile radius involving some 600,000 people. There were 4 million litres of contaminated water blown out of the system. Parts of the core had reached 4,300 degrees, and that is perilously close to the melting point at 5,000 degrees. There were millions of dollars needed to pay for an alternative supply of energy, while figures for the clean-up were initially set at somewhere between $200 and $500 million although the real costs far exceed those estimates ($1,000 million by 1979 – *Observer*, 9 April 1989). Over ten years later, the clean-up is still going on. The United States had narrowly escaped its Chernobyl.

Comment

As in many analyses of industrial accidents and disasters there emerges here a somewhat familiar scenario of a *chain of circumstances* which actors did not fully comprehend at the time and which, despite warnings of impending problems, led step by step, with an awful feeling of inevitability as one reconstructs the events, to crisis. The commission of inquiry set up by President Carter concluded that, given the industry as it was, 'an accident like Three Mile Island was eventually inevitable' (*Observer*, 9 April 1989).

This too is the position of Perrow, who has investigated 'normal accidents' associated with modern high-risk technologies and who has focused on the interactive complexity and tight coupling as *system characteristics* which, in turn, generate a large measure of *incomprehensibility* in operators when things go wrong. In essence, we encounter a complex interaction between human, organizational, and technical factors which is often rationalized away by concentrating on the catch-all rationalization of 'operator error' or 'human factor' (Perrow, 1984: 26; Mokhiber, 1988: 424). As such, any analysis aimed at understanding the processes and mechanisms leading to accidents, disasters, and crises must illuminate the multiplicity of the factors involved and their accumulation into unique circumstances that surprise and overcome participants because events are unexpected and unanticipated (Wagenaar,

1992). To dissect the accident at Three Mile Island fully would require attention to the following:

- *The nature of the industry*: private, competitive, and capital-intensive. The North American branch of the industry was imbued with optimism, with frustration at regulatory restrictions, and with hopes of becoming world leader in the construction of nuclear plants. Multiple actors, all with strong commercial motives, were involved. Babcock and Wilcox was a relatively small company compared to the giants Westinghouse and General Electric.
- *The nature of regulation*: on the surface the industry was strangled by minute, nit-picking regulation but, in practice, there was latitude allowed by the NRC which adopted a conciliatory approach to the start-up problems of a new industry in an immensely complex technological area. Just to get a nuclear plant 'on line' involved running 'a fifteen year gauntlet' (Gray and Rosen, 1982: 47).
- *The nature of the plants*: the actual plants were massive displays of near science-fiction dimensions that were, in fact, a result of a complex chain of interactions between design, construction, and operating branches. Once in operation the personnel went through a collective learning experience to iron out flaws and to discover how to deal with day-to-day operations and maintenance. Because of the risks involved, specifications had to be exact and safety features had to be multiple in order to forestall possible accidents.
- *Running the plants*: although safety was the reassuring leitmotiv of the industry, the firms involved had sunk enormous investments into the plants and non-performance was incredibly expensive. This doubtless meant that there was an element of keeping on line if at all possible and of trying to avoid interruptions in the supply of energy. This could help to explain why warnings were ignored and why the dimension of accidents tended to be played down. The virtual brain-washing on safety also seems to have led some of the supervisors at Three Mile Island into ignoring and misinterpreting signals as if they could not face up to the potential seriousness of the situation (refusing to consider that the core was uncovered and ignoring the hydrogen explosion).
- *Reacting to crisis*: faced with an emergency the operators reacted with behaviour ranging from coolness to panic, disbelief at the readings on their instruments, and trying desperate measures which only worsened the situation. They were faced with an unexpected and unanticipated situation which they could not fully comprehend because the system was giving off false, confusing, and contradictory signals, and also because they could not trace the origin of the defect and could not observe directly the consequences of their remedial action. In all this two aspects are of importance:

1 personnel, training, supervision, communication;
2 the physical lay-out of the control room with its banks of panels making

a complete overview difficult and with certain important controls virtually hidden from view.

- *Organizational reactions and communications*: three of the main actors involved (Babcock and Wilcox, Met. Ed., and the NRC) reacted in a defensive fashion which was exacerbated by multiple failures in communication. All endeavoured to avoid blame for the accident. Met. Ed. sued Babcock and Wilcox and the 'vendor returned the favour by charging that the utility was incompetent to run their machine' (Perrow, 1984: 16).
- *Media interest and formal inquiries*: media attention was intense and critical and exposed the actors involved to hostile scrutiny. Some five commissions investigated the accident so that Three Mile Island is one of the most thoroughly analysed industrial accidents that has ever occurred. Gray and Rosen (1982) have written an excellent blow-by-blow account based on investigative reporting, and Perrow (1984) has produced a highly illuminating analysis placing the accident in the context of high-risk technology.
- *Paradoxes of control*: however, the most essential element in the analysis of the accident is that it reveals how difficult it is to exert effective control over a vastly complex and new industry. Indeed, there is a vital factor involved in terms of paradoxes of control that makes such an industry vulnerable:

  1 the industry may come to believe its own propaganda on safety (it was working on a forecast of one minor accident in 200 years of working with 200 plants);
  2 the operators may become mesmerized by the overwhelming paraphernalia of control surrounding them;
  3 the immense burden of paper-work involved in regulation may easily mean that signals are lost and warnings played down amid the sheer volume of information and documentation;
  4 but, above all, the minuteness and complexity of the rules doubtless means that it is difficult to operate without breaking some regulation; this must make it difficult for operators to know when, and when not, to break rules in order to keep the plant going. Probably any investigation of a plant would uncover these in themselves trivial violations which might, however, be dangerous under a certain set of circumstances.

Finally, the consequences of the accident were dramatic and devastating for the American nuclear industry, which basically has been frozen by political and public opposition and by the dire example of Three Mile Island. When cleared of radioactive debris, Unit Two will remain in quarantine for thirty years until it is dismantled as planned along with Unit One, which will then have reached the end of its working life. Until 2020, then, Unit Two at Three Mile Island in the middle of the Susquehanna River will remain a silent sentinel to a disturbing case of incompetence, dishonesty, complacency, and cover-up. A complex interplay of human, technical, organizational, and communication factors had brought America to the brink of a nuclear catastrophe.

In some cases of corporate misconduct the deviance is deliberate and planned. In the literature of accidents and disasters there are other factors at play. High-risk, capital-intensive plants are normally enmeshed in rules, regulations, and an aura of safety. In practice, as can be seen in the cases of Piper Alpha (and the North Sea oil industry in general: Carson, 1982), Bhopal, Seveso, and Flixborough (Allison, 1993), there can develop an emphasis on production over safety. The engineering mind in a production facility, geared to ironing out technical troubles, when allied to the managerial mind tending to the avoidance of undue losses, can spell out the ignoring of warning signals and the determination to maintain production. In post-mortems on accidents it is almost always the case that warnings were given, that mishaps had occurred that pointed towards trouble, and that some managers were aware of defects. But the bringer of bad news is not welcome in many organizations. Creswell, someone who did put his conscience before his job, was subject to strong informal control in an attempt to play down or deflect his message. This sad pattern can be discerned time and again in organizational failures and disasters. Why do organizations ignore the warning signs? Why are people who try to bring the truth to the attention of senior management so often reviled and informally sanctioned? And what mechanisms would have to be put in place to guarantee the right of employees to blow the whistle? Or do we have to accept that, on occasions, the complex organization simply defies control and gets beyond our grasp?

Case No. 6: Wall Street: Fallen Wizards in the Land of Milken Honey

> In the highest of high finance, as we have seen recently once more, the paths of presumed financial intelligence lead regularly, if not to the grave, at least to the minimum security slammer.
>
> (J.K. Galbraith, 1988: 12)

Markets and Morals

In the early 1980s the American economy was in the doldrums. The second oil crisis, recession, the Japanese challenge, the costs of regulation, and the maturing of smoke-stack industries, all conspired to send American management reeling. The arrival of Reagan as President, attempts at deregulation, and a new competitiveness (fanned by the chauvinism of the likes of Iacocca and the revivalist ideology of *In Search of Excellence*), sponsored a shake-out in the economy and a revival in certain sectors. Nowhere was this more evident than in the financial markets. The 'restructuring' of corporate America through mergers and acquisition altered the ground rules for managers, as raiders put companies 'in play', provided us with a new vocabulary (greenmail, poison pill, shark repellents, crown jewel options, and so on), and made substantial work for financiers, lawyers, and accountants.

One man, and one company, seemed to symbolize the rapid expansion of Wall Street; and their demise was taken to mark the end of an extraordinary decade and even of a spectacular era. The Wall Street scandals, centred on Michael Milken and Drexel Burnham Lambert, were related to practices such as 'insider trading', and the resulting prosecutions reveal a great deal about the internal and external control of financial institutions. How can we explain the growth of criminal practices in Wall Street, how were the cases tackled, and what impact has the scandal had in financial circles?

The details of the case are intricate and extensive; the scandals have inevitably generated a considerable literature (Zey, 1993; Stein, 1992; Stone, 1990; Shapiro, 1987; Levine, 1991; Vise and Coll, 1992; Reichman, 1993). Perhaps the significance of those heady and much-publicized events can be put in a broader perspective in relation to two general features. But before pursuing those two points, let me first emphasize that financial institutions have always been vulnerable to individual crime, such as embezzlement, directed *against* the organization. The stereotypically successful employee can build a protective shield of respect, autonomy, and social space that banks and investment firms seem to give high performers; the largest banking fraud in Canadian history was carried out by the charming Brian Molony, whom everybody trusted; he filched $10 million (Canadian) from under the noses of his colleagues at the Canadian Imperial Bank of Commerce to feed his insatiable gambling habit (Ross, 1992).

My first point, then, is that the Wall Street scandals revealed 'for the first time the organizational dimensions of what had traditionally been under-stood only as individual trust violation' (Reichman, 1993: 55). Reichman's emphasis on this new *organizational dimension* means that we have to take a dynamic new view of institutional and organizational change, alterations in the working of the markets, the development of new technologies, and the emergence of new players. She argues, furthermore, that these 'new forms of insider trading sought to corrupt the market itself, to change its very dynamic' and that this exposed an 'industry at risk of participating in its own destruction' (1993: 56). In short, Wall Street needs to be located within the shifting structures of the financial world.

Second, the scandals raised the issue of *personal ethics* and *collective moral-ity* within organizations and within the financial community. Was it possible to remain straight in that environment? What happened to personal integrity and professional respectability in financial circles? How did the players justify rule-bending to themselves? And what are the implications for ethics and integrity within business organizations?

The Industry

The financial world revolves around information, people, and trust (it is a 'transactional world based on tipsterism, rumor, gossip and eavesdropping':

Shapiro, 1984: 88). Its institutions tend to be characterized by respectability (symbolized by their recruitment from elite circles), because a reputation for trust and integrity is essential to generating the confidence which is instrumental in handling large sums of money for other people. As lubricators of the interests of both industry and of governmental tuners of the economy, they are powerful players who enjoy an advantageous position that makes others highly dependent upon them. Their very respectability is a guarantee of considerable autonomy on the grounds that 'gentlemen' can best be left to supervise their own affairs, within a general framework of regulatory guidelines. The financial industry, then, is generally perceived as exhibiting respectability, autonomy, and trust; by exuding these qualities, other people are persuaded to entrust deals, involving often vast sums of money, to traffickers in information and in capital. The persona of the financial expert is often staid, conservative, reputable, and reliable; his character must convince people that he possesses these qualities as an individual and, in the tight community of finance, is expected to invest in long-term relationships with clients. He, and generally it is a he, can be trusted to deal honestly and to respect a confidence. You can rely on him.

In the 1980s a number of developments occurred in the New York financial centre, Wall Street, which altered that image dramatically and which raised acutely the whole issue of controlling the world of financial dealing, which is difficult to penetrate. There was a substantial measure of deregulation of financial institutions. Corporate America entered a period of considerable restructuring based on mergers and acquisitions. As the economy recovered from recession (aided by the decline in the value of the dollar) and shifted into a higher gear, the stock exchange experienced a 'bull market' that brought unprecedented growth (which was dented, but not undermined, by the 'hiccup' of 'Black Monday' – 19 October 1987 – when the Dow-Jones index fell by 508 points and when $500 billion was wiped off the value of shares).

But above all, the period was characterized by the emergence of a financial 'wizard', Michael Milken, who breathed life into the 'junk-bond' market. The so-called 'junk'-bonds, high-yielding bonds with relatively small backing, were employed to engineer a wave of huge takeovers (for example, in 1989 Drexel co-managed the issuance of $4 billion in bonds to fund the leveraged buy-out of R.J.R. Nabisco Inc: *Business Week*, 26 February 1990: 23). Within five to six years, the junk-bond market was claimed to have generated $75–100 billion and to have shaken up many a complacent managerial board within corporate America. And the cornerstone of junk-bond takeovers was the eagerness of once conservative institutional and foreign investors to acquire this paper in 'vast amounts' (Rohatyn, 1987: 22).

This new, complex, and dramatic development was, we now know, imbued with dishonesty (Stewart, 1991). But at the time it was revelled in as symptomatic of a new-found élan and flair in American financial circles. Its exposure brought about a vigorous spring-cleaning operation that was reminiscent of the 1930s. Then, the financial world took some of the blame for the 1929 crash and this was strengthened during the New Deal era when it emerged that the traditional and extensive self-regulation in the banking, investment, and securities markets had conspicuously failed. The Securities and Exchange Commission (SEC) was one response, and it was founded in 1934 as an antidote to the revelations in public hearings on these markets of incompetence, irregularities, and fraud; and essentially it became the overseer of a network of 'sro's' (self-regulating organizations). For example, the National Association of Security Dealers (1939), and the stock exchanges, became responsible for the effective regulation of securities with the SEC acting as a 'referee' of substantial self-regulation. This inevitably meant that a large degree of reliance on the industry itself was unavoidable. Following a series of scandals, a round of Senate hearings, and new legislation (the 1975 Securities Act), the SEC became more powerful from around the mid-1970s. Within a decade the SEC had gone from being a 'small, reactive caretaker office' to forming a 'large, specialized, pro-active, self-initiating office, constantly expanding the boundaries of enforcement policy and serving as a leader and model for activities of the regions' (Shapiro, 1984: 140).

In her research on the work in that period of the SEC, Shapiro (1984) has indicated that the annual case-load was around 300 and a case averaged about $400,000; she concludes that many offenders were small, new, companies, and also repeat offenders, and that the SEC was not particularly effective at getting at major offenders in an early stage of a dubious deal. In the early 1980s the SEC was under attack from deregulators, who proposed a massive cut in its staff and budget (*The Economist*, 31 January 1981); and its maximum fine for a criminal violation had stood at $10,000 for some fifty years, leading to Shad's calling for sanctions that were three times the profits of the transaction (Shad was then head of the SEC: *The Economist*, 23 April 1983). Its intelligence-gathering Shapiro typified as 'passive, haphazard, and fortuitous' and there was a preoccupation with enforcement to the neglect of detection. However, the SEC did enjoy considerable administrative authority and cases were heard by judges specialized in SEC hearings. In practice, the SEC exerted a form of licensing power, in that enforcement could lead to deregistration of the offender, and also civil injunctions not to repeat an offence. Clarke (1990: 158) also maintains that the SEC 'lacks a really substantial detective capacity and is reliant upon cases coming to light by one means or another. . . . viewed in a positive light, it can be seen as a licensing watchdog over sros's'.

In the 1980s, however, conspicuous deregulation of financial services fostered widespread abuses; and one response to this was the criminalization of 'insider dealing' ('The Insider Trading Sanctions Act', 1984; insider dealing/trading involves the use of inside, confidential information, that is not known to the general public, when trading in securities, leading to personal gain or gain for associates). Until then SEC enforcement policy had largely been that prosecution was a control method of last resort (while until the late 1980s very few major figures in the industry had been involved). Of the cases examined by Shapiro (1984) some 15 per cent were classified as non-violations while in 40 per cent of cases, where a violation had been established, no legal action was undertaken at all. But then the Wall Street scandal broke.

The Players

In endeavouring to explain the dramatic developments on Wall Street, it is clear that new players entered the market who helped to change the rules of the game (Bruck, 1988; Auletta, 1986). Drexel Burnham Lambert was, for instance, a relative newcomer which built its rapid expansion on junk-bonds and was transformed from a 'mediocre investment bank into a Wall Street colossus' with profits of $800 million in 1986 (*Business Week*, 26 February 1990: 21). But a great deal of attention has been focused on the stars who shot into prominence – and later into prison. They were said to be young, thrusting, mercenary, and untroubled by conscience (Lewis, 1990). These 'freewheeling financial samurai' took advantage of deregulation, new technology, and the merger craze, and were said to have entered the game with cynicism, greed, and gusto: 'Too much money is coming together with too many young people who have little or no institutional memory, or sense of tradition, and who are under enormous pressure to perform in the glare of Hollywood-like publicity' (Rohatyn, 1987: 21).

This new boisterous generation was no better typified than by Ivan Boesky's now infamous speech praising greed before an audience of students at Berkeley (which was echoed by Gekko's address to shareholders in Oliver Stone's film, *Wall Street*). His remark extolling greed, which attracted both applause and laughter, symbolized the rampant materialism of this new high-pressure, high-profile elite engaged in mergers, block trading, and arbitrage. Boesky commanded about $3 billion; his office had 300 phones and he had three in his car; he owned a 200-acre estate in Westchester County, NY; and he may have earned $400 million from Drexel (*Time*, 21 December 1987). Dennis Levine (33 years old in 1986), nicknamed 'Mister Diamond', had a Park Avenue apartment, a red Ferrari, and in 1985 took home $3 million in salaries and bonuses. Siegel (37 years old in 1986) enjoyed a 'soaring lifestyle'; besides keeping a posh Manhattan apartment, he and his wife built a 'spectacular cedar-and-glass beachfront home on Connecticut's Long Island Sound, complete with tennis court and gym. He typically commuted to work in a chartered helicopter' (*Time*, 2 March 1987: 48). Milken (39 years old in 1986) is said to have made over a billion dollars within a five-year period, and his personal earnings in 1987 would have ranked him sixty-fifth in the Fortune 500 if he had been a company (*de Volkskrant*: 31 January 1989). Furthermore, Milken was said to have had an 'uncontrollable commitment to work', rising before 5 o'clock and controlling his Wall Street dealings from his West Coast base in Beverly Hills, California; 'the view held in many circles is that of a rapacious, malicious megalomaniac who will blow away anyone who gets in his way' (*Business Week*, 28 November 1988: 51).

Four features of this brave new network are relevant here. First, for the participants it must have been an exciting, almost intoxicating adventure of power in which a privileged few could create the illusion that they could steer great corporations and even influence the entire economy. Second, the suspects were not all young, although the youthful aspect was accentuated by the media which elevated some of them to near pop-star status. But several suspects were twenty- to thirty-year veterans of Wall Street who were in their fifties; it was *not* only the young who succumbed to temptation. Boesky, for instance, was 50 years old. Third, although the major spotlight was turned on the financial houses, it also emerged that several law and accountancy firms were closely implicated in the charges, so that collusion, illicit alliances, and illegal networks were developed. And, fourth, this unprecedented surge of success for the brash, aggressive, competitive newcomers inevitably attracted resistance from the established order and suspicion from the authorities.

Rohatyn (senior partner in the investment firm Lazard Frères) fulminated against the 'cancer' of greed that had contaminated the 'street'; and, in nigh apocalyptical terms, spoke of greed, avarice, and corruption as a financial 'time-bomb' that could easily unleash a 'vicious backlash' (1987: 22). And the highly publicized manoeuvres of the 'investment bankers, raiders, and arbitrageurs seemed to be too orchestrated to be wholly legitimate' and the SEC began to sense a conspiracy (*Business Week*, 28 November 1988: 49).

When the scandal began to unfold, the question that is always raised on such occasions was posed as to the extent of the deviant practices. One investment banker was adamant: 'the "bad apple" speeches are crap . . . this case [Boesky; MP] is illustrative of the general wretched excess on the street. The line between what's right and wrong has been blurred. This is Wall Street's Watergate' (*Newsweek*, 1 December 1986: 48). Others were more cautious:

> Many experts believe the really blatant cases of insider profiteering are, despite the hubbub, rare. 'The vast majority of the people on Wall Street are not doing it,' says Edward Brodsky, a Manhattan securities lawyer. 'Those who are, however, infect the integrity of the whole marketplace.' Maintaining that integrity has been a difficult challenge in the deregulated, hurly-burly Wall Street of the 1980s, where traders have been tempted to use insider tips to maintain their competitive edge. (*Newsweek*, 1 December 1986: 48)

But whether or not we are concerned with a few rotten apples, or a totally rotten barrel, there is a crucial meta-issue in terms of the impact of scandal on the perceived health of financial dealing. As Rohatyn expresses it, 'the integrity of our securities market and the soundness of our financial institutions are vital national assets. They are being eroded today' (1987: 21).

Internal and External Control

What emerges with stark clarity from the Wall Street affair is that internal control – both within individual corporations and the separate branches of the financial community – failed abysmally. Although the top man at Drexel reacted with horror at Levine's arrest, it had been the case that he granted almost unlimited autonomy to his rising stars, with Milken even working out of California and not New York. The nature of their work also involved accountants and lawyers, and it would be mighty strange if some of them had not noticed that the rules were being bent. And where was the New York Stock Exchange in all this? In the end, it was an anonymous tip that started the house of cards tumbling; as each suspect was nailed he bargained by offering knowledge about his former colleagues; and once the ball started to roll, the SEC received government backing to launch a major investigatory campaign (Vise and Coll, 1992).

The securities legislation is geared to achieving three fundamental aims: full disclosure of basic financial information, the equal treatment of all shareholders, and refusal to permit manipulation of the market. Financiers are prohibited from profiting from advance information of which they hear in the course of their work, and that information is also not for the ears of others; so-called 'Chinese walls' are meant to dam in the flow of confidential information within companies. But what had developed by the mid-1980s was a conspiratorial circle of key players who passed on confidential information about forthcoming mergers and acquisitions, who speculated on the anticipated rise in share value, and who engaged in practices to conceal this from their employees and the authorities.

For instance, Levine had dummy Panamanian companies and flew on day trips, so as not to draw attention to his absences, to the Bahamas in order to run his shadow corporations. Boesky engaged in 'parking' his money with a colleague, and this brought down Boyd Jefferies in the subsequent investigation. The players were engaged in a sophisticated, intricate, long-term conspiracy that was not exposed by internal control. It was left to the SEC, in tandem with the Department of Justice, to tackle Wall Street.

Some said the SEC 'witch hunt' reminded them of the McCarthy period, and it was seen as the 'blockbuster' securities case of all time (*Business Week*, 28 November 1988: 48). Certainly in comparison with some other control agencies, the SEC is viewed as a relatively sophisticated, tough, and effective agency. But then it does have the considerable advantage that to a large extent financial services and securities require public and investor confidence and are thus painfully hurt by scandals and exposures: 'The success of the SEC can be attributed to the fact that unlike most of the other regulatory agencies . . . it enjoys strong business support' (Coleman, 1985: 172).

To a certain extent personalities can also help to explain the shift in enforcement policy to going for big fish and to opting for prosecution. Shad was a forceful leader at the SEC, and the US Attorney for Manhattan, Giuliani, made such a furore with his dramatic enforcement policies that he was urged to run for the presidency (and did become Mayor of New York). His previous 'crusade' had been against Mafia bosses, and he said that both groups, the Mafia and the financiers, were similar: 'the only difference is that the Wall Street suspects are better informants – and the work is safer' (*de Volkskrant*, 4 April 1987).

Shad at the SEC initiated investigations into Wall Street and insider traders. Such campaigns rely on tips, transaction records, subpoenas, and dogged investigative research that may lead to 'paper trails' of suspicious deals and to cooperative witnesses. An anonymous tip set them off on the right track. Someone from Merrill Lynch's Caracas office informed company headquarters in New York that two brokers in Caracas were scoring surprisingly high in a number of takeover deals. This information was passed on to the SEC where computer records of some suspect deals were checked on an account at Bank Leu in the Bahamas. The data enabled the SEC to gain cooperation from the Bahamian and Swiss authorities (Bank Leu was Swiss, and usually Swiss banks are renowned for being secretive about clients' accounts). The name that emerged was that of Dennis Levine (*Newsweek*, 2 December 1986: 35). And his cooperation caused other tongues to loosen. It also meant that the SEC was beginning to reach elite members of the business community.

Following Levine, other traders came to the attention of the SEC and the judicial authorities, and of these Martin Siegel, Michael Milken and Ivan Boesky figured prominently in investigations; they all worked for, or with, the renowned firm of Drexel Burnham Lambert, and all had been involved in illegal transactions and insider trading in the security exchanges of Wall Street. Boesky offered his cooperation to the SEC and agreed to pay a $50-million fine and $50 million restitution of illegally earned profit on share transactions; he was also sentenced to three years' imprisonment. Siegel agreed to pay $25 million to the SEC without admitting guilt; Levine received a two-year sentence and paid back $11.5 million in illegally gained profits; Milken initially evaded prosecution but was forced to leave Drexel as part of an agreement with the authorities. Since then he has plea-bargained a deal by admitting guilt to six charges, and by agreeing to pay $600 million in fines, in return for the dropping of almost ninety other charges (*de Volkskrant*, 23 April 1990). Eventually he was sentenced to ten years' imprisonment but was released within a few years. The company, Drexel Burnham Lambert, then came to an agreement with the authorities to pay $650 million partly as a fine and partly as a fund for investors who can claim compensation for losses incurred.

These are spectacular cases – and severe penalties – by any standards and they brought malpractice in Wall Street, and by association in the City of London, into the international spotlight; and the reputation of Wall Street was certainly not enhanced soon after by photos of financiers in handcuffs being taken from their offices on charges of cocaine use. Giuliani left no doubt that he considered the corruption to be widespread if not systemic: he stated that Boesky had 'given the government a window on the rampant criminal conduct that has permeated the securities industry in the 1980s "and that such conduct is at the heart of a substantial amount of market activity by established securities industry professionals"' (*Business Week*, 28 November 1988: 48).

There had plainly been extremely close cooperation between the SEC's investigatory staff and the judicial authorities; and, given the sensitive nature of financial institutions in the health of the economy, there must also have been approval from the government.

Sanctioning and Impact

It should not be underestimated, however, how difficult such a series of investigations and prosecutions are for control agencies. Agencies are faced with complex conspiracies that are not easy to unravel (although the new electronic technology of financial dealing can be used to trace 'audit trails' in a search for discrepancies), and that require considerable investment of people, resources, and time. The suspects are protected by top lawyers, by using every delaying tactic in the book, and by the intricacies of their offshore secret holdings and dummy corporations. In essence, prosecution is facilitated by the willingness of suspects to talk, by plea-bargaining, and by a combination of civil and criminal cases.

This may lead to a critical stance where some people argue that the Wall Street cases are all too typical of white-collar crime prosecution with the defendants getting off comparatively lightly. The suspects were made to appear as solid citizens misled by a turbulent and tempting situation; they were released on bail ($5 million in the case of Levine); they eventually cooperated with the authorities (Boesky was praised for this by the judge) and contritely expressed their regrets; they received relatively light prison sentences (Milken was the exception); and, despite the large sums involved in fines and repaid profits, the assumption is that these are still wealthy men (who can claim tax relief on part of their fines). And an investigation, seen as a 'witch hunt' on Wall Street and publicized as an attack on widespread illegal and corrupt practices, ended with the prosecution of a few figureheads and initially an accommodation with Drexel. The power of Drexel to maintain delaying actions in the courts, and the difficulties of proving cases against the company, meant that at first a compromise was reached that shelved all further investigations. And in the interests of other businesses the complaints against the company were kept secret.

One way of interpreting this is to say that the SEC and the Department of Justice booked a number of successes but failed to clear out the stable. After a ritual cleansing, and a hiccup on the stock exchange, people went back to business and, while Drexel had its reputation and its balance sheet badly dented, it continued to do business for quite a while until it subsequently folded.

Another way of looking at this affair is to see it as a fairly typical case of regulatory control. The SEC and the Justice Department had flexed their muscles in a very tough and sophisticated area to investigate, they had brought in a considerable 'bag' in financial settlements and had nailed some big names (of importance to the public career of someone like Giuliani); and, above all, had sounded a strong, unqualified signal to the financial community.

Given the criminal nature of the conspiracy, and the large sums of money involved, it might be felt that the sentences were lenient. This ignored the authorities' reliance on suspects' cooperation to provide information on deals and to name names, and on the time-saving mechanism of plea-bargaining which short-circuits endless delays and appeals. Furthermore, the suspects could be portrayed as model capitalists – industrious, intelligent, and initially respectable – who got carried away by an intoxicating situation. Certainly this element would be accentuated to the full in the court-room where defendants would be coached to play the role of contrite but basically moral citizens.

For instance, it was said of Milken that, 'he was intense, fiercely competitive, often arrogant, and driven by a desire to control his environment'; but that this side of his personality would be played down in court, where he would be portrayed as 'deferential, modest, unpretentious' (*Business Week*, 28 November 1988: 51). Although he was unable to avoid a stiff prison sentence this was sat out in a minimum security prison where he was given light work and where he readily gained remission of sentence for good behaviour (being released after twenty-two months: *Business Week*, 13 December 1993). And despite having paid fines totalling $650 million, he is still reported to be an extremely wealthy man.

Prior to sentencing, Boesky appeared before US District Judge Morris Lasker in a Manhattan court-room:

> Once Wall Street's most aggressive speculator in take-over stocks, Boesky was a picture of contrition in court. 'I am deeply ashamed,' he said. 'I have spent the last year trying to understand how I veered off course.' Boesky's lawyer pointed out that the defendant has been pursuing rabbinical studies at the Jewish Theological Seminary of America, near Columbia University, and working under an assumed name at a project to aid the homeless run by Manhattan's Cathedral Church of St John the Divine. Lasker praised Boesky for his 'remarkable co-operation' with authorities but indicated that a jail term of more than six months was unavoidable because his crimes have aroused the 'passions of public opinion'. Much of the public indignation was stirred by allegations that Boesky has emerged from the affair with a large part of his huge fortune intact, even after paying $100 million as a result of the charges against him. For sure, Boesky is a long way from the plight of the homeless men he has been helping. He still lives in a luxury apartment a few blocks from his company's headquarters on Manhattan's Fifth Avenue. In the firm's elegant suite of offices, his personal secretary continues to answer the telephone, while a guard hovers near a reception area decorated in gold colors and Far Eastern art. 'Boesky now uses the office as a private club to meet with his lawyers,' says a source familiar with the investor's activities. (*Time*, 21 December 1987: 37)

Levine received a two-year sentence but could have faced up to twenty years,

> on four counts of securities fraud, perjury and income-tax evasion. 'I beg you, let me put the pieces of my life together again,' he implored US District Judge Gerard Groettel before the sentencing. In deciding on two years, Groettel cited Levine's 'extraordinary cooperation with investigators, which had helped them uncover a "nest of vipers" on Wall Street'. (*Time*, 2 March 1987: 47)

Not only were the suspects meek before the judges but they also spilled the beans on their accomplices and colleagues when faced with serious charges and long sentences. An anonymous tip led to Levine; he was a 'vein of gold that you keep mining and mining' for the authorities; and Boesky allowed the prosecutors to tap his phones as part of his cooperation with them (he was likened to Joseph Valachi, the well-known Mafia informer of the 1960s); an arbitrageur claimed that it was only safe to talk to someone in a sauna where you could see they were not bugged (*Business Week*, 28 November 1988: 48; *Fortune*, 9 November 1987: 105). Clearly there was no code of silence, nor of honour, among the Wall Street thieves.

It is difficult to assess the impact this will have on their lives. They have been arrested, hand-cuffed, processed through the criminal justice system, exposed to the glare of negative publicity, fined, and imprisoned. But, while they will never return to their previous pre-eminent positions, having been banned for life from the securities market, it is quite conceivable that they will come back to business as free-lance consultants and may even profit from publishing their memoirs (Levine, 1991; Kornbluth, 1992; while Milken teaches management at UCLA: *Business Week*, 13 December 1993). In the eyes of their peer group they have almost certainly served as a deterrent:

> Securities lawyer David Martin, a former SEC special counsel, says that the deterrent effect of a case like the Boesky scandal can be enormous: 'One guy goes down, and 10 people clean up their act – that's the real benefit'. (*Newsweek*, 1 December 1986: 36)

Doubtless it was also salutary for the financial world to see the mighty Drexel Burnham Lambert come tumbling down in the end. On 13 February 1990, Drexel filed for bankruptcy proceedings under Chapter 11 and went out of business. Initially it had seemed to be able to weather the storm. There were at first remarkably few defections from its portfolio; it invested $150 million in engaging the very best corporate lawyers; and it even managed to survive the fine of $650 million paid to the SEC. But the cases represented a severe drain on management; headhunters moved in to tempt away key personnel; morale slumped; and the CEO, Frederick Joseph, was said to have made a number of serious errors of judgement. Supporters of the charismatic Milken felt that he would have found a way to rescue Drexel and that Joseph's biggest mistake was in dropping him. For some people Joseph was too soft in pleading guilty and in not fighting it out with the authorities.

But there was an old piece of legislation that was shrewdly used to pressurize Drexel and to bring it to its knees. That was 'RICO' – the Racketeer Influenced and Corrupt Organizations Act. This had been used against organized crime, and particularly drug-dealers, and had a double sting; it was aimed at seizing illegally gained assets and also opened up the possibility of civil action for the recovery of assets. If Giuliani had gone after Drexel with RICO then it would have crippled the firm, and under its threat, Joseph buckled and gave in. But that was not the end of it because there was still the impending risk of civil litigation and considerable damages. Ironically, Drexel had become dependent on the junk-bond market (and psychologically dependent on Milken) and had never managed to develop into a full-service investment bank. To a large extent it had revelled in its image as the 'renegade, street-smart firm that could outmanoeuvre the Establishment', but now

that image came home to roost, leaving Drexel with few admirers, and all the
desperate rescue efforts failed:

> If Drexel hadn't been reviled on Wall Street, someone might have lent support dur-
> ing the liquidity crunch. 'You have to ask, if it were Morgan Stanley, would it have
> gone under?' NYU's Smith says. No, he says: 'It would have been saved by the
> Federal Reserve, the stock exchange, the banks, or someone. But Drexel had no
> friends'. (*Business Week*, 5 March 1990: 41)

Drexel was 'arguably the "bad boy" firm on the playing field'; its employees
cultivated an image of the 'hard men' or 'badasses' of Wall Street (Reichman,
1993: 88). By threatening the traditional power structure Drexel was almost
inviting prosecution (according to Stone, 1990: 35):

> The country's corporate elite disliked Drexel for a simple reason: The firm was
> sticking its nose where it didn't belong. Investment bankers were supposed to give
> advice, gentlemen to gentlemen, on financing and friendly acquisitions; they were
> supposed to be charming, well bred, and low handicapped. They weren't supposed
> to raise money for hostile takeover artists. And they sure as hell weren't supposed
> to think up hostile takeovers and then go looking for someone to replace current
> managers.

In brief, the Wall Street scandal had repercussions for individuals, for
companies (including some abroad, a number of them in London), for the
victims, for the Wall Street business community, and, even to a certain extent,
for the market itself. It brought talk of ethics, morality, integrity, and reform
to the foreground. Perhaps a certain amount of the ethical rhetoric hit a
holier-than-thou, hypocritical note but its aim was plainly to bolster faith in
financial institutions:

> I would emphasize the broader issue involved, namely the ethics of a profession
> where integrity has to be fundamental. After all, the word 'credit' comes from the
> Latin meaning 'to believe'; belief in the integrity of our financial system is certainly
> open to question at this time. (Rohatyn, 1987: 23)

In addition, institutions set about tightening control. And, while leaders of
the financial community were busily making pious statements of disbelief,
and condemnation, memos were rapidly being distributed in offices remind-
ing traders of their legal, and ethical, obligations; and the Stock Exchanges
promised tighter auditing via new computerized controls (*Newsweek*, 26 May
1986). The NYSE invested $55 million in improving its data-base and its sur-
veillance potential while virtually every investment bank tightened their
internal control measures and swiftly codified some new rules where appropriate (*Fortune*, 9 November 1987). Some arbitrageurs even changed their
professional title to 'money managers' to escape the opprobrium attached to
arbitrage. Even tougher requirements were being considered in terms of
reporting deals to the SEC; one proposal was for quarterly returns but
another was for information *on demand*, which clearly alarmed the Street.
    There can be no doubt but that the whole affair had sent tremors through
the Street and internal and external control had suddenly become prominent.
Wall Street would never be the same again. Or would it?

Comment

The Wall Street scandals, and subsequent court cases, opened up a window through which we can glimpse the growth of systemic deviant activities in the financial markets of the 1980s. Let us return to the three questions posed at the beginning of this case; how can we explain these developments, how were they tackled, and what impact did they have? In order to seek explanatory variables it is necessary to touch on a whole series of interrelated factors (cf. Zey, 1993).

The Industry, the Companies, the Work, and the Personalities   The nature of the securities industry was influenced by a number of features – such as deregulation, new technology, and merger 'mania' – that helped to create an exceptionally buoyant market situation. This opened up new opportunities for relative newcomers like Drexel and also for a number of shrewd and sharp innovators who came to dominate the meteoric rise of the junk-bond market. Then they started rigging that market for their own benefit. There is, then, a structural explanation – relaxing of rules, new technologies, a bull market, and so on – concerning the conditions which shaped an environment in which it became acceptable, and highly rewarding, to bend or break the rules. The trust inherent in transactions in the industry made it vulnerable to infiltration by people who profited precisely from abusing that trust.

Drexel shot up from nowhere and subsequently took most of the heat of the investigation (it was said that it 'grew too fast, grew too narrowly, and cut too many corners': *Business Week*, 26 February 1990: 21). Although it appears to have played a pivotal role in many of the dubious transactions that came to light, there were several other companies implicated, including law firms, and these were perceived as fostering the work-style of the deviants. The firms imposed extremely high, perhaps even unrealistic expectations, on key employees which other, younger workers then tried to emulate; the salaries and bonuses proffered reached 'outlandish heights'; and companies no longer gave their people a grounding in the old-fashioned values of integrity (*Time*, 2 March 1987). What they did give was almost unrestricted autonomy. To a large extent companies can become deeply dependent on a handful of 'stars'. In 1986 Milken brought to Drexel a phenomenal $61 billion in business; and his reward was near total autonomy from Drexel as he operated from his Beverly Hills base on the West Coast.

There appears, then, to have been a culture of freedom, ambition, exceptional rewards, guru status for a few, and of unlimited trust. That the latter was abused can be attributed to individual personalities but it can also be located in the structural conditions of work, expectations, and rewards. For instance, the mechanism of 'Chinese walls', separating the investment and trading divisions of firms, depends on deeply ingrained norms of integrity in order to protect confidentiality; but it is obvious that the walls had become distinctly porous and that information easily seeped through them (for example, Michael David, who did not even work on mergers, just went to a loose-leaf folder at Paul, Weiss, Fifkind, Wharton and Garrison and could easily figure out likely takeover candidates: *Business Week*, 23 June 1986: 46). Although it may have been largely self-justification for his own offences, Foster Winans (of the *Wall Street Journal's* 'Heard it on the Street' column who had been jailed for leaking the contents of his column to a stockbroker so that they could benefit from stock-trading in response to his column) said that *everyone* cheated on Wall Street (*Newsweek*, 22 September 1986: 44).

The environment in which people worked was one of high pressure and potentially high rewards. The New York Stock Exchange handles deals amounting to $50 billion a day, and work on the Street is often character-ized by a frenetic pace, by vast amounts of money, and by an irreducible element of risk-taking. Arbitrage, for instance, is a high-risk venture where you walk a constant tightrope and which is definitely not for the faint-hearted. What emerges with sharp focus from this case is that this bullish environment not only sponsored a stretching of conventional rules but it also encouraged the emergence of a fresh group of players who were some-times relatively young (although not exclusively) but who seemed deeply enmeshed in a world of pressure, excitement, risk, high status, and high living. There is a near obsessive element to the multi-million-dollar deals:

> Ivan was like an addict and his drug was capital. Milken played the role of pusher. (*de Volkskrant*, 31 March 1989)

> They worked incessantly and displayed a 'relentless desire to accumulate money at whatever cost'; the pressure was sometimes dissipated by drink and drugs. (Galbraith, 1988: 12)

Milken was supposed to have enjoyed the 'game' and 'got joy from the adren-aline, from the action' (Stone, 1990: 45); Levine described his involvement as virtually intoxicating:

> Something deep inside me forced me to try to catch up to the pack of wheeler-deal-ers who always raced in front of me. . . . It was only in time that I came to view myself as an insider trading junkie. I was addicted to the excitement, the sense of victory. Some spouses use drugs, others have extra-marital affairs, I secretly traded stocks. (Levine, 1991: 390)

Like Gekko in Stone's film, they must have revelled in their power to make things happen and to have major corporations dancing to their tune. They may, too, have enjoyed the combination of cloak-and-dagger meetings, brief-cases full of cash, the extravagant life-style, and the publicity. One central explanatory plank, then, is the development of a new working style that inter-acted with the characters of the main actors and their near addiction to deals, double-dealing, and to quite staggering material rewards.

What should not escape attention, moreover, is that these people engaged in a *double* violation of trust: they cheated their companies and also their col-leagues and clients in the market. And, of course, they also broke the criminal law.

Control, Investigation, Sanctions   Without a shadow of a doubt, corporate and professional control had failed conspicuously and had allowed deviant practices first to grow and then to run rampant on the Street. If order was to be restored in the financial community then it would have to come from external control.

For the cases themselves involved very serious offences indeed, and the prosecutions were not as easy as they may appear to be in retrospect. What if the Swiss bank in the Bahamas had stuck to its country's usual attitude to secrecy and Levine had not been 'fingered'? The cases variously concerned tax evasion, criminal conspiracy to violate the security laws, fraud on Drexel's own clients, insider-trading and stock manipulation, failure to disclose beneficial ownership of securities, 'parking', obstruction of justice, perjury, and persistent infringements of corporate rules and of regulatory codes of the financial markets and exchanges. The amounts of money involved were extremely high, certainly compared to 'ordinary' crime. Given the seriousness of the offences, the sums involved, and the potentially severe penalties, it could be said that the defendants got off fairly lightly.

But this 'leniency' was largely a result of plea-bargaining; in order to save time, continual delay, resources, and even the chance of failure, the authorities offered relatively mild sentences in return for cooperation. An additional factor in sentencing was the usually impeccable background of the suspects, bolstered by carefully constructed court-room personas and contrite acts of good work with the needy, and the unlikelihood that they would ever repeat their crimes (partly because they would be debarred from ever having the chance to work in the same position again). Even so, several judges made the point that they had to give sentences of several years both as a deterrent and because public opinion had been critically aroused by the cases. The success of the investigations and prosecutions was based on anonymous information, breaking banking secrecy, the cooperation of the main actors (who 'sang like canaries' to save their own skins), breathing new life into old but tough legislation (with RICO as a potent weapon), new technologies for tracing share movements, the personalities of the main prosecutors, the increasing sophistication of investigatory staffs, and the uniquely close cooperation between the SEC in Washington and the prosecutors in New York. These in turn were encouraged by Senator Proxmire of the Senate's Banking Commission, and there was clearly a feeling that Wall Street itself was on trial and that this campaign was a thorough house-cleaning operation to be compared with that of the 1930s.

In many respects, the SEC and the 'feds' had fought an exemplary campaign. They had shown that they could collectively mount a concerted investigation and prosecution in a tough, sophisticated area; could powerfully foster prevention and claim deterrence; and yet they had not substantially damaged the industry. What more could a regulator ask?

Impact and Implications   Obviously it is difficult to pin down precisely the impact that the cases will have had on the conduct of daily business activity. Information is the key to success in financial dealings and this will always mean a world replete with rumours, gossip, and tips; the line between legitimate and illegitimate gathering and use of information is difficult to draw in reality and possibly much of what went on was fairly common practice. '"There is a lot of ordinary conduct on Wall Street that is very close to things that can be characterized as improper," says former SEC Commissioner Stephen J. Friedman' (*Business Week*, 28 November 1988: 50). We are, then, dealing with an intrinsically fuzzy area.

It is not just the case that norms of conduct may have slipped generally – and such norms may be sensitive to 'control cycles', being enforced when the heat is on and becoming relaxed when pressure reduces or becomes routinized – but also that there was considerable dispute about the personalities, methods, and consequences that emerged from the cases. To some, the buccaneering junk-bond dealers had forced companies into unnecessary restructuring, had put people out of work, had pushed corporations into excessive debt, had encouraged managers to think in the short term at the expense of the long term, had side-tracked business from investing in new products, and had undermined the climate for healthy investment. Others alleged that they had even weakened American competitiveness in relation to Japan (cf. Rohatyn, 1987). To Galbraith (1988: 12), they had even put capitalism itself at risk.

Yet to others these people were heroes who had given American business a long overdue shake-up. Indeed, the scandals have not materially affected the financial markets and, while people have definitely become more cautious and discriminating about junk-bonds, there is still a public for buying speculative stock: 'The continued strength of the market shows that most investors do not believe the system is evil' (*Time*, 2 March 1987: 47). The market did dip following Boesky's exposure in November 1986, but when Levine was arrested, and the cases threatened to spread more widely, the market scarcely blinked and went on to record new heights in February 1987 as institutional and foreign investors continued to put their money into New York. And the American public, according to a poll, was not that much bothered about insider dealing (*Business Week*, 25 August 1986: 114).

There can be no doubt, however, that Wall Street was severely shaken by the scandals. A conspicuous reimposition of internal and external control measures took place that may form a peak in a control cycle that will eventually be relaxed as business returns to 'normal'. But in response the Street reverberated with declamations about ethics and integrity. This is not surprising in the sense that this sober and respectable world had been turned on its head by a bunch of whiz-kids and particularly its leading light, Michael Milken:

> For the past half-dozen years, it [the junk-bond market; MP] has been a creature less of rational financial precepts than of mindful thinking, artful promotion, and, above all, illusion and magic. Instead of free interaction of buyers and sellers, the market was ruled tightly by sorcerers – Michael Milken and his apprentices at Drexel Burnham Lambert. The magic began to fade last year when several big junk deals fell apart. . . . Yet the end of the Drexel/Milken era is basically good for the beleaguered junk market: a return to reality, to logic, to sanity. Surely, junk under Drexel had salutary effects. In enabling raiders to launch bids against major corporations, it stirred ossified managements to take

needed reforms. Too often, though, junk was used to grease deals whose chief justification was the availability of financing and the avarice of the financiers. . . . To
foster junk's use in take-over financing and promote active trading in securities
that are inherently risky and liquid, he [Milken; MP] functioned as a kind of junk
Federal Reserve, the fixer of last resort. Using billions of Drexel's capital and his
famous network of junk buyer-cronies, he more or less controlled prices, and, when
Drexel deals faltered, found ways to avoid defaults. He created the illusion that the
market was almost as safe and liquid as high grade corporate debt. To many in the
investment business, Milken had a larger-than-life image as a wizard capable of
wondrous feats of financial wizardry. (*Business Week*, 26 February 1990: 26)

Milken was variously described as a financial genius, as the ultimate charismatic salesman, and as ruling with an iron grip; and also as an 'impresario
staging a Wagner opera' who 'had tirelessly worked the controls of a vast network of junk-bond issuers and buyers' (*Business Week*, 26 February 1990: 21).
Stone (1990: 119) asserts that 'all the people who worked for Michael Milken
believed him to be honest, they think the laws are wrong'. His power was that
he persuaded the respectable and reputable to believe in him and in his ability
to move mountains. And even people who doubted him could still profit from
following him and his acolytes. For instance, it was said of Wall Street that 'the
righteous wrath at Boesky didn't quite square with the fact that all through his
meteoric career at least part of his power and influence could be traced to his
cultivated image of being just a bit crooked, enough that when he made a
move, his rivals would buy in too, on the theory that he must know something'
(*Newsweek*, 1 December 1986: 32). Galbraith (1988: 12) disdainfully put down
a book by Boesky stating that it 'could not have won him a mail-order MBA
from the most primitive correspondence college'! In essence, the power of the
wizards was based on mystique, sleight of hand, and impression management.

No wonder the Street went in for penitential breast-beating; it had been
conned by a superior con-man. In retrospect, the scandals appear like a
watershed moment that somehow signals the end of a mercenary generation
and a greedy decade. Typically Giuliani had a phrase to sum it up: 'This is a
lesson to people who want to be millionaires in their thirties: better do it
legally' (*Time*, 23 February 1987: 50).

Some Key Concerns   By standing back from the details, it is possible to discern a number of major issues that emerge from this case. First, there is the
question of how you maintain a healthy financial community in the long-term
interests of the national economy; and, second, who has the right to control
that community? Third, what does the Wall Street affair tell us about the
dynamics of financial markets and the likelihood of these violations occurring
again? Fourth, what justifications were used? Fifth, how do these activities
relate to other forms of crime? And sixth, what can we learn about ethics and
integrity in business?

The Financial Community   Financial markets depend considerably on relationships lubricated by trust and are severely damaged by anything that
undermines that trust. The intense rhetorical smokescreen that enveloped

Wall Street in the wake of the scandal, with its emphasis on character, integrity, and ethics, was aimed at restoring confidence in its somewhat tarnished reputation. The stakes were high in a global economy, with London, Tokyo, and New York fighting for world hegemony. Belief in the integrity of the system had to be restored:

> Evidence of such a conspiracy [on insider-trading; MP] could set off a crisis of confidence in the stock and bond markets that would devastate the economy. American business runs on money, and Wall Street is the throbbing heart that pumps it through the system. If the public begins to believe that the markets are rigged, the flow of cash will dry up. (*Newsweek*, 1 December 1986: 33)

The rules had failed, and that meant a resort to an emphasis on 'good' people; a new generation had not respected the traditions and had to be taught new mores: 'We have to rely on the ethics and character of our people; no system yet invented will provide complete assurance that all of them will behave ethically' (Rohatyn, 1987: 21). The message was that you need good people to run a good system.

Control and the Watch-dogs   The scandals opened up the possibility of more severe external social control. The Street was calling for tougher internal controls whilst lobbying powerfully at the same time *against* increased external surveillance. The reformatory verbal response of the leaders of the financial community represent salvoes in a battle to keep the power of controlling Wall Street firmly in the hands of the financial institutions. The insistence that the traditionalists would clear up the Street themselves, and would restore ethics and integrity, was an essential exercise in damage control designed to preserve a large measure of regulatory autonomy. For the really central element that emerges with overwhelming clarity from the Wall Street scandals was that the primary 'watch-dogs' – the sro's at the heart of the traditional internal control system – had failed abysmally.

The Financial World and the Future   Reichman (1993) maintains that we should not retain a static picture of financial markets but should examine them in terms of systemic change. The traditional pattern of individual offences had shifted by the mid-1980s to a more organizational element which in turn is related to structural changes in 'the market, the incentives for misconduct, and the distribution of power among potential players' (1993: 71). Furthermore, Reichman (1993: 66) states:

> The thesis is advanced that deal making in the securities industry is constitutionally vulnerable to insider trading by virtue of the abstract, information-driven commodities it 'produces', the complicated networks of transaction-oriented exchanges that organize 'production', the changes in information technology that promote the free flow of information across jurisdictional (regulated) space, and the competitive drive to be on the 'leading edge' of financial innovation.

This leads her to the observation that we are likely to face new developments, new opportunities, and new incentives for deviance in relation to the structural changes that have occurred in the 1990s; her prediction is that 'the financial transactions that dominate the 1990s are likely to generate new sources of inside information and new networks for trading'.

Justifications   The players made justifications and rationalizations to reduce any moral inhibitions about engaging in criminal behaviour. Hirsch (1986) has written of game metaphors that aided the participants in perceiving their activities as normal, routine, and acceptable; Levine said:

> All too often the Street seemed to be a giant Monopoly board, and this game-like attitude was clearly evident in our terminology. When a company was identified as an acquisition target we declared that it was 'in play'. We designated the playing pieces and strategies in whimsical terms; white knight, target, shark repellent, the Pac-Man defense, poison pill, greenmail, the golden parachute. Keeping a score-card was easy – the winner was the one who finalized the most deals and took home the most money. (1991: 19)

Some of these reflect the techniques of neutralization used by delinquents (Benson, 1985), and this is emphasized by Reichman (1993: 81):

> In this kind of environment, many of the rationalizations identified by Sykes and Matza (1957) as important supports for otherwise law-abiding individuals to engage in unlawful conduct flourish: 'You gotta do it,' Levine told Wilkis [part of Levine's insider trading ring]. 'Everybody else is. Insider trading is part of the business. It's no different from working in a department store. You get a dis-count on clothes you buy. You work at a deli. You take home pastrami every night for free. It's the same thing as information on Wall Street.' [When Wilkis contin-ued to balk, Levine said,] 'I know you want to help your mother and provide for your family. This is the way to do it. Don't be a schmuk. Nobody gets hurt.' (Frantz, 1987: 64: Frantz used the technique of reconstructing conversations from interviews with participants).

Criminals   It is interesting to note that some of the rationalizations approx-imate to those used by common criminals. One commentator, who wrote on Milken, was in no doubt about the significance of these white-collar criminals and their violations:

> Mr Stein's verdict is emphatic. Junk bonds in his view were a classic Ponzi scheme built on treachery, lies and strong-arm tactics that owed more to Murder Inc. than to sound economics. 'Milken was no capo', Mr Stein says, 'but he certainly applied the general mind-set of the gangster to finance.' (Taylor, 1992: 14; Ponzi schemes are named after Charles A. Ponzi who massively defrauded investors in America in the early 1920s; the fraud was based on simply 'borrowing' money from early investors, to promote new investment schemes that attracted a strong flow of cash to pay off the most pressing creditors, and particularly to line the pockets of the fraudeur; Bosworth-Davies, 1988: 85.)

In addition, Reichman (1993: 65) observes, 'Dennis Levine in perhaps a self-serving account of his own motivation describes his behaviour in terms of the quest for action, a motivation not unlike the stickup men described by Jack Katz in 'The Seductions of Crime' (1988).' Although these were violations based on genteel financial transactions, there is an element of action, excite-ment, and intoxication that is reflected in the images used by 'ordinary' criminals to describe their criminal activity.

Ethics   A central plank in this case – indeed, in many of the cases – is the morality of managers. Traditionally the financial world of banks and investment houses is characterized by strong informal social control, integrity, respectability, trust, and codes of ethics. What social processes make executives and business people set their conscience aside and engage in deviant behaviour? And what mechanisms would need to be in place to emphasize ethics and to promote integrity? Jackall (1988) maintains that the condition of work generates moral consciousness and moral rules-in-use. Building on this insight, Reichman (1993: 80) argues that

> the structural conditions of deal making, that is the competition, loose authority relations, and the need to cultivate information networks generally, influence the cultural rules that guide the behaviour of deal makers. Most significant, the structure of deal making allows for, supports, and, in some instances, facilitates the construction of meaning systems favorable to rule violation, or, at the very least, favorable to blatant disregard for the rules systems and their agents.

This draws our attention to work and organization as shapers of moral climate. But our emphasis on the collective should not obscure the fact that each individual makes moral choices and is responsible for the consequences of those decisions. Why do some managers seem to leave their consciences behind when they enter the doors of the corporation?

Case No. 7: Thalidomide – the Drug that Deformed

Tough-minded Managers and Competitive Markets

In some cases the question arises, Why do executives bring an unsafe product on the market?; a corollary to that is, Why do some companies react to controversy in such a hard-nosed, aggressive, and penny-pinching manner? Some companies, such as Revco, do react positively in an accommodative and conciliatory way when faced with investigation, whereas others – for instance, Robins in the Dalkon Shield affair – behave in a tough, mean, almost vindictive style. What makes some managers seem heartless? For example, in the litany of corporate wrongdoings, there is one case that is especially horrifying and that raises powerful emotions and strong feelings – Thalidomide. More than 8,000 children in nearly fifty countries were born deformed because a drug had been brought on the market that was unsafe for use by pregnant women. Once more, it was the *Sunday Times* Insight Team that researched the matter in depth (Knightley et al., 1980). They raised the question whether this was not perhaps one of those inevitable accidents that occur when drugs are marketed, because all drugs, even the most benign and widely used, contain some risks for some people. But they argue cogently that this tragedy was not inevitable; that the law proved not to be particularly benevolent for those seeking compensation; and that recourse to the media (in the UK) was denied to parents by legal restrictions which clouded the scandal in a veil of secrecy.

As in all the cases it is vital to locate the case in the structure of the industry. Several authors, notably Braithwaite (1984), have written of the drug companies as having a particularly poor record in many respects (such as fraud in testing, intimidating critics, price-fixing, providing perks for medical practitioners, for insufficient warnings on promotional material, for 'drug-dumping' and drug-testing in Third World countries). The industry is characterized by intense competition, by large initial development costs (on average $125 million for a new drug), by long delays in getting a drug through the control agencies, and by potentially huge profits. Pharmaceuticals is very big business (prescription drugs in the USA are worth $28.3 billion per annum). In the USA it can take up to fifteen years to get a drug from lab to market; the considerable development costs may end up with no return on investment; but a popular drug that becomes an over-the-counter item can make a company a fortune. It is an industry characterized by often aggressive marketing techniques; not only are the representatives visiting major purchasers, such as hospitals, intensely competitive but they also engage in much munificent present-giving to sweeten relationships.

In the Netherlands, chartered plane-loads of GPs and specialists are whisked off to Cambridge colleges, or sunny resorts in southern Europe, where they are wined, dined, and serenaded; they can shop and go on sight-seeing tours, they can – if they wish – attend a number of presentations on new pharmaceutical developments, and they return laden with samples from the sponsoring company. The industry clearly feels that it is worth wooing medical people by spending relatively large sums of money on such trips in order to gain a competitive advantage for their products. (When I asked a Dutch medical specialist if he had any ethical qualms about going on these jaunts he looked at me as if I was deranged.) The competitiveness may even have been increased by the growing concentration of firms in the industry. The nature of the industry and the fierceness of the competition imply a degree of conflict between the medical research side of the enterprise, and the commercial side of maximizing profits and entering new markets. That conflict was exemplified by the Thalidomide affair.

The Origin: Germany

Thalidomide was a drug that could be taken as a sleeping pill or tranquillizer. It was developed by Chemie Grünenthal in West Germany as a drug with virtually no side-effects. Grünenthal did not enjoy a particularly strong research tradition; no other laboratory has since reproduced its research findings on Thalidomide; and research records are no longer available. But in 1957 Grünenthal jumped into the market with a powerful campaign containing phrases such as 'completely non-poisonous . . . safe . . . astonishingly safe . . . non-toxic . . . fully harmless' (p. 44; hereafter page numbers refer to Knightley et al., 1980). If true, the company had a near miracle drug on its hand. But it was not true. And Grünenthal should have known that it was not true.

For after laboratory tests the drug was sent for clinical trials to a number of doctors (some of whom had financial arrangements with Grünenthal) for testing on humans. In some patients symptoms of giddiness, nausea, constipation, and peripheral neuritis (loss of feeling in fingertips and toes) were recorded and forwarded to the company. Yet the marketing strategy for the drug was to stress that thalidomide was 'completely non-poisonous' and 'completely safe' and this dramatic element, as no sedative had ever been claimed to be entirely safe before, was heavily pushed in advertisements, circulars, and letters to doctors. Sales of the drug rocketed (90,000 packets of Thalidomide a month by the end of the first year in over-the-counter, 'OTC', sales). The incredible sales figures continued to rise in 1958 but so did the complaints.

However, Grünenthal did not reveal the contents of previous reports and continued to *step up* their sales-promotions efforts. Its representatives called on 20,000 doctors, and 250,000 leaflets were issued containing assurances ('non-toxic', 'completely harmless even for infants', and 'harmless even over a long period of time'; p. 46). The Grünenthal people were clearly concerned that the drug would be put on prescription, thus substantially reducing sales.

One tactic to support the drug was to have positive reports published swiftly and also to discourage negative publications by putting pressure on the medical journals. Grünenthal had clearly swung into an aggressive campaign to save the drug. It adopted something of a 'battle mentality' and the attitude was 'we intend to fight for Contergan [one of the trade names for the drug] to the bitter end' (p. 53). Even when the company applied for its drug to be put on prescription, it stepped up its marketing and promotion campaigns. Another response was to alter the label, which now stated that symptoms of 'hyper-sensitivity' would disappear on withdrawal from use of the drug; but this was simply not correct and Grünenthal should have been aware that it was not true. Doctors who criticized Grünenthal's posture were vilified as trouble-makers and one was even shadowed by a private detective. But by 1961 critical articles had begun to appear and sales began to drop.

What, in short, had been Grünenthal's reaction to negative reports about the drug? When doctors wrote asking if there had been any signs of this sort of side-effect before, this was never acknowledged. According to the Insight Team (p. 61), Grünenthal defended its product by emphasizing favourable reports and downplaying negative ones, with the hope of preventing the drug going on prescription.

Thalidomide and Pregnancy

Of pivotal significance in this case is the fact that Thalidomide was also said to be safe for pregnant women. In the mid-1950s it was not universally known and acknowledged that certain substances could pass through the placenta and affect the foetus in the womb. Grünenthal had not carried out clinical trials to test Thalidomide's safety for pregnant mothers and it had also not conducted reproductive tests on animals, although some other companies at the time were using such studies. In Germany, Professor Lenz, head of a children's clinic in Hamburg, took up the case of the disturbing number of deformed children being born and sought to determine whether Thalidomide could be the cause. He was soon visited by Grünenthal representatives and, when he took the issue to the Hamburg health authorities, he was threatened with legal action for 'an unjustified attack on our firm', 'for behaviour damaging to our business', and for 'the murder of a drug by rumour' (p. 136).

The arguments shifted to the Provincial Ministry of the Interior in Düsseldorf, with Grünenthal still threatening Lenz and still issuing circulars describing the drug as a safe medicine. A report in a Sunday newspaper echoing Lenz's objections to the drug swung the issue and Grünenthal capitulated. The ministry issued warnings of danger if the drug was used during pregnancy and these were relayed via the media. Grünenthal continued to dismiss those who opposed the company as 'troublemakers, opportunists, and fanatics', and endeavoured to dismiss Dr Lenz as a fanatic (p. 143). Even when the company, using radioactively controlled Thalidomide in mice, discovered that the drug could pass the placenta and enter the foetus' blood, it contested that this proved that the drug was responsible for the deformities.

Prosecution

In 1961 the Public Prosecutor's office in Aachen began an investigation into Grünenthal and Thalidomide which eventually led to a criminal trial – in 1968 – of nine Grünenthal managers for committing bodily harm and for involuntary manslaughter. In many countries there was simply no legislation on injury to a child before birth being a cause for legal action and this was also the situation in West Germany, where part of the delay can be explained by the fact that there was no precedent in German law. Also, Grünenthal dragged its heels, did not always cooperate wholeheartedly with the inquiry, and refused to surrender certain documents; some documents had to be seized in police raids. Lenz was objected to in court as biased and was further subject to cross-examination by eighteen defence lawyers for twelve days. Grünenthal kept up a public relations campaign during the proceedings and leaned on journalists who wrote negatively about the company. Their aim was to use delay to seek a settlement:

> But Grünenthal's most effective tactic was to suggest that the criminal action was holding up an out-of-court settlement of compensation claims for the German thalidomide families. Representatives of the company declared: 'if we wait to see where the trial gets us, we shall be sitting here in ten years' time and the children will have nothing. If we are forced to, we shall fight to the end, and that, of course, will diminish the resources for any payment by the company'. (p. 168)

After two and a half years of criminal trial proceedings the company agreed to settle out of court on compensation, with Grünenthal providing 114 million marks and the government over DM50 million. This meant that the criminal hearings were suspended, with the agreement of the prosecution, and there was no final verdict. Grünenthal had not been acquitted and neither had it been found guilty but the courts' opinion was unambivalent: 'It was inherently dangerous that a producer of pharmaceuticals would give priority to commercial interests as being of the most immediate importance. . . . The struggle for a market position demanded the emphatic promotion of commercial goals'

(p. 169). Although the criminal trial did not reach a conclusion, Germany was the only country where the government took legal action on behalf of the victims.

The USA, the FDA, and Dr Kelsey

The extent of the Thalidomide tragedy would have been vastly expanded if the drug had been approved for OTC sales in the enormous market of North America. The major reason why that did not happen was the role of the regulatory agency concerned, the Food and Drug Administration (FDA). The company which took on Thalidomide for North America was Richardson-Merrell. An earlier product, MER 29, had brought down 500 civil lawsuits on the company's head, which resulted in around $200 million in damages. A number of irregularities had occurred in the labs, and, as a result, a grand jury brought criminal charges against Richardson-Merrell for 'knowingly making false, fictitious, and fraudulent statements to the FDA' (p. 94). The company was fined $80,000 and three executives were put on six months' probation having pleaded 'no contest' to a variety of criminal fraud courts. The company learned from these experiences and established for the time unusually high standards of auditing for testing and manufacture of drugs; indeed, a lawyer for the company said of Frances Kelsey, 'the FDA scientist who stopped them from marketing thalidomide: "She's a hero [sic]. If it hadn't been for her, we'd be out of business"' (Braithwaite, 1984: 298).

Richardson-Merrell began distribution of the drug in clinical trials some nineteen months before applying to the FDA for permission to sell the drug to the general public. Around 2.5 million tablets were sent to more than 1,200 doctors, who passed them on to about 20,000 patients (this is considered 'massive' for a pre-production programme and distribution began so early before application to the FDA ostensibly in order to get data for the FDA; p. 98). Although the company had no information on the effect of the drug in early pregnancy, it assured doctors that it was safe. It did not carry out animal reproductive tests which might have revealed the horrendous effects that babies might incur from their mothers' use of the drug. The company planned a campaign to launch the drug and were preparing 10 million tablets for distribution.

The application for approval landed at the FDA on the desk of Dr Frances Kelsey, who was tackling her very first case for the agency. Although Richardson-Merrell lobbied the FDA persistently for approval, Dr Kelsey became increasingly critical as she delved into the material, particularly when she came across an article in the *British Medical Journal* linking Thalidomide to peripheral neuritis. The FDA report on the drug 'accused Richardson-Merrell of unacceptable ignorance of what was scientifically legitimate; and contained the admonition, "I cannot believe this to be honest incompetence"' (p. 105). Kelsey was later honoured by President Kennedy for 'saving the nation from the disaster' if the US market had been opened to Thalidomide (Braithwaite, 1984: 71). Resisting pressure from the company, the FDA insisted on a warning label for pregnant women using the drug. Inevitably, the relationship between Thalidomide and deformities in birth gave rise to hotly contested battles in the courts. One case in California went to a jury and the verdict was against the company, while the young girl concerned was awarded $2.5 million damages (which was, however, substantially reduced on appeal). The legal proceedings in the USA were prolonged and tough, but the Insight Team argues that the record there was ultimately quite impressive:

> No one had been denied the right to go to law because of the expense, the lawyers had been vigorous and resourceful, a case had been fought to a jury verdict, substantial settlements had been achieved, and apart from the secrecy imposed by Richardson-Merrell on publishing the amounts of these settlements, the press had been free to report the Thalidomide tragedy in full. The contrast with what was occurring during the same period in Britain could not have been greater. (p. 182)

Britain, Distillers, and the Courts

In Britain, the drug was distributed by DCBL (Distillers Company Biochemicals Ltd). It went on sale in 1958, with advertisements claiming that it was 'completely safe', while in 1961 the company was echoing the message from Grünenthal that 'Distaval (trade name for Thalidomide) can be given with complete safety to pregnant women and nursing mothers, without adverse effect on mother or child' (p. 67). In that same year, a Dr W. McBride of Sydney, Australia, was the first person to pose a direct link between the use of Thalidomide during pregnancy and the birth of severely deformed babies. His first warning to DCBL in Australia was ignored and, apparently, not communicated up the hierarchy in Australia nor passed on to headquarters in London (although there is some dispute on both matters). Eventually Dr McBride sent a letter to a leading British medical journal, *The Lancet*, and it was published in December 1961. This generated considerable alarm within DCBL, and one of its scientists, Dr Somers, experimented in early 1962 with four white rabbits who were given Thalidomide. Of the eighteen rabbits born, some thirteen were deformed. Ironically, Dr Somers was the 'first researcher to reproduce the Thalidomide malformations in animals' (p. 145). Despite resistance from Grünenthal, he published his findings in *The Lancet* in April 1962 and by the end of the year the 'wonder' drug had been removed from the market.

There ensued a legal battle, related to compensation, which took fifteen years to reach a solution (in 1977). This long-drawn-out and complex affair contains three main aspects: the legal contest, the restrictions on publication, and the gradual weakening of the company's position. In this period, the *Sunday Times* itself played a leading role.

In the legal area, the top company lawyers marshalled by DCBL were ranged against the small law firms which provided legal aid lawyers to the parents, and which were relatively inexperienced in such cases. The tactic of the company's lawyers was to seek an early settlement and, if that was not successful, to play for time. The plight of some of the families was desperate as they faced an almost unbearably stressful life caring for a child with multiple handicaps. Some of the deformities were truly extreme and placed an immense burden on parents who had to adjust to the physical and psychological burden of raising children who were severely malformed. And, of course, part of that burden was financial. Of the roughly 400 families involved, a small number gave in to a low offer within a few years. A majority of families later agreed to an out-of-court settlement; but the agreement was valid only if *all* families signed. This placed the parents under considerable psychological pressure. Six families refused to sign, and this meant that DCBL refused to pursue the idea of a charitable trust for the children because consent was not forthcoming from all the families.

By 1967, the *Sunday Times* had become particularly concerned about the Thalidomide affair and began to research its background. In Britain, there are strict rules regarding cases *sub judice*, which prohibit the publishing of information about cases being processed through the courts. The paper did publish an article on Grünenthal but this elicited protest although no legal action from the company. Legal advice, however, was that it was too perilous to bring out anything relating to Distillers. Within the paper opinion began to shift away from the manufacturer of the drug and towards the inadequacy of the settlement as the key issue. In September 1972, the newspaper entered the fray, under the leadership of Harold Evans who had helped to give the *Sunday Times* a strongly investigative and crusading slant, and published an article entitled, 'Our Thalidomide Children: a Cause for National Shame'. Reference was made to a second article, but the paper received a complaint from the Solicitor-General and the High Court banned the second article. It was to be *five years* before that second article reached the printers and the public.

Initially, an official inquiry had been refused by the then Minister of Health in the Conservative government, Enoch Powell. But as concern about the aspect of compensation increased, the cause of the families was taken up by a Member of Parliament, Jack Ashley, who was himself handicapped and who displayed an interest in issues related to the disabled. By taking up the matter in Parliament he was able to use parliamentary privilege to raise interest in the scandal. A sense of outrage grew among an increasing number of politicians.

DCBL had taken up a highly defensive posture, had circled the wagons, and was holding out in the courts for a low settlement. At the time the company was owned by around 250,000 shareholders who held nearly 300 million shares to a market value of £600 million. Unlike a number of other European countries, it is possible in Britain to discover the names of shareholders, and some of them were the local councils of towns and cities. One other institutional shareholder was the Legal and General Assurance Company, and it was potentially embarrassing that an insurance company, advertising with portrayals of healthy families and bouncing children, should be involved with a corporation that was putting the squeeze on the families of severely handicapped children.

The chief executive of the Legal and General – in a 'courageous and unprecedented' move (p. 261) – came out in the open with a plea for higher compensation. Dissent began to escalate and Distillers was faced with a boycott of its products in supermarkets, while Ralph Nader entered the fray and threatened a consumer boycott of Distillers' products in the USA. This negative publicity began to affect share prices; they dropped £11 million in one day and nose-dived £35 million in nine days. The position of DCBL weakened. The company's offer of a £5-million settlement was withdrawn and replaced with a proposal for £2 million per annum for ten years, which the government offered to contribute to in order to offset tax on income that the families would be obliged to pay. In 1972 the courts had been considering a cash settlement of £7,500 per family, whereas within a year that sum had increased to £54,000.

By 1976 the courts had lifted the ban on publication and the *Sunday Times* published an article on Thalidomide. A year later, the European Court of Human Rights decided in favour of the newspaper and against the House of Lords (the highest court of appeal in Britain), so that the original article leading to the ban could finally be published, almost five years later than planned. Some of the Thalidomide children were then in their late teens.

Comment

The Pharmaceutical Industry   The shocking story of the Thalidomide scandal was played out in a global industry, and the consequences were global; some 8,000 children in forty-six countries were born misformed because of the drug. Anyone reading the material on this affair, or examining the distressing photographs, cannot but be moved by this corporate failure that brought about so much suffering. And yet it occurred in an industry that has made an enormous contribution to reducing suffering and to promoting health. How, then, can we explain the cause of this tragedy? How did the companies concerned react to the affair? And have lessons been learned which can guarantee that the errors will not be repeated?

This case is not confined to one society or to one company so that the actors are many and the factors involved are complex. But the answer to our first question – how could this happen? – must be sought in the nature of the pharmaceutical industry. Pharmaceuticals are big business; modern health services are dependent on drugs (in the UK we are talking of 350 million prescriptions per annum, roughly six to seven prescriptions per person a year, and that is not counting the OTC trade in drugs). The industry is research-based, invests large sums in research, is closely linked to the medical profession, has become tightly regulated – leading to considerable delays in getting regulatory approval for new medicines, and can enjoy considerable profits. (Stanley Adams, the whistle-blower at Hoffmann La Roche, emphasized to my MBA students at Nijenrode that the industry is totally rapacious; he argued that the companies hunger after huge profits, are hardened to the suffering of people, and have no conception of ethics.) It also frequently engages in skilful and aggressive marketing campaigns. There emerges in the material on this industry evidence of a deep ambivalence between commercial interests and the health-caring, medical aspects of drugs (Braithwaite, 1984).

One aspect of the dynamic of the industry is an impatient and even aggressive stance when a company believes it has a winner – a successful new product that can relieve pain and make a handsome profit – and this can mean that high initial investment in research and development sponsors a desire to recoup that investment, an impatience with the delays for approval via regulatory agencies, and a haste to break into the market. There are doubtless wide differences between companies, and some firms may consciously seek an impeccable record on testing and safety (for example, Merck), but the above dynamic seems to underpin the Thalidomide tragedy. Grünenthal thought it had produced a pharmaceutical miracle, found that the wonder drug was generating huge profits, played down negative reports, and fought to keep the drug on the market by adopting a combative stance towards critics and regulatory agencies.

The next feature of the industry is that humans are used as guinea-pigs. Following laboratory testing with animals, a drug is brought into limited circulation via clinical trials with physicians. There is no completely safe drug (significant adverse drug reactions occurring in Britain are estimated at over 1 million per annum). Opren, an anti-arthritic drug, passed all the hurdles of pre-market testing but was withdrawn after nearly 100 deaths had been attributed to it. In fact, it is often said that laboratory animals enjoy more legal protection than human 'guinea-pigs', who may be unaware that they are being experimented upon (and this may be exacerbated by the ignorance of general practitioners about the flood of drugs that company representatives dump on them). Apart from these factors, there is an additional feature that may hinder an objective, purely scientific response from the participating doctors, and that is the possibility of commercial and/or financial relationships between company and physician.

Commercial Interests, Testing, and Regulation   The financial rewards for doctors of having links with the drugs industry may seem to impugn the medical practitioner's professional and ethical ethos. And yet the medical world is permeated with commercial interests. Research is sponsored by companies, medical journals rely considerably on advertising revenues, and individual doctors may receive retainers from companies in return for services. In short, the companies have a number of pressure points in the medical world which they can exploit via financial rewards to pursue their own interests.

This intertwined relationship of mutual benefit may also penetrate regulatory agencies. At one stage the FDA employed someone who had previously worked for the industry, and who became known as 'the company doctor'. As Associate Director of New Drug Evaluation, this person was rumoured to be somewhat favourably disposed towards a company and one of its drugs (despite critical reviews on the drug a new warning requirement was dropped; the drug was given an 'effective' rating despite a scathing report; and scientists

who were too critical were taken off the review: Dowie and Marshall, 1982).
When, in contrast, a regulatory agency is seen as slow, bureaucratic, and critical, then the industry may shift to persistent lobbying of the agency (as
occurred with Merrell's application to the FDA for approval for
Thalidomide).

Another aspect of importance is the changing standards of laboratory testing. This case commences in the 1950s, since when testing procedures have
changed considerably. At that time testing generally involved guinea-pigs and
mice, whereas nowadays monkeys and rabbits are used. As it was not universally acknowledged then that drugs could cross the placenta, reproductive
tests in pregnant animals were not always carried out. But even given these
changes, we are still highly reliant on the standards of self-reporting among the
researchers in the laboratory. For instance, no one has ever managed to reproduce the laboratory findings of Grünenthal with regard to Thalidomide. Since
then there have been significant changes in auditing and testing, but
Braithwaite, writing in 1984, was able to indicate a disturbing number of fraud
cases in testing drugs within the pharmaceutical industry (he drew on trial
transcripts, industry data submitted to regulatory agencies, and government
inquiries including congressional 'oversight hearings': 1984: 8).

Victims and Compensation   Given that this is an industry with a measure of
risk involved in its products, there are inevitably victims. How, then, did companies react to the consequences of marketing an unsafe drug? Grünenthal
ignored warnings, fought opponents, influenced the medical community, and
fought a long legal battle before eventually settling out of court. Distillers,
having taken on Thalidomide on the strength of Grünenthal's recommendation, fought a very tough, penny-pinching campaign on compensation and
only capitulated when the scandal began to hit them hard on the stock market and when politicians began to generate a sense of outrage in Parliament.
The response of the companies tended to be tough, calculating, adversarial,
and even aggressive towards victims. For instance, Pilger (1989: 67–73), an
investigative journalist, details how the publicity was focused on the group of
severely deformed children; almost unnoticed and unreported was the battle
for compensation for a second group of less severely deformed victims, and
here the company tenaciously and ruthlessly fought for every penny. Outside
the glare of publicity Distillers' lawyers were tough and aggressive in fighting
to minimize awards to deformed children.

Although the tragedy developed on a global scale, three countries in particular played a leading role. In Germany, the state was prepared both to
tackle Grünenthal with a criminal prosecution and to set up a compensation
fund for the victims of drug-related injuries (with contributions from the drug
companies based on a percentage of their sales). In America, the FDA was
capable of keeping the drug off the market; the media were unhindered in their
reporting; and parents of victims could gain access to top lawyers because of
the contingency-fee practice ('no cure, no pay' and a percentage of awards). In
Britain, in contrast, the media were muzzled and the courts proved to be a far

from benign arena for parents seeking compensation. Top corporate lawyers battled tooth and nail against some relatively inexperienced legal-aid lawyers, and put parents under considerable psychological pressure, in order to force a miserly settlement on people in deep distress. The cases dragged on for years. The government refused an inquiry, was initially tardy and meagre in its offer of compensation, and was eventually moved only by an escalating public outcry. The implication is that we have to take into account, in examining societal reactions to corporate deviance, the *national* culture in which government, regulatory agencies, courts, media, and companies are imbedded. The British experience was not particularly edifying.

Could it Happen Again?   The third question – can we learn from this terrible experience and prevent it happening again? – is answered by the Insight Team in strong and unambiguous terms: all the lessons have *not* been learned and, somewhere, it could all be happening again. The team's view is based on the analysis that drug monitoring is still fairly primitive (Opren revealed the inadequacy of pre-market testing and the need for post-marketing surveillance); that a number of European countries still have relatively unsophisticated schemes for releasing drugs; and that companies use expanding Third World markets as opportunities for testing and 'dumping' drugs. In effect, the Thalidomide tragedy could be repeated; but most likely it would happen in a developing country.

Hard and Blinkered   Finally, let us return to the central issue – how could a company bring an unsafe drug on the market and how can we explain the apparent heartlessness of the company's response? The key to Grünenthal's behaviour seems to be that they were a small company hoping for a breakthrough into the big league; Thalidomide promised a miracle drug and huge profits; and that negative signals drove them into a siege, or battle, mentality of fighting for their product. Managers closed their eyes to the evidence that threatened to disconfirm their belief in the wonder drug; indeed, they *redoubled* their efforts. For instance, when Grünenthal was forced to apply for Thalidomide to be placed on prescription, because of criticisms that focused on peripheral neuritis, the company also decided to *intensify* its marketing and promotion campaign (p. 56). As in other cases, the commercial commitment to a successful product seems to have the psychological effect of blinding people to negative signals and to sponsoring a highly adversarial stance. This leads to a form of cognitive dissonance in which disconfirming evidence elicits an even stronger belief in the product. In essence, an irrational element of blind and blinkered commitment emerges in a defensive stance of psychological closure that leads to hard, tough, and aggressive reactions to 'opponents', however vulnerable they may be.

This virtual self-conscious blindness to critical responses seems also to foster a determination to protect the reputation and continuity of the company by a secretive attitude to the media and a tight-fisted policy on compensation. There seems to be little consideration for the human and ethical aspects of the tragedy, and only intense pressure brought about change in the response of the companies; and in Distillers' case this was only when a stockholder's revolt made their share value tumble on the stock exchange. In the end, it was economic pressure, and not the public and parliamentary outcry, that forced the Distillers' change of mind. They were prepared to invest psychologically and financially in a prolonged legal and publicity battle; but severe loss on the stock market is clearly a different kettle of fish in the managerial mind. This defensiveness might appear to be a standard and understandable company response to protecting its long-term commercial interests in the face of potentially debilitating compensation claims.

But the difference with a 'standard' situation is that here the victims were severely deformed babies whose lives would be overshadowed by multiple handicaps. And faced by the dreadful consequences of their 'safe' drug on young lives, and on the lives of their parents, the companies reacted as follows: denial, secrecy, discrediting opponents, delay, employing extensive legal powers, and grudgingly minimizing compensation.

Case No. 8: 'Guinnesty' – the Guinness Affair and the City of London

My word is my bond.

(Motto of the London Stock Exchange)

Change and the City

The square mile of the City of London is the financial nerve centre of Britain. Cheek by jowl are housed the banks, insurance companies, investment houses, brokers, Lloyd's, the Stock Exchange, and the Bank of England. Traditionally the City has been linked socially to the British establishment and its leading lights have represented inherited wealth, family names of repute, and upper-class values; indeed, many followed the path of public school, Oxbridge, and the armed services before engaging in the noble practice of making money. Much has been written about the social cohesiveness of financial circles, the masculine and clubby atmosphere, and the informal nature of control based on trust, reputation, personal knowledge, and, above all, the idea that gentlemen should be left to discipline gentlemen (Clarke, 1986). The City could run itself. And if that cosiness was at all threatened – perhaps by some tiresome Labour politician haranguing the City about reform and interference with its prerogatives – then there were always powerful allies within the Conservative Party to mount a counter-attack.

This picture altered dramatically in the 1970s and 1980s due to complex forces that not only fundamentally changed the structure and culture of financial services in London but also raised in an acute form the issue of effective control and regulation in these radically new circumstances. It became a long, intricate, and constantly shifting battle between traditionalists and reformers that was fuelled by scandals, unprecedented media attention, and often vitriolic political and ideological debate between Conservatives (in office continuously since 1979) and Opposition (principally the Labour Party). The Guinness affair in the second half of the 1980s, involving an illegal share-support scheme, exposed serious skulduggery in the most prestigious circles of the City and accelerated the pace of reform and external control.

London in the 1970s was forced to change in order to remain a major financial centre that could compete with New York and Tokyo (and also with Paris and Frankfurt). The globalization of the economy, and the increase in international financial dealings, led to an influx of foreign banks into London. New style financial 'supermarkets' emerged that offered a wide range of services and that combined activities previously conducted in separate institutions and following established rules. Those rules were put under scrutiny as a Conservative government propagated 'popular capital-ism' and a 'share-owning democracy' and demanded a relaxation of the restrictions which had strictly channelled financial transactions previously. The Conservatives' encouragement of entrepreneurial activity also led to a mushrooming of new companies seeking venture capital. Then, as the coun-try emerged from the recession of the early 1980s, there were a series of mergers and takeovers that mirrored practices made familiar somewhat ear-lier in the USA. 'Deregulation' was said to have sponsored a resurgence in the British economy and the City was seen as a major employer, a crucial generator of wealth, and a vital guarantor of Britain's continued economic health. Confidence and trust in the probity, professionalism, and compe-tence of London's financial institutions were of eminent importance both economically and financially.

It was with considerable embarrassment, then, that the City found itself harried by a series of damaging scandals (that made the City a 'byword for speculation, inefficiency and cheating': Hutton, 1995: 5). These potentially weakened its position in the international arena while they also encouraged external reform. Revelations of fraud, incompetence, mismanagement, and corporate law-breaking emerged in relation to secondary banking, the com-modities market, Barlow Clowes, Johnson Mathey, and massive tax avoidance by companies, while even the seemingly impeccable reputation of Lloyd's was severely tarnished by a number of scandals (Hodgson, 1986). These drew increasing attention from the media, and the financial news began to move from specialized pages to the front page of newspapers. Scandal also pro-moted government scrutiny and increased regulatory control, with Labour endeavouring to make political capital out of every corporate mishap. The City was inundated with a truly unprecedented stream of reports, inquiries, new legislation, and threats of new regulatory mechanisms.

This new blitz on London came, ironically, from the Conservative govern-ment, which was determined to maintain international confidence in the City while also opening it up to an equity-owning democracy (that would then presumably go on to vote the Conservatives into yet another term in office).

The City had to be seen to be clean and efficient even if this meant a conflict between natural allies. The City put up a spirited defence; one commentator wrote:

> I am firmly of the belief that there is a body of opinion in the City and the financial establishment which will resist change at any turn. There is a powerful lobby actively engaged in an attempt to weaken and dilute the effective strength of the proposed legislation for financial regulation. (Bosworth-Davies, 1988: 10)

In essence, the central issue became the power to define the rules of the game in a world financial centre, and hence the conduct and ethics of the City of London were placed centre stage. Was the City a healthy, self-regulating financial community of impeccable virtue and palpable honesty or was it an uncontrolled playground for scams, fiddles, sharks, and for the 'greedy, unscrupulous, and the enviable wealthy' (Kochan and Pym, 1987: xx). It was in that context of change, turmoil, opportunities, new financial conglomerates, deregulation, internationalization of the economy, and conflicts over effective self-regulation that the Guinness affair unfolded.

The scandal shattered many assumptions about the gentlemanly conduct of British corporate affairs, revealed serious flaws in the regulatory controls, and hastened reform. For these were not sly fixers making a quick killing among gullible speculators, and then hoofing it to a haven free from extradition, but were the core of the establishment. And some of the most prestigious and reputable companies in the City were shown to have dirty hands.

Guinness and Saunders

Guinness was a traditional, family-dominated firm which had originally owed its success largely to the dark ale, or porter, that originated in Ireland and that became the symbol of the firm. By the 1960s it had begun to expand considerably abroad and to diversify widely, but it experienced some difficulty in managing a messy gaggle of companies from plastics to fish farming:

> By 1980 the company had acquired a motley array of products – after over 200 years with just one – and a management which did not know whether it, or the family baron, were really at the helm. Amidst this chaos salvation was at hand. Or so, at least, it appeared when a strong new manager came on the scene in 1981. (Kochan and Pym, 1987: 8)

The saviour of Guinness was Ernest Saunders, who had arrived in Britain from Austria in the late 1930s and who had become one of the new-style marketing-orientated managers. His expertise was in marketing, advertising, and international business and it led him to Nestlé, where he established an influential network through contacts on the managing board and achieved the 'status of international globe-trotting manager' (Kochan and Pym, 1987: 13). Saunders was recruited by Guinness in 1981 and swiftly claimed for himself the position of managing director. By all accounts he did a superb job reviving the ailing company by pruning the loss-making firms, focusing on the core business, and building up the core's strengths. At the height of his power a leading Sunday newspaper wrote that Saunders 'can now stand beside the

modern legends of British commercial success' and there was no sign that the
Guinness board and shareholders were anything but happy with his performance. Epithets used to describe Saunders included 'charming', 'exciting',
'stimulating', 'aggressive', 'a born salesman', 'ambitious' and a 'dedicated
workaholic'; it was also said that he was solitary, used people, and was not
always straight with you (preferring to employ others to do his dirty work for
him); but then as Kochan and Pym (1987: 3f.) note, 'Managers do not succeed
by being nice, and no one claims that Saunders was a particularly warm or
engaging man.'

What is clear from a number of sources, however, is that Saunders han-
kered after power, prestige, and worldly success and that he saw in Guinness
the ideal instrument to achieve his ambitions. He was determined to turn it
into one of the leading drink companies in the world.

Saunders turned Guinness around with incisive cuts and imaginative
advertising; at the same time he established a strong power base for himself.
The prestigious consultants, Bain and Company, were brought in and rushed
all over the company; a number of directors resigned and were replaced by
acquaintances of Saunders; and Saunders was prepared to switch advertising
agency, merchant bankers, brokers, auditors, or lawyers if the occasion
demanded. Among the people he came to rely on were Oliver Roux (the
financial man on the board although he was employed by Bain), Thomas
Ward (an American lawyer whom Saunders had met at Nestlé), and Roger
Seelig (corporate finance director with Morgan Grenfell). Having regalva-
nized Guinness, Saunders looked around for a company that could be
acquired to strengthen his position domestically.

Whisky Galore

His eye fell on Arthur Bell and Son, makers of Scotch whisky and market
leader in Britain. The company was run by Raymond Miquel, who has been
described as 'highly individual and ferociously independent', as a maverick
who won few friends but who easily offended people, as being uncomfortable
with journalists, and as someone who ran the company as his own 'fiefdom'
(Kochan and Pym, 1987: 27). In utmost secrecy Saunders set up a takeover
team that worked assiduously and meticulously in a planning 'bunker' at
headquarters to prepare the campaign. The Guinness people were furious
when news reports suggested their interest in Bell's but it was possibly a deliberate leak. In June 1985, Miquel was phoned in Chicago that Guinness was
after his company. He was taken completely by surprise. Miquel was not well
organized to reply and found himself increasingly friendless. In the heat of
battle his banker of twenty years, Morgan Grenfell, went over to Guinness at
a crucial moment and a member of his board, Peter Tyrie, came out openly
against his boss: 'The festering antagonism between these highly capable and
single-minded executives led to the now infamous split during the take-over
battle which Guinness was able to exploit so effectively' (Kochan and Pym,
1987: 30). Tyrie claimed to be acting in the best interests of the company, in

a manner that he was entitled to take in the interests of the shareholders, and in a legitimate fashion as his statement had been cleared with the Takeover Panel (Kochan and Pym, 1987: 53).

Guinness was remarkably well informed about 'enemy movements' and could anticipate them at every stage. The campaign had all the hallmarks of Saunders' style. He carefully cultivated the media and, in particular, the Scottish media; he persistently lobbied the key interest groups (including the Scottish financial establishment which Miquel had earlier alienated by his antics) and the politicians; and he managed to avoid any awkward interference from the regulators that might have seriously stymied his efforts. At Guinness a smoothly functioning team, working around the clock in an atmosphere of 'fun' and 'stimulation', seemed to get everything right and people began to sit up and take notice.

> Accompanying the high-level lobbying campaign, was a well-planned public-relations effort. The dull world of City take-overs was taken by surprise. It was highly orchestrated, meticulous and energetic. The focus of the campaign was the Scottish press and Guinness were able to field three media experts, all of whom were Scottish. (Kochan and Pym, 1987: 41)

Almost inevitably Saunders reaped the benefits of a sophisticated and ingeniously planned takeover scheme, which skilfully played the media and never neglected local interests, and he won the battle for Bell's in August 1985 with some 70 per cent of the shares. Ernest Saunders' 'star was at its highest and brightest' (Kochan and Pym, 1987: 55).

Distillers and a 'Friendly' Takeover

It all might never have happened if Argyll had not made a crucial decision leading to delay in its takeover bid for Distillers; if Saunders had been initially *more* ambitious and gone straight for Distillers rather than the smaller Bell's; and if Saunders had kept his word. But then there was always Boesky; and Saunders had had his appetite whetted and could not resist going after Distillers. For these were exciting times in the City as American-style practices – 'long working hours, high salaries, big-money deals and enterprising take-over tactics' (*Newsweek*, 12 January 1987: 34) – crossed the Atlantic; some had to adjust painfully to the new rules of the game while others rushed in energetically and, as it transpired, illegally.

Distillers, which had been severely shaken by the Thalidomide scandal (see Case no. 7), was the major drinks company in Britain, was led by 'gentlemen' who considered themselves the elite within the Scottish business establishment, and considered itself immune from predatory intentions. Yet it was described as a 'dinosaur' and as 'one of the worst-run large companies in Britain. In its way it is a classic British failure' (according to the *Daily Telegraph*, quoted by Kochan and Pym, 1987: 87). Its product line contained many established brands – thirty whiskies (including Dewars, Johnnie Walker, Haig, and Buchanans) as well as gins, cognac, vodka, and Pimms. This made it a tempting target for a takeover.

James Gulliver – a non-conforming, classical entrepreneur who had once been dubbed 'Young Businessman of the Year' – had built up the Argyll Group of companies with food and supermarkets at its core. He found Distillers, a Scottish-based company that he had known since his own youth in Scotland, irresistible despite the fact that it was three times the size of Argyll. Gulliver's acquisition team worked in top secret and were perturbed when their plans leaked out sending Distillers' shares upwards. Lacking crucial support at a vital moment Argyll, in consultation with the Takeover Panel (which regulates the rules of mergers and acquisitions), issued a statement that it would not be making an offer for Distillers at the 'present time' (in fact Argyll had agreed to wait three months). This 'stupid statement' probably resulted from over-caution and from lack of realization that this was a new era of leveraged bidding; but Gulliver was acting on the advice of City experts (and 'heads rolled' at Lazards, the City's 'most true-blooded bank,' and Lazards was dropped by Argyll: Kochan and Pym, 1987: 72–6). It is quite possible that Argyll could have taken Distillers there and then but the delay, pinning Gulliver to the three-month period, proved fatal.

It seemed as though Saunders had been too preoccupied with digesting Bell's and had been distracted from much larger and tastier prey. At Guinness it was back to the secretive 'bunker', the Bain team was put on full alert, and all holidays were cancelled. Gulliver meanwhile had gone head-on for Distillers and set out to swamp the Scottish media; the finance director of Argyll recalled, 'It was almost like fighting a war in terms of intensity and deployment of resources' (Kochan and Pym, 1987: 89). The snobbish, golf-playing gentlemen at Distillers were rudely awakened and became horrified at the thought of an upstart food retailer daring to bid for their company. The Office of Fair Trading recommended that the proposed merger should not go to the Monopolies and Mergers Commission and, when the minister concerned accepted this position, the way was open for Argyll. Distillers also felt there were leaks and this was the start of 'dirty tricks' tactics which emerged during the campaign (there were checks for bugging devices at Distillers, offices were carefully cleaned, and a private detective was assigned to investigate Gulliver).

In somewhat of a state of shock the board of Distillers decided to approach Guinness in the hope of finding there a 'white knight'. John Connell, chairman of Distillers, was an 'intensely shy' person and not perhaps well equipped for the tough times ahead:

> He was a gentleman to the core, an absolute gentleman, but absolutely stunned by what he saw happening around him. He just had not anticipated or expected the activity to be what it was, the hours that were required, the drive that was required, the innovation that was required. (An adviser to Distillers quoted in Kochan and Pym, 1987: 90)

Saunders initially proposed Connell as chairman of the merged company with a new holding board and the two existing boards operating at a secondary level. He also suggested that the headquarters would be in Edinburgh, that the name of Guinness would be changed, and that he would work as CEO with Connell. He later reneged on all these promises and crudely pushed Connell aside by recruiting Sir Thomas Risk (Governor of the Bank of Scotland) to chair the new combined group. But when the Distillers' board accepted the proposed deal its members were still convinced, 'foolishly as it now seems, that this was indisputably a benevolent meeting of two like-minded companies. We were certain that that was a better future than with Gulliver' (Kochan and Pym, 1987: 104).

In January 1986 an article in *The Times*, by a journalist with good access to Saunders, speculated on Guinness' interest in Distillers. Saunders had earlier denied any interest in Distillers to Gulliver and he repeated this denial now on the phone. But it did not prove difficult to discover that Morgan Grenfell advisers were around at Guinness' office, on a Sunday, and that Connell's Jaguar car was parked outside. When it hit Gulliver and Argyll that Guinness was a serious contender, a string of legal initiatives were launched to hinder the merger. Saunders' vigorous and concerted response bore many of the characteristics of the previous Bell's effort.

First, he surrounded himself with advisers – merchant bankers, lobbyists, stockbrokers, PR experts, lawyers, and advertising people ('such an array had never been seen before in a take-over campaign': Kochan and Pym, 1987: 106f.). There was Seelig as his right-hand man; at Morgan Grenfell he was the 'take-over star', the 'inveterate dealmaker', and he aggressively 'pushed to the limit take-over legislation and practice'. The smiling American Ward had behind a 'veneer of great charm' a determination that matched Saunders' with a 'no holds-barred', 'go-for-the jugular' style that fitted him for the new-style fray of corporate battles. The bankers and lawyers were all from prestigious firms with considerable clout in the City. Second, Guinness took on board 'some of the best known and influential lobbyists to put their case' (p. 114; page numbers hereafter refer to Kochan and Pym, 1987). Pressure was put on Members of Parliament with Scottish connections, on ministers (the Minister for Trade and Industry, Paul Channon, had to rule himself out of bounds because he was a member of the Guinness family), and on the regulators. The Office of Fair Trading was considering referral to the Monopolies and Mergers Commission as the new company would have too large a portion of the home market. Guinness skilfully offered to sell off a number of brands and checked this proposal with Judge Le Quesne of the MMC; he met the Guinness people on his own and had 'never experienced such unrelenting pressure':

> Guinness and Morgan's very skilfully knew their man. There's no break for coffee, or lunch, or dinner with Saunders, he's the general in the field, it's attack, attack, attack. He did it with the OFT and he did it with Quesne. (According to a former minister at the DTI and later an adviser to Argyll; p. 118)

Saunders and Guinness had outgunned the regulators.

Third, Saunders was highly sensitive to the role of the media and the battle was fought out in the public arena with full-page advertisements proclaiming the protagonists' positions. *The Times* and the *Sunday Times* were generally well coached by the Guinness people and Saunders was not averse to leaning on editors, waving his advertising power under their noses, particularly when he became 'obsessed with bias' in the *Daily Telegraph* and the *Sunday Telegraph* (p. 125). Fourth, there was the increasing use of dirty tricks as the battle progressed. Leaks were used to darken the reputation of opponents (Gulliver's Harvard degree in *Who's Who?* was traced to a four-week course in marketing, while Saunders' Nestlé background was raked over); private investigators were employed; legal actions were mounted; and 'Certainly all the main players had their offices swept for bugs. It was considered almost par for the course that there would be bugging, bribery and leaking and there were no complaints, however excited the press got about the stories.' (p. 128)

This was heady stuff for the British public as American-style tactics emerged in a frenzy of takeover activity in Britain and they were entertained by financial soap operas containing 'character assassination, duplicity and double-standards worthy of a Borgia' (or a Ewing, one might add: Bosworth-Davies, 1988: 76). Clearly there were new rules for the corporate game, and behind the gentlemanly façade it had become something of a rough-and-tumble, mud-slinging, stab-in-the-back, free-for-all:

> While the judicial game was being played in the public forum up front, bands of mercenaries employed by both sides were sniping in a guerrilla war. While the tactics used may have seemed shocking to the outsider, the men at the front knew this was the way take-over battles were being fought and few hands stayed clean at the end. (p. 123)

But behind the tactics and skirmishes the real conflict would be decided by the mobilization of financial muscle and by the reactions in the money markets. What is not allowed, however, is that a company assist in purchasing its own shares in order to bolster its position (this is illegal under the Companies Act 1985). With both sides using top brokerage firms, there commenced a see-saw battle for shares and control of Distillers. At Guinness there emerged an 'inner-cabinet' centred on Saunders, Ward, Roux, and Seelig which met separately from the team of advisers. In a very close run race Guinness shares went from 280 pence to 380 pence. There had been massive buying of Guinness shares, and Bank Leu of Zurich took £130 million worth – the bank's 'biggest single purchase came on 17 April, the penultimate day of the bid battle. It was enough to tip the balance at a crucial stage' (p. 139).

On Friday, 18 April 1986, Saunders could proclaim his victory, with Guinness holding 50.7 per cent of Distillers' shares. Gulliver was 'gracious in defeat', writing to congratulate Saunders; but suspicions had been aroused about share manipulation: 'From this moment onwards we saw this massive buying of Guinness shares and we found it very hard to accept that it was traditional investment buying' (according to Rupert Faure Walker of Samuel Montague who advised Argyll; p. 130). Once more Saunders had come out on top.

Victory Turns Sour

Ernest Saunders was effectively king-pin of a company valued at £3.7 billion, making it the fifteenth largest public company in the UK. But within a relatively short period of time the success story began to unravel. It commenced when he reneged on many of the promises he had made and when it became clear that he wanted complete control for himself over the new, powerful conglomerate. The Distillers' board was not allowed to remain the same and six directors resigned; Connell did not become executive chairman; Guinness was not going to change its name; company headquarters were not to move to Edinburgh; and, despite statements on offer documents and to shareholders mentioning Risk as chairman, he was elbowed aside by Saunders.

Saunders and his cronies – Roux, Seelig, and Ward – were running the show and they were backed up by a swarm of consultants from Bain. Even the Guinness board was being kept in the dark. As Saunders treated the old guard at Distillers with contempt, it became apparent that the white knight had been nothing else than an enemy corporate raider in sheep's clothing;

> I think from that point onwards it suddenly dawned on us that we were dealing with somebody who was not going to honour an undertaking. I called it a breach of faith. We then knew that the fundamentals of the merger agreement were as dead as a doornail. (According to a Distillers' director; p. 154)

But insistent signals were being transmitted to the DTI and the Bank of England about 'bad faith' and possible breaches of the law. It was said that the DTI was close to an inquiry but the watch-dogs proved surprisingly supine. Saunders was meeting some opposition but he made handy use of the media to get his version across and to undermine potential opponents. And in the background there was always Ward – 'rough, ruthless, bullying, threatening' – to lean on people (p. 157). The publicity paid off because at an Extraordinary General Meeting of the new company's shareholders held at a London hotel, which was 'very efficiently stage-managed' (p. 165), Saunders' resolutions were overwhelmingly accepted. Saunders doubtless basked in his triumph but the negative noises were mounting as the Labour Opposition maintained that the City had proved once more incapable of regulating itself – Saunders and Guinness had run a 'coach and horses' through the regulations (in the words of Opposition spokesman John Smith; p. 161). By pushing things to the limit Saunders was grasping tantalizing opportunities but at the risk of raising fundamental issues of deep concern to the financial and corporate world: 'The City was being tested on its power to regulate. Saunders, again, had got his own way and by-passed the City. The scale of his victory at the meeting at the Mount Royal Hotel must have further convinced him of his immortality' (p. 166).

The way in which Saunders had first conned and then humiliated Distillers led to bitter resentment; a gentleman simply did not conduct a hostile takeover under the guise of a friendly merger – it was just not done; as one embittered shareholder of Distillers' remarked: 'I think his subsequent behaviour shows that this is precisely what he intended to do, and of all the things that he's done, that is the biggest crime of all – it did more to ruin his own name, the name of Guinness and the name of the City than all the other things' (p. 167).

The Inspectors Call

The City might have swallowed it, and Saunders might have evaded attention, if Boesky had not fallen from grace and mentioned Guinness. It was at the prompting of the SEC that the DTI finally reacted and sent inspectors to Guinness's headquarters on 1 December 1986. This must have sent shock waves through the management board, and the fall-out was not slow in coming. It emerged that Guinness had invested $100 million in a Boesky venture. Saunders turned to a new public relations agency to handle the press and engaged the lawyers of Freshfields to tackle the DTI. Then, anticipating a battle in the courts, he released them in favour of lawyers with more criminal law experience. 'Mr Saunders had found Freshfields unsympathetic,' according to Oliver Roux who, following a dispute with Saunders, left the office (p. 170). Morgan Grenfell resigned as Guinness's bankers and Seelig also departed from the merchant bankers. In a letter to Guinness's lawyers, Roux effectively implicated Saunders and offered to cooperate with the authorities. The 'Roux letter' was circulated to the Guinness directors. Saunders protested his innocence and was to do so persistently; it was around this time that people began to detect symptoms of megalomania. The Guinness family, which had always fully supported Saunders, began to doubt him and he agreed to stand aside during the DTI inquiry. The accountants Price Waterhouse were called in and unearthed evidence of a massive share-support scheme. Saunders was dismissed. His cronies were unloaded from the company. It was the beginning of the end and the journalistic hunt was on to trace the shares, to unmask the culprits, and to unravel the juiciest morsels about the real activities of the corporate high and mighty.

What emerged from the DTI inquiry and subsequent criminal prosecution in the courts was the allegation that a number of leading figures in the City had engaged in the illegal share-support scheme. This conspiracy during the bid was also matched by a 'large-scale clean-up operation with Bank Leu [in Zurich] as the mop' after the bid to ensure that there would not be a wide-scale dumping of Distillers shares. Bank Leu was effectively 'warehousing' some 41 million shares (p. 147).

As these revelations were exposed there were internal inquiries and resignations at many of the prestigious and highly reputable firms involved. Morgan Grenfell, Woodmac, and Bain had all been seriously embarrassed and went in for a house-cleaning. Cazenove, the 'most powerful and reputable stock-brokers in the land' (p. 137), used solicitors to conduct an inquiry and simply left it at a press statement admitting connections with Boesky and Schenley. Then on the 6 May Saunders was arrested, and after a night in the cells, he was released on bail. At a press conference he was defiant. It was to become a familiar refrain.

Trial and Sanctions

When the trial came to court in 1990 it was dubbed 'the Fraud Trial of the Century' and it elicited unparalleled media attention. Indeed, there were to be several trials, but Guinness I lasted some seven months and it and the investigation cost in excess of £20 million. Saunders and three other businessmen were accused on a number of counts of theft, false accounting, and conspiracy. Saunders, ever conscious of marketing and the media, had carved out a role for himself as 'Mr Clean' and as the 'Scapegoat'. He had applied for legal aid, travelled to court by public transport, and was frequently accompanied by his visibly supportive children (his son wrote a book defending his father and constantly protested his innocence; Saunders, 1989). In a lecture to business students at INSEAD he quipped that he had gone from Rolls-Royce to a bicycle so fast that it ought to be in the *Guinness Book of Records*.

In fact, records were broken in terms of length and cost of the trial and the sentences. It proved to be the longest trial in English legal history. A lot has been made of the role of juries in prolonged and complex fraud trials on the grounds that they are not well qualified to follow the intricacies; the counter-argument is that they are there principally to decide on the honesty or dishonesty of the defendants. They heard of holding companies and accounts in Panama, the Dutch Antilles, Switzerland, Austria, and Jersey; and of money that sped around accounts 'faster than traffic around Piccadilly Circus' (p. 182). In the end the members of the jury simply did not believe Saunders on the evidence presented to them.

Against advice Saunders insisted on testifying. His version was that everyone was lying except him; that he had done nothing criminal; and that he contested statements made by his co-defendants to the DTI. Saunders was long-winded, rambling, and repetitive. His performance in the box was disastrous (*The Times*, 29 August 1990). It was as if his ego and arrogance could not allow him to admit a mistake but, in the end, his own insistence on purity undermined his credibility (*Sunday Times*, 2 August 1990). His fervent denials conflicted with the testimony of his co-defendants when all three had informed the DTI that Saunders knew everything and approved everything (*Observer*, 22 July 1990).

All the defendants were found guilty. The sentences were five years for Saunders, prison sentences and fines for two other defendants, and a £3 million fine for the fourth defendant whose age and illness were taken into account in not sending him to jail. These were high sentences for white-collar criminals and the fine of £5 million (plus nearly £0.5 million in costs) for one defendant was a record, exceeding tenfold the previously largest fine for an individual. The judge's words on sentencing were effectively an indictment of City practices and morals:

> The sentence I pass must send a clear message that persons who seek commercial advantage by acting dishonestly can expect little mercy from the courts. . . . The vice with which we are dealing is the corruption of public and commercial life. We are dealing with the problem against the background of the climate in the City in 1986.

Takeovers that went on at the time were often regarded as battles.

> In such battles the stakes are high, the pressures intense and the rewards of success
> potentially corrupting. The danger is that when men are hell-bent on victory and
> greed is in the saddle, all normal commercial propriety and respect of the law are
> cast aside in the rush and the individual voice of conscience cannot be heard.

He said that the evidence had shown that aspects of the Distillers takeover
were neither within the letter or spirit of the City's takeover code:

> 'These activities were an attack on the integrity of the market. That corruption led
> quite predictably to personal corruption: the payment of vast sums of money to
> those not entitled to them.' . . . Turning to Saunders directly, the judge said the jury
> had found him guilty of dishonesty on a massive scale in his privileged position. He
> was quite satisfied that Saunders was 'at the heart of the dishonest conduct which
> occurred in Guinness at the time. I doubt whether you were the inventor of the ille-
> gal share support scheme, but without your knowledge that scheme would not
> have gone ahead. You gave support to it and you encouraged it. But for the exis-
> tence of that scheme the outrageously high payments would not have been made.
> These rewards exceeded the dreams of avarice. You knew of them and you sanc-
> tioned them. You acted dishonestly.' The judge described Saunders as a
> single-minded man who would have been determined to win at all costs, but he
> added: 'I am satisfied that you would not have been sucked into dishonesty but for
> the ethos of those days.' (*The Times*, 29 August 1990: 1)

'The 'ethos of those days', 'greed in the saddle', 'hell-bent on victory',
'ambition', and 'greed'; those were the catchwords that echoed outside the
court. Two other themes that emerged in the commentaries were that life in
the City had become tough and mean and that rules could be broken almost
with impunity because the watch-dogs were toothless (or were napping at
crucial moments). The *Guardian* newspaper focused on the dangers of excess:

> The six month trial has lifted the lid off the seamy side of the City, exposing a sor-
> did story of greed, manipulation and total disregard for take-over regulations. . . .
> Excess in the shape of an unfettered drive for corporate power through hostile take-
> over bids in a rising market. Excess in terms of the exercise of fiduciary
> powers and personal greed.

And it castigated 'the lengthy and dishonourable supine tradition' at the DTI
and pilloried the Takeover Panel as 'more suited to running a gentleman's
club than curbing the excesses of the rising young Turks' (28 August 1990:
9–12).

After the trial the convicted criminals were shunted off to open prisons.
Saunders was released early on grounds of ill health; the others gained full
remission as 'model prisoners'. At Guinness II Saunders was considered too
ill to stand trial. After five months the judge dismissed the jury on the
grounds that one defendant was 'mentally unwell and unable to continue to
conduct his own defence', and that it would then be unfair to continue proceedings against the other defendant. Subsequently, the Attorney-General
dropped any further prosecutions against the two, which meant that their
cases could not be reopened. The prosecution case in Guinness III collapsed
when, before trial, the prosecution decided to offer no evidence against a

stockbroker and others as conviction had become 'unrealistic'. One of those involved complained of the stress of five years of waiting to be tried – 'they don't keep murderers waiting all that time'. And he added, 'the truth is I have never made any personal gain out of Guinness – over-zealous, yes. Criminal, no' (*Observer*, 16 February 1992).

Some commentators spoke of the 'establishment' taking care of itself whereas others felt that the prosecutions and trials had simply been burned (*Observer*, 16 February 1992: 31). And Guinness IV was meant to bring Ward to book but he was acquitted by the court in 1993 and then turned around and went on to sue Guinness for wrongful termination, loss of income, and libel (*The Times*, 6 February 1995). In the earlier trials several key witnesses from Switzerland had declined the invitation to testify in court. In the end the SFO's Guinness campaign more or less fizzled out as if the prosecutions had become something of an embarrassment to the authorities (*Observer*, 16 February 1992: 31), who were shown once more to have considerable difficulty in prosecuting major fraud trials (*Daily Telegraph*, 24 December 1994).

Yet one thing had emerged with clarity. The City had proved incapable of policing itself. Even so there was a temptation to restore face after the serious embarrassment of the Guinness scandal and to return swiftly to business as usual. For instance, the chairman of a Conservative Party committee on trade and industry opposed further regulation; he stated, 'We have to be very careful with the City that we do not damage a national asset and one of the most important markets in the world' (*The Times*, 29 August 1990).

Comment: Causes and Lessons

New Rules of the Game   The 1970s and 1980s in Britain witnessed significant changes in the business community as a result of developments in the markets of the global economy. New financial conglomerates arose and the ground rules were fundamentally altered as a Conservative government sponsored 'deregulation' of financial markets to open them to international opportunities and to attract a much wider participation in share ownership. New, tempting possibilities were grasped by some companies and some leading managers to innovate in terms of mergers and acquisitions. This ushered in a period of takeover battles that reflected a range of practices and manoeuvres familiar in the USA. Part of the new style of corporate warfare was the unusually tough and even dirty tactics employed (with leaks, smears, private detectives, and burglaries being used to undermine one's opposition). The 'sleazy undercurrent of corruption' in the City (as one Labour politician expressed it; *The Times*, 2 February 1987: 8) was exposed by a series of scandals that lifted the lid off the eminently respectable image of the City.

Until the Maxwell and BCCI affairs broke, the most spectacular scandal was the share-support scheme illegally operated by Guinness in the takeover battle for Distillers, in which Argyll had to be defeated. 'Deadly Ernest' and his co-conspirators had manipulated on a massive scale and this was reflected in the sentencing at their trial, which was heavy and clearly intended as a

warning and as a deterrent. A crucial element in all this turbulence and negative publicity was that business behaviour in general, and in the City in
particular, had become a hotly contested *political* issue. The Conservative
Party represented the establishment and the business lobby (which largely
financed the Party) but was also the party of 'law and order' and of a 'share-
owning democracy'. In office since 1979, the Conservatives had promised to
free the British economy and to create prosperity; much of the economic
renewal was in financial services and it was vital to protect those interests
domestically and to bolster confidence in them internationally. Labour, confined to a long term in opposition, recognized the opportunity to make
political capital out of the series of business scandals and to use them to
embarrass the government seriously.

Casino Economy   Labour politicians contrasted the deleterious consequences of the 'casino economy' with mine closures and unemployment in
traditional industries; the free-market monetarists in government only seemed
willing to intervene, it was alleged, when a bank was in danger of collapse and
needed rescuing; and in debating reform at Lloyd's it could be pointed out
that some seventy Members of Parliament (predominantly Conservatives)
were members of Lloyd's (Clarke, 1986: 63). Thus did fraud in the City
become potentially a major electoral issue (Bosworth-Davies, 1988: 210).
Following heated parliamentary debates the government was forced to intro-
duce a series of measures involving inquiries, legislation, and the
strengthening of the regulatory authorities.

But nothing could disguise the fact that the reputation of the City had
been badly dented. For, after all, those involved came from the most prestigious and reputable firms and they either enjoyed an impeccable lineage or
had developed powerful and well-connected friends. The culprits came from
the top drawer (Levi, 1987). But somewhere along the line these core establishment companies of bankers and brokers had relaxed internal control and
had given full rein to aggressive and innovative managers. This was permitted
because external regulation also proved woefully inadequate and the myth of
self-policing in the City was painfully exposed. The City had fought tooth-
and-nail against further regulation and was vehemently opposed to anything
smacking of an SEC-style institution. Ironically, it was precisely the SEC
that set the ball rolling in the Guinness affair. Indeed, if Boesky had not
started to sing, then no one might have learned of the 'concert-party' in
London.

Finally, in the last resort the main actors were gifted and respected businessmen. The Guinness story – and, indeed the Saunders story – was one of
power and ambition. The stakes were high, the pressures immense, and the
pace unrelenting. Roux (who had bargained his way out of trouble) said he
was 'dead tired' at the climax of the Distillers campaign, that he ended up
agreeing to matters he did not fully understand, and 'I got on a fast train and
it was bloody difficult to step off' (*Sunday Times*, 8 March 1987: 50).
Takeovers were seen as total, and dirty, wars where all is fair and where

'driven, rich and powerful men' flouted the rules (*The Times*, 29 August 1990). Opponents were smeared and humiliated, critics were intimidated or shunted aside, the media were cajoled and bullied, regulators were aggressively harried, and interest groups were persistently lobbied. Someone remarked that there was everything in the scandal except sex. And it worked brilliantly – until the actors became exposed to investigation and trial.

Guinness was exceptional – in terms of the stakes involved, of the highly reputable people implicated, and of reshaping the image of the British businessman as an aristocratic gentleman exuding trust, confidence, fairness, and integrity. The Guinness scandal was also held to be exceptional in that 'first, the perpetrators of the offences were caught, and second they were convicted' (*International Herald Tribune*, 8 September 1990: 21). The irony of that statement is that the four defendants in the Guinness I trial may have their convictions quashed. Saunders has successfully appealed to the European Court of Human Rights that evidence from statements he had made to the DTI impaired his ability to defend himself at his trial.

> The European Commission of Human Rights has declared admissible the applicant's complaint that he was deprived of a fair hearing as a result of the use at his trial of incriminating statements obtained from him by the DTI Inspectors in the exercise of their statutory powers of compulsion. The applicant argued that Art. 6 (1) ECRM includes the requirement that a defendant is entitled to exercise the right not to incriminate himself. Since the statements which he made under compulsion to the DTI Inspectors were used as a significant part of evidence against him at his trial, he was deprived of the privilege against self-incrimination and the fairness of the proceedings was seriously affected. The Government submitted that the DTI Inspector's investigations were separate from the criminal prosecution, their function being inquisitorial and not judicial and to establish the facts, which may result in others taking action. The Commission was also of the opinion that the right of silence, to the extent that it may be contained in the guarantees of Art. 6, must apply as equally to alleged company fraudsters as to those accused of other types of fraud, rape, murder or terrorist offences. In the Commission's opinion, the privilege against self-incrimination is an important element in safeguarding an accused from oppression and coercion during criminal proceedings. Whether a particular applicant has been compelled to incriminate himself and whether the use made of the incriminating material has rendered criminal proceedings unfair will depend on an assessment of the circumstances of each case as a whole. The Commission took into account that the refusal to answer could have been punished, on reference to the court, by a penalty of up to two years' imprisonment or by a fine. It was also accepted by the Government that the applicant's evidence to the Inspectors constituted a significant element of the prosecution case against the applicant. In these circumstances, the Commission considered this must have exerted additional pressure on the applicant to take the witness stand rather than exercise his right to remain silent at the trial and leave it to the prosecution to prove its case. In light of the above, the Commission found that the use at the applicant's trial of incriminating evidence obtained from him under compulsory powers was oppressive and substantially impaired his ability to defend himself against the criminal charges facing him. The Commission concluded that there has been a violation of Art. 6 (1) of the Convention. (Vervaele, 1995)

This opened the prospect of an appeal against conviction in the British courts which could also lead to massive payments in compensation. His request for appeal was rejected, which may mean a return to the European Court. 'Deadly' Ernest may not have had the last laugh yet; but he clearly does not give up easily.

Case No. 9: Moneylenders in the Temple: Calvi, Banco Ambrosiano, and the Vatican

> You can't run the Church on Hail Marys.
>
> (Statement attributed to Archbishop Marcinkus)

'Evil Empires'

Many cases of business deviance are concerned with violations in relation to competitors, markets, products, consumers, and the environment. The violations tend to be located within the business community and are not placed in the social, cultural, and political context that surrounds them. For some forms of corporate misconduct may be linked to politics; there may even be connections to organized crime – as with casinos, the construction industry, and with the cartage business in New York (Reuter, 1993). In some societies all three – business, politics, and organized crime – may be intertwined (Mills, 1986). This is unlikely and unusual in a number of western societies but it does occur in other societies. The implication is that we have to look at the context in which business deviance takes place both comparatively and cross-culturally. The recent revelations in Italy have exposed long and intimate connections between legitimate business, the political parties (of left and right), and various branches of organized crime. The interrelations were lubricated by favours, contracts, jobs but, above all, by bribes and sweeteners. This places all legitimate business people in a dilemma: whether or not to swim in the muddy waters. The predicament may be reinforced by threats of violence. It must be particularly difficult for foreign executives who are not familiar with the system and who may have little official leeway from their parent company (meaning they have to massage accounts to create slush funds while concealing that from head office). Such a situation may seem extreme. But in Italy it was for many managers a way of life. And this was not a notoriously corrupt Asian, African, or South American regime but in a southern European country within the European Union and subject to European law. You can drive there in a day from Holland. This intricate web of deceit and deviance was not far away; it was just down the road, in Italy.

The Actors in an Italian Scandal

The transformation of a leading Italian bank into a fraudulent financial empire, and its subsequent spectacular collapse, would undoubtedly have attracted considerable external attention in any event; but the case of the collapse of the Banco Ambrosiano was truly exceptional. For its downfall brought to light a staggering cast of characters that was enmeshed in intrigue, secrecy, politics, and the underworld. It was called 'one of the biggest things in Italian history, because everyone's involved' (Gurwin, 1984: xvii). The most startling of the revelations that emerged was a connection with the Vatican that induced world-wide interest. Archbishop Marcinkus headed the IOR (Istituto per le Operere di Religione; commonly known as the 'Vatican Bank'), which was strongly linked with the Banco Ambrosiano, and, at one stage, he even faced a warrant for his arrest. Sindona was a highly successful banker, nominated by the American Club for the 'Man of the Year Award' in 1974, who built up a web of fraud and falsification in international banking that earned him a twenty-five year prison sentence in the USA. It was he who introduced Calvi, director of the Banco Ambrosiano, to the Vatican Bank. Gelli was an arch-manipulator with strong right-wing sympathies who was associated with the fascists, Klaus Barbie, Perón, and Italian terrorists, and who recruited an impressive cross-section of the Italian elite into his P2 Masonic Lodge (and among them was the banker Calvi). Carboni was a minor businessman yet with strong connections to the underworld and extreme right-wing terrorism, and it was he who accompanied Calvi on his last, fateful trip abroad. In the background was an incredible supporting cast that included politicians, military men, journalists, businessmen, secret agents, and two popes – among whom was John Paul I (who died suddenly in circumstances that excited rumours of poison and cover-up). Indeed, a number of key figures associated with the case were eliminated, while the more fortunate ones merely had to nurse permanently stiff joints as a memento of the Banco Ambrosiano affair.

But the main figure was undoubtedly Roberto Calvi, who had worked himself up from clerk to become head of Italy's largest private bank. At various stages he became involved with Sindona, Gelli, Carboni, and the Vatican. He began to construct a complex network of fraudulent companies abroad. When the bank was under increasingly intense scrutiny in 1982 Calvi fled to London and was found hanging from some scaffolding under Blackfriars Bridge. An inquest jury brought in a verdict of suicide, but this was altered to an 'open' verdict at a second inquest which indicated that the death could have been caused by murder (an opinion widely held in Italy and apparently confirmed later; *de Volkskrant*, 27 January 1989). Calvi bequeathed a bankrupt bank, the collapse of which then represented the worst financial scandal in post-war Italian history, and which led to the exposure of a trail of devious and dubious connections within the highest echelons of society and, by implication, the Vatican. There were shock-waves throughout the international banking community.

The setting for this intricate and tantalizing drama was an Italian society that had recovered in near miraculous fashion from the rubble of war. The newly buoyant economy, however, was still faced with numerous pre-war regulatory restrictions, while standards of auditing and accounting did not keep pace with developments; in addition, the small Milan stock market was easily manipulated by a few major players. Generally, commentators note that modern Italian society has been continually dogged by the lack of strong central government, by the favouritism ('clientelism') of party politics, by the failure of many regulatory and government agencies effectively to implement legislation, and by behaviour posited on 'secrecy, back door, personal connection, special allegiances, private codes of honour and justice' (Johnson, 1983: 12), out of which grew the Mafia and its Neapolitan counterpart, the Camorra. Furthermore, it is maintained that the 'amassing of personal fortunes by individuals, and the exploitation of public life for this end, is part of the fabric of Italian society' (1983: 12). Italy is, then, a modern industrial democracy, yet there is a deep ambivalence running right through institutional life in terms of a powerful hidden economy, a perception that to get things done one needs access to submerged power, and that in some respects the structural weaknesses politically, economically, and socially are compensated for, or manipulated by, hidden societies and by the pious façade of religion.

The rich ingredients of the Calvi case – with interconnections between politics, terrorism, and the banking world – are not unique to Italy, as the BCCI scandal informs us (see Chapter 1). Ambition, connections, favouritism, and deviousness are also not monopolies of Italians. And yet the story of the Banco Ambrosiano does strongly reflect certain elements of Italian society and these have to be taken into account in placing the case in its proper cultural context. One essential factor, for instance, in explaining the prolonged success of the bank's dubious transactions lies precisely in the relationship between the Vatican, as a sovereign state, and Italian society. The Vatican's special diplomatic status, and its other-worldly religious allure, are a central component in explaining how it provides an opportunity to be exploited by those who wish to outfox the international banking world.

The Bank and Calvi

The Banco Ambrosiano was founded by a priest in 1896 as a Catholic bank aimed at counteracting the 'lay' or non-Catholic banks (that in late-nineteenth-century Italy were often associated with freemasonry). It became known as the 'priests' bank' and its stronghold was Milan in the industrial north of Italy, far from Rome (the seat of political power), and even further from the south and Sicily where other norms applied and which was treated by northerners as virtually a separate country (with sayings such as 'That's where Africa begins'). The bank was small, conservative, and solid. People had confidence in it.

Roberto Calvi joined the Banco Ambrosiano in 1947 and made rapid progress up the hierarchy due to his capacity for hard work, and also because the industrious young man was fortunate to find a powerful patron in the chairman. His rise also coincided with the strong expansion of the Italian economy in the 1950s that provided new opportunities and that Calvi seemed able to anticipate with fresh, innovative plans. In 1963, for instance, a holding company was opened in Luxembourg that later became known as Banco Ambrosiano Holding (BAH) and that was to play a central role later in

Calvi's schemes. The bank grew both domestically and internationally. In 1975 Calvi reached the top when he was elected chairman. Because of the religious origins of the bank and its connection with the Vatican, Calvi was colloquially referred to as 'God's Banker'.

By all accounts Calvi was a highly gifted banker. At the same time he is described as somewhat one-dimensional in that he was aloof and secretive, lacking the silky skills of the traditional patrician bankers. He came from a modest background and retained a strong insecurity that was cloaked by reserve, coldness, suspicion, and secrecy. He never felt at home with his fellow Milanese bankers, not to mention the wheeling and dealing politicians of Rome, and found solace within his close family circle. Some people even felt that he was basically naïve (Gurwin, 1984: 36).

Ambitious he certainly was, and he set about transforming this sleepy, provincial bank into an international merchant bank. In so doing he attracted the attention, admiration, and fear of others – 'at the height of his power he was described as the "most feared, hated and courted private banker in Italy"' (Gurwin, 1984: xvi). Employees were proud of the bank's success, the press dubbed him dynamic and innovative (the only 'real' banker in Italy), and he received an award for his contribution to the economy from the hands of the Italian President. On the surface Calvi was a supremely successful banker representing the new generation of fresh-thinking entrepreneurs cast up by the country's economic revival. He could have enjoyed an outstanding career.

Behind the scenes, however, in the heavily guarded and secretive enclave of his fourth-flour office at the headquarters building in Milan, Calvi had three concerns which ultimately led to his downfall and that of the bank he had built up so assiduously. First, the law was an obstacle to his plans. There were restrictions in force on the export of currency and it was illegal for banks in Italy to own industrial companies. To realize his ambitions Calvi had to bend the law. Second, he wanted personal control of the bank, and, to ensure that no shareholders could challenge him, he devised a secret plan by which the bank would virtually own itself with shares Calvi had 'parked' in companies abroad. Third, and crucially, he felt vulnerable to interference from the world of government, with which he was not familiar, and which he believed was dominated by shadowy cliques of powerful men. He became convinced that the real power in Italy was hidden – *potere occulto* – and that he had to insure himself against it.

> To a certain extent all Italians are aware of the existence, and importance, of hidden power, the 'sotto-governo' (undergovernment) – whatever it is called. But to Roberto Calvi, a particularly insecure and personally isolated man, it became something of an obsession. He was convinced, says one banker, that 'in the world, only a few obscure persons command and decide, and that it's important to have connections and friendships with these circles'. Carlo Calvi [his son; MP] said that his father 'was fascinated by secret societies'. (Gurwin, 1984: 36)

Calvi came to dominate the Banco Ambrosiano completely. His ambition brought him to bending the law in order to achieve his ends, while his isolation, insecurity, and ostensible naïvety led him to seek allies to negotiate and to manipulate for him in those areas where he felt himself a clumsy stranger. The first 'fixer' to spot Calvi's combination of flair and vulnerability was the banker Sindona.

Sindona

Sindona was a Sicilian (and, like Calvi, of modest origins) who was brought up with an empathy for those two vital institutions in the south – the Church and the Mafia. He developed a powerful ambition for wealth, power, and connections. Sicilians traditionally like to think of themselves as 'sly, nimble, quick-witted . . . to be naïve is ultimately to be "fesso" . . . the opposite of "fesso" is "fuerto" or "scaltro" – the sly knowingness which is able to fox authority, to get things done, to bend rules' (Steinberg, 1989: 13). Sindona set out to evade the country's banking, tax, and foreign-exchange controls in order to construct a financial empire based on companies in fiscal paradises, such as Luxembourg and Liechtenstein, through which he could operate on the Italian stock exchanges. Basically the idea was simple, and it was to be copied by Calvi later. Money circulated through a 'shell' company abroad to an offshore investment company and then back into Italy. This enabled him to evade Italian laws and to smuggle millions of lire out of Italy.

Sindona was like Calvi in possessing a 'memory of steel, a swift imagination, and a capacity to keep a secret' but in contrast to Calvi he was a good communicator with 'charm, sparkle, humour' (Cornwell, 1984: 39). At home and abroad Sindona was regaled as a great banker, a dynamic entrepreneur, and 'the only financier in our country who has a modern and dynamic mentality: a modern vision of business' (Gurwin, 1984: 18); Andreotti (the ex-prime minister) even extolled him as the 'saviour of the Lira'.

In the rise of Sindona there are ingredients and characters that recur in the case of Calvi. Sindona cultivated the Vatican, turned to Licio Gelli to lobby for him, had underworld connections, and sought a mentorlike relationship with Calvi. In essence Sindona built a fortune based on illegality. When one particularly ambitious Italian venture came to nought, however, he turned his attention to the USA and bought control of the Franklin National Bank. Basically he was engaging in 'enormous and reckless foreign exchange speculation and falsifying records to cover up the resulting losses' (Gurwin, 1984: 23). When his empire collapsed, the demise of the Franklin National was until then the biggest failure in US banking history, there were severe reverberations on the Milan Stock Exchange (which needed several years to recover), and the collapse contributed to the international financial crisis (that had followed the first oil crisis of 1973).

Sindona had offered his tutelage, his contacts, and his connection with the Vatican to Calvi. But from being a widely fêted banker he had become a bankrupt facing criminal charges in Italy and in the USA. In 1974 warrants for his arrest on grounds of fraud and falsification were issued in Italy but he fled to Taiwan. In his absence he was sentenced to three and a half years in jail. Later he received a twenty-five year prison sentence in the USA, and was extradited to Italy where he died in prison when poison was placed in his coffee. The Vatican had its financial fingers severely burned by the collapse – there were reports of amounts varying from $30 to $300 million – and the escapade, potentially so damaging to the Holy See's reputation, should have acted as a severe warning. Yet somehow the dubious connection – Sindona, the Vatican, Calvi, and Gelli – did not prevent a similar scandal occurring a decade later.

This is especially remarkable because Sindona himself actually helped to open the can of worms about the Banco Ambrosiano. In their relationship Sindona clearly felt that he had strongly favoured Calvi, and for a Sicilian a favour implies an obligation; but when Sindona was in deep trouble Calvi – and the Vatican – dropped him like a hot brick. Sindona then engineered a highly embarrassing rumour campaign in pamphlets and posters which displayed remarkably accurate information about Calvi's dubious share transactions and secret Swiss bank accounts. Apparently Calvi paid off Sindona and the campaign ceased, but an even more potent barb had proved irreversibly damaging in that Sindona had sent a most compromising letter for Calvi to the Italian Central Bank. In the aftermath of the Sindona scandal it was likely that the regulatory authorities, in order to bolster international confidence in Italy's tarnished financial market, would mount a sharpened control campaign. And now the authorities had been alerted to the shadow side beneath the glitter of the Banco Ambrosiano and Roberto Calvi.

The Vatican

The Vatican is a tiny state within a state, its 109 acres being considered sovereign territory. Although it enjoys a religious aura of piety and respectability as the focal centre of the world's Catholics, it also has mundane preoccupations like salaries for its staff and expenses for its upkeep. In the 1970s it was in need of money for a number of reasons and sought alliances with bankers. A key figure in this development was Archbishop Marcinkus, a tall, sociable, sporty American who became a highly visible organizer of papal tours abroad and who took over the running of the IOR, the Vatican Bank. Much earlier, in the 1940s, the Vatican had enabled wealthy Italians to export capital and it was the Vatican's status as virtual 'offshore' haven that soon made it attractive to businessmen:

> 'IOR is the best off-shore bank you can think of,' notes Umberto Venturini of the business weekly 'Il Mondo'. 'Instead of having the unsavoury reputation of a bank in the Caribbean, they have the moral backing of the Church. They are not answerable to any central bank governor, there's total secrecy – and no pope has ever been elected for his financial acumen.' (Gurwin, 1984: 11)

In effect, people like Sindona and Calvi used the IOR as a conduit for moving currency out of the country in a way that evaded effective control. The obsessive secrecy of the Vatican, allied to their privileged status outside of Italian law, means that accurate information on the actual workings of the IOR are meagre (cf. Raw, 1992). At one stage, when Calvi's world was tottering in

1981, he approached Marcinkus for support and received 'letters of comfort', which have no legal status, but which were used to reassure a number of anxious bankers abroad. Marcinkus issued them in return for a letter from Calvi absolving the Vatican of financial responsibility for any subsequent claims. Furthermore, when the scandal broke, the Vatican denied knowledge of the ghost companies which were at the centre of the Ambrosiano affair – but Calvi's son clearly thought otherwise (Gurwin, 1984: 172). This negative publicity was potentially enormously damaging to the Vatican. The embarrassment was heightened by the arrest warrant issued against Marcinkus in 1987 for 'fraudulent bankruptcy' (*Time*, 9 March 1987). The Vatican refused to accept the warrant and for a period the Archbishop remained confined within the Vatican's precincts. Later, the warrant was declared invalid by the highest judicial organ in Italy, against which no further appeal is possible (*de Volkskrant*, 18 July 1987). Marcinkus' career was irretrievably damaged – he was not made a cardinal, no longer accompanied the pope on his travels, and eventually resigned from the IOR in 1989.

The Vatican had been implicated in two major financial scandals involving Sindona and Calvi. The Vatican's response was one of pained innocence; it had been taken for a 'colossal ride' and its 'sins were those of naïvety and inexperience' (Cornwell, 1984: 229). In effect, it had been duped by Calvi. But there can be no doubt that the Vatican had been used for criminal purposes in two successive scandals and these had left an unhealthy impression of secrecy, and even duplicity (1984: 247).

Gelli and the P2

Licio Gelli was one of these slippery power-brokers who emerge to lubricate the byzantine world of Italian politics. He was a past master at *sotto potere* (hidden power) based on information and contacts: and he was associated with 'intelligence agencies, Latin American dictators and death squads, arms dealing, and right-wing terrorism. His dubious reputation as an arch-manipulator earned him the nickname of the "puppetmaster"' (Gurwin, 1984: 53). He was associated first with Sindona and then embraced Calvi. While investigating Gelli's relationship with Sindona the authorities unearthed a membership list of the P2 Freemasons Lodge of which Gelli was Grand Master. He had proved able to draw in 962 prominent people whose names, when made public, staggered even the Italian public who are reared on a juicy diet of scandals:

> Over a period of about ten years Gelli was able to recruit to his most secret of secret lodges in Italy three Cabinet ministers, 40 MPs, the head of every branch of the Armed Services, the head of the Intelligence Services, and senior officers in banks and corporations, who between them gave access to and, information being a form of power, some control over an enormous array of deals, contracts, preferments, and appointments. (Moorehead, 1984: 19)

Roberto Calvi was on the list. He seems to have been initiated into the lodge by Gelli in 1975 and at some stage he started paying him. Gelli had powerful friends in almost every area of public and economic life and he could valuably lobby to protect Calvi's interests. But at a price. For there was an element of blackmail, and even of a massive protection racket, in his dealing with people and the 'protector' of Calvi soon became his manipulator. Gradually Calvi was drawn into a web which ensnared him in increasingly dubious transactions which saw Banco Ambrosiano money flowing to Latin America and being slushed to Italian political parties (allegedly to the tune of 88 million lire) and to the Swiss bank accounts of Gelli. The puppetmaster had found another victim.

Gelli fled Italy in 1981 when his secret files were uncovered. Later, disguised and with a false passport, he personally attempted to transfer $100 million from one of his Swiss bank accounts and was arrested and imprisoned to await extradition. He escaped from the allegedly 'escape-proof' prison of Cham Dollan near Geneva by bribing a guard and with the help of a helicopter (*de Volkskrant*, 19 May 1990). It was hinted that some members of the Italian secret services were involved in the escape and that later, in France, he was protected from arrest at the hands of pursuing Italian officials by elements of the French secret services. The Italian authorities now formally acknowledged that there was a link between the P2 and the Banco Ambrosiano and that Gelli was in possession of $100 million of Ambrosiano money (Gurwin, 1984: 165). After several years in Latin America Gelli gave himself up to the Swiss authorities in 1987. In Italy he has been sentenced to eighteen years in prison for offences that included involvement in the 'bloodbath' of Bologna in which eighty-five people were killed by an explosion at the railway station in 1980. Because of 'heart trouble' he has been released provisionally from prison. Some sources maintain that this is the result of his continuing influence. Many of those mentioned in the P2 list still hold high office. Indeed, it is even insinuated that he has set up a new P2 and protests in his autobiography – *The Truth* (*sic*) – that P2 was legal and respectable (*de Volkskrant*, 19 May 1990).

Gelli represents the dark and sinister side of Italian society and his influence on Calvi was malign. The isolated and insecure banker, ambitiously determined to protect his empire, was vulnerable to an unscrupulous manipulator who drew Calvi deeper and deeper into intrigue and illegality.

Front for Crime

Up until the early 1970s Calvi had advanced his own career and built up the Banco Ambrosiano in ostensibly impeccable fashion. There was no evidence of criminal practices. But in his desire to seek external protection, and to realize his continuing ambition, Calvi sought the company of people like Sindona and Gelli – and later Carboni – who had strong connections with illicit business deals and even with the underworld. In effect, Calvi allowed the Banco Ambrosiano to be appropriated for criminal ends.

It began with the Sindona-Vatican connection and led to an intricate international network of deception. Like Sindona, Calvi set up holding companies in Luxembourg and Liechtenstein, where supervision was weak and the Italian Central Bank had no authority. There was a chain of holdings, subsidiaries, and ghost companies in Zurich, New York, Nassau, Nicaragua, Panama, and other Latin American countries. The holdings sprouted a profusion of shell companies with strange-sounding names (they were 'little more than an entry in a lawyer's books': Cornwell, 1984: 70) that were managed by Calvi but owned by the IOR, which put the companies beyond Italian scrutiny. On paper they were worth millions of dollars but they could be started with a token capital of $10,000. For instance, 'Andino' in Peru contained 'assets' of $890 million in 1980 but its board meetings were held in Switzerland or Luxembourg while decisions were effectively made in Milan; several of the ghost companies' directors were Ambrosiano employees – among them the telephone operator at a Bahamas bank (Cornwell, 1984: 34). The basic tactic was simple:

> Calvi would purchase Italian shares and then re-sell the shares to a foreign company secretly controlled by him. He would then buy the shares back at an artificially high price. The result: several million dollars have been smuggled overseas – in violation of Italy's foreign exchange control laws. (Gurwin, 1984: 20)

The essence was to conceal control and to evade regulations. This enabled Calvi to buy into Italian companies against the law, to manipulate the stock exchange, to strengthen his own company illegally, and to create opaque channels for illicit transactions probably related to arms, drugs, terrorism, and bribes.

In this high-risk game two issues were crucial. One was that the authorities should not be able to uncover who had real control; and the other was that there had to be a measure of sound financial decision-making behind the deceptive façade to ensure that economic reality would not eventually intrude to thwart the banker's intricate constructions. Three factors contributed to Calvi's downfall and the bank's demise. First, he used illegal transactions to gain control of two banks and a large insurance company in Italy. Second, he spirited some 15 per cent of the shares of Banco Ambrosiano through his overseas maze out of the country at a cost of $60 million, giving him control of the bank. Third, Calvi was induced to buy into the Rizzoli media group – which published the influential daily newspaper *Corriere della Sera* – and this originated with Gelli and the search for influence and political clout (this involvement in a newspaper was illegal). Indeed, Calvi stated 'all my problems began when I bought Rizzoli', and Gurwin (1984: 54) maintains 'in making the loan to the ailing Rizzoli company Calvi had violated every principle of prudent banking'. All three could have got Calvi into trouble, although perhaps not of such a catastrophic kind, but in a sense it was the perfidious influence of exploitive figures in his career that led Calvi increasingly to take decisions that should have been directly opposed to his banking acumen.

Somewhere along the line he had started paying money to those devious people in his life. There were 'commissions', loans, bribes, and questionable transactions which no one at the bank really dared to question. Millions were funnelled away to obscure destinations (and, after the collapse, some $400 million remained unaccounted for). Was Calvi fully conscious of what he was doing or had he lost control and was he in the grip of people who were squeezing him? For as each shady figure passed on – first Sindona and then Gelli – there seemed to be another one ready to take his place; thus did Flavio Carboni appear, and he inveigled himself into Calvi's confidence. Carboni had some very tough companions, and Rosone (second man at the BA) said, 'these people make you afraid just by looking at them'; he received gun-shot wounds in the legs that reinforced his point (his attacker turned out to be an underworld figure, who was then shot by bodyguards and who it transpired had been sent by Carboni to act as a 'frightener': Gurwin, 1984: 86). Later it turned out that Calvi had paid Carboni around $14 million. But precisely for what remained obscure. Calvi was not only keeping bad and dangerous company but also a number of his illicit schemes were on the point of unravelling.

The Regulatory Response

To a large extent the machinations of Sindona and Calvi were made possible by the weaknesses of the regulatory mechanisms in Italy – the small Milan Stock Exchange was easily manipulated, the banking and currency regulations were not difficult to side-step, and the Italian Central Bank was powerless to investigate the Vatican's IOR and the shell companies abroad. And, of course, they were made possible by the structural opportunities offered by the near uncontrollable network of offshore financial institutions. For instance, although the Luxembourg holding was called a 'bank', it was not in fact one and consequently the Luxembourg banking authorities were not empowered to control it. However, the increasing linkage of formal financial markets meant that Italian scandals could have rapid and severe international consequences while the Italian economy needed a measure of stability and confidence in order to attract capital. In the mid-1970s the lira was in difficulties, the country faced mounting deficits and high inflation, and the Communist Party grew in strength, which brought a stronger left-wing influence in the political spectrum. One measure that was passed, designed to stem the flow of illegal currency exports, was Law 159, which criminalized the offence and, crucially, made its enforcement *retrospective*. The aftermath of the Sindona affair, moreover, was bound to bring parliamentary and press attention and a revived regulatory alertness. Increasingly, there were indications that the Banco Ambrosiano warranted investigation. Sindona's venomous letter to the Central Bank had sowed the seed of distrust.

The Bank of Italy, responsible for the supervision of about 1,000 banks, is a professional and highly respected institution. In 1978 it sent twelve inspectors to the Banco Ambrosiano. The Bank's subsequent 500-page report was scathingly critical. In brief, it displayed concern about lack of information, weaknesses that could affect other banks, suspicions on the chain of control, the weakness of the organizational structure, the level of undercapitalization, breaches of the banking laws, 'supine and acquiescent auditors', and it concluded with the necessity for restructuring the bank (Cornwell, 1984: 91f.). Two breaches of the currency regulations were attributed to Calvi personally, and this information was passed on to the judiciary.

At this stage the regulators were closing in on Calvi and the Bank. There then occurred a most disturbing episode. The military-style police, the Carabinieri, entered the Central Bank and arrested the principal inspector for the Banco Ambrosiano case on the grounds that he had concealed evidence in another inquiry; only the advanced age of the Governor saved him from a similar humiliation. Given that banks in Italy are all connected to political allies, and tough inspection will elicit enemies, it can only be assumed that this was a 'counter-attack to teach the bank a lesson' and the 'inspector had been muzzled' (Cornwell, 1984: 99, 101). Inevitably, this gross interference in the investigatory wing of a central bank in a major European country brought powerful protests from home and abroad (and the various charges were dropped and the officials concerned were later rehabilitated). This crude warning to the Bank of Italy meant only a stay of execution for the Banco Ambrosiano.

For within a short time the authorities had regained their confidence and were prepared to launch an assault on the financial world when thirty-eight bankers were arrested in 1980 in relation to a savings bank scandal. The financial police, the Guardia di Finanza, also turned up at the Banco Ambrosiano, demanded the surrender of Calvi's passport, and warned him that criminal charges were imminent on the grounds that he had failed to report share-dealings as demanded in Law 159. This must have been a severe psychological blow to Calvi, who was used to attending the key meetings of the international banking world. In addition to stricter regulatory control related to the declaration of interests held by Italian banks abroad, there was a new regulatory regime at the Milan Stock Exchange where the supervisory committee, CONSOB, was pushing, under new leadership for consolidated balance sheets, the disclosure of true shareholdings in quoted companies, and other trading rules as found elsewhere in Europe (Cornwell, 1984: 130). All these were signals that the regulatory net was tightening around Calvi.

The pressure increased on him in 1981 when it was revealed that he was a member of a secret society (the P2 Lodge), and when it emerged that he was improperly involved in a newspaper and had also broken currency regulations. Calvi was arrested and spent two months in jail, which proved shattering for this very private man; he even attempted suicide, although this was interpreted by some as merely a tactic to generate sympathy for his plight. But he was exposed as vulnerable to pressure and under interrogation he had declared himself ready to reveal names with regard to politics, the IOR, and the P2 ('I'm just the last wheel on the cart', said Calvi, 'try to understand, Banco Ambrosiano is not mine. I'm simply in the service of someone else': Gurwin, 1984: 74). However, he retracted much of his statements, although this episode may have alerted his 'good friends' to his weakness and to the threat he posed if he should talk. He was sentenced to four years in prison and was fined 16 billion lire but was released on appeal. The board at the bank then reconfirmed his position unanimously; thus a man with a criminal conviction hanging over his head went on running the largest private bank in Italy!

The Roof Caves In

From his conviction onwards Calvi was a man trying to stave off the inevitable. The Vatican Bank helped out with the 'letters of comfort' but would assume no financial liabilities. There was a short-lived involvement of Carlo de Benedetti, the dynamic entrepreneur who had revitalized Olivetti; but he left after sixty-five days complaining of encountering a 'wall of rubber' and airing his grievances to the Bank of Italy. When there was the first full disclosure on the Milan Stock Exchange the stocks of Banco Ambrosiano declined precipitately. Rosone, the deputy chairman of the bank, was shot at in the street. And, significantly, Calvi was for the very first time defeated at a boardroom vote. Soon afterwards, he was smuggled out of the country. News of his disappearance set off a landslide, and Rosone said later, 'banks deal in confidence, and we just ran out' (Cornwell, 1984: 186). It soon became clear that Ambrosiano was bankrupt and appeals for a rescue to the IOR fell on deaf ears. In his absence Calvi was stripped of his powers, the central bank was notified, and Ambrosiano was placed in the hands of commissioners. Calvi's secretary jumped to her death from a window in the bank's building. Inevitably, some sceptical Italians asked whether she was perhaps helped on her way.

London

Calvi left Italy in the company of some rather unsavoury companions, and via a circuitous route he arrived in London. He had once more talked of revealing all, of naming names, and of implicating the Vatican. He warned his family to get out of Europe and to go into safe hiding; he told them, 'something really important is happening, and today and tomorrow all hell is going to break loose' (Cornwell, 1984: 196). With him always was a black brief-case containing his most secret documents. On 18 June 1982 his body was discovered hanging from scaffolding under Blackfriars Bridge. His body was partly immersed in the Thames and his pockets were filled with money and stones. There were possible elements of masonic symbolism in the manner of his going. Much later there were indications of Mafia involvement, suggesting that Calvi was considered dangerous, in that he was threatening to reveal too many secrets, so that he was expertly strangled and was then left hanging on the scaffolding (*de Volkskrant*, 27 January 1989; *Daily Mail*, 14 August 1991).

Once more the Italian pattern of potential witnesses being prevented from disclosing unpleasant truths had been repeated; and Calvi's black bag had disappeared (later a bishop was indicted in Italy on charges of receiving stolen property in relation to buying back from criminals potentially incriminatory documents for the Vatican; *Daily Mail*, 14 August 1991). During this period Calvi was accompanied by Carboni and some of his cronies. Carboni was later arrested and charged with a number of crimes, including involvement in the shooting of Rosone (deputy chairman at BA, presumably because he was getting too inquisitive). Calvi spent his last days as a fugitive, in the company of criminals; on the eve of his death he informed his daughter that

> he was on the verge of completing it (a deal) – and that it could solve all his problems. 'Things are going ahead slowly' he said, 'but they are moving. . . . A crazy marvellous thing is about to explode which could even help me in my appeal. It could solve everything'. But the conversation also contained an ominous note: 'I don't trust the people I'm with any more.' (Gurwin, 1984: 117)

The next day the man who was once hailed as Italy's leading banker was ignominiously dangling from scaffolding with a rope around his neck, not far from one of the world's financial centres, the City of London, that he had frequented as a highly successful businessman. The career of 'God's Banker' had come to a sad and violent end in a grotesquely visible manner.

The Mess

The dimension of the collapse that emerged after these dramatic events was on a scale that threatened to damage severely international confidence in Italy's financial institutions. The Luxembourg holding company was revealed to have a loss of $1,000 million and total debts were in the order of $1,200 million. It was now clear that Ambrosiano was facing a terminal crisis of both solvency and liquidity. There followed a spate of lawsuits among the various parties involved in the crash. The Bank of Italy, for instance, was refusing to honour all the debts because much of the activity of BA took place in areas where the bank had no control. A rescue attempt by a consortium of Italian banks failed. The Vatican was sanctimoniously denying any responsibility for the débâcle but it did take the unprecedented step of appointing three 'wise men' to investigate the Vatican's financial operations. Later the Vatican was forced to admit that it owned a string of tiny companies that owed the BA some $1,100 million. A joint commission of Italian and Vatican experts also began an inquiry (Cornwell, 1984: 247).

But the Italian government was seeking a political agreement with the Vatican on long-standing issues, and the IOR scandal, with the Vatican still vehemently denying responsibility, stood in the way of a settlement. In 1984 a Concordat was signed between the Italian government and the Vatican after years of delicate negotiations, and it was preceded by a settlement between the Vatican, the Italian authorities, and 120 foreign creditor banks, including a $250-million contribution from the Vatican towards claims.

Comment

> 'In this country everything depends on the "good friends"; my "good friend" is sure that you will get the job you want, so you can go ahead and apply for it. This is our way of doing things. This is our mentality.' In other words the Sindona, P2 and Calvi scandals are products of a mentality and

a system. As a government official puts it: 'Unless we change the rules of the game, another Calvi can be born.'

(Gurwin, 1984: 199)

The complexities, and multiple layers, of the Calvi affair almost beggar analysis; but it tells us something about international banking, Italian society, personal ambition, and the shadowy interlocking world of politics, finance, and religion. In similar fashion the subterranean part of international finance has links to terrorism, drugs, organized crime, arms-smuggling, right-wing regimes, and secret services (cf. the BCCI case; and Mills, 1986). And it reveals that certain segments of banking are indispensable conduits for the dubious and hidden transactions of the underworld, and indeed the 'upper-world', to the extent that a respectable and thriving bank can even become a criminal institution.

Financial Structures   The key to the schemes of Sindona and Calvi lies in the convoluted network of 'offshore' tax havens that evade external control, impose minimal internal inspection and external auditing, and espouse secrecy as fervently as Switzerland. In Europe (Luxembourg and Liechtenstein), the Caribbean, and Latin America there are possibilities for legitimate business – but also for crooks (and government agencies engaged in crooked business) – to seek maximum fiscal advantage with a minimum of supervision. The consciously created loopholes, and inviting weaknesses, in the international banking system are central to this case, which illustrates the 'ease with which a natural deceiver could exploit the opportunities offered' by that 'system' (Cornwell, 1984: 248).

Italian Society   The context for this drama was a post-war Italian society that experienced a fluctuating economic recovery from the war and a long period of political instability (with left- and right-wing terrorism, the murder of Aldo Moro – a former prime minister) and a number of scandals that brought down governments (such as the Lockheed affair of the early 1970s and the oil scandal of the late 1970s). Everything in the country – favours, jobs, contracts, and protection from interference – depends on the shifting bases of power between the contending political parties; and their absorption in negotiation and manipulation (and in reaping the fruits of their favours) almost precludes a strong, serious, and responsible control government (so that Italy is sometimes referred to as a 'blocked democracy' and the stranglehold of the parties on public life as 'partyocratie': *de Volkskrant*, 27 July 1991). There is, too, a very powerful duality running through Italian society between the surface 'front' presented to the outside world and a submerged world where the 'real' business is conducted – in the underground economy (*economica sommersa*), the hidden power structure (*sotto potere*), in secret groups (*potere occulto*) and in the underworld (*malavita*). Notorious examples of the latter are the criminal organizations of the Mafia and Camorra, which reflect and propagate widely held notions of honour, secrecy, silence (*omertà*), and revenge. This means that in Italian society nothing is quite what it appears to be and that public figures have to engage in a constantly shifting and intricately subtle role-play.

Personal Motives   The Calvi case is almost a Faustian morality play related to power, ambition, and greed. First, Sindona and later Calvi were both highly ambitious; they decided at some stage that illegality was necessary for them to achieve their ends. Probably the duo could have had successful and unblemished careers by following legitimate paths, but they clearly wanted more than those paths offered.

In terms of criminal careers, and of identifying potential criminal behaviour in business, it is important here to note that Sindona and Calvi were internationally respected bankers with whom many major banks were only too willing to do business and who were regaled as geniuses (even as saviours of the economy) and as daring innovators. Their strategy was to employ a solid, respectable façade behind which they constructed a fraudulent empire; but they were able to conceal that criminal core until a very late stage in their career. Until exposed, they were identical to successful, straight bankers and indistinguishable from them.

To take the concept of 'career' a little further, there is an element of adoption and tutelage in the case in that Sindona took Calvi under his wing and taught him the financial wizard's bag of tricks; when Calvi was looking for 'good friends' to protect him in places of power and influence he soon found Gelli, and later Carboni, courting him to provide their services. Calvi's ambition led him to illegality and to keeping bad company because he became a captive of the people, and processes, that came to dominate the hidden part of his existence. In those circles 'friendship' tends to be conditional, manipulative, and exploitive; Sindona went from mentor to bitter enemy and Gelli from protector to blackmailer. At the end Calvi – 'a stiff, formal man with a highly developed sense of conspiracy, fascinated by secret societies and the occult' – had become a victim of his own ambitions, his own suspicions, and his own compatriots; he lived in a '"continuous passage from one bunker to another", from armoured car to fortified building, surrounded always by bodyguards' (Moorehead, 1984: 19). He was the captive of forces he could not control.

The Global Multinationals of Crime   Calvi claimed at times to be only a small cog and that others controlled him. His story often raises the feeling that beyond the visible antics of the well-known players in such cases, there is a much deeper, sinister web of connections that somehow interlinks the worlds of finance, politics, religion and ideologies, the media, terrorism, arms-smuggling, drug-trafficking, secret services, right-wing regimes, and organized crime (Mills, 1986; Martin and Romano, 1992; Pearce and Woodiwiss, 1993). It is an area that is obviously difficult, and dangerous, to investigate and it is open to the wildest of fantasies and conspiracy theories. Here, one can only touch on the subject, and hint that there are characters and connections in this case which raise disturbing but near impenetrable questions. These are related to the death of Pope John Paul I – was it because he was investigating the IOR (Yallop, 1984)?; the Catholic Church's aims in eastern Europe and Latin America; the support of dictatorial regimes and the direction of their death squads; the sale of Exocet rockets to Argentina via the illicit arms market at the time of the Falklands/Malvinas crisis; the activities of extremists in western espionage agencies (with or without covert political support); the activities of left- and right-wing terrorists and the support they derive from governments and/or politicians in east and west. And then there are the new 'multinationals' of crime – the old, agrarian criminal societies such as the Mafia which have grown into extensive syndicates with global tentacles – which profit from this finance-politics-international crime nexus because they are of value to both sides of the ideological divide and will operate as dealer, trafficker, launderer, pimp, bag-man, intimidator, burglar, or executioner.

Religion   We do not generally associate bishops with investment banking and it appears strange here to find prelates and cardinals becoming entangled in financial intrigues. But the Vatican is a sovereign state with instrumental ends and mercenary needs; the heightened activities of the Catholic Church in the 1970s created a demand for funds; and the Vatican does own a bank. So religion is an essential thread running through this case. The Banco Ambrosiano had been born as the 'priests' bank' in terms of promoting Catholic against lay banks; its statutes required shareholders to produce evidence of their baptism and a recommendation from a priest; and it became linked with the Vatican. And it was precisely that connection – between high finance and the money needs of the Holy See – which added such a powerful element to the scandal. There is no doubt that the reputation of the Vatican was severely tainted by all this and that its obtuseness, secrecy, and denials clashed starkly with its other-worldly moral ethos. The machinations of Sindona and Calvi could not have taken place if the IOR had been run as a proper bank; behind the walls of the Vatican it operated as an offshore bank, beyond Italian supervision and auditing.

Control   There are three aspects of control that I wish to touch on here. First, the regulatory context of the case is embedded in post-war Italian society where the expansion of the economy was not matched by equivalent developments in legislation. Some of the control measures dated from before the war and were designed to deal with different circumstances; later, they were hindrances to businessmen who operated under more restrictive measures than elsewhere in Europe. In a sense the failure to match legislation and control with the developments in the economy, and with mechanisms in use elsewhere, meant that Italian businessmen were encouraged to bend the law in order to get things done while, at the same time, they could easily avoid supervision.

Second, it is clear that Calvi was pre-eminent at Ambrosiano and that there was no real internal curb on his activities. There was no effective control by board, shareholders, or accountants, that might have checked his absolute power, particularly when his decisions began to stray from sound banking logic.

Third, external control was revealed to be amenable to political persuasion and interference. The most notorious example was the punitive raid on the Bank of Italy in order to 'muzzle' it. The magistrature, particularly in Rome, was also shown to be liable to bend under external pressure. In addition, CONSOB, the supervisory organ of the Milan Stock Exchange, failed conspicuously to curb the manipulation of the market.

In brief, the regulatory environment could be said to have stimulated rule-bending and to have proved incapable of exerting effective control of financial markets. This was exacerbated by Calvi's total dominance at Ambrosiano, which simply subverted internal control, and by an external control structure that was vulnerable to political interference.

Victims   The crimes of Calvi created undoubted victims. There were the 40,000 creditors of Ambrosiano who had been encouraged to invest in the bank; there were the employees (a new Ambrosiano was resurrected from the old one but it was reduced in size); and there were the many foreign creditors who had been 'burned' and who found the Bank of Italy and the Vatican reluctant to help them out. Then there were the opponents, critics, journalists, magistrates, and regulators who faced humiliation and intimidation or worse if they were too inquisitive or too energetic. Threats, blackmail, and violence run darkly through the case and are a significant aspect of trying to unearth deviance in Italian society. Finally, there was Calvi himself, who paid with his life for his involvement with Sindona, Gelli, Carboni, and with some shadowy figures from the underworld. His initially brilliant career ended with him as a fugitive scuttling across Europe, and with a faked suicide that spelt out a warning to all those who threatened to lift the veil on certain powerful, underground forces. It can cost you your life.

The Media   The subterranean activities of politicians, officials, and businessmen may be partly checked by revelations in a tough, independent, and investigative media not open to external influence and manipulation. Calvi was able to own, illegally, the most influential newspaper in the country and Gelli had journalists tied up in his P2 network. When the scandal journalist Mino Pecorelli published incriminating stories on Gelli's past he was murdered within hours (Gurwin, 1984: 64). One element of control – independent and fearless media – was difficult to operationalize in Italy.

Trust and Confidence   A major 'victim' of substantial financial crises is confidence in the international system linking banks and within the banks themselves. The international system and its outlet in stock exchanges and markets is a highly sensitive and delicate instrument that is sometimes all too responsive to various political and industrial tremors. The so-called 'secondary banking crisis' following the first oil crisis of 1973 was definitely exacerbated by the Sindona scandal. The collapse of the Franklin Bank in

1974 was then the biggest default in American banking history and the Federal Deposit Insurance Corporation was forced to fork out $2 billion in compensation.

Calvi and the Ambrosiano affair severely dented the reputation of the Milan Stock Exchange, undermined confidence in Italian financial institutions, and even had international repercussions. The Milan Exchange lost 4 trillion lire, then around $3 billion, in what was called the 'Calvi' effect; the Bank of Italy had suffered severe loss of face; and in the early 1980s the world banking community was once more facing a spate of bleak news related particularly to the growing foreign debt issue. Then it was hit by the Ambrosiano crisis, which was one of the largest bank failures since the war (Gurwin, 1984: 78); and as Rosone stated, 'a bank sells confidence, only confidence'.

Victims of the 'System'   Finally, the case reveals the convoluted, multilayered aspects of a complex, major scandal; of course it is a story of greedy men and overweening ambition, but it is also a lesson about finance, politics, and regulation in the rich cultural context of post-war Italian society. The roles were played out, and the script enacted, according to specific conditions at specific times; what unfolded was related to shifting coalitions of power, control, and submerged forces that constantly changed the parameters of the 'system', even though the players were aware of the culturally bound rules of the game that enable people to negotiate the shifts and ambivalences between 'front' and 'back' in Italian public and corporative life.

There are a number of dualisms running through Italian society – between north and south, between clarity and intrigue (representing two conflictory mentalities, according to the journalist Piero Ottone: Gurwin, 1984: 87), between piety and cruelty, and between surface government and hidden groups with ostensibly the 'real' power. In a sense Calvi fell prey to those dualisms – he was a cold northerner not at home in Rome and a world away from Sicily; he was the brilliant banker with an obsession for secrecy and for hidden power; he was a dominating figure in his own circles but became apparently *fesso* (naïve) to be preyed upon by those who were *scaltra* (quick-witted). Personally and professionally he even began to lead a double life. A lawyer for Calvi at his trial in 1981 maintained that

> Calvi's fatal flaw was that he had a dual character or, as Mazzola put it, 'two brains'. . . . 'Brain number one is good. It's the brain that has built Banco Ambrosiano into a big, solid, prosperous, well-run bank. Brain number two thinks that the world is run by conspiracies.' Calvi's dual nature was reflected in the financial empire he created. 'It was two banks,' says an American banker in Milan. 'One was a normal Milanese bank, heavy in deposits. And then there was this other institution (the foreign network) that nobody understood.' (Gurwin, 1984: 199)

Initially a gifted and feared magnate, he set in chain events that took control of him and led remorselessly and tragically to his own downfall and death. As such the events have to placed, in the context of that 'system' to which he was responding:

Ambrosiano was the ultimate example of what could go wrong with the system at large. It was a mutant child of an imperfect financial structure, of the political parties' unquenchable thirst for money, of the secret ramifications and connivances of a distorted state, of the unresolved relations between Italy and the tiny sovereign state of the Vatican, planted in the heart of its capital. (Cornwell, 1984: 25)

Systems are in a sense no more than the people that comprise them. Yet they can assume reality in the eyes of people who attribute powers to them ('you can't beat the system' or 'the system will get back at you'). And people also get highly involved in the 'system'. The deep emotional attachment of people to their work, and their powerful ties with the organization to which they devote much of their lives, was expressed by Rosone. With a somewhat melodramatic Italian touch he said, 'I did what I could to save the bank. I loved it the way one can love a woman.' More prosaically, Calvi summed it all up when he commented bluntly, 'for that amount of money, people will kill' (Gurwin, 1984: 203, 104).

Case No. 10: the RSV Débâcle in the Netherlands

> I realize now that you cannot keep your hands clean in politics.
>
> (De Quay, Dutch politician of the 1960s, quoted in
> *Elseviers'*, 2 February 1985)

Dutch Deviance

This case builds in two extra dimensions to the series of cases. One has been emphasized before, and that is cross-cultural variations in patterns of deviance and reaction to it. In Europe there are still major differences in legal traditions and enforcement patterns between countries despite attempts at greater coherence and unanimity through European Union legislation. But underlying the legal order there are layers of moral and social order, and examination of these reveal that attitudes to crime, law-breaking and use of power and privilege do differ characteristically between nations (Braithwaite, 1989; Fisse and Braithwaite, 1993). It is easy to fall into stereotypes of countries (apparently there is a documentary on the Netherlands circulating in the USA at the moment called *Sex, Drugs and Democracy*), but it does appear to be the situation that Dutch society, for historical and structural reasons, is fairly tolerant towards business deviance. Some might argue that the Dutch are tolerant of many things, particularly if the deviant behaviour is restrained, segregated, and subsidized (van Dijk and Punch, 1993). This could be related to the tight-knit nature of Dutch society where many major decisions include a wide range of parties which then are in some way implicated in the consequences of those decisions. And, although on the surface the Netherlands is a highly rule-bound and over-regulated society, there is a great deal of forgiveness for the miscreant if he or she can profess a legitimate excuse. Prince Bernhard was treated remarkably mildly in the aftermath of the Lockheed affair, in which it was claimed that he had accepted a 'sweetener' in relation to ordering combat planes for the Dutch Air Force, and the former Prime Minister, Ruud Lubbers, was swiftly forgiven when he admitted to continuing financial contacts with the family business when he was Minister of Economic Affairs (Boulton, 1978; *de Volkskrant*: Lubbers then severed all links with the business, and parliamentarians and the press chose not to dwell on his oversight: 19 February 1986). Thus one central issue is: how do societies differ in the patterns of corporate deviance that develop in them and also in their enforcement strategies as well as their 'tolerance levels' for particular forms of corporate misconduct?

The second important element, and the specific contribution of this case, is that here we can look behind the façade of a major corporation and witness an organizational and managerial shambles. Some corporate deviance is consciously planned and breaks the criminal law; in other cases there may be systematic neglect and unjustified risk-taking that foster accidents; yet there is also a category of cases where the deviance may not be criminal and may not be disastrous, but where the ideal of competent and rational management gives way to incompetence and mismanagement. The latter may, in turn, generate infringements and violations of administrative, civil, and regulatory laws. Mismanagement may encourage milder forms of the 'collective embezzlement' and 'covering up' that Calavita and Pontell (1990) mention in relation to the S & Ls; a significant number of bankruptcies reveal procedural and administrative offences (as well as criminal offences) that were resorted to when the company began to disappear down the tubes. The imagery here would be that of the 'slippery slope', of control deteriorating and malpractice growing almost imperceptibly as a corporation gets into trouble, until the actors discover that matters have gone too far but there is no way back. Fatalism, demotivation, defeatism, demoralization, and predatory cynicism may lead to deviance and may aid in justifying it. There are examples of projects that fail, dramatic cost overruns, and of bitter board-room politics that almost destroy companies (as in the recent battle at Saatchi and Saatchi). In Britain there has been a series of grand failures – cost overruns on the supersonic plane Concorde, delays and escalating costs for the new British Library – and some, such as the collapse of a new computer system for the London Ambulance Service, have even been said to have cost lives. This takes us closer to our experience of everyday organizational deviance, where we may perceive our working environment to be a messy, uncoordinated 'garbage can' (Weick, 1976). An examination of incompetence, mismanagement, and organizational failure takes us into an arena where we can see why things go wrong in organizations and why sometimes managers lose control of the processes they are meant to steer. And managerial or organizational failure may be the harbinger of significant deviance.

Background

Dutch shipbuilding led the world in the 1930s. This was a matter of national pride for a small country that had industrialized relatively late; and it symbolized the Netherlands' intimate relation with the sea. After the war, which left large parts of the country devastated, there was a remarkable economic recovery and Dutch society was seen as stable, affluent, and tolerant. An impressive range of welfare provision was constructed; delicate coalition politics was based on negotiation and compromise; there was tolerance for a wide range of social and political ideas, tastes, and behaviours (notably with regard to the media, sex, euthanasia, abortion, and drugs); and the criminal justice system was enlightened and lenient in a land of relatively low crime (particularly violent crime). Some of the negative characteristics, according to critical outsiders (and also some insiders), are arrogance, complacency, hypocrisy, too much willingness to compromise in order to avoid conflict, avoidance of painful issues, and an inability to take decisive action that would alienate or offend some significant group.

Indeed, there have been analyses of the Dutch character that focus on Asiatic qualities – 'the Dutch are the Chinese of Europe' – which are said to make them shrewd and inscrutable bargainers; that perceive outward bourgeois respectability as a façade beyond which considerable private deviance is permitted (the 'underside' of public and business life is not heavily scrutinized by the media) and progressivism as laced with a degree of calculation – 'the true Dutchman having the heart of a chartered accountant' (De Baena, 1957). But generally the Dutch have been viewed positively as reliable, trustworthy, and free of corruption (Blanken, 1976).

Indeed, a preference for harmony and a feeling for balance had helped establish an enviably stable society. Industrial unrest was rare and business grew from the sober 1950s to the successful 1960s and approached the exciting 1970s with optimism. There had been a wave of mergers, and several Dutch corporations endeavoured to keep up their international competitiveness by following the slogan 'Big is Beautiful'. In that heady and buoyant atmosphere, the shipbuilding conglomerate RSV was born in 1971 and it grew to employ some 33,000 workers at its height. It was to be a showpiece of industrial policy – bolstering quality Dutch shipbuilding against the inroads of cheaper Asian yards – and also of industrial democracy, with a strong element of consultation with the workers.

Yet just over a decade later the company was a demotivated shambles facing bankruptcy; there was talk of serious mismanagement and of mounting a public inquiry; reputations had been scarred and many jobs had been lost; and the state had ended up expending some 3,500 million guilders (almost $2,000 million currently) of the taxpayer's money on an enterprise that proved as fragile as a house of cards. How could this have happened? Who was responsible? And how could it have happened in Holland, the country of reliable managers and accountable politicians?

In fact, you could argue that it was a *typically Dutch* scandal in that no one outside the country has ever heard of it; everyone seemed to be involved in it (it's difficult to discover what Dutch people can do on their own); nearly everyone got something out of it; no one was sanctioned; almost no one was blamed for it; and the state subsidized it. It is almost as if the RSV scandal was talked into oblivion at the time in order to protect the guilty. Since then, however, the RSV affair has come to symbolize more than just the failure of management, unions, and government to work out a viable macro-industrial policy for a declining industry. Rather, it can be seen as a watershed between the 'soft' values of the socially inclined 1970s and the tougher, more entrepreneurial stance by business with government less prepared to hold out a costly safety net. In retrospect, it can also be viewed as raising serious questions about the quality of management, and the effectiveness of political control, at the highest levels of Dutch society.

Background and Personalities

After the war many Dutch shipyards, and related firms, had to watch as precious orders increasingly went to more modern and productive firms in Japan, Taiwan, Singapore, and even Sweden. Yet they failed to modernize so that production methods became obsolete, working conditions were poor, and costs remained high. Above all, the fragmented industry was pervaded by strong feelings of local chauvinism leading to, on the one hand, intense and even bitter rivalry and, on the other hand, to the difficulty for government of advantaging one locality without enraging the others. For instance, three major centres of shipbuilding – Rotterdam, Amsterdam, and Vlissingen – jealously guarded their own interests and built local and national networks to guard their autonomy and continuity. This made cooperation between the yards problematic; rather, the relationships were characterized by 'hatred and envy'; and the bosses of the time were described as 'all of them [being] particularly awkward gentlemen' (Harren and van den Bos, 1984: 13). They all seem to have hated one another's guts.

One of the several commissions which endeavoured to get a grip on the industry reported in the mid-1960s that a major reorganization and rationalization of the yards was essential. Out of the Keyzer Commission's (1965) proposals flowed an amalgamation of several companies into the 'Rijn-Schelde' Group. But there was an entrepreneurial maverick in Dutch shipbuilding, Cornelis Verolme, who was determined to build mammoth tankers to take bulk oil around the Cape of Good Hope (following the closure of the Suez Canal after the 1967 Arab–Israeli War) and who planned to build a vast dry dock to realize his considerable ambitions. He was described as having the attributes of the 'average dictator', did not attempt to disguise his contempt for the traditional shipbuilders 'with all those nice old surnames', and was consequently cold-shouldered by his peers (*Haagse Post*, 2 April 1983). A witness before the later commission of inquiry into the affair stated, 'the relationship between Verolme and the rest wasn't exactly friendly'; Verolme referred to the others as 'fellows with no backbone'; but he was himself 'extremely difficult' and 'he allowed no-one to contradict him' (Harren and van den Bos, 1984: 13–14). When he ran into financial difficulties in supporting his ambitious schemes he approached the Ministry of Economic Affairs in 1967 for credit guarantees. There the policy-makers agreed on the condition that Verolme would accept a 'shotgun marriage' with the Amsterdam yard NDSM which was in acute difficulties. This political decision, geared to avoiding unemployment, set in train a cycle of industrial difficulties, leading to constant pleas for further governmental support.

For within a year Verolme was once more in financial trouble, and he effectively 'blackmailed' the government by threatening to close the Amsterdam yard; many politicians still had vivid memories of the recent turbulence in Amsterdam, with severe rioting in 1966 (and the subsequent ignominious departure of the Mayor and Chief of Police), and decided to ignore the signals that Verolme's position was nearly hopeless by offering him another hand-out. Then the Winsemius Commission (1971) argued for further concentrations in Dutch industry generally, and in the wake of its recommendations Verolme was pushed into yet another merger with his arch-rival, Rijn-Schelde. In his 1971 memoirs he poured bitter scorn on the merger (which led to his swift departure from the scene as the 'organization men' took over from the prickly one-man band), and predicted that it would prove a 'horrible débâcle' (Blom, 1984: 18).

Thus RSV (Rijn-Schelde-Verolme) was born. Its inception was based on optimism, arguments for economies of scale and restructuring, hopes for continuing employment, a belief in a coherent industrial policy, and it also contained an element of chauvinism: 'from a feeling of national pride, shipbuilding should and would be preserved in the Netherlands. The craftsmanship must not be lost and it would be a scandal if the Netherlands would allow the branch, in which it had such a glorious past, to simply disappear' (Harren and van den Bos, 1984: 89). In practice, the conglomerate became an organizational 'dinosaur', which not only defied rationalization but also voraciously devoured money.

In order to steer this unwieldy corporation, a few top people turned to Allerd Sticker. He was a part of a trio – Sticker, Molkenboer, de Vries – that came to dominate the RSV story, while later two politicians, Minister of Economic Affairs G. van Aardenne and C. van Dijk (Member of Parliament and chair of the commission of inquiry into the affair, respectively), played prominent roles (with a bizarre side-show furnished by the American businessman, J.D. Stacy). Sticker was the son of a Minister of Foreign Affairs, had earned his spurs in the chemical industry, and came to shipbuilding with no experience in the heavy capital-goods industry, but with a reputation as a 'golden boy'. He was described as 'smooth' and 'sphinx-like', and even cynical, while he proved incapable of coping with opposition within his board. He displayed a strong, near rigid faith in his plans for reorganization to a divisional structure and somehow remained eternally optimistic, reassuring people even in the bleakest times with speeches that echoed the theme 'next year we'll be out of the red and we'll be earning a fortune once more' (Blom, 1984: 9).

To oversee the government's interest in the concern a highly experienced civil servant was attached as 'observer' to the Supervisory Board. J.

Molkenboer was a supremely confident, somewhat pompous, man who had been used by politicians in several tough assignments (so that he was referred to as the 'pope of industry'). In essence he was to oversee the use of taxpayers' money. And then there was J. de Vries, President of the Supervisory Board. De Vries had built up a reputation as an extremely tough businessman when he ran a construction company – leading to his nickname 'Mister Concrete' – and after his retirement he had led the supervisory board at RSV. Here was a no-nonsense entrepreneur, exuding arrogance, who surely would not fear putting the brakes on the Executive Board if it stepped out of line. Sticker came to reorganize; Molkenboer was there to keep a wary eye on things; and 'Mister Concrete' could steer matters if anything threatened to drift off course. So what went wrong?

What Went Wrong?

Of course it is possible to blame everything on the first oil crisis of 1973 which altered the world dramatically for so many western companies. It certainly was a devastating blow to Dutch shipbuilding (although the Norwegians managed to shift production successfully to offshore projects). World shipping faced overcapacity, the market for mammoth tankers capsized, and Verolme's brain-child – a vast new dry dock – was never completed. But the fundamental factor underpinning RSV's demise was the persistent failure of management to get a grip on the organizational structure and to transform its traditional culture. The conglomerate was shaped by accumulating a set of problems which were merely exacerbated, rather than solved, by the merger.

Corporate management failed to impose a sense of direction on what remained a hotch-potch of diverse companies (according to the official report of the public inquiry; *RSV Report*, 1984). Parochialism, based on old loyalties and traditional vendettas, remained to bedevil reorganization. Overcapacity, obsoleteness, internal competition, communication difficulties, and persistent losses dogged RSV. Managers who were meant to cooperate simply continued to thwart one another in relationships described as 'hate and distrust' (*Haagse Post*, 2 April 1983); orders that should have been passed on to other yards internally were instead put out to third parties at higher rates. Orders were taken on at below an economic price; use was made of 'black workers' controlled by illegal sub-contractors because it was cheaper than to employ one's own workers elsewhere who then stood around idle; and ships were even built on the assumption that a buyer would turn up for them.

The imposition of a divisional structure, imported by Sticker from his previous chemical multinational, proved unworkable in practice and the idea of meshing a commercial with a technical culture proved stillborn. A new centralist structure had been imposed on a highly decentralized industry and the proponents of the two styles began battles on policy in the board-room. Sticker obstinately stuck to his guns and two of his top men resigned. By now Sticker was refusing to listen to counter-arguments and two more of his opponents left as a result of the continuing power struggle. This was a serious loss of managerial talent and Sticker now began to surround himself with 'yes-men'. By 1979 he himself wanted to leave but was persuaded to stay on.

And each crisis led to yet another meek procession in the direction of the government ministries in The Hague. If one focuses on the negotiations there between the three partners – government, industry, and labour – and examines their tactics and manoeuvres, then it is possible to elucidate how all the actors were in at least one double bind of some sort and the cumulation of concealed ambivalences and hidden agendas led to decisional paralysis, irrational defensive measures, strange coalitions, the squeezing out of opponents, manipulation of statistics and accounts, and the withholding of full information from Parliament. A vicious circle of circumstances was set in motion that the top of RSV was unable to retard and which gradually drew into its web prime ministers, cabinets, and many ministries (including Economic Affairs, Social Affairs, Financial Affairs, Defence, and Transport). The actors became judge, guard, and prisoner of the processes they set in motion and played different roles at different stages. The concept of a strategic 'political-industrial policy' foundered on the tactical reactions and realignments of the actors who manipulated the situation by continually switching the arena, the agenda, and the timing of the debate (Wassenberg, 1983).

Successive governments thought of forthcoming elections and poured public money into a bottomless pit while distancing themselves from responsibility. Molkenboer was distrusted at RSV, was denied essential information, and had no authority to interfere with decisions. The *six* ministries involved had different cultures, styles, and motives and sometimes they worked at cross purposes. The union leaders colluded with changes that they might otherwise have viewed critically but instead meekly accepted in the interests of preserving jobs. Members of Parliament turned a blind eye to suspicious gaps in information and patent weakness in policy as long as shipyards were maintained in areas they felt responsible for or because their workers meant votes for their party. Fundamental underlying insecurities bred implicit non-aggression treaties, informal circuits of information, and the constant attempt to stymie rivals. Those who knew their way around the government corridors of The Hague, and who could readily gain the ear of a minister or senior civil servant, were at a distinct advantage in these games. What were almost tribal identities – comparable to the emotions surrounding hard-fought football matches between Ajax (Amsterdam) and Feyenoord (Rotterdam) – brought a further level of emotion and irrationality beneath the surface sobriety of Dutch committee rooms and the ostensible politeness of Dutch political games. Sticker stated later that 'the largely gruelling and drawn-out discussions in the various commissions became characterized by often an almost rancorous atmosphere and usually got bogged down in problems at the micro level' (*Elsevier's*, 23 April 1983: 150).

In the last resort Dutch government, industry, and labour could not clarify issues of power, authority, and responsibility, and became increasingly enmeshed in an intricate trap of illusions laced with cynicism as the actors endeavoured to divide the 'spoils' and to set up 'protection rackets' (Wassenberg, 1983). An unspoken conspiracy led to the construction and conservation of chaos. The results were truly calamitous.

Deeper and Deeper

Whatever was tried, and however hard men worked, RSV seemingly refused to gel as a coherent, cohesive organization. As if cursed, every expedient seemed to fail. A downward spiral of losses only seemed to lead to more and more risky ventures (and to more begging missions to the politicians in The Hague).

Parts of the conglomerate, for instance, had a strong tradition of naval shipbuilding and could usually rely on orders from the Ministry of Defence. But even here RSV proved accident-prone. A substantial order from Iran was cancelled when the Shah was forced to flee the country; an order for two submarines from Taiwan provided work but caused diplomatic rumblings with the People's Republic of China; Portugal dawdled endlessly about its order for ships; and just when the Minister of Economic Affairs was losing patience with RSV, and the writing should have been on the wall for all to see, the Defence Ministry unexpectedly stepped in with funds in 1980/81 which only served to put off the inevitable.

A large contract for a huge movable dredging unit was dogged by delays and technical hitches. In exasperation, the contractors Volkers Stevin refused to accept the intricate contraption and demanded 300 million guilders as compensation (Blom, 1984: 105).

Hopes were also set on providing important components for the nuclear industry at home and abroad. However, Dutch doubts about the expansion of nuclear plants in a tiny environmentally-conscious country spelt out delays in Holland. But then there emerged a potentially massive order from South Africa for substantial parts for two nuclear power plants involving 2.7 billion guilders. Several ministers reacted enthusiastically to the prospects of exports and employment, and argued insistently for an export licence. However, the centre-left coalition of the time was led by the socialist, Joop den Uyl, who felt emotionally divided on the issue, while many Labour Party members strongly opposed the deal. Eventually the Cabinet, by the narrowest of margins, came down against licensing the contract and people at RSV were furious and frustrated at seeing this life-buoy whipped away from their desperate grasp.

A subsidiary of RSV entered into a contract with Algerian state oil and electricity companies for complex technical work in the desert for which it was not particularly well suited. Poor legal advice meant that the contracts were dangerously one-sided; prices had not been based on adequate cost calculations; and technical setbacks did not elicit an adequate response from the parent company. In 1981 a trouble-shooter reported expected losses of 300 million guilders: 'The news was devastating. This time RSV could not blame the government or the depressed shipbuilding sector for its misfortune. This was a clear case of incompetence, mismanagement and lack of corporate

control over the subsidiaries' (*RSV Report*, 1984: 508). Attempts to renego-
tiate the contracts failed and RSV was forced to abandon the sites, scurrying
away with the projects unfinished. Some of the workers had to be smuggled
out of the country illegally and ignominiously in order to avoid being
arrested. RSV's reputation was further blemished.

Yet another doomed venture was the plan to build and export a complicated thin-seam coal-mining machine. Through intermediaries a Mr Stacy
was found as a partner for the American side of the operation and the deal
eventually amounted to some 200 machines. On paper the American firm
promised golden prospects that were 'finger-licking good', and held out
dreams of billions of dollars in coal profits with 200 machines eventually in
operation (for the machines were to be paid for by those profits). The first
machine displayed defects and had to be modified drastically. RSV rashly
decided to commence serial production of thirty machines – 'before a single
machine of the new type had been shipped, tested, accepted let alone paid for'
(*RSV Report*, 1984: 509) – and (fatally) ordered the components for a further
fifty machines. But the whole enterprise foundered on delays and technical
difficulties while Stacy continually found ways of not accepting the machines
for which therefore he did not have to pay. RSV tried to oust Stacy, who was
too well protected legally, and continued to manufacture and ship the
machines which no one wanted. The Dutch were left to carry the can to the
tune of some 400 million guilders. Stacy – who had run up substantial fees for
his efforts – later revealed that the acronym for his company, MMWOPS,
stood for 'Making Money While Other People Sleep'. And it was clear whom
he felt was caught napping.

This run of disasters might seem enough to have sounded the death-knell
of RSV (although it must be said that the firm recorded a profit up to 1976
and that the second oil crisis of 1979, and subsequent world recession, hit
many other companies hard as well). There were repeated signals that all
was not well. But the government was always prepared to man the pumps and
find new subsidies. For instance, the Minister of Economic Affairs, Ruud
Lubbers (later Prime Minister), mounted yet another commission on the
industry which reported that little had been achieved in terms of modernization and which led to the Minister offering 250 million guilders to tide the
industry through the 'valley' of difficult years.

His successor, Gijs van Aardenne, inherited a crisis-prone industry and
handed out 430 million guilders as a rescue operation for RSV. His plan to
close the loss-making Amsterdam yard NDSM raised such a cacophony of
protest that he backed down. When RSV then tried to close two yards in
Rotterdam the government was caught between escalating costs and the unat-
tractive prospect of unemployment and political repercussions. The Cabinet
dallied, Parliament argued for a life-line, and eventually the Minister of
Economic Affairs 'lost control over the financial consequences of his involvement in the shipbuilding industry'. He sank 250 million guilders into a new
'Rotterdam Offshore and Shipbuilding Combination' which was soon
stranded; and in 1979 'he promised to reimburse RSV for all losses incurred

in the large ship-building and off-shore sections, retroactive as from January 1st 1979 (despite the fact that he knew that RSV itself had no control over these losses). His commitment was open-ended and unlimited' (*RSV Report*, 1984: 506). The full details and implications of the privately agreed 'blank-cheque' element in this deal were then not adequately and openly conveyed to Parliament.

Apparently Van Aardenne saw this as a final settlement but RSV was pleading for support again in 1980 and 1981, and, once more, politicians could not face the consequences of closures, while bankruptcy was simply unthinkable. Funds from the Ministry of Defence allowed a breathing space and then further pleas for support were bought only with the enforced resignation of Sticker. By now other ministries, particularly Finance, had become obstreperous, the banks were wary, and a government-imposed external investigation revealed a shocking state of affairs at RSV where only a few subsidiaries made a profit, most were in trouble, and almost none were free of danger. Effectively, the government pulled the plug on RSV and in February 1983 the company 'suspended payments' and went into bankruptcy.

Managerial Response

Whatever external forces there were to plague RSV, its demise must be seen as a substantial failure of management. With a measure of self-justification, and an element of paranoia, Sticker spoke of a 'combination of circumstances' that proved calamitous while the 'carefully constructed campaign by outsiders' against the new set-up led to a 'self-fulfilling prophecy'. The parties involved in setting up RSV had also helped to dig its grave. The 'underdogs' were protected and the 'top dogs' were attacked. Inside and outside there developed an increasingly hostile atmosphere, the last months were characterized by damaging gossip and leaks, and the situation became uncontrollable (*Elsevier's*, 23 April 1984).

Above all, the remarks of Sticker convey the predicament of a management that has simply lost control of the organization it is meant to be running. RSV ran loose and became unmanageable:

> RSV found itself in a stressful position and you could see all sorts of people who couldn't cope and who started to do funny things. Under those circumstances some people began to behave in very strange ways. Because of that situations became unpredictable and there grew a feeling of impotence. (*Elsevier's*, 23 April 1984)

And with chilling frankness Sticker informed the public inquiry of his ominous feelings at the time:

> The shivers run down my spine again if I think back on it. *We had completely lost our grip on the organization.* Of course, as long as you have management it remains responsible for the business. But the circumstances under which projects had to be completed were the worst imaginable in an industrial set-up. RSV was damaged, battered and in many respects humiliated. There was total demotivation. We had a completely worn-out management, not because of age but because of the way things went throughout those years. The organization was not capable of coping

with the issues. Losses which in an incredible manner got completely out of hand. Impotence – industrially a really tragic development. It was a terrible time. (Harren and Van den Bos, 1984: 174–5; emphasis added)

Rarely has a manager conveyed so vividly the feeling of powerlessness when an organization is perceived to be *beyond the control* of its masters. What the top people did manage to do was to feather their own nests. At a time when embittered workers were being laid off and the rest were being beseeched to make sacrifices, their bosses were ensuring that they at least would not suffer financially because of the crises. In the first year that there was no profit the board members were threatened with losing their bonus, so some of them simply sought a construction that raised their salaries to compensate for the amount. Sticker earned in excess of 7 million guilders over ten years (which was then quite high by Dutch standards), including an alleged million guilder 'golden hand-shake' (Blom, 1984: 9). All of this merely added to the feelings of bitterness and recrimination that surrounded the whole unseemly affair.

But Sticker departed from the scene, giving up his business interests completely and turning to the solace of Taoism, with the lament that in RSV people had created a vulnerable 'dinosaur' of human organizational development that evolution had passed by; its relic remained as a painful reminder from the past (*Elsevier's*, 23 April 1983: 151).

Public Inquiry

The seriousness with which the RSV case was taken can be determined by the fact that a special parliamentary commission of inquiry was appointed (and that the last time this had happened was thirty-six years previously, when aspects of the exiled Dutch government's conduct in war-time London were examined). The public and televised hearings became a major media event attracting unexpectedly large numbers of viewers. Typically for the Netherlands, a sober, even boring, politician headed the inquiry, which was restrained, generally polite, occasionally searching, and almost without histrionics. Yet it proved riveting – almost a Dutch Watergate (or perhaps 'Madurogate', in reference to Madurodam – the famous Dutch miniature town, is more appropriate) – as the Prime minister and ex-Prime Ministers, ministers and ex-ministers, directors and ex-directors, senior civil servants, trade union officials, American partners, accountants, and lawyers filed into the sombre arena to be questioned on oath about their conduct and motives.

The overwhelming impression left by the inquiry is of multiple actors who never were fully in control of complex events and processes. In an almost surrealistic, Kafkaesque manner the reams of dossiers coughed up by numerous committees seem to have taken on a life of their own; and it is almost as if the players became unwitting puppets who constructed escalating chaos by committee. No one, inside or outside the concern, could break the interlocking set of vicious circles.

Sticker never managed to get a grip on the organization and blamed circumstances and internal resistance; Molkenboer was aware that not all was kosher at RSV but cleverly managed to hide behind his ministers who were in his eyes primarily responsible for intervening; and 'Mister Concrete' De Vries, apart from running up apparently exorbitant expenses, admitted that he was fully conscious of overseeing a 'socially supported workplace' (a reference to government-run centres for the unemployed). Ex-minister Van Aardenne had egg all over his face but braved it out by trying to justify his policies and by using vacuous language. For instance, in 1976 Van Aardenne proposed to support RSV with a 'BAGL' amounting to 600 million guilders; the 'baggel', as it was soon called, was a 'special retrospective loan' that involved no interest and no repayments and which could even be transferred into 'baggel-certificates' that could be used to colour the balance sheet favourably (Blom, 1984: 24). There were also 'waggels' (WAGLS) and 'aggels' (AGLS) which were verbal smoke-screens for virtually no-strings handouts which only encouraged dubious bookkeeping transactions at RSV and which no one at the Ministry fully understood – while Parliament blissfully nodded assent (Harren and van den Bos, 1984: 72).

Few people emerged with credit, and the unseemly side of padded expenses, dubious pay rises for managers, creative accounting, misjudgements, gross incompetencies, evasion of responsibility, and ministerial economies with the truth were even seen by some as something of a 'witch-hunt' against business, while Van Aardenne had been permanently blighted in terms of a political future. The one attempt to pass on evidence for a criminal prosecution – based on the commission of inquiry's conclusion that De Vries had perjured himself (the public hearings are conducted with witnesses under oaths) – came to nothing when the Public Prosecutor declined to pursue the case.

No heads rolled, but for a seafaring nation – with a centuries-old tradition of shipbuilding – the legacy of deserted wharves, idle cranes, forlorn slipways, dilapidated jetties, and the bitter faces of the redundant left a nasty taste in the mouth. Trustworthy managers, responsible politicians, involved unions, and a caring welfare state were unable to prevent millions of guilders of tax-payers' money disappearing down the drain. RSV had been scuttled by good intentions and its sinking left a feeling of guilt and disappointment. It had been a collective failure of huge proportions.

Comment

Mismanagement and Forgiveness The RSV affair was one of the major post-war scandals in the Netherlands; it elicited an enormous press coverage and led to terms like 'drama', 'trauma', and 'tragedy'. Both business and politics were pilloried, while Parliament was made to look as if it was peopled by supine, deferential, and totally non-critical incompetents. Almost no one emerged with much credit as experienced politicians and top businessmen were exposed to searching scrutiny. The 'moral smog' which hangs above the political machinations of the Hague went into the alarm phase as a result of this 'stinking affair' (as one leader of an opposition party called it); but after some 'super-calvinistic' breast-beating in public the scandal subsided and no heads rolled (van Luijk, 1985). This was typically a domestic scandal, bounded by local rules, in which no one died, no one was actually caught with his hand in the till, and no one went to prison. What, then, is its value as a case on business deviance and control?

In essence, the RSV case reveals a situation of *gross mismanagement* where people in charge almost completely lose control of the organization they are running. Conspiracies, for instance, require both a highly conscious and coordinated web of actions by participants and insightful manipulation of the organization to achieve illicit ends. Here the managers *lost* control and were swept along by events. Politicians were caught between several fires and resorted to prevarication, obfuscation, secret deals, withholding information, and unwarranted personal initiatives in order to evade facing up responsibly and definitively to painful choices. And virtually every control mechanism – internal and external – failed. But the overwhelming impression left by the scandal was that an unworkable structure was created for political reasons and that no one proved capable of getting a grip on the organization. In the RSV case the villain (and, indeed, the victim) was the *organization* itself which, like a rogue elephant (or perhaps more appropriately rogue 'dinosaur'), defied its masters and ran wild, leaving a trail of lost jobs, a shattered industry, vast debts, and tarnished reputations. Managers, whose essential task is to steer the organization, simply *lost control of the company.*

The affair, because of the publicity it attracted, also revealed a great deal about weaknesses in Dutch politics and business and, as such, brought to light a wide range of interesting issues. The two images which emerge constantly are of 'vicious circles', representing powerlessness, and of a 'circus' which implies a constant, manipulative round of negotiations leading to factional gains but also the unconscious perpetuation of the circles ('everyone tries to prevent what the other one wants, and what finally emerges is something that no one really wanted', as Engels put it, quoted in Wassenberg, 1983: 209). The traumatic element is that this happened in the Netherlands, the land of long-term planning, a strong shipbuilding tradition, respectable politicians, and ostensibly of order, control, and predictability. What variables in particular can be highlighted to explain this dramatic débâcle?

1 The structure of the industry was fragmented and inefficient and, despite several high-powered commissions that argued insistently for modernization and rationalization, it continued to defy streamlining. The gentlemen industrialists who ran it were tough and prickly potentates who viewed their wharves as fiefdoms and who were scarcely open to amicable cooperation with former rivals. The yards themselves had resilient, particularistic cultures that made the merger a paper exercise which never generated a collective identity or a willingness to coordinate with the 'enemy' (in Amsterdam, Rotterdam, Vlissingen, or wherever). Thus structure, personalities, and culture perpetuated weaknesses that went on to

undermine the enterprise. As Sticker put it, the very people who helped set up RSV also worked to effect its demise (*Elsevier's*, 23 April 1984).

2 RSV entertained a constant stream of consultants who invariably diagnosed severe problems and proposed stringent measures. These exercises were designed to placate external stakeholders and to illustrate the fact that using consultants under these conditions leads to little improvement because the management is chronically unclear as to the path to be taken and is quite unable to use the advice for genuine reorganization.

3 Parliament failed in its controlling task and seemed to sleep while events took place outside without members applying any brakes; the official inquiry spoke harshly of a Parliament that was 'absent, inattentive, and forgetful' (*RSV Report*, 1984).

4 The Ministry of Economic Affairs proved too generous in the affair. The Minister himself took unwarranted initiatives; the representative of the Ministry, Molkenboer, had too much autonomy and proved largely ineffective; and there was poor communication between Economic Affairs and the other five ministries involved. There were rumblings that the Minister should leave office ('Van Aardenne Must Go', *de Volkskrant*, 11 December 1984), when the 'blank cheque' aspect of his relationship with RSV was revealed. But he was saved by the possible damage his departure might cause to the ruling coalition. His skin had been saved by the intricacies of Dutch political culture, although he became something of a 'lame duck' and left politics later. Since then he has assembled a number of non-executive directorships in business. In other political systems he would almost certainly have been forced to resign for misleading Parliament (but it is rare for a minister to resign in the Netherlands).

5 The two-tier system of management in the Netherlands – with a supervisory board of non-executive directors (*commissarissen*) that ostensibly checks and controls the board of directors – did not function effectively. It never exerted a salutary brake on the policies of the management and must be held partly responsible for that management's failure. The management was also 'at war' with Molkenboer, the minister's representative, and antagonistic to the works council. The unseemly aspect of managers rewarding themselves handsomely while their company was haemorrhaging jobs was reinforced by the revelations of de Vries's exorbitant expenses (and he was chair of the non-supervisory board that had to approve the rises and the 'creative accounting' involved).

6 Finally, the Dutch public had been treated to a well-publicized public inquiry that brought forth a sixteen-volume report and had unprecedented television coverage. The language of the official report was tough. It spoke of a 'tragic' tale of 'confusion, extreme inefficiency, shame and disenchantment'; it described RSV as exuding 'despair, disillusionment, demotivation and doom'; and it roundly concluded that 'the concern was undermined by fatal external developments, lack of vision, personal weaknesses, shortage of courage and absence of trust' (*RSV Report*, 1984: 497–510). Almost a whole generation of politicians appeared before it and

it looked as if somewhere along the line just about all the big names contributed somehow to the debacle (the later Prime Minister, Lubbers, promised to help RSV out of a 'dip' but it turned out to be 'more of an abyss and he should have known better': *RSV Report*, 1984: 504).

And perhaps that was the key to the scandal. Everyone was involved; there was no one murderer who killed the company, so everyone had to be absolved of final blame. Too much political face was at stake to make heads roll and, therefore, all the players lined up for their penitential performance before the cameras. But, having satisfied Calvinistic decorum, they went back to politics – and turned to business as usual.

Nevertheless, it was clear that this was a collective failure. Weak management failed to control the company, was forced into a cycle of risky decisions and pleas for handouts from government, while politicians failed to control the relationship with the firm and became captured in the downward spiral of RSV. Dutch management and Dutch politics had conspired to achieve a disastrous industrial failure costing billions of guilders and thousands of jobs. And for that the main actors were slapped on the wrist. That 'tolerance' made it a typically Dutch scandal.

PART THREE
CONCLUSION

5

Everything But Temptation

I think the boys could resist everything but temptation.

(General Electric executive following antitrust case: Geis, 1982: 136)

Shadow Boxing: Learning to Live with Ambiguity

This book set out to argue the case that business is criminogenic. This echoes Clarke's contention that 'crime and misconduct are endemic to business and that the key to understanding them lies in recognizing the structure that the business environment gives to misconduct, both in terms of opportunities and in terms of how misconduct is managed' (1990: 8).

This implies that we have to examine the nature of business, the realities of organizational life, the dilemmas of management, and the manners and morals of managers in their daily working lives. In general, the business organization is perceived as making a positive contribution to modern society; and this is enhanced by sophisticated impression management (through corporate communications with advertising, sponsoring, and brochures) and the construction of trust. In contrast, many cases of corporate misconduct reveal the negative side of managers' turning to deviance. The underlying theme of this work is to use such cases to unmask the underlying logic of business and the submerged social world of the manager. When the myth system is cracked open by scandal then it reveals the 'operational code' of how business actually gets done and how deviancy may become 'normal' for managers. As Ross puts it,

> Corporate crime might paradoxically be characterized as both aberrant and normal; it is difficult to repress because its sources are so deep-rooted. It is by definition deviant because it violates the law; it also violates the canons of ethics to which almost everybody subscribes formally. Yet, in many situations, illegal activity is a natural reaction to the conflicts and pressures that afflict much of business. The crimes that we have been dealing with are usually not impulsive or mere expressions of irresponsibility; they represent not aberrations so much as alternative ways of doing business. In many circumstances, illegal methods are as authentic an expression of business mores as legal ones. (1992: 127)

Furthermore, we learn that the ostensibly rational and controlled world of organizational life can generate irrationality and shortsightedness; and even get 'out of control'.

In short, then, this book endeavours to peel away the protective layers of corporate impression management and 'outreach' (Miles, 1987; Useem, 1984) to enter the inner reality of business and the hidden world of 'deviant' managers. To understand the social embeddedness of deviant and criminal business behaviour it is essential to grasp that the business organization is the weapon, the means, the setting, the rationalization, the offender, *and* the victim.

> Collective embezzlement, however, not only is deviance *in* an organization – in the sense that the misconduct harms the viability of the institution – but also constitutes deviance by the organization. Not only are the perpetrators themselves in management positions, but the very goals of the institution are precisely to provide a money machine for its owners and other insiders. The formal goals of the organization thus constitute a 'front' for the real goals of management, who not infrequently purchased the institution in order to loot it. The S & L could be discarded after serving its purpose. It is a prime example of what Wheeler and Rothman (1982: 1,406) have called 'the organization weapon': 'the organization . . . is for white-collar criminals what the gun or knife is for the common criminal – a tool to obtain money from victims'. The principal difference between Wheeler and Rothman's profile of the organization as weapon, and the case of collective embezzlement presented here, is that the latter is an organizational crime against the organization's own best interests. That is, the organization is both weapon and victim. (Pontell and Calavita, 1993: 224)

The organization is the villain; our inability to control it is the essential message of this book and that represents a substantial challenge for society.

There is, however, no question of a blanket assertion that most companies are routinely criminal. Not only is there insufficient evidence to maintain this with any level of certainty (Braithwaite, 1985a), but also there are companies which explicitly set out to conform to the law; they maintain a record of no transgressions, anticipate or even go beyond regulatory requirements, and enjoy a respectable reputation. Generally, explanations for this 'cleaner than thou' performance focus on corporate culture and structure, leadership (sometimes related to the values of the founding fathers), and the nature of the industry or product (Punch, 1992). My position, following the work of Sutherland and others, is to view the violations of rules, codes, and laws that occur in business as examples of organizational deviance and corporate misconduct. These are responses to internal and external pressures that foster deviance from the trivial to the blatantly criminal. This means that there is a wide spectrum of deviant behaviour that is drawn upon at certain times and under certain conditions by managers endeavouring to cope with problems encountered in the corporate working environment.

The sociological and criminological scrutiny of deviance at the organizational level has tended to focus lopsidedly on abuse of power in government and on organized/syndicated crime. Business crime has been neglected for a number of reasons, such as the power of business to deflect research and to resist the deviant label. This work endeavours to make a modest contribution to that field; and, indeed, to a Sociology of Business (which, itself, is pitifully underdeveloped (Calhoun, 1989: 542; Reed, 1989). Modesty is advisable given the complexity of the variables involved that muddy any attempt to specify with clarity why some companies under certain circumstances decide to adopt the deviant solution to a business problem. Analysis would necessarily have to touch on societies, markets, the organizational structure of corporations, the division of labour in managerial work, regulatory regimes, and the mechanisms that lead businessmen to break rules. But the more complex the variables, the more difficult and debatable it is to link with any degree of certainty environmental and structural features to human behaviour. Each case, for instance, can be seen as rich in context, if not unique, and can appear to defy comparison (particularly cross-culturally and cross-nationally).

There is one feature, however, that unites most instances of business deviance and that is *deception* and the accompanying necessity to engage in institutional impression management (through creating a legal, cultural, and social façade as Robert Maxwell so successfully accomplished). Indeed, the deviant manager can be likened to the double-agent in that he or she has to be doubly deceptive, both internally and externally (in contrast to the criminals in an organized crime syndicate). This implies that organizations and managers have somehow to learn to deal with a sort of schizoid existence, juggling with surface appearances and the camouflaged hidden reality. In this chapter I wish to explore that element by utilizing a framework based on structural, cultural, and personality identity variables that can be identified in the business environment. This is a simple way to reduce complexity by highlighting three central sociological elements in explaining human behaviour in organizations. To a large extent that effort will be devoted to the question, why do businessmen break the law? This is not simply an exercise in unravelling motivation but is more an attempt to identify what is it precisely in their working world that induces managers to break rules and laws. The answers, in turn, will have implications for the issue of what we can do about tackling business crime. But first I wish to examine more closely the management of that duality between 'clean' and 'dirty' activities that runs as a central thread through this work. Often it is concealed by constructing a 'shadow' organization.

Organizations are labyrinths of deceit. They create pressures, dilemmas, contradictions, and tensions that induce lies, deception, double-think, moral ambiguity, conspiracies, and devious role-playing (Reed, 1989: 20; Thomas, 1993). To a certain extent I am reflecting the pessimism that runs through organizational studies and that was strongly reflected in the work of Weber (the consequence of 'rationalization' in the modern world 'was to be our imprisonment in the house of bondage – the iron cage of bureaucracy': Clegg, 1990: 4). But, of course, organizations have as well an enormous potential for the positive development of trust, loyalty, élan, personal enrichment, and collective achievement. Yet some rule-breaking is intrinsic to institutional life, and the more respected and legitimate the enterprise, the more elaborate and convincing the façade has to be that conceals clandestine 'back-stage' activities from prying outsiders. To illustrate these insights, drawn from a sociological perspective on deviancy in organizations, let us turn briefly to the social construction of deception and duality involved in cloaking deviance. And let us recall that the cases throughout this book push home a number of key points that should be borne in mind continually when reflecting on the nature and extent of business deviance; that we are often concerned with reputable corporations, with senior managers, and with significant levels of deviance. These are mostly not trivial transgressions or incidental mistakes. Of course, there are considerable differences between the cases. There is variety in the extent of planning; in terms of consequences and victims; and in terms of imposing successfully the label of criminality. Some companies set out to break the law; some end up breaking the law; and some cannot manage the messes they get into. And some were helped along by the multiple failures of regulatory agencies and politicians. But nearly all the cases concern legitimate enterprises that indulged in mismanagement and/or malfeasance and that generally engaged in levels of deception and duplicity.

It could be argued that a measure of duality is inherent in institutional life and this may even be reinforced by certain elements in the business environment. For instance, the majority of major corporations are formal bureaucracies – 'characteristically large companies are therefore controlled by accountants, who manage the financial controls by which head offices execute their policy. . . . Business, especially big business, is about committees and paperwork' (Turner, 1986: 751). Here it is valuable to recall that the modern organization ostensibly promised to rescue us from venality and capriciousness. Weber (1947) maintained in his ideal-type that bureaucracy – based on universalism, expertise, unambiguous rules, and so on – promised considerable advantages over traditional institutions permeated by particularism, arbitrariness, and even rapaciousness. His concern about the negative effects of rationality in organizations was ignored by many later writers who took his views to mean that bureaucracy was actually more 'efficient' than other forms of organization. But all bureaucracies contain within them the seeds of conflict between the impersonal, rigid, rule-bound conduct of affairs and the reality of personal relationships, bending the rules, and the retention of traditional elements of power and authority. In practice the bureaucratic structure may be little more than a façade. While maintaining the pretence of bureaucracy (in the form of a 'symbolic' or a 'mock bureaucracy': Jacobs, 1969; Gouldner, 1954), the 'real' work gets performed in an inherently non-bureaucratic manner.

Many studies (Blau, 1955; Crozier, 1964; Merton et al., 1952) have revealed that organizations deviate substantially from the Weberian ideal-type, posited on the rapid, unambiguous, and efficient dispatch of business, and may even come to exemplify delay and injustice while low levels of incompetence may become institutionalized and informally supported – cf. Goode's (1967) perceptive article on 'The Protection of the Inept'. Organizational reality may unintentionally result in 'vicious circles' (circular chains of actions that produce counter-productive results: Masuch, 1985) or 'crazy systems' (the maddening, Kafkaesque bureaucratic circuits that emerge in institutions and that are based on secrecy, over-regulation, non-responsiveness, and 'semantic obscurantism': Singer, 1980). This inherent ambivalence and duality frequently fosters a discrepancy between institutional appearances and the daily reality of work relationships, and that discrepancy may be skilfully concealed by intricate mechanisms of impression management.

This way of looking at reality focuses on the problematic, ambivalent, dualistic world of everyday organizational life (that most of us would recognize from our own institutional experiences). For instance, recent research on the practice of management has brought forward

> 'the ethical and political dilemmas that managers necessarily face in their struggle to cope with the inherent complexity and contradictions of work organisations. It has also served to emphasise the importance of understanding the social processes whereby these dilemmas are reflected in the makeshift, and often internally contradictory, assemblies of practices that constitute contemporary work organisations as bricolages of partially articulated and half-digested sets of principles or rationalities. (Reed, 1989: 20)

One implication is that there is an intricate pattern of ordinary, undramatic, low-level deviance in organizations in general and in business organizations in particular. There is almost no better example of this than Dalton's classic but sadly neglected book, *Men Who Manage* (1959).

This unique and invaluable piece of research is based on long-term *covert* observation carried out when Dalton actually worked as a manager. He focused particularly on informal networks which enabled managers to get things done to mutual satisfaction while also constructing a system of informal rewards and bargaining counters. Some of the practices he uncovered were as follows: records were 'lost' to someone's advantage; the manipulation of accounts with non-existent personnel on the payroll was used to fund secret operations; informal bargains were repaid with informal favours (such as redecorating offices); people were informed beforehand when inspections would be coming; to improve safety records many accidents were not recorded; and guards on the gates colluded in the removal of the firm's goods. The essence of this material is not that we are witnessing bad men at dubious activities: these managers would have jumped a mile if you had accused them of doing anything 'criminal'. Yet they were effectively being coached in the 'finesses of workable illegalities' (Dalton, 1959: 53).

In brief, these collusive, covert practices were anchored in the daily reality – the pressures, expectations, and mutual agreements – of people trying to survive, to succeed, or simply to get things done without making waves. The 'informal system' could build up rights and obligations which were just as binding as those of the formal system, while the bargaining around the informal power relationship was summed up by one manager who said, 'there's just as much politics here in the plant as there is in Washington'.

Dalton succeeds in getting at the covert activities of management and the meanings assigned to them by participants. He wrote of 'abuses':

> do they not in many cases also reduce disruptive conflict, break the monotony of routine, allow more personal expression, ease the craving for spontaneity, and to some extent catch up all levels of personnel in a system of mutual claims so that aid can be requested and hardly denied? (1959: 215)

As an insider account of everyday managerial reality Dalton reveals that people work on two levels – one for the records and appearances and one, submerged but acknowledged (and which drew people into networks of mutually advantageous commitments), for 'real', for simply getting things done. In effect, managers had to learn how to cope with the shifting negotiations and definitions of this institutional ambivalence. The 'weak' were the rule-bound, 'do-it-by-the-book' types who were handicapped by their own rigidity; the 'strong', in contrast, could 'tolerate dilemmas, make a game of them, turn ambiguous situations to their needs', while also,

> They are promoters and reorganizers in the sense that they do not see the firm as static. To them rules and procedures are not sacred guides but working tools to be revised, ignored, or dropped, as required in striking successive balances between company goals on the one side, and their personal ends and the claims of their supporters on the other. (Dalton, 1959: 247, 30)

Dealing with inherent duality in social life – between appearances and reality, which is a central element in much interactionist work and which played such an important part in Goffman's opus – has been a central thread running through this book. It is embedded in a view of organizational reality whereby actors are required to flit constantly between roles and deftly to change their appearances. This imposes a symbiotic or almost dialectical element on relationships and norms: Bensman and Gerver show this duality nicely in elucidating criminal practices in a factory; the personnel involved maintained public values while at the same time performing those actions necessary to attain the public or private ends appropriate to their evaluations of their positions:

> Thus a form of institutional schizophrenia is the major result of the conflict of ends and the conflict of means and ends. Individuals act and think on at least two planes, the plane of the public ideoloy and the plane of action. They shift from plane to plane, as required by their positions, their situations, and their means-ends estimations. In a sense, it is a form of double-think, and double-think is the major result of means-end conflict. (Bensman and Gerver, 1963: 597; see also Ditton, 1977; Henry, 1978; Altheide and Johnson, 1980)

This inherent duality, based on double-think but also double-act, is captured astutely by Reisman (1979) in his study of commercial bribery. He makes a useful distinction between the 'myth system', which publicly bolsters institutional values, and the 'operational code', which is covered in secrecy and which is concerned with how things are actually done. Bribes are deviations from the myth system, but they may be deemed appropriate under the code which constitutes a private and unacknowledged set of rules that selectively tolerates extraordinary payments as an ordinary and necessary form of doing business.

In short, the cases and the material presented in this book have been concerned with how certain companies, when exposed, reveal to us the 'operational code' of business, and also the extent to which they feel forced to bolster the 'myth system' when the deviant label is imposed. But it is vital to emphasize that we are not concerned with the covert reward systems of informal perks and fiddles (generally referred to as 'occupational crime': Mars, 1982), but with companies choosing or even institutionalizing deviant goals and means (sometimes situationally and temporarily, as occasion demands, but also sometimes permanently). This is far more than an 'informal' system, parts of which may be recognized, innocuous, and widely accepted. In order to encapsulate what I mean I have developed the concept of the *shadow* organization.

In significant cases of business deviance it is possible to see corporations employing a shadow strategy (as when a number of American multinationals set out to bribe their way into markets prior to the Foreign Corrupt Practices Act, 1977: Clinard and Yeager, 1980 155–86); shadow organizational structures (units set up deliberately to conduct deviance, such as in the Revco case); shadow financing (in the smoke-screen of offshore accounts in the Calvi affair); shadow accounting (in the assiduous construction of false accounts in the S & L and BCCI scandals); and shadow personnel management (in selecting pliant managers prepared to cut corners as in the heavy electrical antitrust cases). In other words, some managers in some business enterprises, while keeping up the appearance of legality and probity, may engage in sophisticated, subtle, carefully constructed alternative strategies and structures in order to achieve corporate or group goals by illicit means. This 'shadow boxing' requires skill, ingenuity, and cunning. It can range from the daily deviance of the clandestine but acknowledged reality of Dalton's managers based on meeting organizational goals and expectations, to the criminal empire of BCCI which concealed a 'black' bank within a bank. But in many cases managers have to be at pains to conceal their real motives, conduct, and performance both from internal and external scrutiny, and also be prepared to cover up if the shadow system is threatened.

> The basic rule is that you hope that these kinds of things never occur [using a production process that was potentially damaging to employees' health and opened up the possibility of a 'liability disaster' – MP]. Nobody wants to hurt people. Nobody could ever consciously plan to do something that would endanger people. But when things happen, well, you cover for yourself and your company. . . . The thing that makes . . . the corporation work at all is the support we give to each other no matter what happens . . . . We have to support each other and we have to support the hierarchy. Otherwise you have no management system. (Jackall, 1988: 132)

And it implies that managers constantly juggle with a form of mental and moral double bookkeeping. Bowles (1991), for instance, has written an interesting article on 'The Organization Shadow', in which he uses a psychoanalytical approach for examining negative practices and pathologies in organizations and in management. The piece takes the Jungian notion of shadow. This is related to the 'attempt by an individual to repress those characteristics and aspects which do not fit with self-image. Every human carries a Shadow. It represents the "other side", the "dark brother".' The article applies this shadow particularly to Geneen at ITT, 'one of the most well-publicized examples of corporate management losing itself in a pathological drive for power and profit' (Bowles, 1991: 396).

How do well-qualified, respectable managers in reputable companies actually end up bending rules and breaking the law? And how are they induced to engage in and operate the shifting, and even potentially hazardous, complexities of the 'shadow organization'?

Variables Explaining Corporate and Managerial Misconduct

In this section I shall specify a wide range of variables that help us in explaining why companies turn to deviant solutions and why managers become involved in illicit practices. The number of factors that could be drawn on is almost limitless. In order to bring a measure of order to the task the variables have been divided into three sections based on the concepts of structure, culture, and personality/identity.

Structure

While recognizing that there is a great deal of overlap and entanglement between the variables, I would like to touch on a number of structural features of corporate life that potentially promote deviance.

Markets   All businesses function in response to internal and external markets. The price-fixing in the electrical equipment antitrust case was stimulated by market conditions, and waxed and waned partly in relation to market changes. It is not always easy to specify precisely the relations between markets and corporate misconduct (Shapiro, 1980; Clinard and Yeager, 1980; Cochran and Nigh, 1986), but it is clearly a key factor to be taken into account (cf. Braithwaite (1985a,b) on the 'highly conflicting findings' of studies in this area). The development of the market, and perceptions of it, play a role in most corporate decision-making but that does not imply a mechanistic relation to managerial behaviour, determining certain incomes. The 'bull' market of the early and mid-1980s on the New York Stock Exchange undoubtedly contributed to the conditions to which Milken and Co. responded; but not everyone succumbed to those market forces with criminal behaviour, while similar deviant activities have occurred in the past under different market conditions (Clarke, 1990). In the Revco case the external market seems to have played no significant role at all.

Several authors have stressed the competitive nature of business, the drive for profits as a determining feature of firms, and have made the assumption that poor performance and/or inadequate profits will generate the motivation

to indulge in illegal behaviour in relation to market fluctuations and instability (Herlihy and Levine, 1980; Staw and Swajkowski, 1975; Asch and
Seneca, 1976). Jamieson (1994), who has reviewed studies in this area, comes
to the conclusion that the anecdotal and intuitive material linking illegal
behaviour to profit factors has resulted in weak correlations or none. We can
speculate, for instance, that insider trading and defence procurement fraud
were devices to 'ensure outcomes in an environment of risk and speculation'
(Jamieson, 1994: 19). But those companies that are caught may not be at all
representative of all those engaged in deviant activities in response to certain
market conditions. For instance, a high measure of concentration in an
industry can foster a more successful conspiracy whereby companies can
more easily evade detection and prosecution than a larger collection of firms
which are more readily detectable. As Jamieson notes: 'This may be why
more studies uncover a relationship between medium concentrated industries
and the presence of an offence – or only a weak but positive relationship for
oligopolies' (1994: 48).

In antitrust cases it is the more profitable companies that are prosecuted
for market and price manipulation whereas one might expect that less profitable firms would offend. But, again, the less profitable firms may have
offended; and they may even have initiated the regulatory response in the
hope of reaping substantial damages (private parties can sue for three times
the economic damage of an offence: Jamieson, 1994: 5). In effect, the evidence
indicates that a direct causal relationship between market conditions and
corporate decision-making is difficult to establish and tends to 'generate
more confusion than coherence'; that a wide range of factors, and not solely
profit, probably pushes companies towards deviance (nature of market,
nature of industry, size of company, relationship to competitors, and so on);
and that some firms attract attention because they are poor conspirators and
others because they are a tempting target for the civil actions from 'down-
stream' competitors (Jamieson, 1994).

Thus we cannot know how many companies offend under certain market
conditions; cannot decipher with any great precision the impact markets have
on corporate decision-making; and have to interpret the reasons why some
companies are caught in the regulatory net and some are not. Baucus and
Near (1991: 9), using event history analysis, maintain that large firms operating in 'dynamic, munificent environments were most likely of the firms
studied to behave illegally'. But it is the case that there is a widespread
assumption in the literature that managers in business seek predictability,
growth, and enhanced profits, and that they are influenced by shifts in market conditions that adversely affect their competitive position. And, in
addition, managers tend to refer to market factors to justify their deviant
behaviour. In the heavy electrical goods cases it was 'the chaotic condition' of
the market that sparked off the market-rigging and in the folding carton
industry case of 1976 it was a 'crowded and mature' market that fostered
deviance (Jamieson, 1994: 18). Perhaps some managers are capable of using
any market to rationalize rule-bending.

Size/complexity   Size, complexity, and differentiation in large corporations can contribute to lack of control, to deviant sub-cultures, to lack of communication, and to the obfuscation of authority. Outsiders may assume that 'everyone must know what's going on', but Kanter argues that people's view within organizations may 'be limited and parochial because they rarely get a sense of the whole' (1977: 4). There are social mechanisms that may prevent 'bad news' from reaching the top:

> First, as to getting to the higher-ups information adequate to appreciate the legal jeopardy their company is in, there is a natural tendency for 'bad news' of any sort not to rise to the top in an organization. A screening process takes place, such that if a company has been touting a new drug, and the drug begins 'experiencing difficulties' in the lab, lab employees and their supervisors just 'know' that information about this is to be passed upward, if at all, only in the vaguest terms. If an automobile company has retooled and is geared to produce 500,000 units of some car, a test driver or his supervisor knows that information suggesting that the car turns over too easily is not going to be welcomed 'upstairs'. Worse still, certain sorts of wrongdoing of a more serious sort – for example, price-fixing or other criminal activity – is not just screened out casually; it becomes the job of someone, perhaps the general counsel, to intercept any such information that could 'taint' his president or board chairman, divulging his suspicions only in private, if at all. In this way, the law not only fails to bring about the necessary internal flow of information, it may systematically operate to keep information of wrongdoing away from the very people who might best do something about it. (Stone, 1975: 44–5)

It is possible, then, that size, specialization, delegation, fragmentation of information, and segmentation of responsibility can combine to produce a climate 'that allows the abdication of a degree of personal responsibility for almost every type of decision, from the most inconsequential to one that may have a great impact on the lives of thousands' (Clinard and Yeager, 1980: 44). Of course size and complexity are relative concepts, which in themselves need not spell out ambiguity and diffusion of authority, but they are frequently cited as features that allow deviance to arise and go unchecked. They are also related to industrial concentration, which can mean that accidents have a much greater impact than in the past (Perrow, 1984). The implication is that a behemoth like General Motors, employing some 750,000 people in the USA alone at one stage, must at times have difficulty in exerting control and locating responsibility. In contrast, attention has recently been switched to 'small' businesses where precisely the opposite is argued; namely, that small size, close if not familial relations, and a perilous existence, can all contribute to rule- and law-breaking (Barlow, 1993).

Here I am referring primarily to the internal structures of organizations. In terms of offending and attracting regulations, size also has significance. A large corporation may have the power to defend itself effectively against prosecution and may more easily mount a conspiracy than one between several competitors, who may fall out with one another (see above). It may also 'offend' because it aggressively invites prosecution as it is determined to take on the regulators or as it wants to test the limits of legislation in the courts; and as it is a target for civil suits by others. Thus size and crime form a complex matter open to wide interpretation.

But Bennis (1973) sums up this point in general terms when he writes of the differentiation and specialization of organizations; this means that morality in organizations is the morality of 'segmented acts' that foster indifference and even evasion of responsibility.

Goals The emphasis on goals, and the necessity to achieve organizational goals, may intensify practices where the ends are held to justify the means. As such it could be argued that all organizations – capitalist or socialist, governmental or private – experience pressure to resort to illegal means of goal attainment when legitimate means are blocked (in effect, the Mertonian 'strain' perspective applied to organizations: Braithwaite, 1985a: 8). Plainly, the profit motive is crucial in business, but business organizations also strive for other ends – to control markets, to damage competitors, to enhance their power – and, as Gross states:

> Some organizations seek profits, others seek survival, still others seek to fulfil government-imposed quotas, others seek to service a body of professionals who run them, some seek to win wars, and some seek to serve a clientele. Whatever the goals might be, it is the emphasis on them that creates the trouble. (1980: 72)

In brief, the emphasis on goal attainment – particularly when achievement of goals is elevated to a 'mission' or an end in itself or is blocked in some way – can crucially influence the inclination to seek illicit means to achieve legitimate ends (Vaughan, 1983).

Opportunity Structures/Rewards The opportunities for corporate deviance, and the ability to evade control, generally increase as one moves up the corporate hierarchy. In some respects identification with, and pressure to defend, the corporation may intensify while the material rewards for doing so may become substantial. Why deviance occurs where it does may be related to the opportunity structure – implying that certain locations within the corporation are 'zones of temptation' (such as purchasing, sales, negotiating contracts, or financial controls) – and why it persists may be tied into the reward structure, formal and informal. For instance, when the reward system is strongly geared to the quarterly report in terms of bonuses and share options (as in the USA), this may encourage not only short-term thinking (Jacobs, 1991) but also considerable guile in generating figures that enhance one's rewards. Opportunities and rewards are structural elements of a system but how people view them is subjective; however, the opportunity structure favours those who are put in a position to conduct certain activities (and hence debars others). And, while there can be no mechanistic, computable relationship between the size of rewards and the experience of temptation, it may well be the case that the very substantial financial rewards (particularly bonuses related to the volume of work) in some parts of business are a factor encouraging deviancy for some people (such as in the S & L scandal, and the Wall Street cases).

The Company as a Total Institution   It may seem somewhat fanciful, but it can be argued that the modern corporation takes on some of the structural characteristics and psychological impact of 'total institutions' (Goffmann, 1961). The all-encompassing nature of modern management – the dedication to long hours, the emphasis on appropriate out-of-work socializing (club, Church, and political party membership), the extensive package of social and educational provision for family members, the travel and constant changes of residence, and the dependence on work for friendship – may ineluctably and even imperceptibly lead to a deep reliance and involvement in an institution that pervades your entire life. An executive graphically described life under Geneen's regime at ITT: 'Being an ITT manager is like living in a room with closed-circuit television all around you, and with a bug up your ass' (Sampson, 1974: 142).

Here I have touched on a limited number of structural factors that could contribute in some way to managerial and corporate misconduct. More extensive empirical research might further explore market shifts, company size, product diversification, the nature of strategy, geographical dispersion, growth and profitability, the previous record of transgressions, leadership change, reward systems, and so on (Clinard and Yeager, 1980: 150; Cochran and Nigh, 1986).

Culture   The concept of 'corporate culture' has received considerable attention during the last decade (Deal and Kennedy, 1982); it seems to have been resurrected as a positive force for cohesion and identity in response to new flexible and decentralized forms of business organization (Barham et al., 1988). In its original anthropological sense it refers to patterns of thought and action in a group and, when applied to organizations, it tends to reveal that specific companies, and parts of companies, have often a separate style of doing things manifested in subtle, semi-conscious ways of thinking and acting (Ouchi, 1985). There may be a highly articulated formal culture (with songs, prescriptions for dress, and a specified way of conducting business), an informal culture (norms and behaviour related to unspecified but understood ways of doing or not doing things in a firm), a number of sub-cultures (perhaps based on production, finance, marketing, headquarters, and so on), and even an under-culture (either for or against the organization). We have seen earlier that some industries seem to sponsor a rule-breaking mentality. Clinard and Yeager (1980), for instance, identified the oil, auto, and pharmaceutical industries in their survey of American firms in the late 1970s as 'recidivists', and this record of repeat transgressions is probably related to the fact that these industries had at the time a tough, anti-regulatory ideology and culture allied to a feeling that they were over-regulated with petty rules drawn up by people who did not understand their industries. And it is even possible that seeking deviant solutions becomes imbedded in the corporate culture – particularly if we perceive culture as related to collective understanding in groups about coping with shared problems (Van Maanen and Barley, 1984). For instance, Stone has referred to the 'culture of the corporation' as contributing to illegal behaviour, and enumerates the following factors as possibly fostering illegality:

> a desire for profits, expansion, power; desire for security (at corporate as well as individual levels); the fear of failure (particularly in connection with shortcomings in corporate innovativeness); group loyalty identification (particularly in connections with citizenship violations and the various failures to 'come forward' with internal information); feelings of omniscience (in connection with inadequate testing); organizational diffusion of responsibility (in connection with the buffering of public criticism); corporate ethnocentrism (in connection with limits in concern for the public's wants and desires). (1975: 236)

Although the concept of culture is notoriously diffuse it is employed here to suggest that some elements of the corporate culture (in some companies at some times) may be conducive to deviant solutions to company problems; as Braithwaite (1985a: 9) maintains, 'violations are more likely to occur in some industries, those closely associated with an "industry culture" favourable to unethical and illegal behaviour' (cf. Miles, 1987).

Banco Ambrosiano under Calvi, and also BCCI, could be said to have developed a criminal culture – that became the dominant culture – under the veneer of legality and conformity to rules. Indeed, this leads one to surmise that treating culture as something readily definable and essentially separate from the organization is missing the point that culture can be held to be synonymous with organization and strategy synonymous with culture (Bate, 1994). BCCI pursued a criminal strategy and fostered a criminal culture in certain segments of the bank.

Personality/Identity

A major concern in this work has been to look behind the accounts of well-known cases of corporate misconduct to examine the motives and behaviour of the managers involved. Here I wish to specify some of the socio-psychological factors that help to define the personality and identity of managers and that might contribute to accepting, and engaging in, deviant practices.

Depersonalization   Corporate affairs may be conducted in such a way that managers feel far removed from the consequences of their actions. This may be reinforced by the use of euphemistic language, a retreat into figures (reducing decisions to a question of cost-benefit analysis), and by hostile or dismissive negative stereotypes of competitors, customers, regulatory officials, and government representatives. De Lorean commented on decision-making at General Motors when he worked there; he speaks of moral men making collectively immoral decisions related to loyalty, protecting the system, contempt for customers, and especially the impersonality of large American multinationals where people simply do not count (Wright, 1979: 62).

The implication is that individuals are placed in a conflict situation when their own values are compromised by organizational dictates and that a number of socio-psychological mechanisms have to be employed in order to wean managers from their individual moralities in order to be able to subordinate these to organizational ideologies and practices (Bowles, 1991). One adaptation described by Jackall (1988, 147) is the development of negative stereotypes of 'outsiders'; he portrays his managers as beset with feelings of 'beleaguerment' and as feeling 'under siege'; one response was to construct 'sardonic caricatures of their principal adversaries':

> For example, most government regulators are brash, young, unkempt hippies in blue jeans who know nothing about the business for which they want to turn off the electricity before testing power tools. Consumer activists, the far too many Ralph Naders of this world, want to save the universe but not give up their own creature comforts. Workmen's compensation lawyers are out-and-out crooks who prey on corporations to appropriate exorbitant fees for unwary clients whom they fleece next. Labor activists are radical troublemakers who want to disrupt harmonious industrial communities. . . . Academics who criticize business may be able to conjugate difficult Greek verbs; unfortunately, many of them cannot tie their own shoelaces. Most environmental activists – the bird and bunny people – are softheaded idealists who want everybody to live in tents, burn candles, ride horses, and eat berries.

Braithwaite (1984: 2) researched the pharmaceutical industry and encountered one executive with a sign 'go for the jugular' on the wall behind his desk: 'Another respondent, one of the most powerful half-dozen men in the Australian pharmaceutical industry, excused his own ruthlessness with: "In business you can come up against a dirty stinking bunch of crooks. Then you have to behave like a crook yourself, otherwise you get done like a dinner".'

Impersonality also characterized relations with colleagues; this enabled them to distance themselves emotionally from failures, who were cut adrift, as if they were lepers, quite heartlessly:

> Our motives are purely selfish. We're not concerned about old Joe failing, but we're worried about how his failure will reflect on us. When you pick somebody, say, you invest part of yourself in him. So his failure and what it means to his kids and so on mean nothing. What you're worried about is your own ass with your superiors for having picked him in the first place. . . . What we do essentially when somebody fails is to put him in a little boat, tow him out to sea, and cut the rope. And we never think about him again. (Jackall, 1988: 68)

The psychological and social processes that managers go through in the business organization can lead to repressing feeling, bi-polar thinking, impersonalization, rejection of outsiders, psychological distancing from the consequences of decisions, retreat into figures, and a calculative involvement with colleagues.

Ideology/Rationalizations   The culture of companies and the socio-political values of managers can foster a repertoire of rationalizations (or 'vocabularies of motive') and an ideology that supports significant rule-breaking. For instance, parts of American business have sponsored an anti-government and anti-regulation ideology that could aid in removing restraints to rule-breaking (cf. Clinard and Yeager, 1980). Box maintains that corporate officials may operate in a 'subculture of structural immoralities' (Mills, 1956: 138) which helps to provide them with a 'library of verbal technique for neutralizing the moral bind of laws against corporate behaviour' (1983: 54); and this leads to denying responsibility, denying injury or else blaming the victim, condemning the condemners, and appealing to a higher loyalty. Rationalizations, justifications, and 'vocabularies of motive' (Matza, 1964) tend to revolve around statements that either salve consciences during the activity or justify deviant behaviour on its exposure. Examples usually include the following:

- no one was hurt/we didn't mean to hurt anyone;
- it's a jungle out there/it's dog eat dog;
- it was part of the job;
- those were the rules of the game;
- I didn't know it was wrong (illegal/criminal);
- if I hadn't done it, then someone else would have done it (and I would probably have lost my job);
- the world is a market-place and everyone has their price;
- they had it coming to them;
- we weren't lying, we just weren't telling all the truth;
- everyone was doing it;
- I was only doing what I was told to do = orders are orders (the Eichmann rationale).

The rationalizations and motives defuse the moral, criminal, and negative connotations of deviant practices enabling them to be perceived as normal, routine and morally neutral events: 'Regardless of the manner in which their violations are handled, executive offenders do not, for the most part, think of themselves as criminals; nor do they feel morally responsible for the harm they have caused' (Braithwaite: 1985a: 298). As Sutherland (1983: 217) had noted, 'their consciences do not ordinarily bother them.'

Another element in the ideological underpinning of business is that it can take on the strength of religion. The 'magico-religious' view of management (Cleverley, 1971) draws on parallels with beliefs in primitive societies:

Management, he [Cleverley] suggests, incorporates a set of magico-religious beliefs akin to those found in simple societies. The management world is one in which supernatural forces are at work, and sometimes these operate in capricious and threatening ways. But these forces can be influenced by acting out suitable rituals.

Supernatural entities include the shareholders, the company (or organization) and the market. The company, for example, is personified and is imputed with possessing goals, purposes or missions. It is seen as a sacred object commanding reverence through obedience, loyalty and dedication. These gods are threatening and must be propitiated. So, for example, the shareholders are placated at the ceremonial of the annual general meeting. Moral prescriptions, indicating proper ways of behaving, are also in evidence. Foremost among these is 'Thou shalt seek profits', to which we might add 'And thou shalt seek promotion'.

The religion of management, Cleverley continues, is administered by a priesthood, the accountants, and attended by magicians, the consultants. Its belief system is developed and passed on partly by behavioral scientists, and it embraces a set of rites; rites of passage, invoked during processes of managerial recruitment and promotion, and funerary rites, attendant upon retirement, resignation and dismissal. The belief system also defines certain taboo objects which are to be shunned. Women, for example, are to be avoided for fear of contamination. (Thomas, 1993: 81)

Or as Ray Kroc, founder of McDonald's puts it: 'I speak of faith in McDonald's as if it were a religion. I believe in God, family, and McDonald's – and in the office that order is reversed.' (Thomas, 1993: 56)

Business as War   Perhaps another feature endorsing the above is the growing predilection for seeing business in martial terms related to conducting warfare, engaging in inter-organizational conflict, adopting quasi-military strategies, waging campaigns, and requiring 'commanders' at the top. Of course business has always been competitive, and corporate battles have been fought out in the past, but it is the explicit adoption of martial imagery and military models during the last decade that may have aided in removing restraint in some situations. The definition of war is that you cause enough physical or psychological damage to the enemy to persuade him, or her, to cease hostile activities (while recognizing that in the process you too will inevitably be damaged: Monahan and Novaco: 1980). There can be a subtle side to this, in the judicious injunctions of Sun-Tsu (author of 'The Art of War') but one suspects that many managers lean more towards masculine, tough, macho role-models and prefer to see themselves as Pattons (and one visualizes them continually rerunning George C. Scott's impressive film portrait of General Patton). The marketing guru – Ogilvie (1990) – draws on Von Clausewitz, the German blitzkrieg of 1940, and guerrilla wars (of Tito, Che Guevara, Mao Tse-tung and Ho Chi Minh) to illustrate business strategy. The military analogy also has the advantage that it combines a predilection for order and planning as well as an emphasis on character and personality characteristics – for example, toughness, the will to win and to overcome odds, determination, masculinity, the willingness to cause pain, and the ability to take pain, to respond to challenge, and to orientate to team-effort (Garskombe, 1988).

There are also negative features associated with this style of thinking, which may appeal particularly strongly in some national cultures and in some industries more than others. For example, Rosenberg and Van West (1984) note that if 'people believe they are at war, *winning at any cost* becomes important. Price wars, industrial espionage, and even sabotage of competitors becomes acceptable, desirable, and possibly commonplace.'

But it is the case that many corporate conflicts – related to intense competition or hostile takeovers – have been fought out recently as 'wars' (for instance, the 'cola wars' between Pepsi Cola and Coca-Cola and the 'aspirin wars': Mann and Plummer, 1991). And books based on military analogies have become increasingly popular among managements; the flavour of one can be conveyed by this blurb on the jacket (James, 1985):

If you don't fight, you can't win!
How did BMW overtake Mercedes?
How did Jaguar get back on the road?
How did McDonald's grab the hamburger market?
How did Duracell outshine Eveready?

Today's most successful businesses have survived price wars, mounted aggressive advertising campaigns, formed alliances with other companies. In short they have – through strategic manoeuvring – conquered the battlefields of a highly competitive marketplace.

Now, Barrie G. James shows you how the well-tested tactics of the military can be applied to your business. Using examples from the tragic mistakes and brilliant victories of military history, James draws striking parallels with case histories (both successes and failures) of industries worldwide.

Competition is increasing, and the fight for market shares continues to heat up. Business Wargames offers you the strategies you need. It is the indispensable weapon for every executive in the perilous trenches of market warfare in the 1980s.

Also a publisher's promotional kit sent to US marketing professors was called the 'survival kit', complete with khaki camouflage box, rations, medications, and the adage 'it's a jungle out there'; while a course entitled 'Marketing Warfare' at an American college includes 'dogtags' and 'camouflaged notebooks' for the students (Garskombe, 1988: 47–8). It is difficult to specify what sort of impact this rhetoric has on the values, behaviour, and identities of managers, but it could conceivably reduce restraint and justify tough, and even dirty, combat. This can be related to perceiving contemporary organizations as 'essentially masculine phenomena' (Bowles, 1991: 392); and Hirsch and Andrews (1984) have described how 'organizational takeovers and mergers are often depicted in the form of a love affair or marriage, rape or warfare', and remark that 'in virtually all such formulations, the acquiring executive is macho and the target company is the female gender'. Certainly, part of the underlying logic of business is tough, macho, aggressive, and permeated with martial metaphors (Ramsey, 1987). A small operator, for instance, that forges a niche will be tolerated; if the newcomer begins to threaten the established power structure, however, it is likely to be ruthlessly crushed. Laker, who pioneered cheap transatlantic plane travel, was attacked by British and North American members of the IATA cartel once he had reached a significant market share. He was forced out of business, and took the American and British companies to court claiming he had been a victim of a vicious and relentless 'price war' (his demise was also related to his own cavalier and rashly optimistic decision-making: Banks: 1982).

Fun/Excitement Concepts such as deviance and corruption readily conjure up exotic, conspiratorial imagery. Some managers may be attracted to this aspect of their work, and, like double agents and bent cops (Daley, 1979), come to enjoy it and even revel in it. Some accounts of actually managing the logistics of corporate misconduct are colourful and byzantine and read like fiction; in relation to one company's illegal payments to CREEP (the campaign to re-elect President Nixon), Kanter and Stein (1979: 313) note that 'There were secret bank accounts to launder funds, records flushed down toilets, couriers carrying plain envelopes stuffed with cash, safes left conveniently open at night, packages changing hands behind barns on remote ranches, and executives slugging one another in a sedate upper-crust club.' Furthermore, Stone (1975: 69) notes:

> some may even find covert activity exciting, as noted in the case of Equity Funding. In this environment of fun, excitement, and do-as-you're-told corporate loyalty, the law's threats are simply no guarantee that people are going to comply. Indeed, what is worse, I have a strong suspicion – shared by others who have represented corporate clients in their tangled affairs – that being on the edge of the law can even lend a tingle of 007 intrigue to the life of middle-level corporate operatives.

In effect, that 'tingle of 007 intrigue' induces some managers to engage in deviant practices because it provides fun and excitement. In this respect there is an interesting parallel with some of the explanations given by 'common' criminals for their involvement in crimes (Katz, 1988). There is an element that doing, and getting away with, crime may provide sneaky thrills – or a sense of machismo in beating the competition – for some managers. This feature is further reinforced in Reichman's (1993: 82) analysis of Drexel, where there was a culture of action and chaos that Katz (1988) describes as 'typical of street robbers and stickup men'.

Risk-takers and Gamblers One aspect of the above is that some businesses attract and encourage risk-takers, who begin to behave as gamblers. The emphasis on goals, ambition, achievement, innovation, and entrepreneurship can all aid in reinforcing an attitude and a stereotype of risk-taking as justified and as part of the successful manager's image. The plethora of books on excellence, typified by *In Search of Excellence* (Peters and Waterman, 1982), ushered in an emphasis on 'the winner, the champion, the peak-performer, and the risk-taker'; successful managers and entrepreneurs – for example, Iacocca, Steven Jobs, Victor Kiam, Steven Wozniak, Alan Bond, Kerry Packer, Richard Branson, Donald Burr, Tony O'Reilly, or Bill Gates – have emerged as folk heroes (*London Review of Books*, 21 May 1987: 9). In Britain, Robinson (1985) drew up a list of 'risk-takers', and it is noticeable that when he revisited them five years on several had taken a tumble, either in terms of precipitately declining fortunes and/or a visit to one of Her Majesty's prisons (and since then a couple more, Robert Maxwell and Abu Nadir, have been exposed as fraudeurs). But a positive image emerged of the buccaneering entrepreneur as a 'saviour' of stultified business; he, or occasionally she, did not fit into the conventional corporate environment but was more of a daring innovator, a financial juggler, or a crisis-orientated turn-around manager; they tended to be energetic, single-minded, idiosyncratic opportunists (Robinson, 1990).

But it may well be that certain companies in certain industries at certain times – for instance, the financial and property markets in the USA and the UK in the mid-1980s (Seabright, 1990: 1339) – stimulate risk-taking. Perhaps one reason for the incidence of problems in the financial services industry is that what was predominantly a risk-averse culture became transformed, for a number of reasons, into a risk-taking one during the 1980s (Reichman, 1993; Zey, 1993). Furthermore, an ideology supporting entrepreneurship as wholesome for the economy (as in the 'enterprise economy' of the 1980s in the UK) can imply that risk-taking is precisely an essential element in the entrepreneur's success. Again this contrasts with the rational, even cautious, element in business planning and takes us into the psychology of the gambler and speculator who may easily fall victim to irrational forces. Those could be in response to the euphoria surrounding financial 'bubbles' (Galbraith, 1993), could represent the desperate attempt to dig oneself out of trouble with one last throw of the corporate dice, or it could reveal the addiction of the true gambler who gets his, or her, kicks from the risk – and who is led progressively to raising the stakes in order to feed the habit (which seems to have been a strong element in Robert Maxwell's make-up). This, in turn, reinforces a point made in Chapter 1 that legitimate and powerfully encouraged business activity is sometimes virtually indistinguishable from deviant activity. Several authors have highlighted the similarities between 'the stock market, gambling, and the confidence game' (Leff, 1976; Lejeune, 1984). But here, I'm suggesting that some forms of business attract risk-taking and that some managers replicate the behaviour of gamblers – some of them successfully and legally, some of them successfully and illegally, and some of them unsuccessfully and illegally – and even display symptoms of addiction.

Corporate Heroes and Leaders   There are no clear blueprints for success in business and no unambiguous evidence about who gets on in business (Thomas, 1988); but there is a strong mythology and a prevalent stereotype that you have to be tough – and even something of a rule-breaker (Dalton, 1959) – in order to make it to the top. In some senior executives there is a definite element of gaining and using power, control, and dominance over people and resources. As pointed out above, some highly successful entrepreneurs have become role-models for endeavour and flair but, alongside the positive image, there are also unflattering portraits of greed, despotism, ruthlessness, and egoism. For instance, Lee Iacocca (1986) is not someone you immediately associate with whistle-blowing, but nevertheless he gives a savage portrait of Henry Ford II treating one of the major corporations in the world as his family's private property; Ford is shown as doing considerable damage to the enterprise on the basis of his personal whims and phobias (the latter particularly in relation to potentially threatening rivals such as Iacocca). And yet there was no effective mechanism to curb his persistent abuse of power; neither other family members, the board, senior management, nor, indeed, Iacocca himself, proved willing to challenge – or capable of challenging – his absolute authority (and Iacocca admits that he continued to put up with malicious harassment until he was fired). In fact, Henry Ford himself, who built up the Ford Company, was 'unpredictably authoritarian', anti-Semitic, and anyone who invaded his authority was sacked (by the executioner – 'Cast-Iron' Charlie Sorenson – until he too was sacked: Galbraith, 1986b).

In some leaders there is a ruthless element of domination that can lead both to sycophancy among employees and to sadistic and psychologically destructive vindictiveness (Nielsen, 1986). This can manifest itself in vitriolic corporate in-fighting, intrigue, factionalism, vendettas, and the placing of personal loyalty above managerial skills and competence. Geneen, the man who built the ITT empire (Sampson, 1974), was 'an unmitigated swine who regularly terrorised and humiliated his subordinates' (Turner, 1986: 762). And the biographies of Rockefeller, Getty, Onassis, Disney, Maxwell, Hammer, Howard Hughes, Geneen, and similar entrepreneurial, industrial, and commercial titans are replete with the obsessive thirst for power and the frequent abuse of that power (cf. *Business Week*, 1 April 1991: 'CEO Disease: Egotism Can Breed Corporate Disaster – and the Malady is Spreading'). On occasion the personal dominance and animosities of a top manager can sponsor feuds, vendettas, and hatreds that threaten to damage or even destroy the company they have built. The dark, irrational side of business life emerged in the bitter personal battles that brought down the merchant bank Lehman Bros; in the running feud between 'Tiny' Rowland and the Fayed brothers over the sale of Harrods (and Rowland has recently been summarily dismissed from the company he helped build up over thirty years for allegedly undermining his successor: *Daily Mail*, 3 March 1995); and in the fall-out, with writs flying, between the Saatchi brothers and the famous advertising firm of Saatchi and Saatchi (*Daily Mail*, 23 May 1995). Auletta (1986: 43) writes of the demise of Lehman Bros:

> 'what happened at Lehman is a tale of political intrigue unrivalled in Washington, of incompetence unmatched in the civil service, a sordid tale of vanity, avarice, cowardice, lust for power, and a polluted Lehman culture. These human ingredients – not a capital shortage, not impersonal market forces, not deregulated banking, not competition from financial superpowers – are what ultimately crushed an illustrious institution.

Furthermore, Dixon (1994: 307) summarizes the psychological work on the relationship between personality and 'disastrous decisions', and emphasizes an element that has 'probably resulted in more human, misery than all the others put together':

> It is, very simply, that those personality characteristics which take people to the top and establish them as all powerful decision-makers tend to include the very nastiest of human traits – extremes of egocentricity, insincerity, dishonesty, corruptibility, cynicism, and on occasions ruthless murderous hostility towards anyone who threatens their position. Even worse, if that is possible, than the traits which take them to the top are those which they acquire upon arrival – pomposity, paranoia, and megalomaniac delusions of grandeur.

Or as the golfer Ben Hogan was reputed to have said, 'Nice guys come last.'

In effect, there is considerable evidence to suggest that organizations deviate in varying ways from the formal bureaucratic model, that leadership can take on near pathological forms (where abuse of power remains unchecked and where subordinates become servile or else they become highly vulnerable targets), and that businesses may become the emotional and neurotic arenas for the personal battles of managers in relation to power and dominance (Kets de Vries and Miller, 1984; 1987). De Vries and Miller have succeeded in transplanting insights from psychiatry, psychoanalysis, and psychopathology and applying them to organizational malfunctioning.

This is important not only for the sort of people who get on in business but also because there is considerable evidence that the top person can be highly influential in setting the 'moral' tone for the company; that organizational elites indirectly initiate deviant actions by pressurizing middle management to achieve results (and by establishing covert but understood norms for rewards and punishments); and that both the top boss and the elite can be shielded from direct knowledge of deviancy and from the consequences of its exposure. In a survey of corporate ethics, Brenner and Molander (1977) held that superiors were ranked as the major influence on unethical practices; they were often not particularly interested in how results were achieved as long as desired targets were met, while 'respondents frequently complained of superiors' pressure to support incorrect viewpoints, sign false documents, overlook superiors' wrongdoing, and do business with superiors' friends' (p. 60). This indicates not only that the pressure to break the law is frequently funnelled lower down in the organization but that 'when the shit hits the fan' the *blame* can also be passed downwards. While these features make it extremely difficult to prove deliberate intent to choose deviant paths at the top and also to apportion blame justly, it often appears that the top initiates the deviance, the middle gets squeezed, and the non-involvement of the organizational elite in possible blame and exposure is carefully orchestrated. Braithwaite (1985a: 17) states succinctly: 'while it is middle management who perpetrate the criminal acts, it is top management who set the expectations, the tone, the corporate culture that determines the incidence of corporate crime'.

Certain personality types make it into corporate leadership where their dominating style – related to power, control, and egoism – can lead to rule-breaking by themselves, or, by subordinates, on their behalf. Of course, near psychotic megalomaniacs are not confined to business and can be encountered running universities, hospitals, and international sport federations; but a number of corporate criminologists (Clinard, 1983) have argued that top-management strategies are related to misconduct induced by top-down pressure by dominant and all-powerful leaders on lower managers that may increase illegality (Zey, 1993).

Trick and Treaters: Dirty Workers The evidence on exposure of business deviance indicates that some managers are engaged in, and even become specialized in, dirty tricks. There are a number of roles to be played in covert business activities and, presumably, a measure of personnel selection and socialization takes place around 'dirty' deeds.

> Every firm has a 'tough guy' and all large organizations develop specialist roles. It would appear that someone will be willing, pleased, and even anxious to show his courage, toughness, or grit and do 'the job that has to be done'. Superiors may not

wish to know, but they are not necessarily unappreciative. In reply to the question
whether he would fire a worker for paying bribes abroad, a chairman of Booz,
Allen & Hamilton Consultants, replied, 'Hell, no! Why fire him for something he
was paid to do.' (Reisman, 1979: 145)

In short, corporations on occasion need executioners, bag-men, spies, computer hackers, pimps, entertainers, intelligence-gatherers, burglars,
bug-placers, phone-tappers, gophers, moles, frighteners, safe-breakers, forg-
ers, vote-riggers, saboteurs, debt-collectors, garbage rummagers, hatchet-men
and 'escorts'. Executives from another company may require 'entertainment'
and this could involve a weekend on John Wayne's yacht; hitting the fleshpots
of a large city for several nights on the trot with nearly insatiable managers
from abroad; or ensuring that an important customer, with no skill at handling firearms, fulfils his lifetime ambition of shooting a bear (Reisman, 1979).
It's all in the line of business; and of keeping the client happy.

An insight into this area was exposed when it was revealed that one of the
world's leading airlines, British Airways, had become so concerned at competition from Richard Branson's much smaller Virgin airline on transatlantic
and Far Eastern routes that some of its staff set up a disinformation campaign (*Business Week*, 25 January 1993: 21). Virgin was a small independent
carrier but moved into areas usually dominated by the large airlines, for
example business passengers, inter-continental flights, and the major airfields
(such as Tokyo and Heathrow), while it began to pick up accolades for service. In this 'increasingly cut-throat and dirty field' Virgin was in the eyes of
some getting too big for its boots.

> For British Airways, Virgin's progress was a source of immense annoyance, and no
> little concern. In terms of size, Virgin were a mere flea besides British Airways' ele-
> phantine operation, yet the flea seemed capable of inflicting a disproportionate
> amount of discomfort and irritation. (Brown, 1994: 471)

Out of this commercial animosity a campaign was set up to discredit Virgin.

> The battle between BA and Virgin had now settled into a trench warfare of claim
> and counter-claim, accusation and innuendo. The battle was being fought in the
> corridors of the CAA [Civil Aviation Authority], the government – even the
> European Commission – and in the colums of the national press. . . . Such incidents
> [where an advertisement had mentioned Branson as the owner of 'Britain's
> favourite airline' and BA had complained, unsuccessfully, to the Advertising
> Standards Authority] were knockabout fun, the sort of mischievous hype which
> Branson had always delighted in; par for the course. Much more serious, however,
> was the question of the rumours that had begun to circulate about the state of
> Virgin's financial health. (Brown, 1994: 482)

A number of television programmes, such as *This Week* on Thames Television
in February 1992, focused on the practices used in the BA–Virgin rivalry
which were alleged to include entering Virgin's computer space and poaching
passengers. The producer of *This Week* went on to write a book on the
methods allegedly employed in the campaign: Gregory (1994).

Richard Branson openly accused BA of dirty tricks; BA counter-claimed
that Branson was merely seeking publicity. BA's in-house paper, *BA News*,

had published 'an attack on Virgin under the heading "Branson Dirty Tricks Claim Unfounded", accusing Branson of fabricating claims in order to garner publicity' (Brown, 1994: 485). Incensed, Branson sued for libel and BA issued a counter-claim. The 'battle' had begun to heat up when in January 1991 Branson went to the European Commission complaining of BA and alleging that BA was abusing a dominant market position. The libel trial was expected to last three months, was looked forward to as the 'mother of all trials', and was expected to be a tough legal battle with a lot of mud-slinging. In the event, BA decided to climb down and effectively capitulated. It offered an unqualified apology to Branson, paid an estimated £3 million in legal costs, and paid £610,000 compensation to Branson and Virgin. When the BA case collapsed in January 1993 Branson also decided to settle and not to push on with his part of the libel action. In the High Court, Lord King and BA issued a statement which apologized

'unreservedly for the injury caused to the reputation and feelings of Richard Branson and Virgin Atlantic' by the articles in BA News' and Lord King's letters. The statement went on to admit that [a freelance consultant] had attempted to place 'hostile and discreditable stories' in the press, and that aspects of BA's conduct gave Branson 'serious concern about the activities of a number of British Airways employees and of [the consultant], and their potential effect on the business interests and reputation of Virgin Atlantic and Richard Branson'. (Brown, 1994: 493)

A number of BA managers departed in the aftermath of the scandal.

One of the world's leading airlines had admitted that some of its people had engaged in a concerted campaign of disinformation against an upstart competitor. Both chairman King and his successor-to-be, Colin Marshall, explicitly distanced themselves from implication in implementing any 'disreputable business practices' (Brown, 1994: 494). Speaking on BBC Radio in early 1995, Colin Marshall, by then chairman of BA, explained that airlines were in a very competitive industry that used highly aggressive marketing techniques; people had made a 'mountain out of a relative molehill'. Branson, like his forerunner Freddy Laker, went on to pursue BA in the courts. Virgin went after BA on three counts: for breach of copyright related to misuse of computer information; for anti-competitive activity before the European Commission; and in October 1991 Branson went to the USA to pursue his interests under antitrust legislation. In the American courts he claimed £325 million for 'illegal anti-competitive and monopolistic activities' with the possibility of gaining treble damages on top of any award (Brown, 1994: 502; Gregory, 1994). That could be quite a molehill!

In the takeover battles of the 1980s in America and Britain there was a range of dirty tricks which the actors accepted as standard practice ('takeover tactics have gotten nastier – and even some of the key practitioners deplore the excesses': *Newsweek*, 9 December 1985) but, like espionage, everyone denies being involved in it until caught red-handed, when one claims it is a regrettable exception (for example, when General Motors admitted in court to tailing Ralph Nader with a private detective; this cost them half a million dollars in damages: Buchholz, 1982: 54). Alternatively, fall-guys or straw-men are selected in advance of trouble; perhaps it is not always easy to recruit managers for the polluted areas associated with dirty work:

> Examples include company presidents appointing 'vice-presidents responsible for going to jail', respectable companies engaging contractors to do illegal dirty work such as disposing of toxic wastes or producing fraudulent scientific data about the safety of a product, or hiring agents to pay bribes. (Braithwaite, 1985a: 7)

For a number of reasons it may be considered politic to call in outsiders to displace the deviant activity to an external agency; private detective agencies or PR consultants are often employed. For instance, when the *Sunday Times* was investigating the BA–Virgin case a private detective was caught stealing rubbish bags at night from the back garden of the managing editor of the newspaper. The bag-snatcher was working on assignment and was unaware of who was ultimately interested in any of the correspondence in the bags (*Daily Mail*, 22 December 1992).

In many cases, 'old-style' legwork and rubbish-rummaging crops up; when Dr McBride, who had earlier figured in the Thalidomide affair, was preparing to give testimony against a drug company (once more it was a case where a drug was said to have caused deformities in babies), he was warned that he would almost certainly be trailed and kept under surveillance (*Sunday Times*, 21 September 1980). When Edward Safra felt he was being shadowed he mounted a counter-operation which led straight to the headquarters of American Express. Safra had sold his company to American Express but, due to various differences, he had left within a couple of years; American Express believed Safra was intending to compete against them in defiance of an agreement. Safra claimed that he had uncovered a campaign of disinformation against him; he received a public apology, some $8 million was donated to charity on his behalf, and a senior aide to American Express's chairman resigned (Burrough, 1992). In recent years, however, the emphasis in industrial espionage has shifted to sophisticated forms of electronic surveillance and trading in high-grade information. On the one hand, information can be gleaned from computer-hacking, bugging phones and offices, and picking up conversations from buildings by using lasers; on the other, bribery and blackmail can be used to get inside cooperation and information. Here the search is for strategic information or 'competitive intelligence', and less for personal data to discredit an individual. It is not conventional inter-company espionage but the work of middlemen brokers who sell to the highest bidder or who work on assignment. In the Netherlands, for instance, the National Security Service (BVD, the agency for domestic political intelligence) warned that 'malafide information dealers' were preying on large companies and that many companies refused to report these forms of espionage to the police (*Business Week*, 14 October 1991; *de Volkskrant*, 21 April 1994; Broer and Gielen, 1993; Cools and Hoogenboom, 1995; Schaap, 1995).

In effect, companies sometimes need people to conduct dirty work for them and some managers are prepared to engage in it. This probably means preparing to accept an even deeper level of deviousness and duplicity than in more standard and accepted covert practices. Some managers may find this more acceptable than others, but their roles are required at certain times and people are selected and socialized to fill them. This could be a matter of temporary deviance, a role played at a specific time for a specific purpose and then abandoned, or else the assignment is conveniently outsourced to an external agency which can more easily be blamed for any excesses without implicating too many people within one's own company. Box (1983: 42) suggests that managers may not need to be coerced into these positions but slip into them almost as a matter of course:

> it might be more realistic to argue that corporate officials are frequently placed in a position where they are required to choose between impairing their career chances or being a loyal organizational person. That the latter seems to be chosen overwhelmingly testifies not to the existence of coercion, but to careful selection procedures for placing persons in corporate positions coupled with successful methods of persuading them that their interests and the corporation's interests happily coincide – or at least, that that is the most sensible, pragmatic way of looking at it.
>
> As the corporate lawyer put it, when asked why he went along with producing completely bogus insurance policies as part of the Equity Funding Scandal: 'I didn't think anything of it; it was something the company needed done, that's all.'

Pressure and Rewards   Mention was made above of goals, campaigns, and a strong sense of mission in corporate life; this has implications for the type of people who can cope with such pressure and their reactions to it. In many companies there is an emphasis on working long hours, the ability to produce results, and the willingness to take tough decisions; generally the feeble and the soft-hearted do not survive long in this environment. Constant pressure, feelings of stress, and the perception of being in a 'battle' can lead to 'combat fatigue' which lessens restraint in decision-making (cf. Roux in the Guinness case who said he ended up so tired that he did not know what he was doing any more). One form of pressure may be to bend rules. This, in turn, may be linked to legitimate or illicit rewards.

A great deal has been written about the astronomical incomes enjoyed by some American executives (Crystal, 1991). In his best year Milken took home a pay cheque for $550 million and he had amassed a fortune of $1.5 billion by 1990. In recent years CEO salaries have risen precipitously (averaging $3.5 million in 1992), and these have been enhanced by various stock-option schemes (which gave Michael Eisner of Disney Company a windfall of $197 million in 1992: *Business Week*, 8 June 1992; 26 April 1993). This in itself may not form a direct incentive to deviant behaviour. Indeed, it is comforting to read that nowadays the wealthy tend to live frugal if not spartan lives and, with some exceptions, a health-conscious diet keeps them from over-indulgence (Packard, 1989). But the opportunity to gain large rewards was clearly an element in the Wall Street situation and also attracted rapacious predators to the thrifts in the S & L scandal. Attention has been drawn to the short-term reward system in many US companies (Jacobs, 1991), based on the quarterly returns, and this fluctuating feature could induce managers to 'massage' data favourable to their bonuses and to seek other paths for keeping up their level of remuneration if this should be threatened by poor results (as happened in the RSV case). The relationship between performance and bonuses appears to have been an important element in the manipulations of Leeson at Barings.

The crucial point, however, is how managers *perceive* the reward system and *experience* the pressure. On the one hand, there is the oft-repeated but somewhat disingenuous argument that corporate deviants received no direct reward for their activities; but this ignores psychological, covert, or future rewards that may be implicit in conforming to deviant expectations. And, on the other hand, sometimes the stakes are extremely high and a company may be in a make-or-break predicament (for instance, the future of the company may depend on the success of a single product, as sometimes happens in the aeronautics industry). What does that mean in terms of pressure exerted on managers and what is their reaction to that pressure? When *are* the stakes high – subjectively and situationally? It is difficult to conceive of the competitive environment of business without pressure, and without rewards related to performance under pressure. And the assumption is that the response to that pressure is related to personality, motivation, and to certain social contexts.

When is 'enough' enough? The answer generally is that it never is enough, because the reward is a symbol of power or recognition, and that gratifications based on these are, for some people, limitless. And what is someone's 'price'? What sort of pressure and what sort of reward pushes someone into deviance? Greed and temptation are the stuff of business soaps and morality plays but they are also related to specific periods, sub-cultures within companies, cultural expectations, occupational rationalizations, formal and informal rewards, and to certain personality types. In Goodrich the engineers proved unable to resist the pressure; they put their jobs, mortgages, and children's college fees before the lives of test pilots. In Wall Street the financial wheeler-dealers could not resist the temptation, and the kick from 'scoring' on the market overrode wider professional, ethical, and financial considerations to the extent that some accused them of threatening the health of the wider economy. Boesky admitted that he was driven by an illness that he was powerless to control (Packard, 1989).

This section has examined a number of factors that impinge on managers within the business environment and that may shape both a particular way of looking at the world and also a certain personality type and identity. It has also touched on some of the socio-psychological forces that remind us of the irrational element in organizational life and in the darker or 'shadow' side of business (Bowles, 1991). Below an attempt will be made to draw these diverse elements together in a portrait of the managerial mind and personality structure.

The Making of the Managerial Mind

> Finally, those truly adept at inconsistency can also interpret with some
> accuracy the inconsistent machinations of their colleagues and adversaries.

This is not a mean skill. At the very beginning of my fieldwork, the top lawyer of a large corporation was discussing an issue that I had raised when he said: 'Now, I'm going to be completely honest with you about this.'

He paused for a moment and then said: 'By the way, in the corporate world, whenever anybody says to you: I'm going to be completely honest with you about this, you should immediately know that a curveball is on the way. But, of course, that doesn't apply to what I'm about to tell you.'

In a world of cheerfully bland public faces, where words are always provisional, intentions always cloaked, and frankness simply one of many guises, wily discernment, being able, as managers say 'to separate the honey from the horseshit', becomes an indispensable skill.

(Jackall, 1988: 161)

In explaining corporate misconduct, and executive illegality, it is important to see the manager as an actor wrestling with uncertainty and performing in a world of 'conflicting pressures, contradictory alternatives and ambiguous situations' (Thomas, 1993: 84). This negotiation of reality is related to self and identity, accepting institutional logic (even when it is 'illogical'), conforming to expectations, and adapting to a situational morality. The perspective used in this present study encourages us to look not so much at 'bad' people but more at how the condition of work shapes moral consciousness and how ordinary people are induced in an organizational setting to violate laws and rules – cf. Mars's work on 'the normal crimes of normal people in the normal circumstances of their work' (1982: 1). As such it is based on the organizational and managerial work of authors who have helped to illuminate the social world of the executive. Drawing on the discussion earlier in this chapter, this section will focus on a number of features that contribute to the values and behaviour of managers. Potentially the list is endless but I have selected five key factors: *Homo economicus*, organization man, group-think, cognitive dissonance, and the 'amoral chameleon'.

Homo economicus

Business is about functioning in a competitive environment by gearing resources to signals interpreted from that environment. The fundamental concerns of senior management are centred on corporate survival, continuity, power, reputation/face, and profits, although some companies, particularly utilities and family-owned newspapers, continue for years without ever making a profit (Meyer and Zucker, 1989). There is a strong emphasis on gaining profits as a determining feature of business, and it is often mentioned as a factor in illegal behaviour; but 'profit' is itself an ambiguous term open to many interpretations (Thompson, 1967). Through scanning and forecasting managers also seek a fit between external signals and internal response. One crucial domain assumption is that some form of economic 'health' has to be achieved related to indicators designed to satisfy potentially powerful stakeholders; for example, profits, market share, return on investment, turnover, or production quotas. My argument is that the managerial mind is programmed to function in relation to underlying precepts about what business is about as an economic activity – maximizing profits, providing a sound return on investment, reducing unit costs, performance in relation to the competition, investing for the future to ensure continuity, and so on. It is not necessarily the case that managers are obsessed with these matters on a daily base but rather that they underpin decision-making at critical moments. By almost automatically drawing upon them executives may consciously, or even imperceptibly, turn to a deviant solution for a business problem.

For example, rule-breaking may simply be a matter of rational calculation. Let's say a manager is faced with a vast rule-book that makes it difficult to operate without transgressing some law; the chances of detection are small (while non-random inspections mean that he or she can clean up operations until the inspectors have departed); and the level of sanctions is low. Then, the managers, might argue, it makes economic sense to take the low risk and violate the law; and it even militates against the business mentality to comply with the rules. Some rule-breaking may be deliberate, rational, and based on the executive operating as *Homo economicus* (Gross, 1980: 65).

In some cases, however, the instinctive economic mind-frame may push decision-making up to, and beyond, the bounds of rationality. In aeronautics, for instance, the industry is characterized by vast initial investment, a long product life-cycle (aeroplanes continue to operate for many years before they need to be replaced), and a prolonged period before reaching 'ROI' (return on investment). In aeroplane manufacture, in automobiles, and in pharmaceuticals, there are certain conditions which may lead managers to stick with their product almost as a basic, kneejerk reaction. This will especially be the case if it looks like being a 'winner' or there is no readily available alternative. This is based on the business realities of the industry, and of how managers view products and 'ROI,' but it can also mean sticking with a defective product because the managers involved are thinking predominantly economically and managerially (Wright, 1979: 62). This can blind them to other considerations.

Organization Man

Turning to the social world of the manager, there is often an emphasis on loyalty, dedication, and conformity. All groups exact some measure of conformity and here we are concerned with two levels of conformity: one level is conformity to rules, regulations, and laws, and another level is conformity to the corporation, to superiors, and to peers. Whyte (1956) drew attention to the clone-like conformity of managers when he coined the term 'The Organization Man'; loyalty was crucial to success, and unorthodox views or behaviour – even if expressed by a spouse not employed by the company (Seidenberg, 1973) – could be dangerous to career prospects. This was echoed two decades later by Kanter (1977), who showed that selection and socialization perpetuated a culture characterized by lack of introspection, by a bland and easygoing superficiality, by an emphasis on team membership, and by a strong informal code of conduct related to dress, hair-style, verbal expression, and political views.

In particular, Kanter argued powerfully that management was a *masculine* domain and it reflected features to be found particularly in male preserves (an emphasis on comradeship, team effort, ambition, sexually tinged banter, competitiveness, and toughness – 'bottle' or 'balls'); these worked to the detriment of women who wished to move up the corporate hierarchy. Furthermore, Margolis (1979) has argued that constant geographic mobility ties managers, and their families, into corporate life because they never establish roots in a community and because the company caters for virtually all their needs – cf. Sampson (1976: 28–31), on the all-encompassing culture of Shell which provided almost everything for its personnel abroad including transport, housing, schools, and cutlery graded according to the manager's place in the hierarchy.

Above, mention was made of business approaching the impact of a total institution, and in some cases business is organized around occupational communities (Van Maanen and Barley, 1984). It could be that these structural features lead us to exaggerate the impact on personality. Some corporations have loosened their structure, have recruited more women, and have espoused more 'non-conformist' behaviour. Some managers and commentators maintain that the 'organization man' is a stereotype of the past and that he was a peculiarly North American phenomenon (Bennett, 1990). This is a moot point, and could be argued at length, but the pivotal issue is the impact that the group has on individual norms and behaviour, particularly in relation to collectivism in corporations. In some of the business bureaucracies described – and there is a remarkable continuity from Dalton through Kanter to Jackall – there emerges an authoritarianism and collectivism that imposes itself heavily on the individual. You suppress individuality, do not challenge or criticize the hierarchy, and you do as you are told; this might mean that transgressions and violations in business can be likened to 'crimes of obedience' in the military, where the individual feels that the only option is to follow orders (Kehman and Hamilton, 1991). Bennis (1973) also has written of the 'dirty little secrets' in organization life – loyalty, betrayal, and power; and the backbone of organizational life as 'unconscious loyalist behaviour.' Or as one American manager graphically informed me, when I asked him about the reality of his life in a large corporation: 'Well, I guess you learn to eat shit, and to pretend you're enjoying it.'

Group-think

One element that selection, socialization, identification with, and commitment to, the corporation can foster is the phenomenon of 'group-think'. Janis (1985) has analysed the characteristics of group-think as posited around feelings of invulnerability; collective attempts at rationalization; an uncritical belief in one's own values; negative stereotypes of others in the external environment; intolerance of those who think differently; self-censure to help avoid doubts; a shared illusion of unanimity; and the emergence of 'mind-guards' who protect the group against new information (van Dijk, 1989).

Group-think has been used to explain military incompetence, leading to disasters, because the mental and structural rigidity built into the authoritarian military mind and inflexible military organization leads commanders to persist in fatally inappropriate responses, strategically and tactically, to changing circumstances in warfare. Dixon (1979: 397–400), after a review of military disasters, refers to 'the staggering irrationality which can beset the thinking of otherwise highly competent, intelligent, conscientious individuals when they begin to act as a group'; in particular, the symptoms of military incompetence are 'wastage of manpower, over-confidence, underestimation of the enemy, and the ignoring of intelligence reports'.

There may well be, then, a sort of collective conscience, or organizational 'mind', that enables people to lose hold of internalized restraints, because group processes have programmed a manager to the extent that institutional claims on the executive's loyalty are almost impossible to reject (Reisman, 1979: 147). Peter Drucker, one of the leading doyens of management, re-inforces this view when he maintains that 'executive life not only breeds a parochialism of the imagination comparable to the "military" but places a considerable premium on it' (1972: 81). This view of organizational life draws our attention to the inability to learn from experience, tunnel vision, self-deception, and other psychological mechanisms of defence found in groups under stressful conditions (Dixon, 1994: 307).

Cognitive Dissonance and the Road to Abilene

Two of those mechanisms are worth highlighting because they played a role in group behaviour in several of the cases used in this book. One is 'cognitive dissonance', which refers to a psychological mechanism whereby discon-firming evidence of a strongly held belief is not only rejected but also leads to a *strengthening* of that belief (Festinger, 1957). In a number of cases, there is a rejection of negative signals that might have served as a warning, and then a *redoubling* of efforts to market the product. This could be rather cynically seen as an extreme form of rational calculation – 'push it for all its worth until regulation intrudes' – but another interpretation is that the executives con-cerned really did convince themselves of the claims made for their product and that they did this by unconsciously filtering out evidence of a discon-firming nature. In many cases of corporate misconduct there is an almost inexplicable aspect of management which simply does not face up to strong signals that something is seriously wrong (cf. NASA and the Challenger dis-aster; Vaughan, 1988; or a number of blood-bank scandals where officials closed their eyes to the terrible consequences of releasing contaminated blood on the market for transfusions, as happened in France: *de Volkskrant*, 22 December 1992).

Another defensive element – not wishing to disagree with an implied consensus – leads us to places we do not really want to go, such as Abilene (Texas) on a hot, dusty day. Harvey (1988) has called this the 'Abilene Paradox' (which he based on a disastrous family trip to Abilene after which it emerged that everyone had agreed to go because they thought the others wanted to, when in fact no one actually felt like going!):

> Stated simply, it is as follows: Organizations frequently take actions in contradiction to what they really want to do and therefore defeat the very purposes they are trying to achieve. It also deals with a major corollary of the paradox, which is that *the inability to manage agreement is a major source of organization dysfunction.* (1988: 19; emphasis in original)

In essence, this represents a variation on 'group-think' but in terms of 'mismanaged agreement.' The Goodrich test-engineers found themselves on the way to 'Abilene' because no one had the personal strength to persevere with disagreement.

The Amoral Chameleon

> The code is this: you milk the plants; rape the business; use other people and discard them; fuck any woman that is available, in sight, and under your control; and exercise authoritative prerogatives at will with subordinates and other less mortals who are completely out of your league in money and status. *But you also don't play holier than thou.* This last point is as important as all the others.
>
> (Jackall, 1988: 97; emphasis in original)

In the tradition of Whyte (1956), Dalton (1959), and Kanter (1977), there is an important work that sheds illumination on how managers cope in modern corporations. Jackall's (1988) anthropological research is impressive, and his book is valuable and full of sociological insights on management. It deserves to be an influential source of reference for many years. It is difficult to do justice to its richness, but, in a nutshell, he argues that managers who wish to succeed soon discover that hard work alone does not necessarily lead to rewards; they begin to feel that 'politics, adroit talk, luck, connections, and self-promotion are the real sorters of people into sheep and goats' (1988: 3). There is considerable upheaval and insecurity in modern corporations and the key to success is anchoring yourself to your boss and giving him what he demands (figures, favours, deference, and so on). Further, and most vitally, personal morality is shelved in favour of the bureaucratic ethic, the hierarchical imperative, and the corporate dictate. There is a special kind of 'personalization of authority', and people are 'tested' on the way up to ensure that others feel 'comfortable with them' (Calhoun, 1989: 542). Put bluntly, morality is *situational* and the situation is largely defined by your boss: 'What is right in the corporation is not what is right in a man's home, or in his church. *What is right in the corporation is what the guy above you wants from you.* That's what morality is in the corporation' (Jackall, 1988: 6; emphasis in original). The manager learns to live with duality and leaves his conscience at home.

This is an unflattering portrait and Jackall relates it to the 'patrimonial bureaucracy' of certain American companies. Authority is linked to the personal relation with a boss. He needs to 'trust' his subordinates to fit into the amoral manipulation that characterizes the underlying reality of power-play and impression management. The ambition to climb the hierarchy involves 'an endless round of probationary crucibles' (1988: 10) to ensure that the upwardly mobile never challenge the hidden deviousness which is based on the compromises considered essential to corporate existence. Jackall portrays the managers as chameleons, narcissistic, great actors, pragmatic, deferential, and fundamentally insecure ('you're only as good as your last mistake', 'our horizon is today's lunch', and 'I sell everyday: what I sell is *me*', were quotations that conveyed their dependence on fluctuating constellations of power and on pressure for results). Jackall's work doubtless reflects strongly certain American values and behaviour to be found in a select number of large corporations (his research took place in several industrial firms and one PR company). There are bound to be strong cross-cultural variations with other societies (see, for example, van Dijk and Punch (1993); Clegg, 1990). However, it is interesting to note that Leonard (1989: 602) wrote of Marceau's (1989) survey of former MBA students of the prestigious European business school INSEAD, 'it would be difficult to find a comparable group so coldly ambitious and so single-minded in the pursuit of money, power, and prestige'.

But what does emerge powerfully is that Jackall's managers were dominated by expediency, were not prone to make decisions based on moral niceties, and were convinced that achievement alone was not sufficient for success. Performing was always related to fealty in alliance with the powerful and to adopting the socially accepted style of the moment. And, above all, people should be able to *trust* you.

In this environment the manager was an actor, a politician, a manipulator of data, and a short-term operator determined to outrun his mistakes (which were then inherited by his luckless successor). Nothing was quite what it seemed to be on the surface. Beneath the jovial façade these managers were calculating, manipulative, devious, heartless, amoral chameleons.

The Business of Business

> Stay out of the business world . . . take something else . . . you don't have the guts and the guile.
>
> (executive advising his son: Dalton, 1959: 244)

Finally, let me state that I do not believe in an all-encompassing framework that explains business crime and deviance. Attempts at this level merely generate 'platitudinous generalizations' (Braithwaite, 1985a: 6). The complexities are too intricate, the motives too mixed, and the contexts too varied. What is the case, however, is that business crime/misconduct is a sub-section of organizational crime/misconduct. This is because the business organization provides the setting, the means, and the ideology for rule-breaking; and other organizations are victimized. Indeed, in some cases managers may victimize their own organization. In the Revco case the 'perpetrator' even portrayed itself as victimized. To make matters even more complex, the business organization is generally the primary *enforcer* in cases of corporate rule-breaking. And the vagaries of control and regulation have to be analysed at the *inter-organizational* level. In essence, the organization is the perpetrator, is the scene of crime, provides the *modus operandi*, is the location of evidence and witnesses, is the complainant, and may also be the victim (even the unwitting victim, unaware that it has been victimized).

But organizations can be perceived as nothing other than the social constructs of the people who work in them (Thompson, 1967). Throughout this book I have emphasized the complexity of the variables and factors that need to be taken into account in explaining specific cases of major business deviance. Analysis needs to be applied at the levels of society, markets, industries, institutions, organizations, ideology, managerial division of labour, communication, products, technology, internal and external pressures, psychological mechanisms within groups, motivations, and so on. But central to my approach is the perspective that deviation from rules within a business organization requires agreement among managers to deviate, the selection of suitable methods of implementing those decisions, the choice of strategies of defence and concealment, and the inducement for certain people to fill specific roles.

Generally the deviance has to be consciously constructed and carefully camouflaged; managers and corporations may experience a 'moral career' that transforms them from compliers to transgressors (and even back again to compliance). In some cases managers approach deviance instrumentally and temporarily; in others they blunder into misconduct; and in yet other cases they engage in carefully crafted conspiracies over an extended period. This means we are concerned with a world of secrecy, collusion, trust and mistrust, deviousness, implicit meanings, codes, secret languages, reading between the lines, falsification, and fraudulent façades (Clarke, 1990; Box, 1983). In extreme cases companies may effectively become *criminal organizations* where the dominant coalition or leader and the 'shadow organization' espouse predominantly criminal goals and means within a legitimate, legal institutional shell.

What hardly occurs to most businessmen, however, is that what they are doing is illegal, unethical, or criminal. For many of the actors in the cases that we know of the deviant practices were perceived as 'normal', routine (even when concealed), and morally neutral matters. In the heavy electrical equipment antitrust case of 1961, witnesses claimed that price-fixing had become 'a way of life' (Geis, 1967: 144). And following the Lockheed affair, ex-chairman Haughton said of the millions of dollars for foreign payments, 'I didn't do anything wrong. We did it playing the rules of the game as they were then' (*New York Times Magazine*, 26 September 1976: 47). SEC investigations and Senator Church's Subcommittee on Multinational Corporations unearthed the fact that some 500 major American corporations had made 'foreign payments'.

Lockheed pleaded guilty on a number of counts and paid civil and criminal fines; but like most companies it could argue that these were technical offences, related to accounts and taxes, and that the actual 'foreign payments' – in effect bribes – were not declared illegal until legislation was passed in 1977 (Clinard and Yeager, 1980: 156). In effect, what is deviant to others simply becomes the institutionalized, mundane, semi-submerged way of doing business which managers no longer fully perceive as illicit and which they can justify readily to their consciences. A former sales manager for an American brewer remarked candidly,

> The name of the game was sales, pure and simple. You did what you had to do to get the business. A lot of it was small stuff, like an occasional free keg of beer or a case of glasses for a guy who had a bar, but it got a lot bigger, too. If what you were doing was wrong, well, at least you knew you had a lot of company. (Reisman, 1979: 45)

And a beer wholesaler dismissed commercial bribery with the remark, 'But hey, guys in other business, they do pretty much the same things. It's the American way, isn't it?' (Clinard and Yeager, 1980: 160).

A key element in the analysis and the cases has been the view that business provides an arena where managers are weaned from their consciences. In the words of Reisman (1979), they learn to function by the 'operational code' while also espousing the 'myth system'. What this means is that people are coached to function at two levels. For instance, a great deal of emphasis is placed on trust as an essential ingredient in sound business relations (Levi, 1987: 46; Tone Hosmer, 1995). But in business, trust, like so much else, is double-edged. For instance, towards the outside world trust is a *commodity* that has to be bolstered in order to impress significant stakeholders (such as politicians, regulators, institutional investors, the media, and consumers). But internally trust is *relational*, negotiable, and situational: 'Can I trust you to make compromises, to go with the group, not to rock the boat, to keep secrets, to engage in conspiracies, and to get involved in dirty work?' The former is trust in terms of the myth system, as part of externally orientated impression management; but the latter relates to the operational code where deviant paths are chosen and 'partners in crime' are selected. The shadow concerns of managers require coalitions and conspiracies, and the code lays down that these demand secrecy and security. Anyone who cannot be 'trusted' to play by the code is dangerous because he or she could expose the whole show. Thus to get on in this world you have to live by the operational code while mouthing convincingly the tenets of the myth system; that is essential to performing and to managing in the shadows.

This conveys, no doubt, a most unsympathetic portrait of managers. I would argue that much of this applies to organizational life in general and that many of us experience various forms of ambiguity and duality in our own institutional careers. The very nature of business, however, may reinforce organizational duality and moral ambivalence. Business is competitive and even combative; it may accept a measure of 'sharp practice' and may skate a fine line on legality (Clarke, et al., 1994); and it sometimes produces calculating, manipulative, devious, predatory, and ruthless people. Business people are probably more likely to be 'meat-eaters' than 'grass-eaters' (the former have been typified as 'carnivores' – 'the cast of the *Directory of Directors* – the members of the upper and middle classes who believe that if God had not wished them to prey on all smaller and weaker creatures he would not have made them as they are': Frayn, 1964: 331). But it also simply takes ordinary people and asks them to do extraordinary things like bribing, spying, and falsifying data. At some stage these are no longer seen as out of the ordinary but as normal. Ditton (1977: 12) holds it as a general axiom that 'an analysis which portrays a phenomenon as bizarre or strange has failed to understand that phenomenon. People *never* experience their worlds as bizarre or strange: they experience them as wholly ordinary.'

In a nutshell, business deviance can be related to taking an individual, putting him in a group (and mostly it is a 'him'), exerting pressure, confronting him with difficult dilemmas and tough choices, and observing the outcomes. Some do and some do not abide by the law; we cannot say with any accuracy why some decide to stick to the rules and some do not; but we are obliged to take into account the collective circumstances that lead to the deviance because it forces us to acknowledge the seductive power and potent influence of organizational life in general, and corporate existence in particular, on 'good' people (and there but for the grace of God, and a couple of fortuitous exams, go I).

Sometimes it pushes them into doing dirty work. They leave their consciences at home and enter a world where the ends justify the means (and the ends may not even require justification – you just do it). Or, to paraphrase Milton Friedman, the values for some companies at certain times are as follows: 'the only responsibility of business is to make profit – illegally if necessary'. And, 'the business of business is crime'.

6

Tackling Business Crime

As Geis has remarked, the corporation in essence says: 'I didn't do it, but
I won't do it again'.

(Braithwaite, 1984: 15)

The material presented in this book does have implications for that at times
seemingly insoluble issue, how do you deal with business crime/deviance?
(The reader is referred to the following for further detailed treatment of this
area: Levi, 1987; Clarke, 1990; Reiss, 1983; Braithwaite, 1989; Fisse and
Braithwaite, 1993; Tonry and Reiss, 1993; Jamieson, 1994; Wells, 1994.) In the
light of what has been said here it may even seem that corporations are
inevitably and incorrigibly devious and manipulative, that regulation is routinely inadequate, and that effective control of business is, therefore,
unattainable. Indeed, an analysis based on the everyday construction of
deviance in relation to the dilemmas created by organizational life can only
convey an image of near universal and virtually ineradicable processes. And
if Robert Maxwell could rise to the top of a business empire on the basis of
unlimited energy, a drive to dominate, and an ability to cajole or intimidate
colleagues, then it is difficult to see what forces or mechanisms could prevent
similarly forceful business leaders gaining control of companies – for good or
for ill. Sometimes there is a thin line between the brilliant, innovative entrepreneur and the brilliant, innovative corporate crook. There are clearly
resilient elements in the nature of business, organizational reality, inter-organizational relations, and in terms of egos and power that resist reform and
that may continue to promote deviance. It could be argued, in contrast, that
there are forces steering business in a positive direction; cars and planes are
safer, factories are healthier, and consumers are better protected than ever
before. There have also been moves to reform corporate governance, giving
shareholders more power, introducing more outside directors on boards, and
providing more checks on the power of senior executives (Useem and
Gottlieb, 1992; and for the Cadbury Report in the UK on corporate governance cf. *The Economist*, 29 January 1994). And surely companies are smart
enough to have learned from their mistakes?

Yet accidents, disasters, and scandals continue to expose significant business deviance (Allison, 1993). Despite new technologies, based on robotology
and total quality management, General Motors produced a truck with an
almost identical defect to that of the Ford Pinto and has been heavily sued in
court for negligence (*Wall Street Journal*, 5 February 1993; *New York Times*,
17 November 1992). Furthermore, the calculating and manipulative nature of

business is revealed by the transfer of technology to developing countries. This was done for a number of economic reasons, such as cheap labour, but one motive was less stringent regulation. The tobacco industry, faced by falling profits in western countries, is moving production to Asia and accompanying this with a vast advertising campaign to persuade the inveterate smokers of the east to change brands. This doubtless represents 'sound strategy' in corporate terms, is accompanied by sophisticated advertising techniques, and is perfectly *legal*; but it does represent a case of a product, which is under increasing pressure in western countries because of its unhealthy and injurious nature, being shifted to less controlled markets and to societies with a minimal consciousness of the health risk (*Observer Magazine*, 8 November 1992). Braithwaite (1984) had earlier drawn attention to the pharmaceutical industry's tendency to use the 'Third World' for testing and 'dumping' drugs, so that the companies were effectively 'pushers'.

To a certain extent, then, business deviance is exported to less regulated societies and business crime disperses to seek out more congenial environments. This illustrates the difficulty of tackling business crime because its practitioners have the power and acumen to react strategically to the imposition of control. To a degree this is similar to the 'strategic' behaviour of organized crime, which also shifts markets and methods in response to control; it reacts swiftly to new opportunities, like the collapse of the former Soviet Union. Legitimate business is also confronted with fresh possibilities in the very structures that we create; the legal deficiencies and administrative complexities of the European Union, for example, have encouraged massive fraud both from legitimate and illicit business. Newspaper accounts, academic research, and official audits have uncovered substantial manipulation of subsidies related to meat, wheat, milk-powder, cattle, sugar, tuna fish, tobacco, and to non-existent olive groves in Greece, while in Sicily mobile olive trees were constantly moved to create the impression of an industry that only existed on paper. This was estimated to have cost the European Union some £2.5 billion in fraud in 1992 and £5 billion in 1994 (*Observer*, 12 July 1992; *Daily Mail*, 29 July 1994; van der Hulst, 1993; Vervaele, 1993).

In effect, when we enter the terrain of the control and regulation of economic activity we encounter not only intricate and interrelated issues (related to societal, political, and market changes), but also shrewd players who match move with counter-move (Szasz, 1983). And to conduct their illicit business they rely increasingly on professionals – lawyers, accountants, and computer specialists – and on the weaknesses of international regulation. It could be argued that the next decade will be the era of international organized crime and multinational organizational crime; and that national agencies will have to learn to operate internationally and to tackle the *organizational* forms of the 'enemy'.

In those terms it is easy to become demoralized and to feel powerless; surely it is an unequal battle with a predictable outcome? At the macro, global level the picture is disappointing and even depressing. BCCI, for instance, did not just tumble into deviance – it skilfully constructed an illegal empire within a legal shell by exploiting the weaknesses in supervision of cross-border financial services:

> BCCI's ability to evade control was not a matter of luck. The bank concealed its activities behind a thicket of holding companies, affiliates, subsidiaries, insider dealing, shell corporations, front men, buy-back arrangements, fractured corporate structures, and divided audits. (Massing, 1992: 8)

Is there, then, little to be done? In practice there are a number of favourable indicators, and also a series of signs, pointing to potentially effective regulation of business. These are often of a limited, situational nature and have to be placed in the context of the institutional dilemmas facing regulatory agencies. Here I wish to touch briefly on a number of factors influencing regulation, compliance, and control.

Business Cleans up its Act

> Given the great rewards and low risks of detection, why do so many business people adopt the 'economically irrational' course of obeying the law?

(Braithwaite, 1985a: 7)

When the exposure of business crime and deviance damages the reputation of business, then the business community may take action to put its own house in order. In service industries, where customers can easily switch to a competitor (for example, travel agencies and airlines), negative publicity can have a swift impact on economic performance. Financial services, which rely on 'trust', can also be hit hard by scandal. In their study of a 'major North American Stock Exchange' Stenning et al (1990: 115) comment that both regulators and the securities industry had a vested interest in maintaining the perception of fairness and effectiveness in market operations; with increasing internationalization of markets and enhanced visibility of defects in operations, 'the need for any market to have "integrity" is, if anything, becoming more crucial than ever. Loss of integrity invites loss of business, and loss of business invites disaster.' In some cases individual companies engage in a public display of house-cleaning, whereas in others an entire industry may decide to curb excesses and to emphasize branch-wide standards (as the chemical industry has endeavoured to do). In this respect 'clean' business, or the image of cleanliness, is related to self-interest and to the perception of the level of damage done by the revelations of deviance (Clarke, 1990).

In some cases the attempt to attach a deviant label has only led to a tough, intransigent response from the company: Distillers, for instance, seemed to circle the wagons in defiance of external groups in the Thalidomide case. But a company may decide to take an adversarial stance from a range of options; for instance, because it has a hefty contingency fund to fight campaigns or because it is well insured against civil damages. What does hurt, however, is when unfavourable publicity persists and even swells to a campaign with highly visible boycotts of products (as happened with Nestlé and Infant Formula when Nestlé's aggressive marketing of powdered milk for babies in developing countries elicited a long, vitriolic campaign against the company with head-lines like 'Nestlé Kills Babies': Buchholz et al., 1985); when shareholders or institutional investors turn sour, 'revolt', attack the managing board at annual meetings or demand extraordinary meetings, or launch embarrassing share-holder resolutions; and, above all, when share values start to fall dramatically. There is nothing that clears the managerial mind like a quick slide of stock on the markets; it is when their behaviour has consequences for hard economic facts that they may feel obliged to shift from an aggressive, combative, or defensive stance to an adaptive, cooperative one.

In short, business itself may endeavour to control some forms of deviance by setting standards, sanctioning excessive misbehaviour, and even expelling recalcitrant companies from an industry association; this is a form of self-interest that may be encouraged by an industry's sensitivity to painful shifts in market or economic indicators. Indeed, business is often geared to shaping its environment and to generating positive images of it and its products. The same proactive marketing techniques can be employed to enhance the appear-ance of respectability through advertising, issues management, sponsoring of charities and good causes, investing in educational institutions, executives' involvement in public and community service, pushing 'green' products and investments, and so on (Miles, 1987; Buchholz, 1989).

Government as Guardian Angel

The role of government is crucial in relation to the regulation of economic activity. Ostensibly the government is the neutral referee that ensures that the game is followed according to the rules, that the playing field is level, that the goal-posts are not continually moved, and that no one has 'thrown' the game. In the ideal world government is the guardian angel of markets and con-sumers and acts judiciously and fairly in balancing all the competing and conflicting interests in a society. For instance, Wells (1994: 17) states:

> since many of the victims of corporate wrongdoing are unaware of the source of the harm done to them and therefore cannot invoke the criminal justice enforcement system as do victims of burglary, there is a *state obligation* to provide that mecha-nism for them in the form of proactive investigation backed up by effective sanctions. (Emphasis added)

In practice, governments tend to favour various teams or players, change the rules to fit situations, and are far from impartial – and may even be a major offender, as in environmental pollution (Yeager, 1993: 100). At the most fundamental level a government's concern with regard to regulation of business is the question, what is the balance between rules that satisfy the var-ious stakeholders involved in economic activity and the continued health of the economy? (This in turn, is often related to narrow party political inter-ests.) How safe is 'safe'? When is industry over-regulated? What are effective policies, laws, and regulatory agencies? How far do you go in steering markets and protecting consumers (the opponents of product liability legislation in the USA would argue that it has gone to extremes and now represents a potentially crippling nightmare for companies)? These are, at one level, highly practical and even technical matters but, in practice, they are clouded by political and ideological considerations and by the relative power of business and of special interest groups to influence governmental decision-making (Snider, 1991).

What is plain is that effective regulation of economic activity and of business deviance requires political will. The strength of that will can be shaped and distorted by strong connections between business and politics; by bribery and corruption; by reacting to scandals with 'crusades' of 'sound and fury' that appear as if business is being hounded (Reisman, 1979) but without altering fundamentally the underlying practices; and by a belief in 'deregulation' that inadvertently leads to unanticipated consequences (as happened in financial services in the 1980s in the USA and the UK). That will is related to the nature of society, national politics, economic change, and the matrix of power relations between the various players. A number of governments operate openly in the interests of business; they – sometimes in partnership with royal families – strongly support specific trade campaigns; and political parties may rely on contributions from business and draw on business and industry for ministers (while ex-ministers find a ready seat on managing boards).

This opens a vast field that cannot be pursued here; but the central point is that governments play a pivotal role in setting ground rules, in interfering in specific cases, and in determining outcomes in relation to tackling business deviance. Although there is a great deal of evidence that the tenacious and sophisticated lobbying clout of business can help shape the ground rules and can also influence decisions in specific cases, a government may be forced for political reasons to sponsor seemingly 'tough' reform measures to combat business deviance because that deviance is having a party-political impact and because international confidence in business is at issue. This happened in the UK in the late 1980s when the Conservatives, under critical attack by the Opposition, promised to 'clean up' financial services following the series of scandals in the City of London (Clarke, 1990). Even under the ostensibly deregulatory regime of President Reagan there was actually a hardening of public attitudes to the harm caused by companies and a number of tough prosecutory campaigns took place against corporate deviance (Coleman, 1989; Braithwaite, 1993: 25). There can be no doubt that under Reagan some agencies experienced budget and personnel cuts, and business went on to the offensive against a number of agencies (especially OSHA and the EPA: Szasz, 1983), but some prosecutors were prepared to take on business and, later, both legislation and sanctions were strengthened in a 'crackdown on crime in the suites' (*Business Week*, 22 April 1991; Katz, 1988).

But the deregulation rhetoric and ideology – plus the managerial message that 'excellent' companies fought regulation (Peters and Waterman, 1982) – perhaps conveyed an element of moral ambiguity, and these 'mixed signals' may have encouraged the executive behaviour that sponsored the scandals of the 1980s (Reichman, 1993: 82). And in the Savings and Loans scandal the government was accused of entrapment, of being an accomplice, of effectively enticing people into crime: 'A senior thrift regulator in an interview described the cumulative impact of the deregulation: "The government created tremendous opportunity in 1982 for anybody that wanted to engage in any kind of criminal activity or just get rich quick"' (Pontell and Calavita, 1993: 210).

The Short Arm of the Law

Government policies are translated into laws for regulating business conduct. A great deal of attention has been paid to the discrepancy between the 'law in books' and the 'law in action'. Legislation often takes years to enact; laws in such complex areas are intricate compromises that inevitably contain loopholes; and companies scrutinize laws for unforeseen possibilities in implementation to their advantage. Reisman (1979) intimates that some laws are not meant to be fully implemented (*lex imperfecta*). And legislation also has to be tested in court. For instance, the actions that led to the capsizing of the *The Herald of Free Enterprise* at Zeebrugge brought about only the third prosecution for 'corporate manslaughter' in British legal history. But the necessity to prove the direct, conscious link between boardroom decisions and the accident turned out to be too taxing for the prosecution and it was unable to convince the courts (Wells, 1994). A charge of corporate homicide against the Ford Motor Corporation in the Pinto affair also became stranded in court. Outside of the United States the criminal courts are often not a particularly effective arena for tackling corporate deviance; and, even in the USA, it could be argued that a tough prosecutory stance may only elicit an equally aggressive company response, given the adversarial style of some corporate lawyers in that society.

The major issue, then, is recognizing that the law – and in particular the criminal law – may not be a very effective instrument for dealing with business deviance. Wells argues strongly that legal language and practice do not reflect the nature of organizational reality because the concepts of the criminal law are replete with individualism and the language assumes a human, rational, autonomous – and male – body, acting as an individual (1994: 63). It opens the path to adversarial relations where companies have considerable resources to contest cases at length and to convince courts and/or juries of their innocence. This is largely because criminal law is still predominantly shaped on individual behaviour and guilt; it is insufficiently geared to *organizational* forms of deviance (Reiss, 1983; Wells, 1994). Also, executives generally convey a highly respectable image in court that does not coincide with stereotypes of criminals that members of a jury may have in their minds. The same advantageous bias applies to companies: 'Enforcement processes are influenced and partly determined by stereotypes of crime and criminals: corporations are not stereotypical deviant offenders' (Wells, 1994: 12).

In practice, a great deal of regulation is implemented through civil and administrative laws and through 'private' law, while companies will almost always endeavour to avoid the criminal courts in favour of the civil arena (partly because insurance usually does not cover criminal fines or punitive damages). For a number of reasons, we cannot perhaps expect too much from the law in general, and the criminal law in particular, with regard to regulating economic life and combating business deviance. But to the extent that law is used, then the quality of that law is crucial; laws need to be comprehensive, unambivalent, enforceable, and based on a sound knowledge of the industry to be controlled.

This is not an argument for weakening criminal law in relation to corporations. There are two reasons for taking this stance. First, it is unjust if companies because of their power and influence can effectively escape sanctioning: 'The failure rigorously to enforce regulatory schemes taken together with the paucity of available penalties can be used to support the argument that crimes of the powerful are condoned and effectively, or even deliberately, de-criminalized' (Wells, 1994: 29). Jamieson (1994) also maintains that in some antitrust offences it is precisely the larger companies that escape prosecution and conviction. Second, in terms of executive behaviour and fear of its sanctions (generally fines), it does seem to be the case that companies under investigation or audit seek to avoid the criminal *label* – Wells (1994: 147) notes the 'extraordinary efforts corporations frequently employ to avoid conviction'. Executives do not like being treated as criminals and firms endeavour to avoid the negative publicity associated with the criminal courts. As such, Fisse and Braithwaite (1993) argue strongly that regulators should act with a 'pyramid' in mind, with advice, warnings, and persuasion at its base but with corporate criminal sanctions and 'corporate capital punishment' (enforced closure or licence revocation) at its apex. Criminal sanctions then play a role as an ultimate threat and sanction in an escalating ladder of prods, hints, winks, nudges, and warnings (Braithwaite, 1993).

Regulatory Agencies

A great deal has been written about the structural weaknesses of governmental and other agencies for implementing laws and for supervising business. Often, it is said, they are understaffed, poorly qualified, possess feeble sanctions, are loath to intervene, and are overly supine or deferential to the companies they control. There is, too, the 'capture' thesis, which maintains that branches of business exert such a powerful influence over the controllers that they become a pliant extension of the branch, engaged in rituals of enforcement that are benign, toothless, and collusive (Hawkins, 1984). One particular element of this, for example, is the 'revolving door' metaphor which describes the practice of buying the expertise of controllers by offering them attractive terms of employment in private business. And then there is the outright bribery and corruption of officials (Clinard and Yeager, 1980).

In some cases, furthermore, control agencies have a dual function – both to regulate *and* promote an industry – that builds in an inherent conflict of interest. Agencies may also not be immune to political interference either in terms of leadership, staffing, and budgets or even in determining outcomes in specific cases. With regard to inter-organizational relations, there is also the tendency among the formal bureaucracies of regulatory agencies to display poor communication and coordination, to conduct turf wars, for mutual hostility, excessively slow reactions, poaching of cases, and defensive secrecy – as in the 'thrifts' prosecution task forces: Pontell and Calavita (1993: 235). In contrast, the Revco case revealed a willingness to set up a relatively well-coordinated and effective 'control network' that involved a temporary alliance between several agencies with widely different mandates and cultures. And the Wall Street cases showed the SEC successfully at work; this could be taken as a paradigm of effective regulation – well-trained personnel, considerable resources, excellent relations with the justice authorities, a strategy based on a campaign to go after leading figures in the conspiracy, and the grudging cooperation and acknowledgement of the financial services industry that it was targeting (Vise and Coll, 1992). The SEC's successful criminal prosecutions did help to clean up Wall Street (at least for a time).

The reality of much regulation is less heady and far more mundane (say, in controlling hygiene among mobile fast-food vendors). There is a great deal of evidence that agencies do not adopt an adversarial position but rely on a strategy of compliance based on education, advice, personal contacts, warnings, and very reluctant intervention (Yeager, 1993). This is partly because it fits the limited resources available to the agency but it is also partly a philosophy based on what works. The mandate, culture, and historically developed working practices of agencies can foster a coaching, coaxing, mentor-like relationship with business where prosecution is perceived as a *failure*. Indeed, the approach of some agencies is based on doing deals that avoid long and risky trials, that allow restitution of funds, and that do not fundamentally disturb the balance of power in the industry. You have to try really hard to get prosecuted, and Hawkins suggests that what is criminally enforced in the case of environmental regulatory regimes is not so much the pollution itself but more the 'deliberate or negligent law breaking that symbolically assaults the legitimacy of regulatory authority' (1984: 205).

All of these factors have to be taken into account in judging the performance of control agencies. Employees are sometimes coached in the techniques of minimal compliance, as in this example from the pharmaceutical industry:

> Our instructions to officers when dealing with FDA inspectors is to only answer the questions asked, not to provide any extra information, not to volunteer anything, and not to answer any questions outside your area of competence. On the other hand we [the corporate staff – MP] can ask anyone and expect an answer. They are told that we are part of the same family, and unlike the government, we are working for the same final objectives. (Braithwaite, 1984: 137)

In some instances internal regulatory bodies may be seen as more effective – and thus are more feared – than governmental ones because they are more knowledgeable about the industry, including its dark areas, and because their sanctions have a direct impact on perpetrators (as with suspension, exclusion, disbarment, and so on). But these sro's (self-regulating organizations) are also sometimes reluctant to impose the full weight of sanctions at their disposal when colleagues – and here we are concerned with members supervising other members of an occupational group – are cooperative and contrite.

There is a vast literature on the regulation issue and there is considerable debate on the effectiveness of control by agencies. There does emerge a clear picture of what an 'effective' agency looks like – politically independent, well-staffed and well-resourced, and with the will and muscle to grapple with big business. Of considerable importance too is that staff form multidisciplinary teams to deal with the complex material that needs to be sifted in a major investigation. In practice, many regulatory bodies simply do not conform to that model and rely on cajoling, or on bluffing, companies into compliance. This may not satisfy some critics, and may smack of an implicit conspiracy to go easy on business, but it is essential to appreciate, and to analyse, the institutional dilemmas facing such agencies. What is patently evident, moreover, is that control agencies on their own cannot be expected to tackle business in order effectively to curb deviance and crime – except under the most favourable circumstances.

Indeed, the relationships between regulator and regulated are far from simple. For instance, regulation may actually be powerful enough to shape the regulatory response of an industry; but this can be interpreted both positively and negatively. The tough controls of the FDA on the drug industry have pushed companies into installing quality assurance units in their laboratories to monitor research and development; in order to speed up the process of bringing a new drug on the market the industry has learned in the USA that it is best to anticipate FDA standards, to impose them internally and at the earliest stage, to cooperate with the FDA in getting the drug through the approval process and even to use FDA approval as a marketing tool. In nursing homes, in contrast, the burden of bureaucratic control has led many homes to adopt a ritualistic approach of avoiding violations by simply providing the paperwork required and by treating inmates uniformly, but this makes them less humane and less service-orientated than less 'regulated' homes in other societies (Braithwaite, 1993). In effect, relationships between regulators and regulated are sometimes complex, can even shape the nature of an industry's response to regulation, but may have unanticipated consequences that paradoxically achieve the opposite to what was intended. This means that those relationships are contextual, shift over time, and need to be analysed by research that examines in detail the concrete interaction between parties. American nursing homes, for instance, scarcely need to be warned of a violation – if the inspector makes an evaluation, then the comments are taken seriously and the advice is heeded. The homes simply do not want the hassle of a violation; and the ultimate sanction of licence revocation is very powerful indeed because it means you are out of business. This complexity and contextuality must be taken into account when examining the strengths and weaknesses of regulation (Fisse and Braithwaite, 1993; Tonry and Reiss, 1993).

Investigations and Interventions

The above point can be illustrated by examining briefly some of the difficulties of penetrating the cover of an organization engaged in deviance. A control agency may have thousands, if not millions, of companies to supervise and a limited number of enforcement staff; firms can calculate that the chance of a visitation is extremely low. Generally agencies rely on inspections, audits, surveillance, and investigations (Reiss, 1983). Each has its own virtues, and weaknesses, and much depends on the enforcement strategy of the agency concerned; is it reactive or proactive? A great deal of ordinary law enforcement in general is reactive, being triggered by a signal after the event, and regulatory enforcement is little different. Many agencies may wait for a report of a violation before taking action. Inspections and audits are often routine, pre-announced, and ritualistic. Industrial rule-breaking is camouflaged during the visitation and the inspectors are easily hoodwinked; and external auditing by accountants has often failed conspicuously to sound warning bells on deviance. This in turn has brought about a number of substantial suits against accounting firms for not unearthing the deviance behind the data.

> These are bad times for bean-counters. Members of a famously dull profession, in recent years accountants have merged into ever-bigger firms with worldwide links, while striking out into lucrative consulting and corporate finance. Now, however, many say that liability suits arising from their bread-and-butter auditing work threaten eventually to bankrupt them.
> The biggest single suit to date involves Price Waterhouse and Ernst & Young, two of the big six accounting firms (the others are KPMG Peat Marwick, Arthur Andersen, Coopers & Lybrand and Deloitte Touche Tohmatsu). They face an $8 billion claim in a London court arising from their auditing of the failed Bank of Credit and Commerce International (BCCI). In America outstanding claims against the Big Six total $30 billion. (*The Economist*, 26 February 1994)

Random inspections are a much more aggressive instrument, particularly if they are allied to a policy of reporting all violations (as in the American coal-mining industry, Braithwaite, 1985a: 5). But then this is related to the enforcement strategy of a particular agency in its relation to a particular industry; random inspection may be considered inappropriate if not counter-productive (for example, it may foster attempts to corrupt officials in order to obtain advance warning). Police-led raids on legitimate businesses often lead to a storm of protest as professionals are suddenly confined to a building, as their attaché-cases are searched, and as piles of documents are visibly removed by uniformed policemen under the inquisitive eyes of press and public (when Slavenburg's Bank was raided by police in the Netherlands it was compared to the *razzias* in the Second World War when the Nazi occupiers rounded up people at random for forced labour: Blom, 1983).

Surveillance and investigations are labour-intensive and time-consuming.

Attention has repeatedly been drawn to the time-consuming nature of corporate crime investigations. As two US federal prosecutors summed up the position:

> Economic crimes are far more complex than most other federal offences. The events in issue usually have occurred at a far more remote time and over a far more extensive period. The 'proof' consists not merely of relatively few items of real evidence but a large roomful of often obscure documents. In order to try the case effectively, the Assistant United States Attorney must sometimes master the intricacies of a sophisticated business venture. Furthermore, in the course of doing so, he, or the agents with whom he works, often must resolve a threshold question that has already been determined in most other cases: *Was there a crime in the first place?*

> If anything, this understates the difficulties which arise. Prosecutors are confronted with what amounts to a network of complexities: tortuous legislation, intricate accounting practices, convoluted organisational accountability, amnesia among witnesses, and jurisdictional complications. (Fisse and Braithwaite, 1993: 37; emphasis added)

In general they are reactive in relation to indicators from the external environment (such as anonymous tips from informants, data provided by a whistle-blower, or physical evidence of pollution that comes to light). In fact an agency's investigation has usually been preceded by an *internal* investigation that has led the company to call in the controllers (such as the police in a case of fraud or embezzlement). Proactive surveillance has sometimes been employed by other law-enforcement agencies with a more aggressive stance, such as the FBI, DEA, IRS and Customs (in the USA). This has led them by means of scams, undercover methods, and concealed videotaping of transactions, to stumble on business crime (as in the BCCI case). These investigative agencies are usually more interested in organized crime than crime by legitimate companies, while their methods may be controversial; the Justice Department, as was noted earlier, failed to prosecute successfully John De Lorean on the basis of video-taped evidence of his involvement in drug-dealing (his defence successfully claimed entrapment and he was cleared of the charges: *Newsweek*, 27 August 1984). In one case four FBI investigators went undercover as brokers in the commodity futures trading pits at the Chicago Board of Trade and the Chicago Mercantile Exchange. They had to learn the trade, win the confidence of other brokers, and build up incriminating evidence against them (Greising and Morse, 1991).

There are, then, considerable technical, logistical, and legal aspects to intervening in organizations. Corporations produce masses of data, and regulatory personnel need the expertise to sift through this and to seek promising leads. An expert on tracing fraud within organizations argues that there nearly always are identifiable traces. Although Bologna (1984) was principally concerned with deviance *against* the organization (namely, occupational crime), his remarks apply equally to tracking deviance for the organization. He notes that criminals usually exploit human and system weaknesses and that controls are merely an obstacle – if not a challenge – to be overcome:

> But the variations in techniques for fraud against or on the behalf of a company are limitless. The human mind, when unleashed against an accounting or internal

control system, seems to be at its highest point of inventive genius. It is a game most people find fascinating, but to the avowed criminal it becomes a passion. (1984: 30)

These deviants are often intelligent, trusted, motivated, loosely supervised, have the power to manipulate controls, and engage in conspiratorial networks; but they inevitably leave traces or a 'paper-trail'. Bologna employs the acronym 'MOMM' to focus on motivation, opportunity, means, and methods. Essentially he is talking of forensic accounting where multidisciplinary audit teams set out to dig out deviance; the starting-point is that you have to be able to identify closely with the mind and methods of the deviant. And that means looking *upwards*, because that is where the opportunities for deviance are located and the social power to influence control exists. Bologna's approach assumes that deviance has taken place and that the data can be unravelled to expose it. This is a totally different approach from most formal auditing where deviance is not assumed, where explanations for discrepancies from the hierarchy are readily accepted, and where commercial considerations – in terms of not wishing to alienate a good client – may play a strong role (Clinard and Yeager, 1980; this is particularly the case as mergers have reduced the number of large accounting firms and competition among them has increased considerably).

But if we accept Bologna's standpoint that, despite the seemingly bewildering maze of data, deviance *can* be traced, it requires multidisciplinary investigative teams; it involves entering the deviant's mind; and investigators should look *upwards*. In some cases, the success of an investigation may depend on whether the regulators' accountants, detectives, computer experts, and lawyers are smarter and sharper than those of the company. Clearly, a proactive 'trawl' of a company is a tougher nut to crack than a reactive response to scandal, exposure, or bankruptcy; for instance, investigators who work alongside liquidators have the advantage of leads, leaks, signs, 'footprints' and possibly confessional and cooperative managers. Although one may think that major companies can control overwhelming expertise to cloak their deviance, it is increasingly the case that firms specializing in forensic accounting are becoming feared opponents (McMurdy, 1992); to them it is a promising new market and they are quite prepared to hire out their expertise to investigatory agencies for a price.

Deterrence and Sanctions

If we examine the corporate deviant, collectively and individually, then there is some evidence that both may react positively to the imposition of controls. The key point is that deviance can be an instrumental, temporary adaptation to a specific dilemma. When warned by exposure and prosecution, companies may move people, reimpose control, give assurances, and generally engage in housecleaning; Fisse and Braithwaite (1993) maintain that 'substantial reform' can be achieved even without a criminal conviction, because companies react positively to 'informal publicity, prosecuting threats and negotiation with inspectors' (see also Braithwaite, 1985a: 9). For mixed motives, then, legitimate companies are sometimes amenable to control because trust, confidence, reputation, and 'face' have to be bolstered and a deviant label has to be resisted. Baucus and Near (1991: 34), however, argue from their data that

> firms with prior violations were more likely to commit additional illegal acts. Apparently, the current standard of punishment does not deter illegal behaviour – quite the opposite, it appears that committing illegal acts may teach firms how to further violate the law.

Under President Bush the reaction to the deregulation of the Reagan era had fostered a 'crackdown on crime in the suites', particularly in the areas of antitrust, banking, securities, and the environment; penalties rose and executives were jailed. This wave encouraged prevention and rewarded it; a company that had consistently endeavoured to take measures to ensure compliance was likely to be treated more leniently if caught offending. The government issued guidelines on prevention:

An Ounce of Prevention . . .

- Set mandatory standards and procedures for employee behaviour
- Appoint a high-level manager to ensure compliance
- Publicize all codes of conduct through brochures, mandatory employee training sessions, and other means
- Be wary of delegating authority to employees who may abuse it
- Take all reasonable steps to ferret out criminal conduct by setting up auditing systems and a well-publicized mechanism for workers to reveal suspected crimes without fear of retribution
- Enforce standards consistently through apt disciplinary measures
- After a crime, take all reasonable steps to prevent similar offences.

Data: US Sentencing Commission. (*Business Week*, 22 April 1991)

And if companies can be deterred and even 'rehabilitated', then this is equally true of individual executives, if we assume that the deviance is 'part-time crime' involving the part-time self of the manager – rather than a permanent, expressive involvement in crime. Then exposure is a considerable shock when the executive is faced with the 'criminal' label (as was evident in the heavy electrical equipment antitrust case). On the one hand, the corporate executive often possesses a battery of positive attributes – status, respectabilty, money, a career, a comfortable home, a supportive family (Chambliss, 1967) – that mean he is seen in court as an unlikely 'criminal', and certainly is unlikely to be perceived as a potential recidivist, so that the manager can expect a light or a suspended prison sentence, bail, and probation. On the other hand, this also implies that the executive has a lot to lose and is unlikely to repeat an offence – certainly compared to many 'common' criminals, although Weisburd et al. (1995) challenge this conventional view with their data on recidivism among white-collar crime offenders.

In other words, there is a case to be made that 'white-collar' criminals as corporate deviants may not be always readily deterred but they are relatively easily rehabilitated. This indicates, furthermore, that tough sanctions as such are not an important deterrent factor; exposure, shame, the criminal label, the stigmatization of being processed and incarcerated as if a common criminal (even if only for a night or two), are generally traumatic and have more impact than the threat of long sentences (with the plight of Sherman McCoy in Tom Wolfe's *Bonfire of the Vanities* being enough to send shivers up most middle-class spines). Indeed, for some committed deviants the higher the sanction the more the challenge may be to outwit the authorities; more likely is the scenario that corporate conspirators simply assume their infallibility and cannot conceive of ever being caught (or else they rely on the knowledge that severe sanctions are rarely fully imposed).

Tough sanctions are also problematic in relation to corporate entities because many criminal sanctions are inapplicable – you cannot imprison a company, cannot punish it for speeding, and it has 'no soul to damn, no body to kick' (Wells, 1994: 85) – and fines are pitifully small in relation to corporate turnover or resources. In Britain, for instance, the only sanction against a company is a fine, and generally these are small even for serious offences causing considerable harm (Wells, 1994). A small fine may have no impact and a large fine may simply be passed on to the shareholders or consumer, causing another form of injustice. In America there is a tendency to employ a wider battery of measures – probation, adverse publicity, equity fines, community service, making a company lend an executive to a charity for a year, direct compensatory orders, and punitive injunctions; while European antitrust law allows a sanction equivalent to 10 per cent of the previous year's turnover (Wells, 1994: 33–5). In an unprecedented judgement a judge in Virginia sent a company to 'jail' for involvement in price-fixing (*The Economist*, 10 September 1988):

> Judge Doumar made it clear that he did not actually expect to have the company incarcerated, but said that he could have all [the company's] facilities padlocked for the full three years of the sentence. He said that it was unfair for a company to make large illegal profits and then get away with a simple fine. In the event, Mr Doumar relented a little. He suspended the sentence (and $50,000 of the $1 m fine), placed the company on probation and ordered four of its senior executives to work full-time for the community for up to two years.

For firms it may well be that withdrawing a licence, recalling a product, and bankruptcy are more effective threats than a criminal prosecution with the threat of fines and imprisonment. Incapacitation and rehabilitation, putting firms effectively 'on probation', may be preferable to a frontal criminal prosecution. And as with individuals, companies are sensitive to exposure, shame, loss of face, negative publicity, and regulatory pressure (Braithwaite, 1989, Fisse and Braithwaite, 1993). Indeed, Braithwaite and Petit (1990) have developed a 'republican criminology' which seeks to reintegrate corporate offenders; in other words, conventional criminal sanctioning not only stigmatizes but rejects companies rather than offering mechanisms of reparation and reintegration. Braithwaite draws a distinction between reintegrative and stigmatizing shaming:

> Reintegrative shaming is issued by actors who maintain bonds of respect for the offender and who terminate episodes of shaming with gestures of reacceptance or

forgiveness. Reintegrative shaming is focused on the evil of the deed rather than on the evil of the actor . . . Stigmatization, in contrast, is disintegrative shaming in which no effort is made to reconcile the offender with the community. Offenders are outcasts; their deviance is allowed to become a master status trait; degradation ceremonies are not followed by ceremonies to decertify deviance. (Braithwaite, 1989: 341)

It is not always easy to see how these concepts would be applied in practice to organizations in western societies (Makkai and Braithwaite, 1994). Yet there is no doubt but that Braithwaite is one of the most prolific and innovative researchers on corporate deviance and control and his ideas require careful consideration. In particular, he emphasizes the point that efforts to induce compliance are likely to be more effective in general and in the long run than those that aim to deter via prosecution and tough sanctions (Braithwaite and Ayres: 1991). His belief in 'friendly persuasion', backed up by increasingly unfriendly measures, represents a positive approach that is refreshing in a field deeply imbued with pessimism and even cynicism.

However, the law, and especially the criminal law, encounters difficulties, as we have argued, when trying to specify the criminal intent of an organization. In extreme cases this may seem to let corporations off lightly. On the one hand, the corporation may evade sanctioning because the prosecutory focus is on individuals; on the other hand, individuals may escape punishment because they can 'hide behind' the corporate entity (Wells, 1994). But in many cases it does seem that companies and executives are amenable to control and without necessarily having to resort to the criminal law. The key is the extent to which the deviance is a part-time, situational, instrumental choice from a number of alternative scenarios which implies that the deviance can be relatively easily pruned or avoided while the corporation continues in legitimate business. BCCI, for instance, had essentially become a criminal organization and it was 'executed' by the Bank of England, which put it to death, albeit slowly and reluctantly. Other companies – Guinness, for example – can rapidly recover from the stigma of a criminal investigation and go on to prosper (on the grounds that the affair was confined to a limited and temporary involvement of a few top people, who could be exorcised allowing business 'under new management'). In corporate crime a measure of deterrence and rehabilitation can be obtained – at least for a time – and often without resorting to the toughest measures. Many companies have survived scandal, disasters, high civil damages, and criminal exposure. Organized crime, for instance, is usually quite ruthless and heartless about the consequences of its criminal conduct (for example, in relation to drugs-trafficking, environmental pollution, arms-dealing, and trading in nuclear materials and radioactive waste). Companies also sometimes react in a heartless fashion and strongly contest accusations of wrongdoing. But in the long-term interests of continuing in legitimate business they may feel forced to espouse reform, to impose new controls, and to assure external stakeholders of their contrite determination to stay on the path of virtue.

The extent to which this is genuine, and not just cosmetic, needs to be judged on a case-by-case basis. In an industry that routinely engages in illicit practices – such as kick-backs, rigged bidding, padded contracts (as in pharmaceuticals, building, and defence procurement fraud respectively) – then a clean company may feel that it is being pushed into uncompetitiveness; reform may, then, simply be part of a 'control cycle' whereby a company keeps its nose clean until it is considered safe to go back to 'business-as-usual'. Bribes and sweeteners, for instance, seem to be an ineradicable part and parcel of the arms trade; currently, several Belgian politicians are under a cloud of suspicion because the Italian firm Augusta deposited some funds in their party's coffers in the hope of influencing the choice of a helicopter for the Belgian armed forces (*de Volkskrant*, 24 February 1995). In the USA a retired Air Force colonel, who observed the purchase of weapons whilst serving in the Pentagon, argued 'that moral and ethical corruption, incompetence and overweening ambition characterized the process' and concluded that buying weapons is 'a corrupt business – ethically and morally corrupt from top to bottom' (Burton, 1993: 2).

Corporate Leadership

It has been suggested that the top executives in a firm set the 'moral' tone, generate the pressure for deviance, and are sometimes closely involved in illegal practices (while cunningly avoiding direct blame or responsibility: Clinard and Yeager, 1980; Clinard, 1983). By implication, the reverse is true and, generally, strong symbolic leadership is required in a 'clean' company where the top manager is a role-model for integrity and he, or she, publicly espouses compliance with laws and ethical codes. The 'mission statement' of Levi Strauss, for instance, encourages 'leadership behaviour that epitomizes "standards of ethical behaviour"' (Kanungo and Conger, 1993: 45). A reading of Jackall (1988) does not make one optimistic about the corporate executives (in the American companies he studied) embracing honesty and integrity; in fact, his major theme is to argue that corporate mobility meant jettisoning one's own personal moral values in favour of the demands of the collective. And there have been cases where managers who had taken an explicit stand on ethics were later found to be deeply involved in deviance.

Anyone researching this area can hardly be anything but sceptical, and, yet, there are corporate leaders who do explicitly reject dubious methods, do respect the environment, and do preach compliance (and even go beyond compliance; cf. Punch, 1992). Some of their companies even perform extremely well, so that we are not just talking of marginal 'do-gooders' who produce 'green' products – for example, Prudential Insurance, Johnson and Johnson, Control Data, Dayton Hudson, Procter and Gamble, Johnson Wax (Tuleja, 1987). Anita Roddick's Body Shop chain has been extremely successful while also making her shops virtual action centres for progressive, humanitarian, and environmental themes. Johnson Wax has a history of excellent employee relations, environmental consciousness (sometimes in advance of legislation), philanthropy, and sponsoring of the arts and culture (Punch, 1992). (Sam Johnson, CEO of S.C. Johnson and Son, Inc., told me that if he had been president of Exxon then he would have been up to Alaska in a flash, would have got a small sea-plane to fly him out to the *Valdez* accident, and would have been seen visibly helping to rescue and clean birds and other animals covered in oil within the first day). Sometimes this is referred to as 'enlightened self-interest' in the sense that certain consumer, retail, and health companies – because of the nature of their industry and of their products – are rewarded for a clean image; and, once attained, it would be highly injurious to lose that aura of probity, as happened with Sears whose pro-consumer reputation took a deep dent when its car-repair services were exposed for systematically over-charging customers (*Wall Street Journal*, 1 November 1993: A15). The point is not so much to ascertain how many corporations are clean and how many are not so clean, for that is unknowable; but rather to assert that reform of a corporation is dependent on many matters, of which an important one is leadership (Walton, 1988; Cannon, 1992). If the power and influence of the top person is so strong as has been maintained, then any genuine and lasting change – in relation to compliance, integrity, and morality – is pointless without convinced and convincing support from the CEO. This places a heavy burden of moral leadership on executives, but without it corporate social responsibility and accountability are virtually a dead letter.

Ethics and Whistle-blowers

'Business ethics' (for some the exemplary oxymoron) has become a growth industry, many companies have embraced an ethical code, and the subject is widely taught in business schools (Matthews et al., 1985; Mahoney, 1990). Almost every company in the Fortune 1000 list has an ethical code, and companies like Caterpillar, Texas Instruments, and S.C. Johnson & Son, Inc. have led the way (Ferrell and Fraedrich, 1991). There is no necessary relation between a code and behaviour, however, and one can be highly sceptical of a code's impact (companies may cynically exploit an ethical code for its PR impact). There are, however, a number of positive aspects to this trend in that merely the debate on formulating a code can raise the consciousness of managers on ethical issues and can make taboo subjects a matter of open discussion (Silk and Vogel, 1976). Also, middle managers, who tend most to be confronted with the pressure to bend and break rules, can employ the code to set limits to a business relation. For example, they can refuse profuse hospitality and gifts, and reject claims for bribes, by saying that their hands are tied by explicit corporate policy; possibly this has the effect of not making the refusal or rejection personal and offensive, and not allowing the client to manipulate the business interaction by plying managers with excessive hospitality or gifts.

But ethical statements are usually abstract and general (Hartley, 1993; Ferrell and Fraedrich, 1991; Buchholz, 1989; Donaldson and Werhane, 1979).

There is evidence that the majority of companies with codes do not often actively engage in 'ethics oversight'; some federal contractors, however, have mandatory ethics training that has to be backed up by 'monitoring, discipline, and effective communications', while these effects must be 'diligently documented' in order to impress regulators and to gain 'sentencing credit' (*Business Week*, 22 April 1991). To implement them a company needs an ethical committee that is perceived as legitimate within the firm and that can handle cases brought to its attention in confidence. Some employees may feel the need for anonymity and this needs to be guaranteed (Westin, 1980). People in an organization are generally sensitive and astute about any weaknesses in the selection of personnel or the operational functioning of such a committee and may even be highly sceptical of its value. This, in turn, is related to corporate policy and practice in supporting ethical behaviour and in not sanctioning, formally or informally, 'whistle-blowers' (Fisse and Braithwaite, 1993: 56). It is plain that corporations dislike people who threaten to expose their dirty linen in public and may hound them. In Switzerland the attempt to blow the whistle on Hoffmann La Roche's illegal conduct led to Stanley Adams's imprisonment on charges of espionage (Adams, 1984). And companies – as well as regulatory agencies, it must be said – have a whole range of mechanisms for stereotyping, deflecting, defusing, and expelling potential troublemakers who pose a threat with regard to unearthing and passing on dirty data (Eagleton, 1991; Ewing, 1977).

In the USA in public administration there is a measure of legal protection for whistle-blowers, and there is a case for offering similar support to those in private business who bring to light information on the criminal and/or harmful conduct of business (Perrucci et al., 1980). Companies who have taken the positive step of implementing such schemes include Mobil and ATT. The Conference Board, a forum for senior executives, has issued a model policy that illustrates their advice in this area;

A Model Whistle-blower Policy

Shout it from the rooftops: Aggressively publicize a reporting policy that encourages employees to bring forward valid complaints of wrongdoing

Face the fear factor: Defuse fear by directing complaints to someone outside the whistle-blower's chain of command

Get right on to it: An independent group, either in or out of the company, should investigate the complaint immediately

Go public: Show employees that complaints are taken seriously by publicizing the outcome of investigations whenever possible

Data: The Conference Board. (*Business Week*, 27 July 1992)

In reality, there are doubtless a battery of social pressures and informal processes that militate against ethical behaviour and whistle-blowing. Ethical codes and protection of whistle-blowers are two ways of combating this tendency to demand of the individual that he or she sacrifices individual conscience to the collective 'good'. We can remain highly sceptical of the impact of all this on actual business behaviour but these do form two potential mechanisms that can play an incremental role in building a rule-abiding corporation. In the last resort, of course, we are reliant on individuals and their ability to resist pressure and to suffer the consequences of taking a stand-point (with Creswell in the Three Mile Island case saying, 'You can always find another job but you can't always find another conscience'). Some may have a mercenary motive: under the False Claims Act whistle-blowers in the USA can receive up to 25 per cent of any money recovered by the government; and some have an axe to grind – disgruntled executives sometimes hit back at the corporation that they had served for many years. As well-informed insiders with high-level information they are difficult to refute. Former General Electric Vice-President, Edward Russell, accused the company that dismissed him of price-rigging and stock-packing, and he claimed to have the data to prove it (*Business Week*, 10 August 1992). As a result GE pleaded guilty and paid a substantial fine.

But however commendable ethical codes are, and however laudable the actions of whistle-blowers, much of the material in this area highlights the willingness of people to submerge their wills, and shelve their consciences, in the interests of the organization. Many of the cases in this book indicate the 'ethical numbness' of corporate executives and the 'pragmatic structural amorality' in business (Wells, 1994: 94). The individual succumbs to the collective and allows the organization to shape his or her morality. The implication is that you have to change the nature of the organization.

The Media

One element in the effective control of corporate (and governmental) conduct is the existence of strong, independent media. Frightened whistle-blowers, desperate victims, and irate consumers need to be able to find a ready response in the media for their tales of corporate misconduct. This is particularly the case because legal redress is often a long and expensive road, with the company often holding the initiative and the resources. The influence of the media is often vital in keeping controversial issues and specific cases in the public arena. Some parts of the media specialize in investigative reporting, which involves a proactive delving into deviance in the hope of unearthing a scandal. But investigative reporting is expensive, haphazard in terms of results, unpredictable, and likely to elicit a combative corporate response (Doig, 1983). The news industry that takes on the business world has to be prepared for court cases, legal battles, and possibly to pay high damages; Distillers effectively muzzled the *Sunday Times* in the Thalidomide scandal and then with the full backing of the law in Britain. And scandals are related to specific national cultures, styles of reporting, and differential impacts, and can engender a successful counter-campaign of cover-up and damage limitation. In practice, furthermore, the media itself are responsive to commercial pressure, in terms of sponsorship and advertising revenue, to political influence, and to inter-connections between the media and business world. In this respect the concentration of the media industry in the hands of a few magnates in several western societies is a cause for concern. The investigative stance of the *Sunday Times* was tempered by Rupert Murdoch's arrival, and Maxwell was said to have had a diluting influence on the *Daily Mirror*'s tradition of tough reporting against vested interests (Evans, 1984; Pilger, 1989).

Some companies do dig in their heels and are determined to fight an issue over a long period of time. But prolonged negative publicity is painful to experience. This is allied to the fact that 'upper-world' crime and deviance has received increasing space in the media. Sutherland's contention that much corporate deviance is ignored no longer holds. Many American managers believe that the media are hostile to business – and they fear the *Wall Street Journal, Mother Jones*, and TV shows such as *Sixty Minutes* and *Donahue* in which executives sometimes get a roasting – and in Britain the scandals of the City, for instance, were full-blown, 'sexy' stories that were extensively covered by the serious and tabloid press (Levi, 1993). The Guinness affair, for example, was front-page news, and the popular tabloid newspapers, especially, went to town on catchy headlines that included, 'The Thieving Millionaires', 'Down and Stout', and 'Guinness Crook of Records', while they also carried extensive sections on the trial, defendants, and sentences (Levi, 1994).

It is probably no more than one of the 'platitudinous generalizations' that Braithwaite was referring to, but it is plain that one crucial element in investigating and controlling organizational deviance and corporate misconduct is strong, independent, well-resourced, and fearless media. Other mechanisms, such as legal redress or public inquiries, are expensive and slow and may not reach to the core of an issue. However imperfect an instrument of control, the media are vital in spotlighting bent business and crooked corporations. The media are also an important resource for victims and survivors of corporate malfeasance – the relatives of disaster victims, the duped pensioners in the Maxwell scandal, the victims of dangerous drugs, and those that have suffered harm from defective products – who may face years of frustrating campaigning for redress against a recalcitrant company where their only ally is the media.

Finally, it is possible to conclude that we require honest politicians, unambivalent laws, well-resourced regulatory agencies, business leaders of integrity, ethical codes, and crusading media in order to tackle corporate misconduct successfully. Clearly, these are ideals and they are rarely realized in practice. In the cold light of analysis it does appear as if business has the power and resources to defy and outwit effective regulation and control; and this is particularly true of cross-border trade where international regulation is often patchy if not toothless (Levi, 1987: 277). The best guarantee of compliance is not so much having powerful control bodies and hefty sanctions but rather in shaping a business strategy of compliance based on corporate self-interest in partnership with sophisticated and resourceful regulators. Despite the conspicuous failure of self-regulation in several cases it is almost certainly the path of the future, as governments cut back on public spending and endeavour to 'liberate' business from restrictive rules. One can be deeply suspicious and highly sceptical about all this, as cases of business deviance continue to emerge. But business does potentially have the power and resources to implement effective control through *private* systems of justice under the supervision of external authorities. The scepticism arises because time and time again business deviants have proved capable of side-stepping internal control and undermining external control, and because they have submerged their consciences in the will of the corporation.

The Future

There have been significant changes during the last decade in the economy and in the structure of the corporation, which mean that we have to rethink many assumptions about business and other organizations (Useem, 1990, 1993; Reed and Hughes, 1992). There has been the development of the global economy, most noticeably in terms of a global financial system that is closely interlinked and that allows the rapid transfer of information and money; transnational corporations have transferred technology and production to countries with cheap labour and weak regulation; and western countries have encountered slow growth, high unemployment, and the decline of traditional industries. The Japanese challenge, followed by the rise of a number of Asian economic 'tigers', issued a fundamental jolt to western economic hegemony. This combination of forces has led to a drastic restructuring of many businesses – and, indeed, non-profit-organizations. Downsizing, re-engineering, and restructuring usually meant leaner – and 'meaner' – companies that were flatter, delayered, with the 'fat' cut out (usually at the expense of middle management and central staff units), and with the emphasis on self-managing teams, shifting networks, and pressure for innovation and performance (Kochan and Useem, 1992). Organizational boundaries were redrawn in the form of shamrocks, doughnuts, and pizzas (Handy, 1990). Information technology meant that work need not be related to a central office and that teams could work with considerable geographic dispersion. The 'virtual corporation' promised excellence, opportunity, redefinition of work and core competencies, no borders, and the promotion of 'brain-wave' in these 'nutty times' (Peters 1989).

It is not easy to comprehend the implications of these developments for deviance in corporations and its control. In terms of organized crime there does seem to be a shift in the direction of more organizational sophistication, more use of experts, more infiltration of financial institutions, and a strong level of 'globalization'. Possibly its activities will shift more to trading high-grade intelligence, to peddling nuclear information and radio-active materials, and to a global black market in human organs (Ward, 1991). Almost certainly, the professions will become more deeply involved in criminal activities as the 'underworld' comes increasingly to rely on the expertise of lawyers, investment bankers, and computer specialists. We await the first major fraud conducted via Internet. And as business enters new, expanding, and relatively unregulated markets, then we can expect fresh scandals in eastern Europe and the Far East. As advanced economies shift from traditional 'smoke-stack' industries to light industry, new forms of production, service industries (and financial services in particular), it is highly probable that industrial accidents will occur in less developed and regulated societies and that business crimes will take place in the expanding financial markets of Singapore, China, and Russia where newcomers from outside will get burned. In trade and finance cases information technology will undoubtedly play an increasingly important role. Pontell and Calavita (1993: 241) noted that, as 'money replaces production as the locus of profit making', the nature of business crime has altered correspondingly, with increasing incidences of 'insider trading, junk bond scams, insurance fraud, and securities violations, as well as thrift and banking fraud.' And Reichman (1993, 65) predicts that 'the financial transactions that dominate the 1990s are likely to generate new sources of inside information and new networks for trading'.

What is evident, however, is that concepts of organizational boundaries, competition, market, profit, control, culture, bureaucracy, and corporate identity are altering dramatically. (To more phenomenologically orientated academics they were already largely seen as social constructions and these concepts were felt to be reifications: Thompson, 1967.) At one level there are industrial and financial conglomerates, highly concentrated and operating flexibly and adaptively across national boundaries, while at another level there are near autonomous teams with low hierarchy and low formal control but with considerable responsibility related to pressure for results. It is surely no coincidence that several major business scandals in the last decade have been in the financial world of investment banks and security firms (Franklin, 1990; Foot, 1992; Taylor, 1993). Previously, 'when investment banking was the province of an elite community of financiers, informal controls based on reputation and loyalty worked fairly well'; but in response to changes in the market environment many of these firms have become, 'self-designing organizations' with 'a high degree of autonomy', 'dispersed authority structures', and a reward structure based on bringing 'resources (profits, clients, etc.) into the firm' (Reichman, 1993: 76). Ostensibly, information technology was meant to lubricate the cyber-system with instantaneous data and to allow effective control of transactions. But, as we have seen, the transformation in structure, culture, style of work, and orientation of personnel to the generous reward system meant that small groups of deviant mavericks could grasp the autonomy, evade the controls, and exploit the rich opportunities presented by the new set-up (Reichman, 1993; Zey, 1993).

In tough times, with the recession of the early 1990s biting, competition increased between firms; but now there was much more competition *within* companies as profit centres and business units were created, as budget responsibility was devolved, and as teams were rewarded for performance. For instance, Fisse and Braithwaite note the management guru Mintzberg's views on new-style organizations replacing old-style formal bureaucracies:

Mintzberg shares with many futurologists the view that the Adhocracy is the type of organisation which is the wave of the future. It is the form of structuring best adapted to innovative high-technology industries. If all this is right, then the problems of designing a coherent jurisprudence of corporate crime will become even more perplexing than today. At least in the past, the greater organisational complexity resulting from increased size has been tempered by the tendency for larger organisations to opt for greater standardization of policies, procedures and roles. Accountability in the twenty-first century will be an acute problem if there is a trend to Adhocracy while the tendency for economic activity to become more concentrated in larger organisations which transcend jurisdictional boundaries continues. The problem of allocating responsibility for fraud in the development and safety testing of pharmaceuticals by transnational corporations (which tend to Adhocracy in their research divisions) is perhaps a window into the future. (1993: 108)

One can speculate that these new and varied organizational forms will foster fresh and innovate deviant practices that will provide unexpected challenges for internal control and external regulation (especially as some control agencies are themselves pressurized to change along the same innovative lines and perhaps even to privatize). The positive view would be that people in small units, based on trust and strong peer control, will feel less tied to the formal organization and more free to speak out; they have been encouraged to take responsibility, to take risks, to admit mistakes, and to reduce the social distance with superiors, so that it should be easier to raise problems and issues related to deviance (cf. Johnson and Johnson, whose successful handling of the Tylenol crisis – a painkiller that had been contaminated with cyanide leading to the deaths of several consumers – was related to the company's decentralized structure, emphasis on innovation, positive leadership, and willingness to admit mistakes, *Business Week*, 26 September 1988; 4 May 1992; Frederick, et al., 1988).

The implication is that we will have to undertake a profound rethinking of our conceptual and legal vocabulary in relation to organizations, business, and deviance. At the macro level, BCCI revealed graphically the inherent weaknesses of the world financial system. At the other extreme, Nick Leeson, apparently on his own, was able to blow blue-blooded Barings to pieces with just a few taps of the keyboard. Traditional regulation is geared to the formal organization working within national boundaries. Clearly, it experiences considerable difficulty in tackling the transnationals, who can export their dirty tricks, dirty products, and 'clean' investments with impunity (Ives, 1985; Weir, 1987; Jones, 1988); and now it will have to face diffuse, amorphous, shifting networks of companies and sub-units that can rapidly switch location, personnel, data, composition, task, and contractual basis of employment. In fact, the two levels may collude in devious and concealed ways to mutual advantage. The virtual corporation in a global economy spells out rich, new opportunities for corporate deviance and a potential nightmare for regulators burdened with the control of corporate and economic activity.

In conclusion, this book is about work, organizations, environments, power, and abuse of power, managers, and morals. It has argued that, to understand business crime and deviance, we have to pay attention to the nature of business, the realities of organizational life, and the dilemmas facing management. The analysis uncovered two major themes; first, that managers in the business organization are induced by organizational pressures and mechanisms to subjugate their personalities and their consciences to the collective, and this leads them to bend and break the law; and second, that business organizations frequently abuse the fiduciary relationship of trust with stakeholders by choosing deviant solutions to problems and by skilfully and consciously fabricating a façade of normality and of compliance with the law (Fisse and Braithwaite, 1993: 38). In a nutshell, managers perceive pressures in their internal and external environments, they select deliberately or semi-consciously illicit means and/or ends, and they endeavour – with varying levels of care and sophistication – to create a shadow reality to undermine control and mislead watch-dogs. The intricate patterns of misconduct encountered in the business world also need to be placed in a context of cultural embeddedness (in terms of professions, industries, and societies) as well as in the changing features of dynamic market places (Reichman, 1993: 71; Hutton, 1995). And, above all, they need to be perceived as arising out of the values and practices of ordinary business; the deviance grows out of, and is justified by, normal commercial conduct.

In the past, the standard literature on this area tended to emphasize business crime as arising from a rational pursuit of economic goals and as being shaped by behaviour on behalf of the organization. In contrast, I have drawn on a number of sources, and a series of cases, to explore two fresh insights on corporate misconduct. One is that the literature on disasters and pathologies in business alerts us to the dark and even irrational side of organizations in relation to incompetence, neglect, ambition, greed, competition, power, domination, and leadership. The other is that the motives of managers may be related not to deviance *for* the organization but in deviance *against* the organization – they abuse it, loot it, and even destroy it. They 'murder' the company by exploiting it to death. This means that we are concerned with *organizational* crime and deviance and our focus should be on the organization as a weapon, a target, an offender, a scene of crime, a justification, an opportunity, a means, and as a victim.

My interest throughout this work, then, has been on how organizations misuse their power and how they manipulate managers into deviance. By peeling away the myth system to expose the operational code we can witness a wide range of deviant practices that are stimulated by the underlying logic of business as a competitive activity, in a conflictual and adversarial context, requiring 'hard', predatory, and manipulative conduct.

In essence, then, this book has argued that business provides a criminogenic arena for some managers at certain times and under certain conditions. The managerial talent that they display in rule-bending is strongly related to their organizational ability to use and exploit their environments for illicit purposes. They have to master the techniques of the shadow organization and develop a high level of skill in order to pull the wool over the eyes of bankers, accountants, investors, shareholders, lawyers, the media, and regulators over an extended period of time. And the legitimate corporation engaged in illegality is often sophisticated and successful at subterfuge, concealment, impression management, and cloaking the inner reality. The con-man inveigles you into trusting him. The corporation engaged in misconduct also manipulates trust and confidence in order to allay suspicion. This indicates that it is right to be wary and suspicious of business organizations. Even more importantly, it implies that organizational deviance and corporate misconduct have to be tackled *organizationally*; the aim has to be to penetrate organizational fronts to expose the concealed core. The central issues then become visibility, accountability, responsibility, openness, trust, and morality. Can the 'transformation' of organizations create structures and cultures that avoid the pitfalls of traditional, formal organizations? And can a new managerial 'revolution' liberate executives from the moral and emotional stranglehold of the institution on their identities and consciences? In terms of regulation this also means more than the snapshot of routine control but deep penetration to the shadow, where the covert action is. This requires a determination and sophistication that equals that of bent business. That is the challenge of tackling business crime. And the more we fail organizationally, then the more organizational crime and corporate misconduct will continue to pay, and to pay handsomely.

Bibliography

Adams, J.R. (1990) *The Big Fix: Inside the S. & L. Scandal.* New York: Wiley.

Adams, J.R. and Frantz, D. (1992) *A Full Service Bank: How BCCI Stole Billions around the World.* New York: Pocket Books.

Adams, S. (1984) *Roche versus Adams.* London: Jonathan Cape.

Adler, P.A. and Adler, P. (eds) (1984) *The Social Dynamics of Financial Markets.* Greenwich, CT, London: JAI Press Inc.

Allison, R.E. (1993) *Global Disasters: Inquiries into Management Ethics.* New York: Prentice-Hall.

Altheide, D.L. and Johnson, J.M. (1980) *Bureaucratic Propaganda.* Boston, MA: Allyn & Bacon.

Asch, P. and Seneca, J.T. (1976) 'Is collusion profitable?' *The Review of Economics and Statistics,* 58: 1–12.

Auletta, K. (1986) *Greed and Glory on Wall Street.* Harmondsworth, Middx: Penguin.

Bakker, M. (1985) 'Scheepsfraude: het onbekende "zwarte gat"', *FEM-Supplement,* 23 (15 June): 47–9.

Banks, L. (1982) *The Rise and Fall of Freddy Laker.* London: Faber.

Barham, K., Fraser, J. and Heath, L. (1988) *Management for the Future.* Berkhamsted, Herts: Ashridge Management College.

'Barings' Report (1995) Report of the Board of Banking Supervision Inquiry into the Circumstances of the Collapse of Barings. London: HMSO.

Barlow, H.D. (1993) 'Directions and strategies in the study of small business crime', Paper presented at Third Fraud, Corruption and Business Crime Conference, University of Liverpool (March 1993).

Bate, P. (1994) *Strategies for Cultural Change.* Oxford: Butterworth Heinemann.

Baucus, M.S. and Near, J.P. (1991) 'Can illegal corporate behaviour be predicted? an event history analysis', *The Academy of Management Journal,* 34 (1) 9–36.

Beaty, J. and Gwynne, S.C. (1993) *The Outlaw Bank: A Wild Ride into the Secret Heart of BCCI.* New York: Random House.

Bell, D. (1973) *The Coming of Post-Industrial Society.* New York: Basic Books.

Benekos, P.J. and Hagan, F.E. (1990) '*Too little, too late: regulation and prosecution and the S & L scandal*'. Paper delivered at the American Society of Criminology Annual Meeting, Baltimore, MD, 1990.

Bennett, A. (1990) *The Death of the Organization Man.* New York: Morrow Books.

Bennis, W. (1973) *The Leaning Ivory Tower.* San Francisco: Jossey-Bass.

Bennis, W. (1976) *The Unconscious Conspiracy: Why Leaders Can't Lead.* New York: Amacom.

Bensman, J. and Gerver, J. (1963) 'Crime and punishment in the factory', *American Sociological Review,* 28: 588–98.

Benson, M.L. (1985) 'Denying the guilty mind', *Criminology,* 25: 583–607.

Berge, D. ten (1990) *The First Twenty Four Hours.* Oxford/Cambridge, MA: Basil Blackwell.

'Bingham' Report (1992), 'Inquiry into the supervision of the Bank of Credit and Commerce International', by Lord Justice Bingham. London: HMSO.

Blanken, M. (1976) *Force of Order and Methods: An American View into the Dutch Directed Society.* The Hague: Martinus Nijhoff.

Blau, P. (1955) *The Dynamics of Bureaucracy.* Chicago: Chicago University Press.

Blom, R.J. (1983) *Slavenburg: De ondergang van een bank.* Utrecht/Antwerp: Het Spectrum.

Blom, R.J. (1984) *RSV: Een financiële scheepsramp*. Utrecht/Antwerp: Het Spectrum.

Bologna, J. (1984) *Corporate Fraud: The Basics of Prevention and Detection*. Boston: Butterworths.

Bosworth-Davies, R. (1988) *Fraud in the City: Too Good to be True*. Harmondsworth, Middx: Penguin.

Bouchier, D. (1986) 'The sociologist as anti-partisan', *Research in Social Movements, Conflict and Change*, 9: 1–23.

Boulton, D. (1978) *The Grease Machine*. New York: Harper & Row.

Bower, T. (1989) *Maxwell: The Outsider*. London: Arum Press.

Bowles, M.L. (1991) 'The organization shadow', *Organization Studies*, 12 (3): 387–404.

Box, S. (1983) *Power, Crime and Mystification*. London: Tavistock (2nd edn).

Boyd, C. (1990) 'The responsibility of individuals for a company disaster: the case of the Zeebrugge car ferry', in G. Enderle, B. Almond and A. Argandona (eds), *People in Corporations: Ethical Responsibilities and Corporate Effectiveness*. Boston: Kluwer, pp. 140–8.

Braithwaite, J. (1984) *Corporate Crime in the Pharmaceutical Industry*. London: Routledge & Kegan Paul.

Braithwaite, J. (1985a) 'White collar crime', *Annual Review of Sociology*, 11: 1–25.

Braithwaite, J. (1985b) 'Corporate crime research', *Sociology*, 19 (1): 136–48.

Braithwaite, J. (1989) *Crime, Shame and Reintegration*. Cambridge: Cambridge University Press.

Braithwaite, J. (1993) 'The nursing home industry', in M. Tonry and A.J. Reiss Jr. (eds), *Beyond the Law*. Chicago: Chicago University Press.

Braithwaite, J. and Ayres, I. (1991) 'Transcending the regulation versus deregulation debate', Paper presented at Second Liverpool Conference on Fraud, Corruption and Business Crime; University of Liverpool (April 1991).

Braithwaite, J. and Petit, P. (1990) *Not Just Deserts*. Oxford: Oxford University Press.

Brenner, S.N. and Molander, E.A. (1977) 'Is the ethics of business changing?' *Harvard Business Review*, 55 (1) (January–February): 57–71.

Broer, J. and Gielen, P. (1993) 'Bedrijfsspionage in Nederland', *Bedrijfsdocumentatie*, 24 (7) (October): 20–3.

Brown, M. (1994) *Richard Branson: The Inside Story*. London: Headline Book Publishing (3rd edn).

Bruck, C. (1988) *The Predators' Ball*. New York: The American Lawyer/Simon & Schuster.

Buchholz, R.A. (1982) *Business Environment and Public Policy*. Englewood Cliffs, NJ: Prentice-Hall .

Buchholz, R.A. (1989) *Business Ethics*. Englewood Cliffs, NJ: Prentice-Hall.

Buchholz, R.A., Evans, W.D. and Wagley, R.A. (1985) *Management Response to Public Issues*. Englewood Cliffs, NJ: Prentice-Hall.

Burrell, G. and Morgan, G. (1979) *Sociological Paradigms and Organizational Analysis*. London: Heinemann.

Burrough, B. (1992) *Vendetta: American Express and the Smearing of Edmond Safra*. New York: HarperCollins.

Burton, J.G. (1993) *The Pentagon Wars*. Annapolis, MD: Naval Institute Press.

Business Week, 23 June 1986, 'Insider trading: the limits of self-policing'.

Business Week, 25 August 1986, 'Why insider trading really is a crime'.

Business Week, 11 August 1987, 'Texaco: Chapter 11?'

Business Week, 26 September 1988, 'At Johnson & Johnson, a mistake can be a badge of honor'.

Business Week, 7 November 1988, 'Did Schwab play fast and loose with its customers' shares?'

Business Week, 7 November 1988, 'Grey markets'.

Business Week, 28 November 1988, 'Just how damning is the case against Drexel Burnham?'

Business Week, 26 February 1990, 'After Drexel'.

Business Week, 5 March 1990, 'And now, the predator is preyed upon'; 'Could Fred Joseph have saved Drexel?'

Business Week, 1 April 1991, 'CEO disease: egotism can breed corporate disaster – and the disease is spreading'.

Business Week, 22 April 1991, 'The crackdown on crime in the suites'.

Business Week, 22 July 1991, 'The long and winding road to BCCI's dead end'.

Business Week, 14 October 1991, 'How some companies spy'.

Business Week, 4 May 1992, 'Johnson & Johnson: a big company that works'.

Business Week, 8 June 1992, 'The Drexel debacle's "Teflon guy"'.

Business Week, 25 January 1993, 'British air: not cricket'.

Business Week, 19 April 1993, 'The aftershock from the Lopez affair'.

Business Week, 26 April 1993, 'Executive pay', special report: 38–56.

Business Week, 26 July 1993, 'It's getting tougher to untangle the Lopez imbroglio'.

Business Week, 23 August 1993, 'Are trade-secret police patrolling your company'?; 'There's another side to Lopez saga'.

Business Week, 13 December 1993, 'Freedom is no picnic for Mike Milken'.

Calavita, K. and Pontell, H.N. (1990) '"Heads I win, tails you lose": deregulation, crime and crisis in the savings & loan industry', *Crime & Delinquency*, 36 (3): 309–41.

Calavita, K. and Pontell, H.N. (1991) '"Other people's money": collective embezzlement in the savings and loans insurance industries', *Social Problems*, 38 (1): 94–112.

Calavita, K. and Pontell, H.N. (1993) 'Savings and loan fraud as organized crime: towards a conceptual typology of corporate illegality', *Criminology*, 31 (4): 519–48.

Calhoun, C. (1989) Review in *Contemporary Sociology*, 18 (4): 542–5.

Cannon, T. (1992) *Corporate Responsibility*. London: Financial Times/Pitman Publishing.

Carr, A.Z. (1968) 'Is business bluffing ethical?' *Harvard Business Review*, 46 (1): 425–41.

Carson, R. (1962) *Silent Spring*. Boston: Houghton Mifflin.

Carson, W.G. (1982) *The Other Price of Britain's Oil*. New Brunswick, NJ: Rutgers University Press.

Chambliss, W.J. (1967) 'Types of deviance and the effectiveness of legal sanctions', *Wisconsin Law Review* (Summer): 703–19.

Charles, M.T. (1989) 'The last flight of the space shuttle Challenger', in U. Rosenthal, M.T. Charles and P. 't Hart (eds), *Coping with Crises*. Springfield, IL: Charles C. Thomas.

Clarke, M. (1981) *Fallen Idols: Elites and the Search for the Acceptable Face of Capitalism*. London: Junction Books.

Clarke, M. (ed.) (1983) *Corruption: Causes, Consequences and Control*. London: Frances Pinter.

Clarke, M. (1986) *Regulating the City: Competition, Scandal and Reform*. Milton Keynes: Open University Press.

Clarke, M. (1990) *Business Crime*. Cambridge: Polity Press.

Clarke, M., Smith, D. and McConville, M. (1994) *Slippery Customers: Estate Agents, the Public and Regulation*. London: Blackstone Press Ltd.

Clegg, S.R. (1989) *Frameworks of Power*. London, Newbury Park, Delhi: Sage Publications.

Clegg, S.R. (1990) *Modern Organizations: Organization Studies in the Postmodern World*. London: Sage.

Cleverley, G. (1971) *Managers and Magic*. London: Longman.

Clinard, M.B. (1952) *The Black Market: A Study of White-collar Crime*. New York: Holt, Rinehart.

Clinard, M.B. (1983) *Corporate Ethics and Crime*. Beverly Hills, CA: Sage.

Clinard, M.B. and Yeager, P.C. (1980) *Corporate Crime*. New York: Free Press.

Clutterbuck, D. (1981) 'Blowing the whistle on corporate misconduct', in A. Elkins and D. Callaghan (eds), *A Managerial Odyssey*. Reading, MA: Addison-Wesley.

Cochran, P.L. and Nigh, D. (1986) 'Illegal corporate behaviour: an empirical examination', Paper presented at Academy of Management Meeting, Chicago (August 1986).

Cohen, A.K. (1966) *Deviance and Control*. Englewood Cliffs, NJ: Prentice-Hall.

Cohen, P. (1974) *The Gospel According to the Harvard Business School*. Harmondsworth, Middx: Penguin.

Cohen, S. (1972) *Folk Devils and Moral Panics*. London: MacGibbon & Kee.

Coleman, J.W. (1985) *The Criminal Elite: the Sociology of White Collar Crime*. New York: St. Martin's Press (1st edn).

Coleman, J.W. (1989) *The Criminal Elite: The Sociology of White Collar Crime*. New York: St Martin's Press (2nd edn).

Comfort, L.K. (ed.) (1988) *Managing Disaster: Strategies and Policy Perspectives*. Durham and London: Duke University Press.

Conklin, J.E. (1977) *Illegal but not Criminal: Business Crime in America*. Englewood Cliffs, NJ: Prentice-Hall.

Conway, B. (1981) *The Piracy Business*. London: Jonathan Cape.

Cools, M. and Hoogenboom, A. (eds) (1995) *Kwetsbare kennis: Over 'business intelligence' en informatiemakelaardij*. Alphen a/d Rijn: Samson.

Cornwell, R. (1984) *God's Banker*. London: Gollancz.

Cressey, D.R. (1953) *Other People's Money*. New York: Free Press.

Cressey, D.R. (1969) *Theft of the Nation*. New York: Harper.

Cressey, D.R. (1972) *Criminal Organization*. London: Heinemann.

Croall, H. (1992) *White Collar Crime: Criminal Justice and Criminology*. Buckingham/ Philadelphia: Open University Press.

Crozier, M. (1964) *The Bureaucratic Phenomenon*. London, Tavistock.

Crystal, G.F. (1991) *In Search of Excess: The Overcompensation of American Executives*. New York: Norton.

Cullen, F.T., Maakestad, W.J. and Cavender G. (1984) 'The Ford Pinto case and beyond', in E. Hochstedler (ed.), *Corporations as Criminals*. Beverly Hills, CA: Sage Publications.

Curran, D.J. (1994) *Dead Laws for Dead Men*. Pittsburgh, PA: Pittsburgh University Press.

Daily Mail, 15 July 1991, 'Bank victims: we need urgent aid'; 'Banks tempt the ethnic entrepreneur'.

Daily Mail, 14 August 1991, 'Breakthrough in nine-year riddle of God's Bank'.

Daily Mail, 5 December 1991, 'How Maxwell kept us in the dark'.

Daily Mail, 20 January 1992, 'New doubts on illness that freed Saunders'.

Daily Mail, 10 March 1992, 'Accused! Report lays the blame for Maxwell pensions scandal'.

Daily Mail, 23 October 1992, 'The Bank is blamed over BCCI "debacle"'.

Daily Mail, 22 December 1992, 'The rubbish bag bandit "who was an industrial spy"'.

Daily Mail, 8 January 1993, 'BA chiefs surrender in Virgin libel battle'.

Daily Mail, 28 January 1993, '£41m scandal of the BCCI conman'.

Daily Mail, 27 April 1993, '£1m bill for spy pair in BP swindle'.

Daily Mail, 12 May 1994, 'Jail but no bill for crook who lied to keep BCCI afloat'.

Daily Mail, 29 September 1994, 'My ordeal by ferry Briton'; 'A crash, and the sea cascaded in'.

Daily Mail, 5 October 1994, 'Bow doors sealed in ferry safety crackdown'.

Daily Mail, 8 November 1994, 'One in three ferries fails the safety test'.

Daily Mail, 23 December 1994, 'Guinness Four win fight for a new hearing'.

Daily Mail, 28 February 1995, 'Where in the world is he?'; 'Blunders behind Barings Straits'; 'Tighter rules must follow Barings crash'.

Daily Mail, 1 March 1995, 'Escape to island hideaway'.

Daily Mail, 3 March 1995, 'Yes, I am the man you want'.

Daily Mail, 12 March 1995, 'Barings auditor to face lawsuit'.

Daily Mail, 4 May 1995, 'Thalidomide victims win £37.5m boost'.

Daily Mail, 23 May 1995, 'Saatchis the winners in Entente Cordiant'.

Daily Mail, 3 June 1995, 'Maxwell's son puts blame on the sins of the father'.

Daily Telegraph, 24 December 1994, 'Fraud office in the dock'.

Daley, R. (1979) *Prince of the City*. London: Panther.

Dalton, M. (1959) *Men Who Manage*. New York: John Wiley.

Dalton, M. (1964) 'Preconceptions and methods in "men who manage"', in P. Hammond (ed.), *Sociologists at Work*. New York: Basic Books, pp. 50–95.

Day, K. (1993) *S & L Hell: The People and the Politics Behind $1 Trillion Savings & Loan Scandal*. New York: Norton.

Deal, T.E. and Kennedy, A.A. (1982) *Corporate Cultures*. Reading, MA: Addison-Wesley.

De Baena, Duke (1957) *The Dutch Puzzle*. The Hague: Boucher.

Dekker, V. (1994) *Going Down, Going Down*. Amsterdam/Antwerp: Uitgeverij L.J. Veen.

Department of Defense Inspector General (1990) 'Seminannual Report to the Congress, 1 October 1989 to 31 March 1990'. Washington, DC: DOD.

Dijk, van, N.M.H. (1989) *Een methodische strategie van organisatie-verandering*. Delft: Eburon.

Dijk, van, N.M.H. and Punch, M. (1985) 'Useful knowledge: management science as dialogue', Public lecture, Breukelen, Nijenrode University, 2 September 1985.

Dijk, van, N.M.H. and Punch, M. (1993) 'Open borders, closed circles: Management and organization in the Netherlands', in D.J. Hickson (ed.), *Management in Western Europe*. Berlin/New York: Walter de Gruyter, pp. 167–90.

Ditton, J. (1977) *Part-time Crime*. London: Macmillan.

Dixon, N.F. (1979) *On the Psychology of Military Incompetence*. London: Futura Publications Ltd.

Dixon, N.F. (1994) 'Disastrous decisions', *The Psychologist*, 7 (7) (July): 303–7.

Doig, A. (1983) '"You publish at your peril!" – the restraints on investigative journalism', in M. Clarke (ed.), *Corruption*. London: Frances Pinter.

Doig, A. (1984) *Corruption and Misconduct in Contemporary British Politics*. Harmondsworth, Middx: Penguin.

Donaldson, T. and Werhane, P.H. (eds) (1979) *Ethical Issues in Business: a Philosophical Approach*. Englewood Cliffs, NJ: Prentice-Hall.

'Donner' Report (1976) *Rapport van de Commissie van Drie*: onderzoek naar de juistheid van verklaringen over betalingen door een Amerikaanse vliegtuigfabriek. ('Donner Commission' that examined the Lockheed affair and the role of Prince Bernhard.) The Hague: Staatsuitgeverij.

Douglas, J.D. and Johnson, J.M. (eds) (1977) *Official Deviance*. Philadelphia: Lippincott.

Dowie, M. (1977) 'Pinto madness', *Mother Jones*, 2 (September/October): 17–19.

Dowie, M. and Marshall, C. (1982) 'The Bendectin cover-up', in M.D. Ermann and R.J. Lundman (eds), *Corporate and Governmental Deviance*. New York: Oxford University Press (2nd edn).

Downes, D. and Rock, P. (1982) *Understanding Deviance*. Oxford: Oxford University Press.

Drucker, P.F. (1972) *The Concept of the Corporation*. New York: Mentor (rev. edn).

Drucker, P.F. (1980) *Managing in Turbulent Times*. New York: Harper & Row.

Eagleton, T.F. (1991) *Issues in Business and Government*. Englewood Cliffs, NJ: Prentice-Hall.

Economist, 31 January 1981, 'SEC: muzzling the watchdog'.

Economist, 24 July 1982, 'IBM pulls the plug on cheap imitators?'

Economist, 10 September 1988, 'Corporate convict'.

Economist, 18 December 1993, 'Trading in hypocrisy'.

Economist, 29 January 1994, 'A survey of corporate governance'.

Economist, 2 July 1994, 'When the fiddling had to stop'.

Economist, 24 September 1994, 'Human rights: unconventional'.

Eddy, P., Potter, E. and Page, B. (1976) *Destination Disaster*. New York: Quadrangle.

Ehrenfeld, R. (1992) *Evil Money: Encounters along the Money Trail*. New York: Harper Business.

Elsevier's, 23 April 1983, 'Analyse van het RSV-drama'.

Elsevier's, 2 February 1985, 'RSV Zaak Opnieuw'.

Ermann, M.D. and Lundman, R.J. (eds) (1978) *Corporate and Governmental Deviance*. New York: Oxford University Press.

Ermann, M.D. and Lundman, R.J. (eds) (1982a) *Corporate and Governmental Deviance*. New York: Oxford University Press (2nd edn).

Ermann, M.D. and Lundman, R.J. (1982b) *Corporate Deviance*. New York: Rinehart & Winston.

L'Etang, H. (1969) *The Pathology of Leadership*. London: Heinemann.

Evans, H. (1984) *Good Times, Bad Times*. London: Coronet.

Ewing, D.E. (1977) *Freedom Inside the Corporation*. New York: McGraw-Hill.

F.E.M., 18 March 1995; 'Het Risico van Barings', feature article, pp. 62–9.

Ferrell, O.C. and Fraedrich, J. (1991) *Business Ethics*. Boston: Houghton Mifflin.

Festinger, L. (1957) *A Theory of Cognitive Dissonance*. Palo Alto, CA: Stanford University Press.

Festinger, L., Riecken, H.W. and Schachter, S. (1956) *When Prophecy Fails*. New York: Harper & Row.

Financial Times, 30 September 1994, 'Ferries in six "near accidents"'.

278   *Dirty Business*

Financial Times, 19 July 1995, 'Controls failure sank Barings'; 'The Barings Report'; 'Barings and the Bank'.

Financial Times, 4 December 1995, 'Singapore may prosecute former Barings executives'; 'Leeson Trial'; 'Singapore moves to defend reputation'.

Fisse, B. and. Braithwaite, J. (1993) *Corporations, Crimes and Accountability*. Cambridge: Cambridge University Press.

Fitzgerald, A.E. (1989) *The Pentagonists: an Insider's View of Waste, Mismanagement and Fraud in Defense Spending*. New York: Houghton Mifflin.

Foot, P. (1992) 'Dirty money', review in *London Review of Books*, 17 December pp. 3–5.

Forbes, 1 August 1969, 'McDonnell Douglas billion-dollar gamble'.

Fortune, 11 September 1978, 'Ford: the road ahead'.

Fortune, 9 November 1987, 'The paranoid life of arbitragers'.

Franklin, P. (1990) *Profits of Deceit: Dispatches from the Front Lines of Fraud*. London: Heinemann.

Frantz, D. (1987) *Levine and Co.: Wall Street's Insider Trading Scandal*. New York: Holt.

Frayn, M. (1964) 'The Festival of Britain', in M. Sissons and P. French (eds), *The Age of Austerity*. Harmondsworth, Middx: Penguin.

Frederick, W.C., Davis, K. and Post, J.E. (1988) *Business and Society: Corporate Strategy, Public Policy, Ethics*. New York: Mc Graw-Hill (6th edn).

Friedland, M. (ed.) (1990) *Securing Compliance: Seven Case Studies*. Toronto: University of Toronto Press.

Galbraith, J.K. (1986a) 'Behind the Wall', review in *New York Review of Books* (10 April): 11–13.

Galbraith, J.K. (1986b) 'Truly the last tycoons', review in *New York Review of Books* (14 August): 17.

Galbraith, J.K. (1988) 'From stupidity to cupidity', review in *New York Review of Books* (24 November).

Galbraith, J.K. (1993) *A Short History of Financial Euphoria*. New York: Whittle Books/Viking.

Garskombe, D.J. (1988) 'Organizational culture dons the mantle of militarism', *Organizational Dynamics*, 17 (1) (Summer): 46–56.

Geis, G. (1962) 'Toward a delineation of white-collar offences', *Sociological Inquiry*, 32: 160–71.

Geis, G. (1967) 'White collar crime: the heavy electrical equipment antitrust cases of 1961', in M.B. Clinard and R. Quinney (eds), *Criminal Behavior Systems*. New York: Holt, Rinehart & Winston.

Geis, G. (ed.) (1968) *White Collar Criminal*. New York: Atherton.

Geis, G. (1978) 'White collar crime: the heavy electrical equipment antitrust cases of 1961', in M.D. Ermann and R.J. Lundman (eds), *Corporate and Governmental Deviance*. New York: Oxford University Press.

Geis, G. (1982) 'The heavy electrical equipment cases', in M.D. Ermann and R.J. Lundman (eds) *Corporate and Governmental Deviance*. New York: Oxford University Press. pp. 123–43 (2nd edn).

Geis, G. and Goff, G. (1983) 'Introduction' to E.H. Sutherland, *White Collar Crime*. New Haven/London: Yale University Press.

Geis, G. and Meier, F.R. (eds) (1977) *White Collar Crime: Offences in Business, Politics and the Professions*. New York: Free Press (rev. edn).

Geis, G., Pontell, H.N. and Jesilow, P.D. (1988) 'Medicaid fraud', in J.E. Scott and T. Hirschi (eds), *Controversial Issues in Crime and Justice*. Beverly Hills, CA: Sage.

Geis, G. and Stotland, E. (eds,) (1980) *White-collar Crime: Theory and Research*. Beverly Hills, CA: Sage Publications Ltd.

Glees, A. (1987) 'The Flick affair', *Corruption and Reform*, 2 (2) 111–26.

Goffman, E. (1959) *The Presentation of Self in Everyday Life*. New York: Anchor Books.

Goffman, E. (1961) *Asylums*. New York: Anchor Books.

Goffman, E. (1969) *Strategic Interaction*. Philadelphia: University of Pennsylvania Press.

Goode, W.J. (1967) 'The protection of the inept', *American Sociological Review*, 32 (1) 5–19.

Gouldner, A.W. (1954) *Patterns of Industrial Bureaucracy*. New York: Free Press.

Gray, M. and Rosen, I. (1982) *The Warning*. Chicago: Contemporary Books.

Greenslade, R. (1992) *Maxwell's Fall*. London: Simon & Schuster.

Gregory, M. (1994) *Dirty Tricks*. Boston: Little, Brown.

Greising, D. and Morse, L. (1991) *Brokers, Bagmen and Moles: Fraud and Corruption in the Chicago Futures Market*. New York: Wiley.

Gross, E. (1980) 'Organization structure and organizational crime', in G. Geis and E. Stotland (eds), *White-collar Crime*. Beverly Hills, CA: Sage, pp. 52–76.

Guardian, 28 August 1990, 'The Guinness trial' (4-page report), 'Guinness Four guilty'.

Guardian, 9 March 1992, 'Maxwell pensions: angry reactions'.

Guardian, 1 February 1994, 'Crime without punishment'.

Guardian, 21 October 1994, 'How store saga engulfed stiff-necked accountant and ambitious right-winger'; 'Tories on ropes over "sleaze"'.

Guardian, 19 July 1995, 'Leeson to carry can over Barings fiasco'; 'The mugging of an old lady'; 'Freewheeling into the Wimbledon abyss'; 'Brown savages the old boys' network'.

Gurwin, L. (1984) *The Calvi Affair: Death of a Banker*. London: Macmillan.

Haagse Post, 2 April 1983, 'Waarom RSV gedoemd was', 14–24.

Hagan, F. and Benekos, P.J. (1990) 'The biggest white-collar crime in history: the great Savings & Loans scandal', Paper presented at Annual Meeting of American Society of Criminology, Baltimore, 1990.

Haines, J. (1988) *Maxwell*. London: Macdonald.

Halperin, M.H. (1977) *The Lawless State*. Harmondsworth, Middx: Penguin.

Handy, C. (1990) *The Age of Unreason*. London: Arrow.

Harren, J. and Bos, J. van den, (1984) *De RSV Show*. Utrecht: Grote Beren.

Hartley, R.F. (1993) *Business Ethics: Violations of the Public Trust*. New York: Wiley.

Hartley, R.F. (1994) *Management Mistakes and Successes*. New York: Wiley (4th edn).

Hartung, F.E. (1950) 'White-collar offences in the wholesale meat industry in Detroit', *American Journal of Sociology*, 56 (July): 25–34.

Harvard Business School, Case 383-129 (1983), 'Managing product safety: the Ford Pinto'. Boston, MA: HBS Case Services.

Harvard Business School, Case 9-383-128 (1984), 'Managing product safety: the case of the McDonnell Douglas DC 10', Boston, MA: HBS Case Services.

Harvey, J.B. (1988) 'The Abilene paradox: the management of agreement,' *Organizational Dynamics*, 17 (1) (Summer): 17–34.

Hawkins, K. (1984) *Environment and Enforcement*. Oxford: Oxford University Press.

Hawkins, K. and Thomas, J.M. (eds) (1984) *Enforcing Regulation*. Boston: Kluwer-Nijhoff.

Hay, G. and Kelly, D. (1974) 'An empirical survey of price-fixing conspiracies', *Journal of Law and Economics*, 17: 13–38.

Hayes, M. and Pearce, F. (1976) *Crime, Law and the State*. London: Routledge & Kegan Paul.

Henry, S. (1978) *The Hidden Economy*. Oxford: Martin Robertson.

Herlihy, E.D. and Levine, T.A. (1980) 'Corporate crisis: The overseas payment problem', in E. Bittner and S.L. Messinger (eds) *Criminology Review Yearbook*, 2: 221–42.

Herling, J. (1962) *The Great Price Conspiracy: The Story of Anti-Trust Violations in the Electrical Industry*. Washington, DC: Luce.

Hirsch, P. (1986) 'From ambushes to golden parachutes: corporate takeovers as an instance of cultural framing and institutional integration', *American Journal of Sociology*, 91: 800–37.

Hirsch, P. and Andrews, A. (1984) 'Ambushes, shootouts and knights of the round table: the language of corporate takeovers', in L.R. Pondy, P.M. Morgan and T.C. Dandridge (eds) *Organizational Symbolism*. Greenwich, CT: JAI Press Inc., pp. 145–55.

Hochstedler, E. (ed.) (1984) *Corporations as Criminals*. Beverly Hills, CA: Sage.

Hodgson, G. (1986) *Lloyds of London*. Harmondsworth, Middx: Penguin.

Hope v. McDonnell Douglas et al., Civ. No. 17631, Federal District Court, Los Angeles, California (n.d.). Quoted in *Harvard Business School*, Case 9-383-128 (1984), 'Managing product safety: the case of the McDonnell Douglas DC 10' Boston, MA: HBS Case Services.

Hughes, E.C. (1958) *Men and their Work*. New York: Free Press.

Hughes, E.C. (1963) 'Good people and dirty work', in H.S. Becker (ed.), *The Other Side*. Glencoe, IL: Free Press.

Hulst, J. van der, (ed.) (1993) *EC Fraud*. Deventer/Boston: Kluwer.

Hutton, W. (1995) *The State We're In*. London: Jonathan Cape.

Iacocca, L. (1986) *Iacocca: An Autobiography*. Toronto/New York: Bantam Books.

Independent, 28 February 1995, 'The breaking of the bank at Bishopsgate'.

Independent, 28 February 1995, 'How one dealer broke the bank that built a family's fortune over centuries'; 'Baring dealer's £1m boast'; 'Barings can't put all blame on "Mr Simex"'.

Independent, 1 March 1995, 'Barings knew of rogue deals'; 'Urgent meetings aim to break up Barings' business'; 'Wall Street aghast at lack of control of traders'; 'A banking tragedy that calls for some purges'; 'We can't bank on trust alone.'

Independent, 4 March 1995, 'Fraud office goes into Barings'; 'Baring the City: breaking the bank.'

Independent, 19 July 1995, 'Barings Report'; 'Bank of England offloads blame for Barings collapse'; 'Three strikes and you're out'; 'Barings makes case for break-up of Bank'.

International Herald Tribune, 8–9 September 1990, 'Guinness affair highlights major problems of investor protection'.

Ives, J.H. (ed.) (1985) *The Export of Hazard: Transnational Corporations and Environmental Control Issues*. New York: Routledge and Kegan Paul.

Jackall, R. (1988) *Moral Mazes: The World of Corporate Managers*. New York/Oxford: Oxford University Press.

Jackson, B. (1988) *Honest Graft: Big Money and the American Political Process*. New York: Knopf.

Jacobs, J. (1969) 'Symbolic bureaucracy', *Social Forces*, xlvii: 413–20.

Jacobs, M.T. (1991) *Short-term America: The Causes and Cures of Our Business Myopia*. Boston, MA: Harvard Business School Press.

James, Barrie G. (1985) *Business War Games*. Harmondsworth, Middx: Penguin.

Jamieson, K.M. (1994) *The Organization of Corporate Crime*. Thousand Oaks, CA: Sage Publications Ltd.

Janis, I.L. (1985) 'Sources of error in strategic decision-making', in J.M. Pennings and associates, *Organizational Strategy and Change*. San Francisco: Jossey-Bass.

Janis, I.L. (1972) *Victims of Groupthink*. Boston: Houghton Mifflin.

Japan Times, 4 December 1994, 'Up to 200,000 permanently affected by Bhopal gas disaster, doctors say'.

Japan Times, 21 December 1994, '25 indicted for insider trading'.

Japan Times, 23 February 1995, 'Shadow of Lockheed lingers. Money, politics, scandals still plague the system'.

Jay, A. (1987) *Management and Machiavelli*. London: Hutchinson (first published 1967).

Johnson, D. (1983) 'God's godfather', review in *London Review of Books* (6–19 October): 12.

Johnson, G. and Scholes, K. (1993) *Exploring Corporate Strategy*. New York: Prentice-Hall (3rd edn).

Johnson, J.M. and Douglas, J.D. (eds) (1978) *Crime at the Top: Deviance in Business and the Professions*. Philadelphia: Lippincott.

Jones, T. (1988) *Corporate Killing: Bhopals will Happen*. London: Free Association Books.

Kanter, R.M. (1977) *Men and Women of the Corporation*. New York: Basic Books.

Kanter, R.M. and Stein, B.A. (eds) (1979) *Life in Organizations: Workplaces as People Experience Them*. New York: Basic Books.

Kanungo, R.N. and Conger, J.A. (1993) 'Promoting altruism as a corporate goal', *Academy of Management Executive*, VII: 3: 37–48.

Katz, J. (1977) 'Cover-up and collective integrity: on the natural antagonisms of authority internal and external to organizations', *Social Problems*, 25 (1): 3–17.

Katz, J. (1979) 'Legality and equality: plea-bargaining in the prosecution of white-collar and common crimes', *Law and Society Review*: 13 (Winter): 431–59.

Katz, J. (1988) *The Seductions of Crime*. New York: Basic Books.

Keeble, J. (1991) *Out of the Channel: the Exxon Valdez Oil Spill in Prince William Sound*. New York: Harper Collins.

Keefe, R.S.E. and Harvey, P.D. (1994) *Understanding Schizophrenia*. New York. Wiley.

Kehman, H.C. and Hamilton, V.L. (1991) *Crimes of Obedience*. New Haven, CT: Yale University Press.

'Kerry' Report (1992) *The BCCI Affair: A Report to the Senate Committee on Foreign Relations*. Report for Subcommittee on Terrorism, Narcotics, and International Operations (under leadership of Senator J. Kerry). Washington, DC: USGPO.

Kets de Vries, M.F.R. and Miller, D. (1984) *The Neurotic Organization*. San Francisco: Jossey-Bass.

Kets de Vries, M.F.R. and Miller, D. (1987) *Unstable at the Top: Inside the Troubled Organization*. New York and Scarborough, Ontario: New American Library.

Knightley, P., Evans, H., Potter, E., and Wallace, M. (1980) *Suffer the Children: the Story of Thalidomide*. London: Futura.

Kochan, N. and Pym, H. (1987) *The Guinness Affair*. London: Christopher Helm.

Kochan, N. and Whittington, R. (1991) *Bankrupt: the BCCI Fraud*. London: Gollancz.

Kochan, T.A. and Useem, M. (eds) (1992) *Transforming Organizations*. New York: Oxford University Press.

Kolb, D.A. (1976) 'Management and the learning process', *California Management Review*. xviii (3) (Spring): 21–31.

Kornbluth, J. (1992) *Highly Confident: the Crime and Punishment of Michael Milken*. New York: William Morrow, Inc..

Kotter, J.P. (1982) *The General Managers*. Free Press: New York.

Krisberg, B. (1975) *Crime and Privilege: Toward a New Criminology*. Englewood Cliffs, NJ: Prentice-Hall.

Leff, A.A. (1976) *Swindling and Selling*. New York: Free Press.

Lejeune, R. (1984) 'False security: deviance and the stock market', in P.A. Adler and P. Adler (eds), *The Social Dynamics of Financial Markets*, Greenwich, CT/London: JAI Press Inc.

Leonard, R. (1989) Review in *The Times Literary Supplement* (2–8 June): 602.

Levi, M. (1981) *The Phantom Capitalists: The Organisation and Control of Long-firm Fraud*. London: Heinemann.

Levi, M. (1987) *Regulating Fraud: White-Collar Crime and the Criminal Process*. London New York: Tavistock.

Levi, M. (1993) 'The victims of fraud', Paper presented at Second Liverpool Conference on Fraud, Corruption and Business Crime. University of Liverpool.

Levi, M. (1994) 'The media and white collar crime', Paper presented at Annual Meeting, American Society of Criminology, Miami (November).

Levine, A.G. (1982) *Love Canal*, Lexington, MA: Lexington Books.

Levine, D.B (1991) *Inside Out: a True Story of Greed, Scandal and Redemption*. New York: Berkley Books.

Lewis, M. (1990) *Liar's Poker*. Harmondsworth, Middx: Penguin.

Luijk, van, H. (1985) 'Politiek en Ethiek', *Elsevier's* (2 February): 54–5.

Lyon, D. (1994) *The Electronic Eye: The Rise of the Surveillance Society*. Minneapolis: University of Minnesota Press.

McDonnell Douglas Corporation, Press Release, St Louis, 21 March 1974.

McIntosh, M. (1975) *The Organization of Crime*. London: Macmillan.

McMurdy, D. (1992) 'Hands in the till', *MacLeans's* (27 July): 22–4.

Mahoney, J. (1990) *Teaching Business Ethics in the UK, Europe and the USA*. London: The Athlone Press.

Maier, J.M. (1992) *A Major Malfunction*. Instructional Module, Binghamton: State University of New York.

Makkai, T. and Braithwaite, J. (1994) 'Reintegrative shaming and compliance with regulatory standards', *Criminology*, 32 (3): 361–83 .

Management Review (April 1990) 'The Alaskan oil spill: lessons in crisis management': pp. 12–21.

Mann, C.C. and Plummer, M.L. (1991) *The Aspirin Wars: Money, Medicine, and 100 Years of Rampant Competition*. New York: Knopf.

Marceau, J. (1989) *A Family Business: The Making of an International Business Elite*. Cambridge: Cambridge University Press.

Margolis, D.R. (1979) *The Managers: Corporate Life in America*. New York: Morrow.

Mars, G. (1982) *Cheats at Work*. London: Allen & Unwin.

Martin, J.M. and Romano, A.T. (1992) *Multinational Crime: Terrorism, Espionage. Drug and Arms Trafficking*. Newbury Park, CA; London; New Delhi: Sage Publications.

Massing, M. (1992) 'The new Mafia', Review in *New York Review of Books* (3 December): pp. 6–9.

Masuch, M. (1985) 'Vicious circles in organizations', *Administrative Science Quarterly*, 30: 14–33.

Matthews, J.B., Goodpaster, K.E. and Nash, L.L. (1985) *Policies and Persons: A Casebook in Business Ethics*. New York: McGraw-Hill.

Matza, D. (1964) *Delinquency and Drift*. New York: Wiley.

Mayer, M. (1990) *The Greatest Ever Bank Robbery: The Collapse of the Savings & Loan Industry*. New York: Scribners.

Menkes, V. (1987) 'Big bang for publishers', *Business*, May: 163–4.

Merton, R.K., Gray, A.P., Hockey, B. and Selvin, H.C. (eds) (1952) *Reader in Bureaucracy*. New York: Free Press.

Meyer, M.W. and Zucker, L.G. (1989) *Permanently Failing Organizations*. Beverly Hills, CA: Sage Publications.

Meyers, G.C. (1988) *Managing Crisis: A Positive Approach*. London/Sydney: Unwin Paperbacks.

Miceli, M.P. and Near, J.P. (1992) *Blowing the Whistle: the Organizational and Legal Implications for Companies and Employees*. Lexington, MA: Lexington Books.

Miles, R.H. (1986) *Coffin Nails and Corporate Strategy*. Englewood Cliffs, NJ: Prentice-Hall.

Miles, R.H. (1987) *Managing the Corporate Social Environment*. Englewood Cliffs, NJ: Prentice-Hall.

Mills, C. Wright (1940) 'Situated actions and vocabularies of motive', *American Sociological Review*, 5: 904–13.

Mills, C.W. (1956) *The Power Elite*. Oxford: Oxford University Press.

Mills, J. (1986) *The Underground Empire: Where Crime and Government Embrace*. New York: Doubleday.

Mintz, M. (1985) *At Any Cost: Corporate Greed, Women and the Dalkon Shield*. New York: Pantheon Books.

Mintzberg, H. (1973) *The Nature of Managerial Work*. New York: Harper & Row.

Mitroff, I.J. (1984) *Corporate Tragedies: Product Tampering, Sabotage and Other Catastrophes*. New York: Praeger.

Mitroff, I.J. (1988) 'Crisis management: cutting through the confusion', *Sloan Management Review* (Winter): 15–20.

Mokhiber, R. (1988) *Corporate Crime and Violence*. San Francisco: Sierra Club Books.

Monahan, J. and Novaco, R.W. (1980) 'Corporate violence: a psychological analysis', in P.D. Lipsitt and B.D. Sales (eds), *New Directions in Psychological Research*. New York: Free Press.

Moorehead, C. (1984). 'Just good friends', Review in *London Review of Books* (2–15 February): 19.

Morgan, G. (1986) *Images of Organization*. Beverly Hills, CA: Sage Publications.

MV *Herald of Free Enterprise* (1987) 'Report of Court No. 8074, Formal Investigation'. London: HMSO.

Nader, R. (1965) *Unsafe at Any Speed*. New York: Grossman.

Needleman, N. and Needleman, C. (1979) 'Organizational crime: two models of criminogenesis', *Sociological Quarterly*: 517–528.

Newsweek, 27 August 1984, 'De Lorean: not guilty'.

Newsweek, 11 February 1985, 'A giant under fire: General Dynamics faces numerous charges of fraud'.

Newsweek, 21 April 1986, 'Counterfeit threat'.

Newsweek, 21 April 1986, 'Grey markets'.

Newsweek, 26 May 1986, 'Greed on Wall Street'.

Newsweek, 22 September 1986, 'A little fish takes the fly'.

Newsweek, 1 December 1986, 'True greed'.

Newsweek, 12 January 1987, 'London gets a cold'.

New York Times, 5 July 1977, 'Bernhard, a year after disgrace over Lockheed, shows no scars'.

New York Times, 17 November 1992, 'Data show GM knew for years of risk in pickup trucks design'.

New York Times Magazine, 26 September 1976. 'The Lockheed affair'.

Nielsen, W.A. (1986) *Golden Donors*. London: Weidenfeld & Nicolson.

NRC Handelsblad, 27 July 1991, 'Italië is geen serieus land'.

Observer, 17 June 1990, 'Ernest Saunders versus the rest'.

Observer, 1 July 1990, 'Saunders: the errors and explanations'.

Observer, 22 July 1990, 'Guinness: the final round'.

Observer, 2 September 1990, 'A creed of greed'.

Observer, 16 February 1992, 'Guinness: Seelig speaks'.

Observer, 4 October 1992, 'How BCCI hoodwinked the Bank'.

Observer, 25 October 1992, 'Bingham blames the Bank'.

Observer Magazine, 9 April 1989, 'Still active: Three Mile Island ten years on'.

Observer Magazine, 10 June 1990, 'Law of the jungle'.

Observer Magazine, 8 November 1992, 'The $225,000,000,000 habit'.

Ogilvie, R.G. (1990) *Krijgen is een kunst*. Leiden/Antwerp: Stenfert Kroese.

Ouchi, W.G. (1985) 'Organizational culture', *Annual Review of Sociology*, 11: 457–83.

Oversight Hearings on the DC-10 Aircraft (1974), 'Subcommittee on Aviation of the Committee on Commerce (United States Senate, 93rd Congress)', Washington, DC: 26–27 March 1974.

Packard, V.O. (1989) *The Ultra Rich: How Much is Too Much?* Boston: Little, Brown.

Packard Commission (1986): *President's Commission on Defense Management*, 'Conduct and accountability: a report to the President', Washington, DC: Ethics Resource Centre.

Passas, N. and Groskin, R.B. (1993) 'Overseeing and overlooking: the handling of money laundering charges against BCCI in Tampa by US Federal Agencies', Paper presented at Third Liverpool Conference on Fraud, Corruption and Business Crime.

Patterson, W. (1987) 'Nuclear power and its opponents', Review in *London Review of Books* (8 January): 8–9.

Pearce, F. (1976) *Crimes of the Powerful*. London: Pluto Press.

Pearce, F. and Woodiwiss, M. (1993) *Global Crime Connections: Dynamics and Control*. London: Macmillan.

Perrow, C. (1984) *Normal Accidents*. New York: Basic Books.

Perrucci, R., Anderson, R.M., Schendel, D., Trachtman, L. (1980) 'Whistle-Blowing: professionals' resistance to authority', *Social Problems*, December.

Peters, T.J. (1987) *Thriving on Chaos*. New York: Knopf.

Peters, T.J. (1989) *Liberation Management*. London: Cape.

Peters, T.J. and Waterman, R.H. (1982) *In Search of Excellence*. New York: Harper & Row.

Pettigrew, A. (1973) *The Politics of Organizational Decision Making*. London: Tavistock.

Pettigrew, A. (1985) *The Awaking Giant: Continuity and Change in ICI*. Oxford: Basil Blackwell.

Pfeffer, J. (1981) *Power in Organizations*. Boston: Pitman.

Pilger, J. (1989) *Heroes*. London: Pan Books.

Pilzer, P.Z. and Deitz, R. (1989) *Other People's Money: The Inside Story of the S & L Mess*. New York: Simon & Schuster.

Pizzo, S., Fricker, M. and Muolo, P. (1989) *Inside Job: The Looting of America's Savings & Loans*. New York: McGraw-Hill.

Pontell, H.N. and Calavita, H.N. (1993) 'The savings and loan industry', in M. Tonry and A.J. Reiss (eds), *Beyond the Law*. Chicago/London: University of Chicago Press, pp. 203–46.

Potts, M., Kochan, N. and Whittington, R. (1992) *Dirty Money: BCCI: The Inside Story of the World's Sleaziest Bank*. Washington, DC: National Press Books.

President's Commission on Challenger Accident (1986) 'Report of the Presidential Commission on the Space Shuttle Challenger Accident', Washington, DC: USGPO.

Price Waterhouse Report (1991) 'Report on Sandstorm SA Under Section 41 of the Banking Act 1987', report into BCCI.

Punch, M. (1981) *Management and Control of Organizations*. Leiden/Antwerp: Stenfert Kroese (inaugural lecture, Nijenrode University, Breukelen).

Punch, M. (1985) *Conduct Unbecoming: The Social Construction of Police Deviance and Control*. London: Tavistock.

Punch, M. (1986) *The Politics and Ethics of Fieldwork*. Beverly Hills, CA: Sage Publications Ltd.

Punch, M. (1989a) 'In the Underworld: an interview with a Dutch safe-breaker', *The Howard Journal of Criminal Justice*, 30 (2) (May): 121–39.

Punch, M. (1989b) 'Researching police deviance: a personal encounter with the limitations and liabilities of field-work', *British Journal of Sociology*, 40 (2) 177–204.

Punch, M. (1992) *Address at the Conferring of an Honorary Degree on Samuel Johnson*. Opening Academic Year 1992/3. Nijenrode University, Breukelen.

Punch, M. (1993) 'Bandit banks: financial services and organized crime', *Journal of Contemporary Criminal Justice*, 9 (3) (August): 175–96.

Punch, M. (1994a) 'Politics and ethics in qualitative research', in N.K. Denzin and Y.S. Lincoln (eds) *Handbook of Qualitative Research*. Thousand Oaks, CA; London; New Delhi: Sage Publications, pp. 83–97.

Punch, M. (1994b) 'Dilemmas in researching corporate deviance', Paper presented at International Society of Criminology, 49th International Course, University of Leuven (May 1994).

Quinney, R. (1977) *Class, State and Crime: On the Theory and Practice of Criminal Justice*. New York: David McKay.

Ramsey, D.K. (1987) *The Corporate Warriors: The Battle of the Boardrooms*. London: Grafton Books.

Raw, C. (1992) *The Moneychangers*. London: Harvill.

Reed, M. (1989) *The Sociology of Management*. New York; London: Harvester/Wheatsheaf.

Reed, M. and Hughes, M. (eds) (1992) *Rethinking Organization*. London; Newbury Park; Delhi: Sage Publications.

Regester, M. (1987) *Crisis Management*. London: Hutchinson.

Reichman, N. (1993) 'Insider trading', in M. Tonry and A.J. Reiss, Jr (eds), *Beyond the Law*. Chicago/London: University of Chicago Press.

Reisman, M. (1979) *Folded Lies*. New York: Free Press.

Reiss, A.J., Jr (1983) 'The policing of organizational life', in M. Punch (ed.), *Control in the Police Organisation*. Cambridge, MA: MIT Press.

Reiss, A.J., Jr and Biderman A. (1980) *Data Sources on White-collar Lawbreaking*. Washington, DC: National Institute of Justice.

Reuter, P. (1993) 'The cartage industry in New York', in M. Tonry and A.J. Reiss, Jr (eds), *Beyond the Law: Crime in Complex Organizations*. Chicago/London: University of Chicago Press.

Richardson, G., Ogus, A. and Burrows, P. (1983) *Policing Pollution: A Study of Regulation and Enforcement*. Oxford: Oxford University Press.

Robinson, J. (1985) *The Risk Takers: Portraits of Money, Ego and Power*. London: Allen & Unwin.

Robinson, J. (1990) *The Risk Takers: Five Years On*. London: Mandarin.

Rohatyn, F. (1987) 'The blight on Wall Street', *New York Review of Books* (12 March).

Rosenberg, L.J. and West, J.H. van, (1984) 'The collaborative approach to marketing', *Business Horizons* (November).

Ross, G. (1987) *Stung: The Incredible Obsession of Brian Molony*. Toronto: Stoddart.

Ross, I. (1980) 'How lawless are big companies'? *Fortune* (1 December).

Ross, I. (1992) *Shady Business: Confronting Corporate Corruption*. New York: Twentieth Century Fund Press.

RSV Report (1984). 'Opkomst en ondergang van Rijn-Schelde-Verolme', Report of Parliamentary Commission of Enquiry under chair of Mr C.P. van Dijk. The Hague: State Publishing Company.

Saito, T. (1990) 'Recruit scandal', Paper delivered at American Society of Criminology Annual Conference, Baltimore, 1990.

Salaman, G. (1979) *Work Organizations: Resistance and Control*. London: Longman.

Salaman, G. and Thompson, K. (eds) (1973) *People and Organizations*. London: Longman.

Salaman, G. and Thompson, K. (eds) (1980) *Control and Ideology in Organizations*. Milton Keynes: The Open University.

Sampson, A. (1974) *The Sovereign State of ITT*. Greenwich, CT: Fawcett Crest.

Sampson, A. (1976) *The Seven Sisters*. London: Coronet Books.

Sampson, A. (1978) *The Arms Bazaar*. London: Coronet Books.

Sampson, A. (1982) *The Money Lenders: Bankers in a Dangerous World*. London: Coronet Books.

Saunders, J. (1989) *Nightmare*. London: Hutchinson.

Schaap, C.D. (1995) 'Bedrijfsspionage en informatie-makelaardij: criminaliteit van de toekomst?', in M. Cools and A. Hoogenboom (eds), *Kwetsbare Kennis*. Alphen a/d Rijn: Samson.

Schrager, L.S. and Short, J.F. (1980) 'How serious a crime: perceptions of organizational and common crimes', in G. Geis and E. Stotland (eds), *White-Collar Crime*. Beverly Hills, CA: Sage, pp. 14–31.

Schur, E.M. (1969) *Our Criminal Society*. Englewood Cliffs, NJ: Prentice-Hall.

Seabright, P. (1990) 'Is life a lottery?', Review in *The Times Literary Supplement*, 14–20 December, p. 1339.

Seidenberg, R. (1973) *Corporate Wives: Corporate Casualties?* New York: Amacom.

Senator Kefauver's Subcommittee on Antitrust and Monopoly (1961) Washington, DC: USGPO.

Shapiro, S.P. (1980) 'Detecting illegalities: a perspective on the control of securities violations', PhD dissertation, Yale University.

Shapiro, S.P. (1984) *Wayward Capitalists*. New Haven, CT: Yale University Press.

Shapiro, S.P. (1987) 'The social control of impersonal trust', *American Journal of Sociology*, 93: 623–58.

Sherman, L.W. (1979) 'Organizational deviance: concepts, scope and theory', Mimeo: State University of New York at Albany.

Sherman, L.W. (1980) 'Three models of organizational corruption in agencies of social control', *Social Problems*, 27: 478–91.

Shover, N. (1976) 'Organizations and interorganizational fields as criminogenic behaviour settings', Unpublished paper, University of Tennessee, Knoxville, TN.

Shover, N. (1980) 'The criminalization of corporate behaviour: federal surface coal mining', in G. Geis and E. Stotland (eds), *White-Collar Crime*. Beverly Hills, CA: Sage.

Shrivastava, P. (1987) *Bhopal: Anatomy of a Crisis*. Cambridge, MA: Ballinger.

Silk, L. and Vogel, D. (1976) *Ethics and Profits: The Crisis of Confidence in American Business*. New York: Touchstone (Simon & Schuster).

Singer, B.P. (1980) 'Crazy systems', *Social Policy* (September/October): 149–67.

Snider, L. (1991) 'The regulatory dance: understanding reform processes in corporate crime', *International Journal of Sociology of Law*, 19: 204–23.

Srivasta, S. and Associates (1988) *Executive Integrity*. San Francisco/London: Jossey-Bass.

Staw, B.M. and Swajkowski, E. (1975) 'The scarcity-munificence component of organizational environments and the commission of illegal acts', *Administrative Science Quarterly*, 20: 345–54.

Stein, J. (1992) *A License to Steal: The Untold Story of Michael Milken and the Conspiracy to Bilk the Nation*. New York: Simon & Schuster.

Steinberg, J. (1989) 'Capos and cardinals', Review in *London Review of Books* (17 August): 13.

Stenning, P.C., Shearing, C.D., Addario, S.M. and Condon, Mary G. (1990) 'Controlling interests: two conceptions of order in regulating a financial market', in M.L. Friedland (ed.) *Securing Compliance: Seven Case Studies*. Toronto: University of Toronto Press, pp. 88–119.

Sterling, C. (1994) *Crime without Frontiers: The Worldwide Expansion of Organized Crime and the 'Pax Mafiosa'*. Boston, MA: Little, Brown.

Stewart, J.B. (1991) *Den of Thieves*. New York: Simon & Schuster.

Stone, C. (1975) *Where the Law Ends: The Social Control of Corporate Behavior*. New York: Harper & Row.

Stone, D.G. (1990) *April Fools: An Insider's Account of the Rise and Fall of Drexel Burnham*. New York: Donald Fine Company.

Stotland, E. and Geis, G. (1980) 'Introduction', in G. Geis and E. Stotland (eds), *White-collar Crime*. Beverly Hills, CA: Sage, pp. 7–13.

Sturt, R.H.B. (1993) 'Memorandum on vicarious liability', Unpublished document by Kent County Coroner used at presentation on the Zeebrugge disaster, Police Staff College, Bramshill, UK.

Sunday Telegraph, 2 October 1994, 'Why these ferries are still not safe'.

Sunday Telegraph, 12 March 1995, 'Barings knew of Leeson ban'; 'Leeson trial "to be in UK"'; 'Cazenove merger plan fuelled Barings' gambles'.

Sunday Times, 21 September 1980, 'Pregnancy drug firm sets private eye to "investigate" expert witness'.

Sunday Times, 8 March 1987, 'Guinness roll out the barrel'.

Sunday Times, 2 September 1990, 'Guinnesty: an everyday odyssey of brewing folk', 'Guinness: the clan keeps its head', 'Saunders, a man convinced he could do no wrong'.

Sunday Times, 5 March 1995, 'Meltdown: how an entire financial system failed to stop a trader's mad gamble that flushed Barings bank into oblivion'.

Sutherland, E.H. (1940) 'White-collar criminality', *American Sociological Review*, 5 (February): 1–12.

Sutherland, E.H. (1945) 'Is "white-collar crime" crime?', *American Sociological Review*, 10 (April): 132–9.

Sutherland, E.H. (1949) *White-collar Crime*. New York: Holt.

Sutherland, E.H. (1982) 'White-collar crime is organized crime', in M.D. Ermann and R.L. Lundman (eds), *Corporate and Governmental Deviance*. New York: Oxford University Press (2nd edn).

Sutherland, E. (1983) White-collar Crime: The Uncut Version. London: Yale University Press.

Swigert, V.L. and Farrell, R.A. (1980/81) 'Corporate homicide: definitional processes in the creation of deviance', *Law and Society Review*, 15 (1) 161–82.

Sykes, G. and Matza, D. (1957) 'Techniques of neutralization: a theory of delinquency', *American Sociological Review*, 22: 664–70.

Szasz, A. (1983) 'Corporate resistance to effective regulation of environmental hazards', Paper presented at American Sociological Association, annual meeting, Detroit.

Tappan, P.W. (1947) 'Who is the criminal?' *American Sociological Review*, 12: 96–102.

Taylor, J., Walton, P. and Young, J. (1973) *The New Criminology: For a Social Theory of Deviance*. London: Routledge & Kegan Paul.

Taylor, R. (1993) *Going for Broke*. New York: Simon & Schuster.

Taylor, W. (1992) 'Adventures in the Junk Trade', review in *The New York Times Book Review*, 15 November 14–15.

Thomas, A.B. (1988) 'Does leadership make a difference to organizational performance?', *Administrative Science Quarterly*, 33: 338–400.

Thomas, A.B. (1989) 'One-minute management education: a sign of the times?', *Management Education and Development*, 20 (1) 23–38.

Thomas, A.B. (1993) *Controversies in Management*. London: Routledge.

Thompson, J.D. (1967) *Organizations in Action*. New York: McGraw-Hill.

Thompson, P. and Delano, A. (1989) *Maxwell: A Portrait of Power*. London: Bantam Press.

Time, 13 September 1976, 'The Lockheed mystery'.

Time, 2 February 1987, 'Fearing that "muck" will stick'.

Time, 23 February 1987, 'A raid on Wall Street'.

Time, 2 March 1987, 'From pinstripes to prison stripes'.

Time, 9 March 1987, 'The Vatican: behind the walls'.

Time, 30 March 1987, 'Serving his clients all too well'.

Time, 30 March 1987, 'Wall Street: more suspects held'.

Time, 20 April 1987, 'Texaco's star falls'.

Time, 28 December 1987, 'Boesky gets an inside trip'.

Times, The, 29 August 1990, 'Guinness three are jailed after Parnes collapse', 'Judge's tough sentencing receives widespread support'.

Times, The, 20 February 1995, 'Problems for Ward in fight with Guinness'.

Times, The, 19 July 1995, 'Calling into question the Bank's role as regulator'; 'Clarke attacks blunders that sunk Barings'; 'Barings Report'; 'Lost Barings'; 'City welcomes reforms in Barings Report'.

Timmer, D.A. and Eitzen, S. (1989) *Crime in the Streets and in the Suites*. Boston, MA: Allyn & Bacon.

Tone Hosmer, L. (1995) 'Trust: the connecting link between organizational theory and philosophical ethics', *Academy of Management Review*, 20 (2): 379–403.

Tonry, M.T. and Reiss Jr, A.J. (eds) (1993) *Beyond the Law: Crime in Complex Organizations*. Chicago/London: University of Chicago Press.

Truell, P. and Gurwin, L. (1993) *False Profits: The Inside Story of BCCI, the World's Most Corrupt Financial Empire*. New York: Houghton Mifflin.

Tuleja, T. (1987) *Beyond the Bottom-Line*. New York: Penguin Books.

Turner, J. (1986) 'In the time of the entrepreneurs', Review in *The Times Literary Supplement* 11 July 1986: 751–2.

Udink, E. (1993) *Criminele Geldstromen*, Arnhem: Gouda Quint.

Useem, M. (1984) *The Inner Circle: Large Corporations and the Rise of Business Political Activity in the U.S. and U.K.* New York: Oxford University Press.

Useem, M. (1990) 'Business restructuring, management control and corporate organization', *Theory and Society*, 19: 681–707.

Useem, M. (1993) *Executive Defense: Shareholder Power and Corporate Reorganization*. Cambridge, MA: Harvard University Press.

Useem, M. and Gottlieb, M.M. (1992) 'Corporate restructuring, ownership-disciplined alignment, and the reorganization of management', *Human Resource Management*, 29: 3: 285–306.

US General Accounting Office (1989) *Thrifts Failures: Costly Failures Resulted from Regulatory Violations and Unsafe Methods*. Report submitted to Congress (June), GAO/AFMD-89-62. Washington, DC: US Government Printing Office.

Vandivier, K. (1982) 'Why should my conscience bother me?; in M.D. Ermann and R.J. Lundman (eds), *Corporate and Governmental Deviance*. New York: Oxford University Press (2nd edn).

Van Maanen, J. (1978) 'On watching the watchers', in P.K. Manning and J. van Maanen (eds), *Policing: A View from the Street*. Santa Monica, CA: Goodyear, pp. 309–49.

Van Maanen, J. (1983) 'Golden passports: managerial socialization and graduate education', *The Review of Higher Education*, 6 (4) 435–55.

Van Maanen, J. and Barley, S.R. (1984) 'Occupational communities', in B. Staw and L. Cummings (eds), *Research in Organizational Behavior*. Greenwich, CT: JAI Press, vol. 6.

Vaughan, D. (1980) 'Crime between organizations: implications for criminology', in G. Geis and E. Stotland (eds), *White Collar Crime: Theory and Research*. Beverly Hills/London: Sage.

Vaughan, D. (1983) *Controlling Unlawful Organizational Behaviour: Social Structure and Corporate Misconduct*. Chicago: University of Chicago Press.

Vaughan, D. (1988) 'Organizational misconduct: a method of theory elaboration', Paper delivered at the American Society of Criminology Meeting, Chicago.

Vervaele, J.A.E. (ed.) (1993) *Bestuursrechtelijke toepassing en handhaving van gemeenschapsrecht in Nederland*. Deventer: Kluwer.

Vervaele, J. (1995) 'Nemo tenetur se ipsum accusare: a interesting decision in Strasbourg. Ernest Saunders against the United Kingdom, European Commission of Human Rights – 10 May 1994', *Agon*, 3 (April): 5–6.

Vise, D.A. and Coll, S. (1992) *Eagle on the Street*. New York: Collier Books.

Vogel, D. (1989) *Fluctuating Fortunes: The Political Power of Business in America*. New York: Basic Books.

Volkskrant, de, 8 March 1978, 'Lubbers als Minister in zaken'.

Volkskrant, de, 25 June 1982, 'Computerdiefstal schokt Japan'.

Volkskrant, de, 27 July 1982, 'Alle remmen los in gevecht computermarkt'.

288   *Dirty Business*

Volkskrant, de, 1 November 1984, 'Milde straffen voor frauderende nonnen in Belgisch klooster'.
Volkskrant, de, 10 December 1984, 'Politiek verloederde RSV'.
Volkskrant, de, 11 December 1984, 4-page special on RSV inquiry's report.
Volkskrant, de, 19 February 1986, 'Premier Lubbers en broers ontliepen belastingheffing'.
Volkskrant, de, 5 July 1986, 'Frauderende yuppies brengen Wall Street in rep en roer'.
Volkskrant, de, 24 April 1987, 'Speculant Boesky gaf beurscommissie valse informatie'.
Volkskrant, de, 1 May 1987, 'Merril Lynch verspeelt kwart miljard dollar'.
Volkskrant, de, 18 July 1987, 'Hoogste hof in Italië trekt arrestatiebevel tegen Marcinkus in'.
Volkskrant, de, 25 July 1987, 'Directie Townsend verantwoordelijk voor ramp'.
Volkskrant, de, 29 October 1987, 'Onderzoek Salem-affaire strandt in Zuid-Afrika'.
Volkskrant, de, 12 November 1987, 'Salem-affaire eindigt met vrijspraak hoofdverdachte'.
Volkskrant, de, 21 December 1987, 'Texaco betaalt Pennzoil drie miljard'.
Volkskrant, de, 23 August 1988, 'Hunts veroordeeld voor manipuleren zilvermarkt'.
Volkskrant, de, 26 January 1989, 'Mike Milken verlaat Drexel'.
Volkskrant, de, 27 January 1989, 'Italiaanse bankier Calvi zou in 1982 toch zijn vermoord'.
Volkskrant, de, 31 March 1989, 'Mike Milken officieel aangeklaagd'.
Volkskrant, de, 19 May 1989, 'De lijdensweg van duizenden vergiftigde Spanjaarden'.
Volkskrant, de, 23 April 1990, 'Milken bekent schuld en betaalt miljard boete'.
Volkskrant, de, 24 April 1990, 'Mister Big dealt slechts in het groot'.
Volkskrant, de, 29 May 1990, 'Belangrijkste verdachten afwezig in proces over Banco Ambrosiano'.
Volkskrant, de, 20 October 1990, 'Bemanning van gezonken Herald gaat vrijuit'.
Volkskrant, de, 29 July 1991, 'Mafia-baas wurgde Gods bankier Calvi'.
Volkskrant, de, 22 December 1992, 'Bloedschandaal bereikt Franse politici'.
Volkskrant, de, 30 July 1993, 'Opel slaat terug: Harde bewijzen voor spionage Lopez'.
Volkskrant, de, 8 September 1993, 'VW-topman Piëch: U stelt toch steeds dezelfde vragen'.
Volkskrant, de, 29 September 1993, 'BCCI-bankier veroordeeld tot zes jaar'.
Volkskrant, de, 21 April 1994, 'Angst voor negatieve publiciteit hindert aanpak bedrijfsspionage'.
Volkskrant, de, 28 April 1994, 'Justitie vindt bewijzen voor spionage bij GM'.
Volkskrant, de, 16 August 1994, 'Volkswagen-computers bevatten duizenden geheimen van Opel'.
Volkskrant, de, 20 October 1994, 'Topman failliete BCCI krijgt elf jaar cel'.
Volkskrant, de, 1 December 1994, 'Boete van 535 miljoen voor cementbedrijven'.
Volkskrant, de, 3 December 1994, 'Overlevenden giframp Bhopal hebben nog geen cent gezien'.
Volkskrant, de, 27 February 1995, 'Faillissement Britse bank treft beurzen'.
Volkskrant, de, 28 February 1995, 'Derivaten-debâcle kan volgens Bank of England iedereen overkomen'.
Volkskrant, de, 1 March 1995, 'Klopjacht op verdwenen Barings-medewerker'.
Volkskrant, de, 3 March 1995, 'Singapore wil uitlevering Nick Leeson'.
Volkskrant, de, 5 April 1995, 'Curatoren Barings wijten ondergang bank aan falend management'.
Wagenaar, W.A. (1992) 'Risk-taking and accident causation', in J.F. Yates (ed.), *Risk-taking Behaviour*. New York: Wiley, pp. 257–81.
Wallraff, G. (1979) *Beeld van Bild*. Amsterdam: Van Gennep.
Wall Street Journal, 30 November 1977, 'Last suit is settled arising from crash of Turkish Air DC-10 near Paris'.
Wall Street Journal, 5 February 1993, 'GM ordered by jury to pay $105.2 million over death'.
Wall Street Journal, 1 November 1993, 'Sears PR debacle shows how not to handle a crisis'.
Walter, I. (1986) *Secret Money: The World of International Financial Secrecy*. London: Allen & Unwin.
Walton, C.C. (1988) *The Moral Manager*. New York: Harper & Row.
Ward, R. (1991) 'The black market in body parts', *International Criminal Justice Newsletter*, 7 (5) (September/October) 1–6.
Wassenberg, A. (1983) *Dossier RSV*. Leiden/Antwerp: Stenfert Kroese.
Weber, M. (1947) *The Theory of Social and Economic Organization*. New York: Oxford University Press.

Weekly Telegraph, no. 80, 8–15 January 1993, '"Dirty tricks" apology after two-year saga'.

Weekly Telegraph, no. 88, 5–11 March 1993, 'Car parks chief cleared in spying case'.

Weick, K.E. (1976) 'Educational organizations as loosely coupled systems', *Administrative Science Quarterly*, 21: 1–19.

Weick, K.E. (1990) 'The vulnerable system: an analysis of the Tenerife air disaster', *Journal of Management*, 16 (3): 571–93 .

Weir, D. (1987) *The Bhopal Syndrome*. San Francisco: Sierra Club Books.

Weisburd, D., Waring E. and Chayet, E. (1995) 'Specific deterrence in a sample of offenders convicted of white-collar crimes', *Criminology*, 33 (4): 587–605.

Wells, C. (1994) *Corporations and Criminal Responsibility*. Oxford: Oxford University Press.

Westin, A. (1980) *Whistleblowing: Loyalty and Dissent in the Corporation*. New York: McGraw-Hill.

White, L.J. (1991) *The S & L Debacle: Public Policy Lessons for Bank and Thrift Regulation*. New York: Oxford University Press.

Whitley, R. (1984) *The Intellectual and Social Organization of the Sciences*. Oxford: Clarendon Press.

Whyte, W.H. (1956) *The Organization Man*. New York: Simon & Schuster.

Wolfgang, M., Figlio, R.M. and Thornberry, T. (1975) *Criminology Index: 1945–1972*. New York: Elsevier.

Wolfgang, M., Figlio, R., Tracy, P. and Singer S. (1985) *The National Survey of Crime Severity*, Washington, DC: Department of Justice.

Wright, P.J. (1979) *On a Clear Day You Can See General Motors*, Detroit, MI: Wright Enterprises.

Wright, P. (1987) 'Excellence', Review in *London Review of Books*, 21 May 1987, pp. 8–11.

Yallop, D. (1984) *In God's Name*. London: Cape.

Yeager, P.C. (1993) 'Industrial water pollution', in M. Tonry and A.J. Reiss, Jr (eds), *Beyond the Law*. Chicago: Chicago University Press.

Zey, M. (1993) *Banking on Fraud: Drexel, Junk Bonds. and Buyouts*. New York/Berlin: Aldine de Gruyter.

Zijderveld, A. (1970) *The Abstract Society*. New York: Doubleday.

Zimring, F.E. and Hawkins, G. (1993) 'Crime and justice and the Savings and Loan crisis', in M. Tonry and A.J. Reiss, Jr (eds) *Beyond the Law*. Chicago: Chicago University Press.

Index